Knowing Our Rights : Women, family, laws and customs in the Muslim World

Women living under muslim laws
Femmes sous lois musulmanes

International Solidarity Network

zubaan
AN IMPRINT OF
KALI FOR WOMEN

First published 2003 in paperback
by Women Living Under Muslim Laws
PO Box 28445
London N19 5NZ, UK

This edition published by
Zubaan,
an imprint of Kali for Women
K 92, 1st Floor, Hauz Khas Enclave
NEW DELHI - 110 016
email: zubaanwbooks@vsnl.net

Reprinted 2006

Printed & bound at Raj Press, R-3 Inderpuri, New Delhi 110 012

Title Design by Tim Simpson, Plunge Productions

ISBN 81 86706 69 0

CONTENTS

ACKNOWLEDGEMENTS

As the largest and longest-running of all WLUML's collective projects, the Women & Law in the Muslim World Programme has involved literally thousands of women and men, spanning over a decade and some 20 countries. Those involved have ranged from participants in focus-group discussions, to typists; from small, voluntary community-based organizations to national non-governmental organizations; from active networkers who conceived, planned and implemented the Programme to outside experts who contributed to country projects and the international synthesis. Warm thanks are due to each and every one of these who shared in the gathering and analysis of information in the belief that they would be helping to increase the options available to women in their contexts.

Here we shall only be able to name individually those who have been part of a changing group of networkers who have directly helped to shape this Handbook. These include participants in the initial W&L Planning Meeting and the three W&L international synthesis meetings, many of whom also continued to provide feedback during the drafting stages: Sherifat Hussein-Abubakar, Maryam Awais, Marieme Helie-Lucas, Homa Hoodfar, Pinar Ilkkaracan, Ayesha Imam, P. Imrana Jalal, Sultana Kamal, Sindi Medar-Gould, Vahida Nainar, Kishali Pinto Jayawardena, Farida Shaheed, Salma Sobhan, Isabelita Solamo-Antonio, Hajara Usman, and Faizun Zackariya; as well as Hanadi Taha and Lynn Freedman for supplementary feedback at the final crucial stages. Also to be thanked are Suhraiya Jivraj, Shaheena Karbanee, Sarah Masters and Caroline Simpson for significant assistance.

However, there was an additional group who not only participated in various synthesis meetings but who also took on concrete responsibilities and provided the essential input that brought this Handbook into its current shape. Without their dedication and insight, this Handbook would have remained a dream. These include Chulani Kodikara, Fatima Seedat, Salbiah Ahmad, Sohail Akbar Warraich, and Sume Epie-Eyoh. Very special thanks are also due to language editor and indexer Kathleen McNeil for her sensitivity and ability to work to an impossible deadline, as well as to Finn, Jason and Tristram Ariss.

A synthesis and writing project of this magnitude and complexity is simply not possible unless one person has the vision, the passion, the skills – and the stamina – to see it through. For us, that person has been Cassandra Balchin. Far more than simply coordinator of the editorial team, Cassandra has been organizer, motivator, designer, and drafter. Her skill as a writer and editor shines through many parts of this Handbook. Her experience as a WLUML networker and activist gave shape and coherence to the collective, substantive decisions that collaborative writing entails. Put simply, her commitment to the Handbook and to its ultimate goal of expanding women's choices, brought this enormous project to its final fruition. From the WLUML network, a huge thank you.

Finally, we extend our thanks to the Andrew W. Mellon Foundation for many years of generous support for the international coordination of the Women & Law Programme as well as the production of this Handbook, and to the many other organizations that have over the years supported the activities of the WLUML international coordination office and networking organizations that participated in the Women and Law in the Muslim World Programme.

Women Living Under Muslim Laws
February 2003

GLOSSARY

Across Muslim countries and communities, there are multiple spellings and different words for essentially the same thing. For example, a judge or other authority who hears cases concerning Muslims is known variously as a cadi/kadi/kazi/kathi/khati/qazi/quazi/qadi/qadhi. In general, the problem arises from the challenge of transliterating and translating Arabic words into local languages. In the text of this Handbook, we have opted for either the version most commonly accepted or that which we believe would be most widely recognized, without implying that there is any one 'correct' spelling.

A

Ahsan
A form of talaq, regarded as the most approved: a single, revocable talaq.

Ahadith/Hadith
Reported sayings of the Prophet Muhammad.

Affinity
Related by marriage, e.g., mother-in-law, son-in-law.

Alim certificate
Qualification regarding basic knowledge of Muslim laws; from 'alim' – one who has knowledge.

Anak dara
Woman who has not had sexual intercourse, whether married or not (Malaysia/Singapore/Indonesia).

Ayat
Verse of the Qur'an.

B

Baligh
Age of puberty.

Bain
Irrevocable (as related to divorce).

Bain kubra/Baynuna kubra
The 'greater finality': parties having been divorced from each other three times are not free to marry each other again until the former wife has undergone a consummated, intervening marriage (hilala) to another man.

Bain sughra/Baynuna sughra
The 'lesser finality': parties divorced from each other would have to undergo a fresh marriage contract if they wished to remarry each other.

Bride-price
Money given by the groom or his family to the bride's family in exchange for her hand in marriage.

Bid'a/Bida'a/Bidat
Literally, a disapproved innovation. Used with reference to a talaq pronounced three times in one sitting or one majlis.

C

Complete separation of property regime
A property regime in which each spouse retains ownership of property they bring into the marriage and property inherited during the marriage, as well as retaining individual control over any earnings or wealth they create during the marriage, with all assets marked as belonging to a specific spouse.

Communal property regime
A property regime in which the spouses surrender all individual ownership of property brought into the marriage and created during the marriage, and which is to be divided equally on dissolution.

Consanguinity
Related by blood or origin; descended from the same ancestors, e.g., mother, grandson.

D

Darar Syarie
Harm or danger in respect of religion, life, body, mind or property. Used in the context of fault-based divorce as a grounds for divorce (Malaysia/Singapore).

Decree nisi
A provisional decree; in relation to divorce it effects a conditional divorce which becomes absolute on the occurrence of a prescribed contingency (usually the passage of a certain amount of time).

Dower
see mahr

Dowry
Trousseau, or the goods (and cash) brought into the marriage by the bride. Although technically the absolute property of the wife, the dowry is often in the form of presents given to the groom and his family and not recoverable by her.

E

'Esma/Ismaa/'Usma
The common term used for the delegated right of divorce/ talaq tafwid in Arabic-speaking communities.

Exchange marriage
Exchange marriage involves the marriage between the brother and sister of one family and sister and brother of another family. In extreme cases, a man may pledge any future daughter to his in-laws in exchange for his own wife. Exchange marriages imply that the fate of one couple is tied to the fate of the other couple, so that if one couple divorces, the other couple automatically has to divorce even if they are happy together. Exchange marriages are often among relatives, compounding the associated problems. Known as berdar in Turkey, badal in Jordan and Palestine, and watta satta or addo baddo in Pakistan.

Ex parte
Court proceedings in the absence of the respondent party, where the respondent has failed to appear for hearings.

F

Faskh/Fasah/Fasakh
Fault-based divorce, generally related to an irregularity in the contract or the violation of a contractual clause. Commonly available only to women through the courts.

Fatwa
Religious ruling, decree or opinion, usually issued by a body of religious scholars or an individual scholar, or even a mosque imam, with or without sanction by the state.

Fiqh
Jurisprudence; generally used to refer to Muslim laws as developed by jurists.

H

Hadanah/Hizanat
Custody; physical care and control of children.

Hadd
Literally, 'the limits'. Used mainly with reference to Muslim penal laws, and the evidentiary requirements and maximum punishments as prescribed in the Qur'an. Note the Hudud and Hudood laws operative in certain states of Malaysia and Nigeria, and Pakistan.

Hadith
see ahadith

Hakam
Arbitrators (family or strangers) appointed to help the parties in a marriage to resolve their differences when there is strife and discord (shiqaq) leading one party to seek a divorce.

Hanafi
A particular School of Muslim thought of the Sunni School attributed to Abu Hanifah Nu'man ibn Thabit. He was born in Kufah, Iraq in 80H; 699 AD and is of Persian descent (d.150H; 767 AD).

Hanbali
A particular School of Muslim thought of the Sunni School attributed to Abu Abdullah Ahmad ibn Hanbal. He was born in Baghdad in 241H; 780 AD. (d.241H; 855 AD). He journeyed to Syria, Hijaz, Kufah and Basrah.

Hantaran/Handaran
Literally, 'sending over'. The goods and cash exchanged between the groom and bride's families on the occasion of their marriage (Malaysia, Singapore).

Haram
Prohibited, illegal.

Harta sepencarian
Jointly acquired matrimonial property (Malaysia, Singapore).

Hasan
A form of talaq, regarded as acceptable.

Hiba
Lifetime gift.

Hilala/Hila
Intervening marriage; bain kubra.

Hudood/Hudud
see hadd

Hukum Syara'/Hukum Syarak
Used in Malaysia, Singapore, Indonesia with reference to the general principles of Muslim laws of the Sunni school.

I

Idda/Iddat/Iddah/eddah
Waiting period which begins from the time a Muslim woman is divorced or widowed. The period varies depending on the type of divorce, whether she is pregnant, whether she is still menstruating or not and whether she is widowed. During this time, she is not free to contract another marriage.

Ijab & Qabul
Literally, 'offer and acceptance'; used to refer to the offer and acceptance of the terms and conditions of a marriage contract..

Ijbar
The power to compel an unmarried virgin into marriage, recognized by certain Schools. The power usually resides in the father and paternal grandfather.

Ijma
Consensus of scholars on an issue.

Ijtihad
Independent reasoning to arrive at a legal principle.

Ila'
A grounds for divorce available to women through the court; it becomes available after the husband has taken an oath of abstinence from sexual intercourse.

Imam
One who leads the prayers, usually male.

Irrevocable
A talaq or dissolution of marriage which has become final. Should the couple wish to reconcile, they will be required to contract a fresh marriage with another mahr.

Isbat/ithbat
A court process to establish the existence or non-existence of a marriage (some Arabic-speaking countries, Indonesia).

J

Jactitation
A court process to silence all claims regarding the existence or non-existence of a marriage.

Jamaat
Mosque committee (some South Asian Muslim communities).

Jehez/jihaz
see dowry

Jirga
A traditional adjudication forum (Pakistan).

Joint property regime
A property regime in which each spouse retains ownership of property they bring into the marriage and property inherited during the marriage, but all assets created during the marriage are to be divided equally on dissolution.

Jumma
A main mosque used for Friday prayers (some South Asian Muslim communities).

K

Kabinnama
Muslim marriage contract (Bangladesh).

Kafa'a/ Kafa'ah/Kaf'a
The principle that parties to a marriage should be equal or compatible. Kafa'a is used mostly in relation to a groom - that he must not be of a lower status than the bride. Although according to jurists the factors to be considered include nobility (hasab), piety (din), lineage (nasab), family (bayt), today economic status is a main consideration.

Kahwin Cina Buta
Pejorative local idiom for the husband in an intervening marriage; see hilala (Malaysia, Singapore).

Kaikuli
Any sum of money paid, or other movable property given, or any sum of money or any movable property promised to be paid or given, to a groom for the use of the bride, before or at the time of marriage by a relative of the bride or by any other person. Kaikuli is to be held in trust by the groom on behalf of the bride and should be returned at any time on demand or on dissolution of marriage (Sri Lanka).

Kalangies
Traditional Sri Lankan weight in gold (or mixed gold).

Khiyar al-bulugh
The option of puberty; a Muslim woman's right, on attaining puberty, to ratify or rescind a marriage contracted when she was a minor, providing the marriage was not consummated. Schools and laws differ over whether the option is available to a woman married by her father or paternal grandfather.

Kitabia/Kitabiyah/Kitabiya
Generally refers to a woman from the 'revealed religions' who are not Muslims, i.e., Christians and Jews. Law and custom varies regarding the precise definition.

Khul'/Khul/khul'u/Khula
Form of divorce available to a Muslim woman, generally on compensating the husband. Interpretations, laws and practices differ regarding the husband and/or court's role and agency, and whether or not this is an irrevocable divorce (bain sughra).

Kwatance
see sleeping embryo (Hausa)

L

Li'an
A procedure leading to divorce. The husband swears on the Qur'an that his wife has committed zina. The wife, in response, swears on the Qur'an that she has not. This process is repeated a further two times and if neither retracts their oath, the court automatically pronounces the marriage dissolved and the paternity of any child who is the subject of li'an proceedings is no longer established. The essence of li'an is that the husband has no proof of his accusation.

M

Ma'azoun/Mazoum
Religious figure who officiates at a Muslim marriage; state employed in Sudan and Egypt.

Madrassah
School of religious instruction with Arabic as a medium of instruction.

Mahr/Mahari/Mehr
Dower. The goods and/or cash to be given by the groom to the bride as a requisite of a valid Muslim marriage. It may be given at the time of the marriage ceremony (prompt), or promised at a later date or to be paid upon divorce or the death of the husband (deferred) or divided into prompt and deferred portions.

Mahr ul mithl
Also known as 'proper dower', mahr ul mithl is due when no amount of mahr was specified in the marriage contract but the wife now seeks to recover her mahr. It is then fixed (by a court or similar authority) as the amount due to the wife either based on the mahr received by her female relatives and/or taking into account the husband's means.

Mala fide
In bad faith.

Maliki
A particular School of Muslim thought of the Sunni School attributed to Malik ibn Anas al-Asbahi. He was born in Medina in 95 H; 713 AD and lived in Medina all his life except for a pilgrimage to Mecca (d. 179H; 795 AD).

Marital rape
Sexual intercourse between spouses where one spouse does not consent.

Masjid
Mosque.

Maskahwin
Dower (Malaysia, Singapore, Indonesia).

Mata'a/Mutaah/Mut'ah
A compensatory payment by the husband to the wife, paid on divorce through talaq or where the 'fault' lies with the husband.

Maulana/Maulvi/Mowlana/Mulla
Term used to denote a person learned in Muslim laws.

Mubarat/Mubara'a/Mubaralat
Divorce by mutual agreement.

Muhsan
Married person.

Mumaiyiz
Age of discernment; generally used in relation to custody disputes and the age at which a child's preference may be taken into account.

Mut'a
Temporary contract of marriage; a concept recognized by the Shia School.

N

Nafaqa/Nafaqah
Maintenance of wife and children.

Nasab
Relations by blood (in the context of marriage-guardians or wilayat al-nikah).

Nazim
Chairman of the lowest tier of government, the Union Council (Pakistan).

Nikah
Marriage ceremony (many Muslim communities in Asia or of Asian origin).

Nikahnama
Muslim Marriage contract (India, Pakistan).

Niza' wa shiqaq
Discord and strife; a grounds for divorce available to both women and men.

Nushuz/Nusyuz/Nashezeh/Nashiz/Nashizah
Disobedient (usually used in reference to wives who do not obey their husband).

P

Panchayat
Traditional adjudication forum; informal gathering of community influentials/family elders.

Pemberian
Weddings gifts (Malaysia).

Polygynous
A marriage in which the husband has more than one wife at the same time.

Prohibited degrees
Those persons related by blood, marriage or fosterage who are forbidden in marriage to each other.

Property regime
The arrangement between a married couple regarding the ownership of property they own (separately and/or jointly).

Q

Qabul
see ijab

Qadiani
A religious sect derived from Islam. Adherents follow a different Prophet other than the Prophet Muhammad.

Qamariah
Lunar month or Lunar year.

Qazi/Quazi/Qadhi
Muslim court judge, or registrar.

R

Rada
Fosterage.

Radjii
Revocation of divorce.

Revocable
A divorce which has not achieved final effect. After the pronouncement of talaq or dissolution, if the couple wish to reconcile they may do so (during the period of idda) and no fresh marriage contract is necessary; revocability is the possibility of the dissolution being revoked.

Rujk/Rujuk/Ruju'
Revocation of divorce.

Rushd
The age of legal majority (related to puberty and the age of discernment).

S

Sadaq
In pre-Islamic Arabia, sadaq was a gift to the wife at marriage. Used in some communities to mean a gift in addition to mahr, and synonymous with mahr in other communities.

Salish
Traditional and informal village mediation body. Usually comprises of village elders, local influentials and occasionally the village mullah.

Separation of property regime
A property regime in which each spouse retains ownership of property they bring into the marriage and property inherited during the marriage.

Shafi
A particular School of Muslim thought of the Sunni School attributed to Muhammad ibn Idris al-Shafii of the Quraysh tribe who was born in Gaza in 150H; 767 AD (d. 204H; 819 AD). He travelled widely to the Hijaz, Yemen, Egypt and Iraq.

Shia
The partisans of Ali; a School of Muslim thought.

Shiqaq
see niza' wa shiqaq

Shurut
The negotiated clauses in a marriage contract/terms of a contract.

Sleeping embryo
The principle recognized by some Schools that an embryo may 'sleep' in the mother's womb and be born many months, even years after the dissolution of her marriage and still be attributed to her former husband.

Statutory rape
Rape with a person who cannot legally have been considered possible of consenting to sexual relations (usually minors and the insane).

Sui juris
Age of maturity; majority.

Sunnah
The practice (acts, deeds/omissions and words) of the Prophet Muhammad.

Sunni
A Muslim sect, traditionally with four main Schools of thought: Hanafi, Maliki, Shafi and Hanbali.

Suo moto
Of the court's own initiative; generally used to refer to a superior court's initiative to take action when an incident comes to its notice.

Surah
Chapter of the Qur'an.

Syed
Descendants of the Prophet Muhammad.

T

Tafriq
Judicial divorce, generally related to problems between the spouses, specifically a spouse's failure to fulfill certain marital responsibilities.

Talaq
Unilateral divorce by the husband.

Talaq bid'a
see bid'a

Talaq Tafwid/talaq-i-tawfiz/Tafweed
The delegation of the husband's power of talaq. It may be delegated to the wife (either at the time of the marriage ceremony or subsequently), or to a third party, and may be conditional or unconditional.

Talaqnama
Notice of divorce (South Asian Muslim communities).

Ta'liq/Taklik
Conditional divorce. The Ta'liq certificate is signed when the marriage takes place. The usual grounds under ta'liq which entitle the wife to complain to the court are cruelty (violence and lack of conjugal relations), non-maintenance and desertion. Upon proof of the complaint, either the court confirms a divorce (faskh) in absence of the husband or the husband pronounces talaq.

Tamkin
The principle that the wife must remain in the marital home, implying 'obedience' and sexual availability.

Thayyib/Thayyibah
A woman who has had sexual intercourse.

Tuhr/Tuhur
The period of purity/cleanliness, i.e. in between menstruations.

U

Ulema/Ulama
Muslim religious scholars or jurists; singular: alim.

V

Vakil
See wakeel

W

Wakeel/Wakil/Wakal/Waqalah
Agent, or representative.

Wali
In the context of marriage, a marriage guardian. Usually recognized by some Schools as the father or paternal grandfather who has authority to contract the marriage on behalf of the bride.

Wali mujbir
Marriage guardian with the power to compel a virgin in marriage.

Wali nasab
Marriage guardian related by blood to the parties.

Wali raja
Marriage guardian with no blood tie. Used with reference to the transfer of the power of wali to the court. The transfer is made where there is no wali nasab to act as guardian or where the wali mujbir has unreasonably held his consent to the marriage (Malaysia, Singapore).

Waliyat/Walayat-al-jabr
The power of ijbar.

Wilayat-al-nikah
The power of guardianship in marriage.

Z

Zar-i-Khula
Compensation due to the husband from the wife in a khul' divorce (Pakistan).

Zihar
A grounds for divorce available to women through the court; it becomes available after the husband has compared his wife to his mother or a female related in the prohibited degrees.

Zina
Sexual intercourse between parties not married to one another. Under Muslim penal laws, zina is liable to hadd punishment: death for married persons or 80 lashes for unmarried persons. Under Muslim penal laws, there are very stringent standards of evidence required to sentence a person to a hadd punishment (four adult, male Muslim witnesses of good character who witnessed the act itself). If such standards of evidence are not available, a court may award lesser sentences under tazir, for which no specific punishments have been fixed in the Qur'an.

ABBREVIATIONS

ADMLA
Administration of Muslim Law Act, 1966 (Singapore)

CC
Civil Code (Iran, Turkey, and others)

CrPC
Criminal Procedure Code (Bangladesh, India, Pakistan, and others)

CF
Code de la Famille, 1984 (Algeria)

ChMA
Christian Marriage Act 1862 (the Gambia)

CMA
Civil Marriage Act 1939 (Cap 41:02) (the Gambia)

CMPL
Code of Muslim Personal Law, 1977 (Philippines)

CMRA
Child Marriages Restraint Act, 1929 (Bangladesh, India, Pakistan)

CP
Code Penale (Senegal)

CrC
Criminal Code

CSP
Code du Statut Personnel (Tunisia)

DMMA
Dissolution of Muslim Marriages Act, 1939 (Bangladesh, India, Pakistan)

FCA
(West Pakistan) Family Courts Act 1964, as amended in 2001 (Pakistan)

FL
The Law on the Family (Uzbekistan) no date known

GAMCOTRAP
Gambian Committee on Traditional Practices Affecting the Health of Women and Children

GREFELS
Groupe de recherche sue les femmes et lois au Senegal

IFLA
Islamic Family Law (Federal Territories) Act, 1984 (Act 303) (Malaysia)

KHI
Compilation of Islamic Law, 1991 (Indonesia)

LM
Govt. Regulation No. 9 of 1975 Concerning Implementation of the 1974 Law on Marriage (Indonesia)

LMA
Law on Marriage Age (no. 56/1923) (Egypt)

LMA
The Law of Marriage Act, 1971, as amended by Act 23/73 and Act 9/96 (Tanzania)

LMPS
Law concerning Maintenance and some provisions in Personal Status (no. 25/1920) (Egypt)

LPS
Law Concerning Personal Status, 1992 (Yemen)

MA
Marriage Act No. 1/1974 (Indonesia)

MCA
Matrimonial Causes Act, (UK, the Gambia, Fiji, Nigeria)

MMDA
Muslim Marriage and Divorce Act, 1951 (Sri Lanka)

MMDO
Mohammedan Marriage And Divorce Ordinance, 1941 (the Gambia)

MMDRA
Muslim Marriages and Divorces Registration Act, 1974 (Bangladesh)

MWRAF
Muslim Women's Research & Action Forum

OEC
Officier de l'Etat Civil

PC
Penal Code, 1860 Bangladesh, India, Pakistan; Sri Lanka

PLRC
Pilipina Legal Resources Centre

SMA
Special Marriages Act (1872 Bangladesh, Pakistan) (1954 India)

SG
Shirkat Gah Women's Resource Centre

WC
Women's Charter, 1961 (Singapore)

WLUML
Women Living Under Muslim Laws

WRAG
Women's Research & Action Group

WWHR
Women for Women's Human Rights

ZO
Zina (Enforcement of Hudood) Ordinance, 1979 (Pakistan)

LIST OF STATUTES

This is a partial listing of statutory provisions relevant to this Handbook, and does not include all laws relevant to issues covered in this volume and procedural laws.

algeria

Law No. 84-11 of 9 June 1984 comprising the Family Law 1984/Code de la Famille (amendments currently under discussion)

bangladesh

Child Marriage Restraint Act 1929, as amended in 1984

Criminal Procedure Code

Dissolution of Muslim Marriages Act 1939

Guardians and Wards Act 1890

Muslim Family Law Ordinance 1961

Muslim Marriages and Divorces Registration Act 1974

Muslim Personal Law (*Shari'at*) Application Act 1937

Special Marriages Act, 1872

cameroon

The Civil Code 1981

The Civil Status Ordinance of 1981

egypt

Civil Code (no. 131/1948)

Decree concerning provisions in Personal Status (no. 25/1929)

Law concerning Maintenance and some provisions in Personal Status (no. 25/1920)

Law of Bequest (no. 71/1946)

Law on Marriage Age (no. 56/1923)

Personal Status (Amendment) Law (no. 100/1985), subsequently amended on 27 January 2000

fiji

Matrimonial Causes Act 1985 (Cap. 43)

the gambia

Christian Marriage Act 1862

Civil Marriage Act 1939 (Cap 41:02)

Matrimonial Causes Act 1986 (Cap 43)

Mohammedan Marriage and Divorce Ordinance 1941

india

Bihar & West Bengal Registration of Muhammedan Marriages Acts 1876

Child Marriage Restraint Act 1929

Criminal Procedure Code

Dissolution of Muslim Marriages Act 1939

Family Courts Act 1984

Guardians and Wards Act 1890

Muslim Personal Law (Shari'at) Application Act 1937

Muslim Women (Protection of Rights on Divorce) Act 1986

Special Marriage Act 1954

The Shariat Act, 1937

indonesia

Compilation of Islamic Law, 1991

Govt. Regulation No. 9 of 1975 Concerning Implementation of the 1974 Law on Marriage

Marriage Law 1974 (no. 1/74)

iran

Civil Code 1928-1935 (amended in 1982, 1992 and 1995)

[Family Protection Law 1967 repealed]

lebanon

The Law of the Rights of the Family 1962

malaysia

Islamic Family Law (Federal Territories) Act 1984 (Act 303)

morocco

Al- Moudawana/Code of Personal Status 1957 (amended by Law no. 1.93.347 1993)

nigeria

Marriage Act 1990 (Cap 218)

Matrimonial Causes Act 1970 (Cap 220)

Shari'a Court of Appeal Act 1967

pakistan

(West Pakistan) Family Courts Act 1964 (amended in 2001)

(West Pakistan) Muslim Personal Law (Shari'at) Application Act 1962

Child Marriage Restraint Act 1929, as amended in 1961

Criminal Procedure Code 1860

Dissolution of Muslim Marriages Act 1939

Dowry and Bridal Gifts (Restriction) Act 1976

Enforcement of Shari'a Act 1991

Guardians and Wards Act 1890

Muslim Family Laws Ordinance 1961

Offence of Zina (Enforcement of Hadd) Ordinance 1979

Qanun-e-Shahadat (Law of Evidence) Order 1984

Special Marriages Act, 1872

philippines

Code of Muslim Personal Laws (Presidential Decree no. 1083 1977)

Family Code (Executive Order no. 209 1987, as amended by Executive Order no. 227 1987)

saudia arabia

Code of Civil Procedure

Judicial Regulation Decree 1975 (no. 64/1395)

senegal

Code de la Famille 1972, amended in 1974, 1979, 1989

Code Penal

singapore

Women's Charter 1961 (no. 18/61) (Muslims exempted from several sections of Charter)

Administration of Muslim Law Act 1966 (no. 27/66), amended in 1999

Guardians of Infants Act 1961 (no. 6/61)

sri lanka

Adoption Ordinance 1941

Muslim Marriage and Divorce Act 1951

sudan

Muslim Personal Law Act 1991

tanzania

Code of Civil Procedure 1966

The Law of Marriage Act, 1971, as amended by Act 23/73, Act 15/80 and Act 9/96:

tunisia

Code du Statut Personnel 1956, also known as the Majalla (amended inter alia by Laws no. 77/1959, no. 1/ 1964, no.7/1981, no. 74/1993)

turkey

Civil Code 2001

uzbekistan

The Law on the Family 1998

yemen

Civil Code (no. 19/1992)

Law Concerning Personal Status/Personal Status Act 1992 (no. 20/1992)

Penal Code 1994 (no. 12/1994)

1a INTRODUCTION

women living under muslim laws and the women & law in the muslim world programme

This Handbook is an outcome of the Women & Law in the Muslim World action-research Programme of the international solidarity network, Women Living Under Muslim Laws (WLUML). WLUML was founded in 1984. Originally, the network was an action committee, formed specifically in response to several specific cases that urgently required attention. In each of these cases, women were being denied rights by those who claimed to be acting in the name of Islam or with reference to 'Islamic' laws. In response, those who initiated the network aimed to mobilize solidarity and protest, particularly from within the Muslim world, with the goal of unmasking the political motives behind this denial of rights and challenging the alleged sacredness of the dictates under which women were being oppressed.

From the outset, we were clear that our sphere of activity would include not just women who identify themselves as Muslims and not just those living in 'Muslim' states. The very name of our network indicates that we also address ourselves to women in secular societies where Islam is rapidly expanding and where fundamentalists are demanding the imposition of laws based on religion; to women governed by minority religious laws; to women from immigrant Muslim populations in Europe and elsewhere; and to women who have chosen other markers of identity but to whom Muslim laws are applied either through their marriages, their nationality, or their birth identity.

While our original mission was action-oriented, we were conscious that our lack of knowledge about the laws applied to us in our own contexts as well as our lack of knowledge about laws in other contexts added to our isolation from each other and inhibited our ability to challenge the denial of our rights. Therefore, we expanded our goals to include the sharing of concrete information and analysis. Such exchanges build solidarity and enable us to develop and articulate politically effective positions in diverse situations. Clearly, we would need to build upon our collective knowledge in order to move towards bringing about lasting change.

Consequently, WLUML supports solidarity actions and information exchanges, and also undertakes collective projects. These enable women from Muslim countries and communities to deepen our understanding of the factors that shape our lives, thereby strengthening our strategies for initiating change. The longest running of these collective projects was the 'Women and Law in the Muslim World' (W&L) Programme, which started in 1991 and formally concluded in 2001. Cross-regional and international syntheses (such as this Handbook) continue.

The need to research laws in Muslim countries and communities was mentioned in WLUML's very first collectively formulated document, the 1986 Aramon Plan of Action. The actual framework for the W&L subsequently evolved organically and crystallized from our experiences during the network's first two collective projects, the 1988 Exchange Programme (in which networkers from one context spent several months in a context completely different from their own) and the Qur'anic Interpretations Meeting of 1990. During both of these collective projects, it was confirmed that there were indeed multiple understandings of Muslim laws, even if this reality has been obscured in each context because women have internalized the locally hegemonic definition of womanhood.

In the W&L action-research Programme, multidisciplinary teams of researchers and activists across Asia, Africa and the Middle East documented how laws and practices - secular, religious, and customary; written and unwritten - are applied to and affect women in Muslim countries and communities (while there are non-Muslim communities in many Muslim countries, they were not the focus of our research). See Annexe 1 for a list of countries covered by the W&L research. The W&L gathered and shared individual and collective strategies to increase women's rights and space, as well as strategies to resist reactionary trends in legal interpretation and community practice.

methodology, principles and premises

The uniqueness and strength of the W&L lies in its methodology, and in the principles and premises which underlay all the W&L research. These reflect WLUML's overall approach of using our strong networking linkages to break the isolation in which we wage our struggles; we identify commonalities while simultaneously challenging the myth of one homogenous Muslim world by identifying diversities across Muslim countries and communities, and all the while we respect the autonomy of the individuals and groups that are linked through the network. Although comparable research took place through the contemporary Women and Law in Southern Africa (WLSA) project, which has now been extended to Eastern Africa, the W&L was certainly unique in the countries and communities covered in this Handbook.

A basic premise of the W&L is that women are constrained from taking action against oppressive practices and/or from accessing our rights by our lack of knowledge of our formal (especially constitutional) rights. Custom and culture combine to govern the possibilities that are open to women in any context. Hence, customary laws and practices were an important component of the W&L research. Additionally, women internalize the construction of womanhood in their societies and are told that these have religious sanction. Hence, we often believe these constructions are the only, or at least the only valid, definition of womanhood. In Muslim communities, such constructions are often defined in reference to Muslim identity and women who challenge or diverge from the prevailing ideal of 'Muslim womanhood' are seen to be challenging nature, religion and community. Thus, the W&L endeavored both to unravel how custom, culture and law combine to structure our lives and to highlight how the dynamics of religion and politics shape these combinations. At the more immediate level, the W&L aims included demystifying what is presented as 'law' to women; examining the options available to us in law; distinguishing between the customs applied to us and the law; and understanding what the processes of legal construction and reform involve. Such knowledge is vital to those taking a critical and questioning approach to rights, laws, and constructions of womanhood.

We also recognize the equally important fact that the reality of law in women's lives cannot be read from legal texts. In certain cases, law is not specified in any single statute or text. For example, certain customary practices can be enforced as law by courts in Nigeria, while in India the Muslim laws governing the Muslim minority are uncodified (though secular courts may rule on them). Furthermore, written laws, particularly those protecting and guaranteeing women's rights, are more often ignored or broken than honoured and enforced. Numerous countries have laws designed to control or eliminate child marriage and polygyny, but these practices have continued while few (if any) violators have been brought to court. Even more frequently, social practices (whether customary or ascribed to religion) enjoy the force of law even though they contravene a written constitutional or other legal provision. In a number of countries covered in this Handbook, the law has done away with the concept of unilateral talaq (repudiation by the husband); but communities continue to regard a couple as 'properly' and effectively divorced if the husband repudiates his wife, regardless of the content of formal law. Likewise, Bangladesh's laws have banned the demanding and giving of dowry, but women have continued to be beaten and killed because of these practices. Hence, in this Handbook, we distinguish between **law** (enacted legislation or legal interpretations established by court judgments), **implementation** (if and how the agencies with the responsibility for enforcing law do so), and **practices** (what women, or other sectors of the community, actually do).

The W&L was also premised on the analysis that essentialist identity politics and policies (often referred to as 'fundamentalism') restrict women's rights and autonomy in the name of religious and/or cultural imperatives. This perspective has been confirmed in the decade or so since the W&L began, as women in several Muslim countries or communities have found their rights (and often lives) at risk as a result. Perhaps the most publicized example has been Afghanistan, where the ruthlessly authoritarian regime of the Taliban denied women even the basic necessities of life, all in the name of their particular brand of Islam. A common characteristic of essentialist identity politics is the assertion that the political proponents of such ideologies have a monopoly on knowledge and truth. Muslim essentialists make the claim that there is only one true Islam and they attempt to gain moral authority for their political activities by claiming that their interpretations represent that one true Islam. Essentialists often obscure the diversity of Muslim communities in order to claim a unified historical precedent for their goals. WLUML has always asserted that the common – and deliberate – myth of a homogenous Muslim world prevents women in our contexts from even dreaming about alternative possibilities.

The comparative and historical approach of the W&L aims to provide important insights that will help us resist these claims to a sole truth or homogenous reality. Concrete knowledge of the wide variety of options available to women in other Muslim countries and communities helps us resist or challenge the imposition of any one way as the sole correct possibility. For instance, polygyny (the marriage of a man to more than one woman) is customarily mandated in some sections of the Muslim community in Nigeria, permitted without restrictions (other than the number of wives) in India; permitted provided the wives are given separate residences in Sudan; permitted only with court oversight in Malaysia; and altogether prohibited in Tunisia. Moreover, all of these systems claim Islam as the justification for their laws and practices. What is assumed to be Muslim in one community may be unknown, or even be considered unIslamic, in other Muslim communities. Knowledge of the range of possibilities under laws supposedly based on Muslim laws is particularly important for women in those contexts (such as the Central Asian Republics or Fiji) where laws are based on other sources and the identity politics and fundamentalisms of various communities are resulting in demands for reforms in personal laws. Often such demands focus on the community's collective right to be governed by allegedly Muslim laws, such as laws that allow polygyny. Inevitably, these demands are for a very limited (and anti-woman) version of such laws.

The historical approach of the W&L highlights the fact that any given law presented as 'Muslim' was nonetheless contextually constructed at a specific historical time and in a particular geographical place - and therefore, like any other law, it is legitimately subject to critique and change. An historical analysis shows that provisions of law said to be 'Islamic' may in fact either be derived from sources other than Islam or be a reaction to a particular historical context. For instance, the defense of provocation to killings of women in so-called 'honour' killings, which is available under the law in Lebanon, was actually borrowed from the French Napoleonic Code. Similarly, much of the 'Islamic law' of the Indian sub-continent was in fact a British colonial-inspired construction and codification and as such can be more appropriately called 'Anglo-Mohammedan law,' rather than 'Islamic law.' This astute observation was made by A.A.A. Fyzee, the mid-20th century jurist. Similarly, the various disparate regulations about what constitutes a valid and complete payment of mahr (dower, see glossary) are very clearly related to diverse pre-Islamic customary practices about marriage gifts (which party gives what to whom, how much and when) in their specific contexts.

diverse contexts, shared themes

Some twenty country projects were planned in order to take into account the following different types of contexts: majority and minority Muslim communities; countries where secular law is the norm and those where Islam is the state religion, and/or where family laws are based on personal laws derived from religious sources; those that formally recognize customary laws, and those that do not; Muslim minority communities where formal laws are secular; situations where citizens can choose amongst varied legal systems, and those where there is no such choice; as well as diverse (and changing) political situations. This variety of contexts reflects the realities facing the networkers who are linked through WLUML and this list is a small indication of just how varied the situational realities are for women in Muslim countries and communities.

The internal diversity within WLUML was also reflected in the composition of the country teams that conducted the W&L in each of these contexts. These teams included social scientists, writers and lawyers, all with a background in and commitment to women's rights activism. The multidisciplinary nature of the country teams brought richness to their analysis that we believe surpasses previous discussions of women's relationships with law, custom and culture in Muslim countries and communities. Building on our strength as an international network, we also intended the results of the W&L to be comparable at the regional and international levels. To date, too few studies of women's status in Muslim countries and communities have been able to draw upon the diversities in our contexts and thus enrich and strengthen the analysis of the socio-economic and political forces that shape our lives. Thus, following the completion of all W&L country projects by 2001, the process of regional synthesis has begun, with regional syntheses almost completed for South Asia and underway for Africa-Middle East. This Handbook forms part of an international synthesis, and we hope that both the regional and international syntheses will feed back into and deepen local analysis.

Although all W&L country teams were informed by the shared principles discussed above, it was still necessary to develop a list of common research themes and a shared understanding of what research methodologies would produce the data most useful to networkers in order to produce comparable data. In 1992, networkers met to work on these issues, and decided that, in line with WLUML's overall principle of respect for the autonomy of networking groups, each country team would be free to develop its own W&L strategies. The principle difference that emerged between country teams was that some included outreach to strengthen women's knowledge of and access to rights as an integral part of the research process, while others conducted outreach after the initial research and analysis. Moreover, each country team was also free to prioritize specific themes and topics from within the list of commonly identified research themes. They were to do so taking into account the issues which were of greatest concern to the group and/or in the national context, and/or the issues which had already been extensively researched in their local contexts.

The W&L focused on three themes, women in the family, women's individual and bodily rights, and women as citizens. Research on women in the family (concentrating on marriage and divorce) was of principal importance because it is in the family that we experience imposed definitions of gender-appropriate roles on a daily basis. It is in the family that customs, cultures and law most vividly come together. Furthermore, it is the area of personal status law that is most frequently governed by reference to religion or custom. In contrast, in other areas (e.g., political participation, commerce, and often criminal law) previous practices have been replaced or modified by laws from other sources (such as colonial laws; or theories of democracy, socialism and modernization). Crucially, it is in the family that culturally specific articulations of patriarchy are most clearly seen, in the Muslim world and elsewhere. Very often laws and customs relating to marriage, rights within marriage, and divorce determine women's choices in relation to the W&L's second theme. This theme dealt more specifically with bodily integrity (including reproductive rights, sexual violence and domestic violence) and issues of sexuality (including the penalties imposed by the state, society or family for transgressions). The final theme for the W&L was women's rights in the state polity, these being defined in reference to the constitutional framework as well as legal rights to work, to seek and be provided with an education, and to participate in economic activities. This Volume of the Handbook addresses the W&L's first theme, and the remaining themes will be taken up in subsequent volumes.

1b INTERNATIONAL SYNTHESIS OF THE W&L PROGRAMME

the handbook process

This Handbook is the result of some 10 years of research and collective analysis, which has at various points involved almost all active networkers linked through WLUML. These many contributors have been indicated in the long list of people and organizations cited in our Acknowledgements.

After a common list of issues to be researched had been agreed upon at a 1992 meeting in Lahore, W&L Country Projects were started in some twenty countries over the next six years. By 1996, Country Projects in South Asia (Bangladesh, India, Pakistan and Sri Lanka), Fiji, Nigeria, and Turkey were sufficiently advanced for us to begin planning a synthesis in the form of an international cross-comparative Handbook on women, laws and practices. Thus in 1996 a meeting was held in Mumbai, India at which we laid the framework for the Handbook and identified those who would be most closely involved. The concept was further refined at the WLUML third Plan of Action meeting in Dhaka in 1997 and we moved towards fruition in 1998 when two networkers, one from Pakistan and one from Cameroon, worked for three months at the then International Coordination Office (ICO) in Grabels, France. They sifted through the primary data and the published materials that had been produced by the W&L Country Projects and identified gaps in the information. In order to manage the vast amount of information generated, tables were developed for each country that covered the laws, implementation and practices (wherever available) that were relevant to the research issues identified in 1992. These were then circulated to Country Teams for feedback and corrections. In 2000, the first synthesis meeting was held in Lahore, Pakistan, bringing together over a dozen networkers from Asia and Africa to begin the intensive process of analysis and cross-country comparison within each topic. The networkers concentrated on discussing the criteria that would be used to rank laws, implementation practices, and other practices as more or less option-giving for women. Working Groups were set up for each of the Handbook themes: women in the family; violence against women and bodily rights; women as citizens. We decided to prioritize the women and family law theme because networkers and those whom they had encountered in their work most frequently demanded information concerning this area. By 2002 work on the Handbook entered a more intensive phase at the ICO, which had recently relocated to London. There the ICO-based Handbook Coordinator and a South African intern were able to devote several months to developing draft sections. Finally, in September 2002, a small editorial group (composed of networkers) met to review and complete these drafts, which were then circulated to the Country Teams for final feedback before a full language edit. The final production process took place in Lahore at Shirkat Gah Women's Resource Centre, the WLUML Asia Regional Coordination Office.

We are aware that the printing of this volume is in many ways not the conclusion of our work, but just a milestone along the way. Not only do two volumes of the Handbook remain to be published, but as discussed immediately below, we insist that the present volume is by no means definitive. Therefore, we expect (and welcome) that networkers and others will be moved to send us feedback and comments, which may lead to a second edition.

scope and limitations

Although other countries were to be included, practicalities limited the W&L Country Projects to the following, which are all represented in the Handbook: Bangladesh, Cameroon, Fiji, the Gambia, India,

Indonesia, Iran, Malaysia, Morocco, Nigeria, Pakistan, Philippines, Senegal, Sri Lanka, Sudan, Turkey; partial research was also carried out in the former Soviet Central Asian republics of Uzbekistan, Kazakhstan and the Kyrgyz Republic.

However, for the purposes of the Handbook, we felt the need to extend our coverage, at least of statutory laws, to include a number of other countries. Egypt, for example, has been included in a number of sections, both because it was among the first to codify personal status laws and also due to the position of Al-Azhar in the Muslim world, which results in Egyptian laws serving as a frame of reference for reformers in many Muslim countries and communities. Similarly, Tunisia has been included as an important example of the possibilities for reform within a religious framework, particularly in the contentious areas of polygyny and talaq, both of which have been banned. Yemen has been included in places because of the significance of its recent history, notably South Yemen's status as a socialist state and the subsequent reunification of North and South Yemen and the changes this has brought in family laws. Occasional reference is made to Tanzania (which has a large Muslim minority governed by family laws that apply to all citizens and which recognize certain aspects of Muslim laws) and Singapore (which also has a Muslim minority, but they are governed by separate laws) where their provisions may provide legal reformers useful inspiration. Finally, Lebanon (where more than a dozen, separate religious communities are governed by distinct family laws) is also occasionally mentioned, notably in the context of a failed 1998 attempt to introduce a uniform civil code that was backed by women's groups. In many of our contexts, where multiple communities co-exist, the question of a uniform civil code has in recent years, especially with the rise in identity politics, become a matter of considerable debate.

Women & Law Projects took place in the majority of countries and communities covered in this Handbook, and our aim was to produce information on laws, implementation and practices that would be comparable at the cross-country level. However, the network's principle of respecting the autonomy of participating groups, combined with the extremely varied capacity and resources of the Country Project teams, has resulted in our W&L material not being strictly comparable. However, where possible, international synthesis has been offered. On the one hand, the Pakistan, Senegal and Sri Lanka Country Projects were all able to research years of case law, interview focus groups and judges, and discuss issues with judges and Quazis/imams (those who implement personal status laws applicable to Muslims). This extensive research led to a comparatively deeper understanding of the statutory provisions as they actually apply in women's lives. On the other hand, the Cameroon Country Project, because of the relatively recent emergence of women's activism; and the Iran and Sudan Country Projects, because of political restrictions, were more limited in the scope of their research. Perhaps the major area of distinction between the Country Projects was the extent to which procedural law and customary practices were examined. Yet, particularly for women who generally face greater problems of access to justice through the formal courts, procedural matters invariably dictate whether the rights and protections granted under a law actually offer anything to women. Similarly, given that the majority of the population in many of our countries lives beyond the scope of the formal system, customary practices may well have greater significance in our daily lives than any rights granted in the formal law. Finally, local resources, opportunities and priorities determined which of the topics within the broad area of personal status law each Country Team focused on in depth; in only one or two instances were Country Teams able to cover each of the topics represented here in similar depth.

In addition to these limitations, there are a number of other factors that cause this Handbook not to be definitive. Firstly, the W&L Programme was undoubtedly a learning experience for all those involved, and our present analysis of the issues, a decade after the W&L research began, is in some instances now ahead of the understandings that informed the research process. For example, originally it may have been sufficient for us to learn that Algerian courts usually grant a relaxation in the minimum age of marriage for girls who are pregnant. However, we now understand that it is important to know whether this flexibility is motivated by social attitudes that regard puberty, rather than the legal age of 18, as the 'appropriate' age of marriage for females, or motivated instead by a desire to ensure that all sexual activity takes place within valid marriage. Secondly, laws, implementation and practices reflect the societies in which they apply and thus have continued to evolve after our research concluded. In some instances we have been able to include recent changes, notably in statutory laws through the process of Country Teams providing feedback on the Handbook drafts. However, we are conscious that even in the historically short time period since our research on customary practices has been concluded, global and local socio-economic changes have impacted customary practices. Thirdly, we acknowledge that, despite the distinctiveness of its perspective, WLUML is by no means the first or the last to have conducted legal research and sociological-anthropological investigations into customary practices in the countries and communities covered by the W&L. While the Country teams may have reviewed research by groups and academics outside the network to inform their work, such background research is not necessarily reflected in the Handbook.

Further limitations of this Handbook stem not from the W&L research itself, but from the nature of the synthesis exercise and the nature of reproducing the research results in a Handbook format. Inevitably, in the process of synthesizing the W&L materials, we had to lose certain subtleties of social analysis and interactions, both between the various statutory laws applied to one community and between laws and practices. We thus envisage the Handbook to be a starting point resource for advocacy and legal reform efforts, an indication of the issues and various laws and practices across the countries and communities that are covered. We have attempted to highlight the main factors and interconnections that activists should consider when engaging in legal reform and advocacy that concerns women's rights in the family. However, we encourage both networkers and others who read this Handbook to go on to consult the resources listed, do their own further research, and contact relevant networking groups in order to look deeper into the issues. (See Annexe 2 for a list of WLUML networking groups who can be contacted for further information.)

Thus, the Handbook is a synthesis of the results of our research, nothing more and nothing less. We are certain, however, that the W&L's distinct focus on the realities of women's lives and its clarity regarding the interrelationship and differences between laws, religion, and customs will result, even within these limitations, in the Handbook being an essential resource for our efforts towards positive change in women's lives and in the lives of their communities.

handbook format and structure

In all, this Handbook covers twenty-six topics relevant to marriage and divorce, including the status of children (paternity and adoption) and child custody and guardianship, in so far as these affect the lives of women as mothers. Although inheritance is a personal status law issue, we have chosen to deal with it in a future Volume of the Handbook (Volume III), which will include a focus on women's economic rights.

Each chapter and section within chapters contains a narrative overview of the main issues in laws, implementation and practices for that topic. It is in this short space that we have attempted to present our position(s), analysis and debates regarding the topic. Where we have mentioned systems in parentheses while discussing a point, these are examples rather than a complete list of countries or systems that illustrate the point. Almost all topic sections also contain a comparative table of laws (codified and uncodified) that govern that topic.

Since this is a Handbook, not just of legal provisions but also of what these legal provisions mean in the reality of women's lives, we had always intended to indicate which provisions were more or less option-giving for women. The law tables in most sections are therefore ranked, starting with the more option-giving provisions, and moving through the middle ground to end with the less option-giving provisions, each separated by boxes and indicated by an accompanying symbol. These ranked tables should provide the reader an immediate visual guide to the provisions. We consciously avoided labeling provisions 'most' and 'least' option-giving, firstly in recognition of the fact that current provisions are rarely ideal from women's perspective – they may be the best options **available** but certainly not the best provisions **possible**; and secondly, due to women's different positioning even within the same community (especially due to class and age factors), what may be generally option-giving for most women, may not be the best possible option for all women, either of that community or for women of other communities. However, at a very general level, we tended to rank as more option-giving those provisions that specify not only the effects of the violation of a right or procedure (e.g., the validity of a polygynous marriage in contravention of permission procedures), but also the penalties which an offender is liable to. Indeed, those laws that set a minimum penalty are even more option-giving, as they can guard against the courts letting violators go without punishment.

The criteria for these rankings were the subject of considerable debate, and developing them proved to be the most challenging aspect of our work on the Handbook. In order to help readers understand how and why we have ranked various provisions as more or less option-giving, we have listed our criteria before each table of provisions. However, we wish to emphasize that these are not intended as a blueprint for reform or even a listing of 'best practices'. They are our understanding, following the W&L research, merely of what would generally most benefit most women at the current historical moment and in the contexts researched. Clearly, the particularities of local circumstances will determine whether or not our understanding of what is more option-giving will be shared by advocacy and reform activists on the ground. In places, notably in reference to the issues of the validity of child marriages, unregistered marriages, and unregistered divorces (see p.124 & p.140), we point out that our discussions of the criteria may have been inconclusive or incomplete.

Moreover, even within one particular context, individual women's circumstances will determine how more or less option-giving a particular provision will be. For example, if a talaq that fails to follow the legal procedure is nevertheless declared effective by a court, this recognition by the court can both advantage and disadvantage women. In the first instance, for a woman who has remarried after an oral, unregistered talaq, court recognition of the talaq saves her from charges of bigamy or adultery. On the other hand, for a woman who does not want her marriage to end but finds that the court has accepted her husband's unregistered talaq, the court's action has worked to her disadvantage.

There are a handful of sections for which we have decided not to rank provisions in terms of more or less option-giving. Some, such as the sections on Marriage Contracts and Registers and Other Forms of Divorce for Women, have not been ranked simply because ranking was not practical or useful. But for others, we decided not to rank provisions as more or less option-giving in order to reflect continuing debate concerning these topics. For example, the women's movement as a whole appears undecided as to whether or not the principle of the husband having primary responsibility for the maintenance of the wife and family works to women's advantage or not (see p.217-218). Similarly, activists in Muslim countries and communities are divided as to whether mahr (dower, see glossary) should be viewed as a useful financial resource for married women or should be viewed as the equivalent of selling a wife's sexual services and a purchasing of her 'obedience'.

Within the categories of more option-giving, middle-ground, and less option-giving, there is no internal ranking of the provisions; in places we have listed systems alphabetically within each category while in other instances, where one system's provision(s) clearly top(s) all others, we have positioned it at the top of a category to indicate that we assess it to be 'better' within its particular category. Similarly, a country or provision that falls right at the bottom of the table may not necessarily be the ultimately least option-giving provision.

We discovered, while conducting the synthesis analysis, that no single system or set of laws stands out as 'the best' to be copied indiscriminately. While for certain issues a system's provisions may fall closer to the top of the rankings, for other issues it may fall to the bottom. Even within a particular issue, various aspects of a system's provisions can fall in different places within the table. For example, the text of maintenance laws may be more option-giving while the procedures for recovery are extremely weak. This presented problems in the process of ranking provisions, especially where we did not have access to information about procedural matters.

In our tables on laws, wherever practicable, we have paraphrased the law or tried to reproduce the language of the text as closely as possible. Although we have attempted to rank most laws, our aim of summarizing all the provisions concerning a particular topic in easily accessible tables resulted in our not always being able to indicate whether or not a provision is actually applied. The tables on laws must therefore be read simply as a summary of the theoretical provisions, except where we have been able to include Landmark rulings and case law that establishes a firm precedent, as well as other notable rulings. Therefore, to understand the complete picture, the narrative overview and information on implementation and practices must also be examined. For example under Senegal's Code de la Famille, at the time of contracting a marriage the husband must indicate whether he has opted for a monogamous marriage, a polygynous marriage limited to potentially two wives, or a polygynous marriage with an unspecified number of potential wives. Information on how far men adhere to this, the position of the courts in the event of violation, and the ability of brides to influence their husband's chosen option will not be found in the tables on laws.

In most sections, information on implementation and practices follows the tables on laws. In 'implementation' we examine the role of state-recognized bodies (generally the judiciary, but also occasionally local authorities and the police) in upholding the provisions mentioned in the laws tables. Where case law reflects unstable or contradictory social or political trends, we have also discussed this in 'implementation.' We occasionally encountered certain conceptual problems in researching case law and attempting to understand whether a particular judgment works to women's advantage or disadvantage. For example, a 'good' judgment does not necessarily arise out of a notion of gender equality and may instead be informed by paternalistic concepts of the need to protect women as 'the weaker sex.' Such a judgment may not serve the longer-term goals of women's rights advocacy, but it may be a useful experience to share for tactical or strategic reasons. Moreover, even within the same judgment there can be elements which work both to women's advantage and disadvantage, and one must be cautious in citing case law when the complete judgment and circumstances of the case are not known.

In 'practices' we have included information about what communities actually do, beyond the scope of or irrespective of legal provisions. This information highlights ways in which communities seek to circumvent or ignore laws – both to promote and to deny the rights that are denied or granted under laws. As discussed earlier, 'practices' refer to those acts and norms which cannot be brought before a formal forum for a decision and are not 'justiciable.' There are a number of important points to note about the information we present in the Handbook on customary practices. Firstly, there can be a distinction between what people say is their community custom and what actually happens in daily life. For example, in some communities both law and custom dictate that the wife must 'obey' the husband, but we all know that within certain parameters (agreed, that are generally not defined by women themselves) and particularly within the domestic sphere, women of that community may wield considerable decision-making power. However, the Handbook and its necessarily summarized descriptions of practices, was not the appropriate forum to discuss these subtleties. Secondly, many of the W&L Country Projects found an immense variety of practices even within a limited geographical area, due in part to variations of class, ethnicity, sect, rural or urban location and even individual family differences. Again, reflecting this diversity for each of the countries where customary practices research took place was beyond the scope of this volume. Thirdly, wherever we have presented a practice as the norm of a particular community, we acknowledge that in each instance there will be exceptions to the rule, particularly where determined and courageous women have resisted a negative practice or insisted on expanding their individual options.

While our initial intention was to rank implementation and practices according to the more option-giving, middle-ground, and less option-giving continuum, the fact that not all Country Teams had researched these aspects forced us to change our plans. Without a more complete range of provisions to compare, it would have been inappropriate to identify any particular country's courts or community's practices as being at the top or at the bottom of the 'league.' Indeed, doing so may have led to unhelpful generalizations and stereotyping. In a number of sections (e.g., Witness & Mahr, Maintenance, Status of Children, Talaq Tafwid, Khul', Hilala/Intervening Marriage, Custody & Guardianship), the lack of comprehensive research data on implementation and practices led us to drop these subsections altogether and instead incorporate whatever information we did have in the narrative overview.

Finally, many sections contain additional information in the form of boxes and case studies. These highlight particular positive or negative trends, illustrate issues and strategies in country-specific detail, or point out the possible pitfalls of reform.

challenging issues and the positions of wluml

Once we had decided to rank at least laws as more or less option-giving for women, we realized that quite apart from the issues on which we 'agreed to disagree' (notably mahr and maintenance, as discussed above), we would necessarily have to take positions on the topics we were analyzing, **as a network**. Those who are familiar with WLUML will know that, given our insistence on collectivity and the need to accommodate diverse positions, this was no easy prospect. This was particularly so since the eight members of the editorial group that finalized the Handbook did not 'represent' the full diversity of network contexts. Our discussions were further structured by a conscious desire to avoid the pitfalls of cultural relativism and universalism. Moreover, taking a position on one topic inevitably impacted our positions on other topics in ways that were not always consistent. However, we feel that our overall determination to highlight a rights perspective ultimately imposed a considerable measure of coherence.

For example, in the section on Capacity for marriage, our aim is to highlight those laws and practices that increase women's options to choose their marriage partner. Meanwhile, in Chapter 4 on Child Marriage, we take a firm stand that 18 years of age is an appropriate minimum age for marriage and that marriages involving girls less than 18 often involve an element of force because the girl may not have the capacity and social position to provide her informed consent. Our firm position on this minimum age was put into question when we considered the position of girls in the 14-18 age group who may want to marry against their parents' wishes. We ultimately decided that the only means of reconciling our positions on these two topics was to support 18 as the legal minimum age of marriage while allowing for exceptions with court, and not parental, permission. However, activists in systems with such provisions note that they can merely serve as loopholes for the continuation of early and forced marriage. Regarding polygyny and mut'a marriage covered in Chapter 6, some argue that these may be helpful for women who might otherwise face being divorced by their existing husband or remaining unmarried. Indeed, there are indications that in some instances women themselves seek such unions. In the case of polygyny (but not for mut'a, for which we did not have sufficient material to inform a decision), after considerable debate we took the position that even while it may be strategically option-giving for women in particular circumstances, overall polygyny reflects gender inequalities in society and therefore ultimately cannot be considered option-giving (see p.198 on the factors behind polygyny).

As the Handbook progressed, it also became clear that we were indirectly calling for a reconceptualization of marriage in our laws and communities. We were critical of laws and practices that deny women choice in marriage; we ranked provisions that imply an exchange of sexual availability and 'obedience' by the wife for maintenance by the husband as less option-giving for women; we repeatedly emphasized in the sections on inherent rights in marriage, dissolution, financial rights and settlements on dissolution the need for mutuality and gender equity; we deliberately gave prominence to mutual agreement to divorce. In all, we rejected several aspects of the present situation where laws and practices are based on a complex interaction of patriarchal secular provisions; narrow interpretations of Muslim laws; and negative cultural practices have combined to limit women's options in the family. We instead demand the right to build relationships based on harmony, respect and partnership.

This Introduction is immediately followed by a chapter in which we define our terms, identify some issues concerning legal and social contexts, and briefly outline the legal frameworks of the countries and communities covered in the W&L Programme. Readers may find themselves repeatedly returning to this latter section on legal frameworks because, as we are all too aware in our diverse network, the socio-legal context behind a particular law or practice is an important point to consider when we seek to access experience of women in other situations.

2a LAWS, LEGAL SYSTEMS AND CHANGE: OUR DEFINITION OF TERMS

what do we mean when we use the term law?

The word law can be used in several different ways. These include:

a) Statements generalizing invariable patterns of occurrence in the physical world. These are often termed natural or physical laws. One example of this type of law is the law of gravity that holds, for instance, that when a ball is thrown up, it will come down again.

b) Rules devised to regulate behaviour. There are two types of these.

(i) The first are norms and practices that are unwritten and taken for granted. An example of such norms is the practice found in almost all societies of giving gifts at weddings. Failure to observe such norms may bring strong social criticism. A practice in a given social context may seem to have the force of 'law' because its breach is punished by the society (possibly even in a violent manner). Even though the consequences of deviating from a socially enforced practice may be serious, a formal court is not involved in such enforcement.

(ii) The second are rules of prescription (what should be done) and proscription (what should not be done or is disallowed), which society regulates through formal systems, such as the police and state courts. An example of these are regulations governing polygyny; a husband may be required to seek court permission before contracting a polygynous marriage, or co-wives may be able to approach the courts to demand equal treatment. There may even be a punishment of imprisonment and/or a fine for husbands who violate the legal requirement to obtain court permission before entering into a polygynous union. Laws that are enforced through state systems may be written (statutory laws) or unwritten (customary laws), but in contrast to (i) above, such laws are always enforceable through the formal system.

This Handbook focuses on b) the laws of society. Moreover, the W&L country projects tended to focus on (ii) through an examination of the texts of laws, archival research of case law, and interviews with judges and/or others involved in implementing the law. However, some country teams, particularly those that had the institutional capacity to conduct large-scale field research, also examined (i) through surveys, focus-group discussions, and fieldwork.

In contrast to (a) physical laws, the laws of society (both customary norms and formal laws) change over time. Taking the example above, the nature and amount of the wedding gifts or who gives what to whom is constantly changing, even though today's practices are frequently presented as "what has always been done." Similarly, laws regulating polygyny and the court's application of such regulations have changed in most of our countries over the past 50 years.

types of laws

There are various types of laws recognized by formal systems, and in the different countries covered in this Handbook, personal status matters may be governed by one or more of these.

1) Statutory laws include all the Acts and statutes passed by legislative bodies (such as parliaments or houses of assembly) in civilian democratic governments, as well as the decrees and edicts issued by military regimes or civilian dictators. In principle, the legislators, particularly if they are the peoples'

elected representatives in government, are supposed to reflect the views of society. However, it is usually the interests of those in power that are reflected.

2)Common law consists of those rules that by long-standing usage have come to be law, as recognized by a court. Common law is a combination of what people are already doing and the recognition of this reality by judges.

3)Customary laws (sometimes referred to as traditional laws) generally include some form of a peoples' pre-colonial laws (customs and practices) and are usually unwritten. By the twentieth century, customary laws had been largely restricted to personal status concerns (e.g. marriage, divorce, custody) and community-derived property (especially land). Customary laws may themselves have been derived from long-established practices (tradition) or from the decisions of bodies that had authority in the past (such as rulers or perhaps village councils). Some practices may also derive from religious sources. When courts recognize customary practices, these will be enforced by the formal legal system. Customary and common law are thus very similar.

In this Handbook, we distinguish between 'customary laws' and 'practices.' We take customary laws to mean those customs which are justiciable (i.e., a court will accept to hear a case based on such customs), while non-justiciable customs are referred to in the Handbook as 'practices.' For example, in Nigeria a dispute regarding promised gifts that are traditionally exchanged at the time of marriage can be taken to a court and decided on the basis of customary laws. However, in Pakistan where exchange marriages (where a man and a woman from one family are married to a woman and a man from another family) are commonly practiced, the courts will not enforce a promised exchange marriage between Muslims because only statutory law governs Muslim marriages.

Different countries have various combinations of some or all of these types of law. In Nigeria, for instance, all laws, whether based on customary, religious, statutory provisions, or common law are enforced by a court system that stretches from area, customary and magistrates' courts in the first instance, all the way up to the Supreme Court. This formal court system, regardless of which type of law is the basis for hearing the case, is staffed, paid for, and enforced by the Nigerian state. However, in India some aspects of personal status matters may be governed by statutory laws enforced through the formal courts while other aspects are governed by uncodified customary and religious provisions, which may or may not be discussed in the formal courts. In contrast, in the Central Asian Republics only statutory laws are applied by the courts, and they do not recognize customary practices.

the sources of law

Human beliefs about how societies should be organized and regulated are the sources of law. These beliefs may be secular (such as pragmatic empiricism, theories of development or Enlightenment, or socialist rationalism), based on community traditions that are not framed with reference to religion, or they may be framed in reference to religion. Religious sources include the reasoning and opinions of religious legal scholars who have based their understandings on divine revelations and holy texts. In Muslim societies these understandings and reasonings form the basis of what is called 'Sharia.' In this Handbook we will use the phrase 'Muslim laws' rather than 'Sharia' to consciously reflect the diversity of such laws and to dispel the myth that there is a monolithic system of 'Muslim law' or 'Islamic law.' Elements derived from Muslim laws may be codified and thus become part of statutory law; elements may also be reflected in the common law and customary laws. Other examples of explicitly religious systems include the Canon laws (laws based on Christian Church rulings) and the Torah (laws based on Judaism).

While these categories may be useful for analytical purposes, the line between 'secular laws' and 'religious laws' is not so clear in reality. There is a distinction between the political-legal authority of those passing the law – be they religious authorities (imams, the Pope) or non-religious authorities (a monarch, a military dictator, a parliament). But even a statute introduced by a secular authority may still be classified as 'religious' because of its reliance on religious reasoning and beliefs for moral authority (as in the new Sharia Acts in Nigeria or the Hudood Ordinances in Pakistan). Likewise, even when a law is passed by secular authorities without any reference to religious authority, it may still have been influenced by the religious beliefs of its makers, whether or not that is recognized. For example in many contexts laws define the normal working week to extend from Monday to Friday. Inevitably, such laws occur in states with dominantly Christian or European colonial histories. In contrast, in other states with Muslim histories, the work week may be defined in the law to extend from Sunday to Thursday.

Colonial laws, which are still important in many of our countries, are good examples of laws that blur the line between 'secular laws' and 'religious laws.' Colonial laws are those laws promulgated by former colonizers (Britain and France, for the most part, but also Spain, Portugal, Holland and Belgium) and imposed on former colonies. Often these, or parts of these, have been retained after political independence has been achieved. Similarly, the former Soviet republics have retained, in large part, Soviet civil and criminal law since their independence in the early 1990s. Colonial laws were themselves derived from the statutory and common law of the colonizers and were based on the beliefs of the colonizers. With the exception of Soviet law, which explicitly attempted to move away from the influence of religion, colonial laws, particularly those relating to personal status matters, were often strongly influenced by a combination of secular and religious beliefs. For example, the Matrimonial Causes Act that several countries have inherited from British colonial rule (and often not reformed in line with changes that have since taken place in Britain), is strongly influenced by conservative Christian traditions. These influences are reflected in the very limited divorce options and the view of marriage as an intrinsically monogamous union.

Because of the problems discussed above with the imprecision of the term 'secular law' (and its common synonym, 'civil law'), we have instead used in this Handbook the terms 'laws based on Muslim laws' and 'laws not based on Muslim laws' or 'laws based on other sources' rather than 'religious' and 'secular' laws. By using the words 'not based on' and 'other sources,' we in no way mean to imply that laws based on Muslim laws should be seen as the norm, what is desirable, or what is 'better'; we are simply attempting to address the issues raised by the above discussion. In contexts where personal status matters (family laws) for various communities are governed by the separate religious and/or customary laws of each community, we have used the term 'personal laws.'

the nature of muslim laws

There are several 'schools' of Muslim laws. The four main Sunni Schools of fiqh, or thought, that exist today were formed through the personal allegiance of legal scholars or jurists to the founders from whom each school took its name - Hanafi, Maliki, Shafi and Hanbali. Consequently, each School has variations according to the cultural, political, and socio-economic contexts in which they were developed and the philosophy of reasoning that was accepted. The Shia Schools of law came into existence following a rift between Muslims after the death of the Prophet. A difference of political opinion subsequently led to doctrinal differences. An eminent jurist of the main Shia School was Imam Abu Jafar.

Even the oldest Schools of Muslim laws did not exist until many decades after the revelation of the Qu'ran and the Prophet's death. Hence the laws they outline are clearly not direct divine revelations from God. Instead, they are laws developed through human judicial reasoning (ijtihad, in Arabic). The fact that these laws are not sacrosanct but are man-made (literally so because women were excluded from the law-making process) is often obscured by those attempting to gain moral and political authority from them. Equally obscured is the diversity of Muslim laws, which reflects the various and changing concerns of the societies from which they emerged. Muslim laws are therefore not unchangeable law, to be accepted unquestioningly by all Muslims. The scholars after whom the four currently accepted Sunni schools were named had no intention of making their views final and binding on all Muslims.

Abu Hanifa said, "It is not right on the part of anyone to adopt what we opine unless he knows from where we derived it." Imam Hanbal urged, "Do not imitate me, or Malik, or al-Shafi, or al-Thawri and derive directly from where they themselves derived." Whilst Imam Malik cautioned, "I am but a human being. I may be wrong, and I may be right. So first examine what I say. If it complies with the Book and the Sunnah, then you may accept it. But if it does not comply with them, then you should reject it" (MWRAF, 2000). Thus, the very founders of the Schools urged Muslims to question, examine, and trust their own reasoning and beliefs.

The unthinking acceptance which today dominates Muslim societies derives from the myth of the 'closing of the gates of ijtihad', whereby for the last thousand years or more, legal jurisprudence has ceased to develop and instead has followed established models. However, it should be noted that this 'closing' was a politically inspired change in approach. Abu Zahra wrote that the acceptance of ijma (a consensus about the Schools of Muslim laws at that time) in the tenth century was only for the maintenance of national unity and to check individual deviations, that ijma was legalized as an "authority after the sacred texts" (MWRAF, 2000). Thus, refusing further ijtihad is not a religious or divinely sanctioned act. It is not required in the Qu'ran or by the Sunnah (the sayings and practices of the Prophet). Indeed, the Shia Schools have never accepted the closing of the gates of ijtihad.

Today, most statute laws and even uncodified Muslim laws applied by courts as 'Muslim laws' are derived from an eclectic mixture of provisions from the various Schools. These are added to an acceptance of the principles of modernization (particularly reflected in the need for state regulation of marriage and divorce) and to remnants of customary practices (for example, the refusal of courts in many systems to recognize women's property rights on divorce). In the W&L research, we also found that frequently judges and communities stated that their application of Muslim laws reflected a particular sect (e.g., Maliki or Hanafi laws), even though people of the same sect elsewhere do things differently.

2b LAWS, LEGAL SYSTEMS AND CHANGE: CONSTITUTIONAL LAW, CEDAW AND INTERNATIONAL HUMAN RIGHTS LAWS AND NORMS

The constitution of any country embodies the basic principles governing that country. Often described as its supreme law, a constitution spells out the fundamental principles which govern relations between the state and its citizens, as well as relations between citizens. While specific laws deal with matters like family issues, crimes and penalties, civil procedure, and so on, a constitution regulates the overall working of the law.

Post-colonial constitutions follow similar patterns. They lay down the form of government that will be followed in the country: whether that be parliamentary, presidential, or even a monarchy and whether there will be a federal or a unitary system. However, the most important parts of a constitution are those which deal with a country's ethos, its guiding principles. Constitutions should be examined to see whether or not they safeguard the rights of individuals and of religious and ethnic minorities, whether or not all citizens, regardless of caste, colour, creed, ethnicity, or gender are equal; to see, indeed, who can be a citizen. (In ancient Greece, the cradle of Western democracy, neither women nor slaves were citizens). One looks to see whether or not the state has arbitrary powers of arrest and detention and whether or not the state can be challenged if it acts unconstitutionally. It is important to see which of the fundamental rights (of freedom of religion and belief, of equality before the law, and of due process) are safe-guarded within the constitution itself. Sometimes it is possible to go to court to have a fundamental right enforced. However, in some cases even when a fundamental principle is laid down in the Constitution, it may not be enforceable in court. In other words, the constitution is saying, "This is what we would like to see happen, but no promises are being made."

Legal equality, even when guaranteed constitutionally, is often negated by the retention of discriminatory personal status laws that are usually derived from an interpretation of religious and customary laws, or even by the constitution's own recognition of customary laws, as in the Gambian Constitution. This point is developed further below.

Equality before the law is not the same as legal equality. The first relates to the processes of law (for example, whether or not women and men are treated equally by the police and courts). The second relates to status (for example, does the law grant women and men equal rights to choice in marriage). Most equality clauses are broad enough to encompass both process and status. However, in practice, in many states the equality clauses in constitutions are narrowly interpreted by the courts, which hold that equality has to be construed in the light of clauses guaranteeing freedom of religion or recognizing customary laws, rather than vice versa, even though the constitution may not say explicitly that these are higher than the fundamental right of equality. The most significant exception to this pattern is South Africa, where a Supreme Court case has established that equality takes precedence. (Women's networks, including WLUML and WLSA, shared with South African allies their concerns and experiences about the dangers of the constitutional recognition of customary laws during in the period of intense debate and constitution-making in the 1990s, and are much encouraged by the current situation.)

In systems where the laws of evidence and criminal laws are based on retrogressive local interpretations of Muslim laws, they discriminate variously against women: reducing the value of women's testimony in certain matters, making females liable to punishment at an earlier age than males, and in some instances providing for lesser compensation for women (either as victims or heirs of victims) under laws of Qisas and Diyah (retribution and bloodmoney).

Thus, even constitutional guarantees of non-discrimination and equality may not amount to much. In this context international conventions have a major role to play.

International Law is the system of rules and regulations by which sovereign states bind themselves to behave in certain ways. The main difference between International Law and national laws is that states only voluntarily bind themselves to uphold International Law. A private citizen may not like the laws of her country, but she will be bound by them nevertheless. States are under no such obligation unless they have entered into an agreement (and they may, if they are powerful or rich enough, withdraw from treaties they have signed). Such institutions as the United Nations and the International Court of Justice (and now the International Criminal Court) use treaties, conventions, and protocols to bring nations into the fold and to protect weaker states against the more powerful ones.

The Universal Declaration of Human Rights was formalized in 1948. Several other conventions followed. Twenty-two developing and Eastern European countries had framed a request to the Commission on the Status of Women in 1963 (U.N. General Assembly A/5606 15 November) to draft a declaration on the elimination of all forms of discrimination against women. These countries included Afghanistan, Algeria, Argentina, Austria, Cameroon, Chile, Columbia, Czechoslovakia, Gabon, Guinea, Indonesia, Iran, Mongolia, Morocco, Pakistan, Panama, the Philippines, Poland, Togo and Venezuela. The Convention on the Elimination of all forms of Discrimination against Women (CEDAW), which eventually came into being in 1985, was thus the expression of the concerns of these states rather than the 'western' imposition it is frequently portrayed to be. In fact, the USA, the leading Western power, is one of the few countries that continues to refuse to adopt CEDAW.

CEDAW is an instrument that women can use to try neutralize the patriarchy inherent in the laws that govern them, including the constitutions of their countries. All but three Muslim majority countries have ratified the Convention, although, like for example Bangladesh, Iraq, and Morocco, often with reservations to Article 2, which commits the state, amongst other things, to an undertaking to amend national laws to bring them in line with international norms. However, ratification with reservations is not limited to Muslim majority countries; New Zealand, on behalf of the Cook Islands, and Britain have both made reservations to CEDAW.

If a country ratifies an international convention, its provisions will not necessarily become law within that country. In some instances there are constitutional provisions that immediately incorporate the ratified treaty/convention. More often, incorporation requires an act of legislation. It is, however, always possible for judges to guide themselves on the basis of an international norm, and activists work on preparing such arguments in writs brought in court. There have been instances where judges have taken cognizance of these conventions and drawn upon them to give gender-sensitive judgments.

2c LAWS, LEGAL SYSTEMS AND CHANGE: LAWS AND SOCIAL CONTEXTS

law and patriarchy

Women have seldom been in a position to pass, elaborate, and implement laws. Thus, laws have been developed, over many centuries from the viewpoints (implicit and otherwise) of men. This applies just as much to laws not based on Muslim laws as it does to Muslim or customary laws. It is therefore dangerous to assume that a move away from religious or customary laws will be free of biases against women. Patriarchy (in its minimalist sense of male-dominated rule) has been around for a long time and continues to influence modes of thought and behaviour.

Laws that are not based on religion are often discriminatory as well; patriarchy is not a construct of religion but is derived from an unequal distribution of resources and decision-making along gender lines. The negative influence of patriarchy is visible even in laws not relating to personal status in countries where family laws are inspired by Muslim laws. For example, often female citizens who are married to foreigners are denied the right to pass on their nationality to their husbands (for example in Egypt, Morocco, Bangladesh, and Pakistan) even though foreign women married to men from those very countries become entitled to nationality. Similarly, patriarchy is a problem in countries where family laws are not based on Muslim laws. For example, often the husband is institutionalized as the head of household; this provision was influenced by French colonialism in secular leaning Senegal and has only recently been removed from the Turkish Civil Code (in 2001).

Moreover, the influence of patriarchy continues to be reflected in contradictory constitutional provisions (as discussed above regarding provisions on gender equality and religious freedoms and/or recognition of customary laws), as well as in the attitudes of state institutions, such as the judiciary, the police, and administrative bodies. For example, even where citizenship laws or family laws do not require it, as in Nigeria, officials may nevertheless ask a woman to produce evidence that she has her husband's permission or consent before they will provide her with a passport.

Therefore, it is clear that legal reforms, in and of themselves, will not be sufficient to change women's status within the family. Whether or not laws afford protection for women's rights depends not only on how the laws are worded, but also on the social relations of the context in which they are to operate. As Farida Shaheed points out, "since the interpretation of law cannot be detached from the specific cultural context in which it is located, norms and accepted practices profoundly affect the application and the interpretation of law" (Shaheed 1998:65). Hence in Pakistan, up to 1990, the defense of "grave and sudden provocation" had been accepted to condone men's murder of female relatives – even when the evidence refuted the claim or there was no evidence at all that there was provocation, never mind sudden or grave. The bare legal phrase had been clothed with socio-cultural norms about men's and women's acceptable behaviour. Male relatives still are acquitted of killing female relatives. Even though the defense of "grave and sudden provocation" is no longer available under the 1990 Law of Qisas and Diyat, changing the attitude of lawyers and judges to ensure that men who murder their female relatives are not given lighter sentences has proved an uphill task.

Undoubtedly, one of the greatest indications of the predominance of patriarchy is women's overall lack of access to justice, whether due to their lack of knowledge regarding their rights or other factors that constrain them from approaching the courts to seek justice. This Handbook's focus on formal laws must be seen in this context: we have attempted to highlight provisions that are more option-giving for women, but we have not always been able to comment on how far these provisions are meaningful in practice.

inter-relationships of laws

One of the complexities of using law reform and access to rights in law as a tool for developing and protecting women's rights and autonomy is that it is insufficient to improve law in one area, without taking into account other areas will be impacted. For instance, laws on divorce need to be cross-referenced with provisions on mahr (is it recoverable or is it returnable?), child custody (will the mother retain custody of her children?), marital property (will the woman be given a share of that property?), etc; provisions regarding polygyny need to be examined in the light of provisions regarding maintenance (can a co-wife approach the courts to demand equal maintenance, is this a condition for polygyny?), registration of marriage (can a polygynous marriage be registered), divorce (can a wife seek divorce if her husband contracts a polygynous marriage in violation of polygyny regulations?), mahr (does it become due when her husband contracts another marriage?), property rights (how is marital property divided in polygynous households?), and the possibility of negotiating stipulations in a marriage contract (can the wife demand that the marriage remain monogamous, or does the husband have to choose whether the marriage will be monogamous or polygynous?). Therefore, when using this Handbook as a tool for discussing reform (whether of the formal law or bringing about changes in community practices) in a particular family matter, it is necessary to be aware of all the related aspects that have to be examined. For this reason, we have attempted to indicate where a section dealing with an issue should be cross-referenced to another section.

Moreover, to analyze the implementation of a particular law and its impact on women's lives, one has to examine a range of interactions of family law with civil law, criminal law, court structures, constitutions, judicial training facilities, etc. For example, the registration of marriages can be interrelated with rules, directives, and laws on the qualifications of marriage registrars; constitutional provisions regarding the right to found a family, or relationships between members of different religious communities; or penal laws on sexual crimes (such as unregistered marriages leaving couples vulnerable to charges of zina).

law as a tool for reform

Those involved in law reform advocacy have to be particularly careful to consider whether or not, and in what circumstances, a change that seems like a clear gain might have contradictory and painful consequences. For example, the rights of wives are usually thought to be better protected when the law requires marriages to be registered formally because when unregistered marriages are not recognized, then forced and under-age marriages are much less likely to occur. However, if the law does not recognize unregistered marriages, but they are nonetheless happening in large numbers, then this might result in the wives from these unregistered marriages being unable to claim inheritance or maintenance, or in their children's paternity being unrecognized (therefore, they are unable to make claims on the putative fathers).

It is not just that reform may have untoward consequences, but also that (as noted above in the discussion regarding patriarchy and social contexts) in certain instances, there are very clear limitations of law reform as a tool of social change. For example, reforms to restrict child marriage and polygyny have been ineffective in many countries, and any change (increase or decrease in the practice) has been in spite of, rather than because of, legal provisions. Similarly, maintenance for wives and children, no matter how protective the legal provisions, is largely unrecoverable especially in undocumented, poverty-ridden economies.

In the context of law reform, there is an on-going debate over whether it is more option-giving for women to have a law which is exhaustive in detail (such as the pre-unification South Yemeni code and many aspects of Malaysian Muslim family laws) or to have laws which lay down certain principles but leave the courts considerable discretion in interpreting these principles. Detailed provisions (if well drafted) have the advantage of leaving less room for endless litigation and the exploitation of loopholes by the more powerful (generally men in the context of family laws) and setting the basic parameters for court's decisions. However, if detailed laws contain restrictive provisions, they can leave women, progressive lawyers, and gender-sensitive judges little room to maneuver. On the other hand, vague provisions leave women vulnerable to court attitudes and changes in the country's political atmosphere while also creating confusion about the intent of the law. Ultimately, when advocating for reform, activists have to be aware of the dangers inherent in either explicit or implicit provisions.

There is also the question of whether or not regulation (particularly retrogressive or poorly drafted provisions) is better than unregulated practices. Where women have a measure of autonomy recognized by the community, a bad law can actually reduce their options. This is starkly illustrated for example in Kerala, India, where divorce among Muslims is completely unregulated. In recent practice, women migrant workers have been sending their husbands 'talaq notices,' and the communities are accepting and upholding these. But, for example, if a law recognizes men's unilateral 'right' of talaq and allows it to be freely accessed apart from minor procedural requirements, while at the same time providing women with only limited access to divorce through the courts, codification and regulation may work to women's detriment. This then points to the need for the involvement of women in the law reform process to ensure that the introduction of regulation (which **generally** works to women's advantage) does not, in fact, remove any previous space for maneuvering that they had in an unregulated system.

Another matter to be considered in the law reform process is whether or not stricter regulation will merely push underground the negative practice it is seeking to control. Yet again, it is clear that law reform and regulation must be accompanied by wider efforts towards social change.

Finally, the local political context will determine which strategic approach is more appropriate when seeking to strengthen women's rights within the family. For example, factors such as the government's concern over the increasing influence of politico-religious parties in Turkey, the overall secular context of family laws, and the high levels of education and employment among women enabled Turkish women's groups to launch a headlong challenge to conservative forces who opposed sweeping and positive changes in the Turkish Civil Code. In other contexts, demanding progressive change in family laws may be a political impossibility because the state is succumbing to the growing influence of identity politics, and a reduction in women's rights is invariably the first concession made to politico-religious parties. Such concessions were made in Algeria's 1984 Code de la Famille, as well as in the abandoning of certain positive provisions introduced in 1979 during family law reform in Egypt in 1985. In such contexts, reform of procedural laws and administrative procedures, which are less in the public spotlight, may offer a more accessible avenue for immediate change.

There are currently contradictory trends within and across countries. On the one hand, factors such as socio-economic developments, greater consciousness, and work by rights activists are widening women's options, forcing more gender sensitive judicial interpretations, and increasing pressure for positive reform. On the other hand, the growth of fundamentalisms and increasingly violent resistance to change on the part of the powerful is leading to a narrowing of options for women. There may be particularly contrasting trends within countries where there are parallel legal systems with different laws applying to different communities. For example, in Sri Lanka, following sustained pressure from rights activists, changes were recently legislated in provisions regarding child marriage. These changes introduced a minimum age of marriage. However, Muslims were excluded from the new law's ambit because of opposition from Muslim conservatives and politico-religious parties (at the time a key factor in the parliamentary balance), so there is effectively no minimum age of marriage for Sri Lankan Muslims. Under such circumstances, states may claim that they cannot 'interfere' in the 'traditions' of a community, even if many members of that community demand reform. Such apparent sensitivity concerning community rights is often, in effect, a very calculated policy of discrimination.

2d LAWS, LEGAL SYSTEMS AND CHANGE: CONSTITUTIONAL AND LEGAL FRAMEWORKS

For the vast majority of women in the countries and communities covered in this Handbook, rights within the family are governed largely by practices operating outside the framework of the formal law. Nevertheless, an understanding of the constitutional and legal framework is essential to our goal of equitable laws and practices, as this framework provides the present limits within which we can work, as well as the boundaries we may want to challenge. This framework includes the following, which can determine the success of individual and collective attempts to access justice:

- **Constitutional provisions,** notably those regarding gender equality, freedom of religion, the secular or religious nature of the state, and the recognition or non-recognition of customary practices (particularly those that violate any fundamental rights guaranteed in the constitution);
- **Provisions determining which laws apply to which community**, and in the case of parallel systems, whether women in Muslim communities must be governed by laws based on Muslim laws or can opt to be governed by laws based on other sources;
- **The court structure** and whether or not there are separate courts to adjudicate on Muslim and/or customary laws, and whether or not women in Muslim communities can approach general courts for the adjudication of family law disputes;
- **The question of whether or not custom is justiciable**, i.e., whether or not the courts will accept cases where relief is sought on the basis of custom.

The legal frameworks in countries covered in this Handbook vary from a single law, not based on Muslim laws, applying to all citizens, irrespective of their ethnic or religious identity (the Central Asian Republics, Fiji, and Turkey) to a combination of coexisting laws including Muslim laws, customary laws, and laws based on other sources within the same state (the Gambia, India), sometimes even complemented by multiple court systems (Nigeria). Because so many of the countries included in this Handbook have different laws for different communities, we have been careful to use the word 'systems' rather than 'countries' while discussing a particular provision of law. In countries where there are different laws for the various ethnic or religious communities and also a supposedly secular law applicable to all citizens, it may be possible for people to choose which law applies to them (India, Nigeria), or it may not (Indonesia, Malaysia, Pakistan, Sri Lanka).

Political change can limit these choices as in Nigeria, where the process of 'Sharianization' that has been particularly evident since 1999 has reduced the space for Muslim women to marry under customary laws or the Matrimonial Causes Act. In another example, the Special Marriages Act found in Bangladesh, India, and Pakistan has been most commonly used as a legal means for inter-faith couples to marry. In Bangladesh, as implied in the text of the Act, any person wishing to marry under the Act must renounce their faith, while any Muslim is automatically obliged to marry under the Muslim Family Laws Ordinance. In India, following a 1954 amendment, any citizen may marry under the Act without having to abjure their faith. But in Pakistan, the choice of marrying under the Special Marriages Act (which has retained its original text as in Bangladesh) has been severely curtailed by 'Islamization' and the possibility that new provisions in the Penal Code regarding blasphemy might be invoked to frame a blasphemy charge should someone renounce their faith in order to marry under the Act.

To add further complications, certain family matters (e.g., marriage and divorce) may be dealt with by courts applying a specific law based on religion or custom, while other family matters (e.g., maintenance, adoption, enforcement of decrees) may be governed by a general law applicable to all communities. For women this can present extreme difficulties. For example, in Sri Lanka a maintenance decree for a woman married under the Muslim Marriage and Divorce Act, 1951 is to be decided by the Quazi Courts, but since the Quazi Courts have no powers of enforcement, the woman has to go to a Magistrate Court for enforcement. And finally, in some countries (Cameroon, the Palestinian community in Israel), the litigant may choose whether to approach a general forum or one which operates on the basis of customary or Muslim laws.

Being able to choose which system is applied to them is usually not an option for most women because of their lack of decision-making power in the area of family matters. Moreover, as the findings of the W&L and the subsequent sections on family matters show, it is hard to categorically state which system is 'better' for a woman. Within each system, her options may be increased in one sphere and decreased in another. For example, marriages under the Matrimonial Causes Act in some West African countries may bring stronger guarantees that the husband will remain monogamous or that he can be punished for polygyny, but divorce options can be more limited than under customary and Muslim laws. Often, it is men who are more able to take advantage of the existence of multiple systems. In India, Malaysia, and Sri Lanka, conversion to Islam is a device used by Christian and Hindu husbands to avail themselves of the easy unilateral divorce or the option of polygyny available to Muslim husbands.

A federal state structure can add further complexities. In federal Nigeria, customary laws vary from place to place but are not coterminous with state boundaries. Meanwhile, since each State's court system is seen as autonomous, positive precedent in one State does not automatically apply in another. In federal Malaysia, family law varies from State to State, and husbands can attempt to evade or side-step the regulation of polygyny by moving their application for permission or conducting their polygynous marriage in another State. However, non-Muslim wives in Malaysia appear to be protected from their husband's manipulation of conversion possibilities under a judgment of the Federal Court, which laid down that any matrimonial disputes must be governed by the law applicable to the parties at the time of their marriage where only one party has converted. But this may not have application across all States.

algeria

Constitution	Other Laws	Muslim Laws	Customary Laws	General Comment
Algeria is a unitary Republic. Article 29 of the 1976 Constitution states all citizens are equal before the law and there shall be no discrimination including on the basis of sex. A. 31 emphasizes the state's obligation to take steps to ensure equality including between men and women; A. 32 states that fundamental rights are to be enjoyed by men and women. Meanwhile A.2 affirms that Islam is the state religion and A. 36 protects freedom of religion, There is no indication as to how any potential conflict between these provisions is to be resolved.	Religious minorities are governed by separate personal status laws, but all family cases are heard by a unified system of general courts.	After a struggle against French colonial rule inspired by socialist principles, the Algerian state emphasized an increasingly restrictive Muslim identity as a means of forging a post-independence national identity. Women's rights have been a major focus of this contradiction, leading to almost two decades of controversial attempts to reform family laws. In 1984 a highly disputed and patriarchal Code de la Famille was promulgated, based on regressive interpretations of Muslim laws.	Customary practices are not justiciable.	An on-going civil war between the Algerian state and armed politico-religious extremists has been raging since the 1990s, leading to the deaths of over 100,000 people. Women have been a particular focus of war crimes perpetrated by the fundamentalist FIS and GIA, while progressives have been persecuted both by the government and extremists.

bangladesh

Constitution	Other Laws	Muslim Laws	Customary Laws	General Comment
Secularism was one of the fundamental principles underlying Bangladesh's Constitution. This principle has since been repealed. Equality provisions in the Constitution are interpreted as being limited by others that protect freedom of religion. In practice, even where a discriminatory law is not based on religious laws, the courts have not used equality provisions to strike the law down.	The Indian subcontinent was under British Colonial rule, for about 200 years, until 1947. During this period English Common Law was imported into the region and codified. Religious communities maintained various personal status laws, some of which were ultimately codified. Following an end to colonial rule in 1947 and independence from Pakistan in 1971, most of Bangladesh's laws continue to be based on English Common Law. Citizens may marry under the secular Special Marriages Act, 1872. However, to do so they must renounce their existing faith.	The various religious communities are governed by separate personal status laws. These include pre-Independence laws such as the Dissolution of Muslim Marriages Act, 1939 and the Muslim Family Laws Ordinance, 1961 (MFLO) as well as the post-Independence Muslim Marriages and Divorces Act, 1974. All Bangladeshi Muslims are to be governed by the MFLO. Although Bangladesh is dominated by the Hanafi School, laws governing the Muslim community are derived from various Schools. There are no separate Muslim Courts or Judges.	For Muslims, custom is not justiciable in the area of family matters.	In the area of family laws, there is an interaction between laws based on Muslim laws and those based on other sources. This interaction includes both substantive and procedural aspects of the laws. For example, the Guardian and Wards Act 1890 which governs all communities, is applied in conjunction with the rules of guardianship under Muslim laws in the case of disputes involving Muslims. A wife's right to mahr is governed by Muslim laws, facilitated by the standard marriage contract established under the Muslim Family Ordinance Rules of 1961. This is enforced through the Family Courts which are not specified as being available only to Muslims.

cameroon

Constitution

Cameroon is a 'decentralized' unitary republic which is secular, democratic and dedicated to social service (1996 amendment to 1972 Constitution). Only those traditional values which conform to democratic principles, human rights and the law are to be recognized. However, equality provisions do not mention gender. There is no state religion in this multi-religious society.

Other Laws

Cameroon has a history of German, French and British colonization before independence in 1960. The judicial system is largely based on the French system although Common Law influence is evident. Since both French and English are official languages all laws are meant to be in both languages but often the French is taken as the authentic version and translation discrepancies occur.

The Civil Status Ordinance governs registered marriages and only registered marriages are recognized.

Muslim Laws/Customary Laws

Spouses must agree to be judged either by (a) the more easily accessible Court of First Instance, which bases its judgments largely on customary and Muslim laws, or (b) by the High Court, which follows the Civil Status Ordinance.

General Comment

The very low number of lawyers and magistrates places a severe strain on the justice system and discourages people from accessing the courts.

egypt

Constitution	Other Laws	Muslim Laws	Customary Laws	General Comment
Egypt is a unitary Republic, and under Article 1 of the Constitution, a democratic socialist state. Under A. 2 Islam is the state religion and Islamic jurisprudence the principle source of legislation. A. 11 qualifies that women's equality with men is to be without violation of the rules of Islamic jurisprudence, while A.12 privileges tradition, national values, scientific facts, socialist conduct and public morality. A. 40 on equality before the law does not specify equality of women and men before the law.	Separate personal status laws exist for the substantial Coptic Christian minority.	Egypt has some of the longest-standing codified personal status laws based on Muslim laws, dating back to the 1920s. These have been amended repeatedly, most recently in 1985 and 2000, and are largely based on the Hanafi School, although provisions regarding divorce initiated by women have been inspired by other Schools. Personal status issues are heard by special sections of courts of general jurisdiction and by judges trained in Muslim laws.	Customary practices are not justiciable.	Family laws have been the focus of attention by extreme Right politico-religious groups. The constitutionality of a Presidential decree, introducing among other provisions, reforms of personal status laws, was challenged in the mid-1980s. Following a compromise with conservatives in Parliament a number of provisions were dropped from the new provisions subsequently adopted.

fiji

Constitution	Other Laws	Muslim Laws	Customary Laws	General Comment
The Constitution is the supreme law of the republic of Fiji, and any law inconsistent with the Constitution is invalid. Article 35 guarantees freedom of religious belief. A. 38 establishes the right to equality before the law and prohibits discrimination including on the grounds of gender.	The Fijian courts continue to accept UK precedent, including in deciding matters under the Common Law based Matrimonial Causes Act.	Muslim laws are not recognized by the courts as a source of law.	Customary practices are not justiciable for Muslims, although lower courts may take these into account while deciding family cases involving Muslims.	A proposed Family Law Bill will introduce significant reforms, notably in the area of divorce although not directly changing the Marriage Act. Although the Bill has been discussed for many years, its passage has been strongly resisted by groups promoting identity politics based on religion and ethnicity, particularly local Christian authorities and Fijian nationalists.

gambia

Constitution	Other Laws	Muslim Laws	Customary Laws	General Comment
The 1997 Constitution is the supreme law of the Gambia and any laws inconsistent with the Constitution are void. The Constitution also contains clauses guaranteeing human rights and fundamental freedoms without distinction as to gender. However, the Constitution recognizes (The laws of the Gambia, 7a-f) 'the Sharia' as a source of law for family matters among Muslims and also recognizes customary laws as a source of law for the laws of the Gambia. Activists believe this undermines constitutional guarantees of gender equality. There have not been any cases to test the equality provisions in the area of family matters.	The largely outdated Civil Code was inherited from British colonial rule. In addition to personal status law and customary laws, decrees passed by the Armed Forces Provisional Ruling Council, and Common Law principles are recognized as the laws of the Gambia. Citizens can choose to be married under and governed by the Civil Marriage Act 1939 (Cap 41:02)and Matrimonial Causes Act 1986 (Cap 43).	The Mohammedan Marriage and Divorce Ordinance of 1941 governs certain family matters for Muslims marrying under the Ordinance, including registration of marriage and divorce. Other family law matters are governed by uncodified Muslim laws. The Cadi Court (established by the Family Code Part 3:137(1-7), relies on a combination of the Maliki School and local custom. Appeal against decisions of the Cadi Court cannot be heard in any other forum.	The Constitution recognizes the unconditional application of customary law without any modification (chapter 2:7(e). Parties married under customary laws are governed by these irrespective of provisions of Muslim laws or other laws. Customary law is based upon the established practices of the various ethnic and tribal groups and is mostly adjudicated by male elders or District Authorities.	

india

Constitution	Other Laws	Muslim Laws	Customary Laws	General Comment
The much-amended 1949 Constitution establishes India as a secular federation. While A. 25-28 guarantees freedom of religion, A. 44 states the aim of establishing legal uniformity in India, including a uniform civil code, now resisted by large sections of the minority Muslim community. A. 15 guarantees non-discrimination including on the grounds of sex, and permits affirmative action by the State to promote women's status.	The Indian legal system is heavily influenced by English Common Law following centuries of colonial rule. Although colonial policy was to leave family laws uncodified, in the late 1800s and early 1900s basic legislation was introduced, including the Guardians & Wards Act 1890 and Child Marriage Restraint Act 1929, applicable to all communities. Muslim personal laws are applied by general Family Courts established under the 1984 Family Courts Act. Inter-religious and secular marriage is possible under the 1954 Special Marriages Act.	Personal laws for Muslims have remained largely uncodified since colonial times. Cases are heard primarily on the basis of Hanafi jurisprudence, although precedent, interpretations by other Schools and custom can be considered authoritative. The Muslim Personal Law (Shariat) Application Act, 1937 merely directs that family laws matters for Muslims shall be governed by Muslim personal laws. The dissolution of Muslim Marriages Act 1939 was introduced following pressure from local religious authorities as many Muslim women left Islam as a means of ending unhappy marriages.	The Family Courts have increasingly rejected negative customary interpretations of Muslim laws, such as triple talaq, on the basis of fundamental rights or reinterpretations of Muslim laws.	Some States have provisions for registration of marriages and divorces such as the Registration of Muhammedan Marriages and Divorces Act 1876 applicable in Bihar and West Bengal. Reform of personal status law for Muslims has become the focus of identity politics since the 1980s and the Shah Bano case. The Muslim Women (Protection of Rights on Divorce) Act 1986 remains highly controversial and subject to varying legal interpretations.

Indonesia

Constitution	Other Laws	Muslim Laws	Customary Laws	General Comment
The 1945 Constitution establishes Indonesia as a unitary Republic. It does not adopt any official religion, but Article 29(1) affirms belief in the One Supreme God. There are no gender equality provisions.	The Indonesian legal system is influenced by Dutch colonial rule and combines Roman-Dutch law, Muslim laws and customary laws. A controversial Marriage Law was introduced for all Indonesians in 1974. Regular courts hear cases for religious minorities while Sharia courts hear personal status law cases for Muslims.	During colonial rule, Muslim laws were applied in family and inheritance law in Java and Madura. Following independence in 1945, the Muslim Marriage and Divorce Registration law of 1946 was enacted. In the 1980s the state issued Compilations on Islamic Law in order to clarify the application of Muslim laws. These are dominated by Shafi interpretations. The 1989 Law on Religious Courts restricted the secular courts systems jurisdiction over religious courts.	Customary adat law was previously recognized under Dutch rule, and continued to be applied in matters of inheritance until the Islamization of laws in the 1980s.	As a concession to the movement for autonomy in Aceh, the Indonesian government has accepted the application of 'Sharia law' in the province, which women activists have reported as detrimental to their rights. Other areas, such as Western Sumatra and South Sulawesi have also been introducing restrictive legislation including for example restricting women's movement after dark.

iran

Constitution	Other Laws	Muslim Laws	Customary Laws	General Comment
Article 1 of the 1979 Constitution establishes Iran as an Islamic Republic. Although A. 12 establishes the Shia School as the official religion, laws may be interpreted according to other Schools either where the party is of such a School or the local area is dominated by another School. Under A. 13 Christianity, Judaism and Zoroastrianism are given official recognition. A. 20 and 21 guarantee equal protection of law for women and women's rights, 'in conformity with Islamic criteria'.	Christians, Jews and Zoroastrians are governed by their own personal laws. Registration of marriage was introduced for all communities in the 1930s.	The Civil Code deals with family matters as well as general procedural law. The 1967 Family Protection Act which amended aspects of the CC introduced the codification and regulation of many areas of family law, although it did not challenge basic patriarchal assumptions regarding gender roles. The provisions of the Act were repealed in 1979, which saw a return to weaker regulation of many aspects of family law. The current CC has been amended on a number of occasions, largely positively and in response to pressure from rights activists.	Customary practices are not justiciable for Muslims.	Operating within the framework of Islam and accessing the 1979 Revolution's slogan of social justice, both modernist and traditionalist women's groups have successfully advocated reform in family matters. A major role has been played by a vibrant women's press.

malaysia

Constitution

Article 3 of the Constitution provides that Islam is the religion of the 13 States that form the Federation of Malaysia. In September 2001 Malaysia was declared to be an Islamic state. This was a politically motivated move to counter the extreme-right politico-religious opposition's assertion that it was 'more Islamic' than the ruling regime. The meaning and effects of this declaration have not been clarified.

In 2001 the Malaysian Constitution was amended to include a gender equality clause. However, other constitutional provisions (notably concerning nationality) contradict the new equality clause, which is yet to be tested. All laws are subject to the Constitution.

Other Laws

The legal system was dominated by English Common Law before Independence from British colonial rule in 1957. The parallel system of laws not based on Muslim laws has since developed independently by means of statute passed by the national parliament and precedent.

Muslims may not access parallel laws based on other sources in the area of family matters.

In 1988, the Civil High Court's jurisdiction over matters in the Syariah courts was removed. Thus, the Civil High Court could no longer hear issues relating to guardianship, probate and property settlements under Muslim laws. The meaning and impact of the amendment continues to be the subject of litigation.

Muslim Laws

Under the post-Independence federal Constitution, the State legislatures may only legislate on Muslim family laws, offences against the 'precepts of the religion', and inheritance. Each State may make Muslim laws without being bound by other States' legislation or precedent. In 2003 a uniform Islamic Family Law proposed by the Federal government is still being debated and resisted by the States.

During the 1980s Islamisation of laws, Muslim family law was codified, and the State Syariah courts were upgraded.

In recent years taazir and hudud laws have been introduced in the States of Kelantan and Terengganu, but remain unenforceable.

Customary Laws

Customary laws refer to the customs of the Minangkabau peoples, mainly in the State of Seremban. In 2002, a federal court recognized the customary land rights of an indigenous community in the state of Selangor.

The colonial courts recognized the 'customs and practices of the natives', primarily Muslim personal status laws. The continuing Islamization of laws appears to envisage the establishment of a 'Malaysian common law' which is largely based on principles of Muslim laws.

General Comment

The parallel system has resulted in a conflict of laws concerning marriages and divorces for example where one of the spouses in an existing civil law marriage converts to Islam; where a Muslim wishes to marry a non-Muslim (in effect not available to women or men); or where non-Muslims who convert to marry a Muslim leave Islam. There is no right to convert out of Islam as this is a crime under State Muslim laws; rehabilitation laws exist in several states for 'deviants' and 'apostates'

In the State of Selangor, when a father converts to Islam, his minor children are deemed to be Muslim. Despite great opposition, this law has not been repealed.

morocco

Constitution	Other Laws	Muslim Laws	Customary Laws	General Comment
Morocco is a constitutional monarchy and unitary state. Under Article 5 of the Constitution, all Moroccan citizens shall be equal before the law. Article 6 declares Islam the official state religion and guarantees freedom of worship for all citizens.	There is no option for Muslims to marry under any other law. Certain procedural laws apply to all citizens and are strongly influenced by French law following a period of colonization. A small Jewish minority is governed by separate personal status laws.	Following independence in 1956, a Code of Personal Status (al-Moudawana) was issued, based on the dominant Maliki School, but also adopting some provisions from other Schools and legislation in neighbouring countries. Major improvements were made to the Moudawana in 1993 following campaigns by activists.	Customary practices are not justiciable.	

nigeria

Constitution	Other Laws	Muslim Laws	Customary Laws	General Comment
The Constitution contains basic human rights clauses (including non-discrimination on the grounds of sex). However, these are non-justiciable. The Constitution itself discriminates against women in the matter of nationality. The Constitution recognizes customary and religious personal laws, and does not comment on whether human rights provisions should take precedent over religious and customary laws. This has not been tested for Muslim laws.	Nigeria was under British colonial rule until 1960. The British introduced laws and procedures based on English Common Law. The system then developed independently by means of statute and precedent. Nigeria has a federal system in which the federal legislature has exclusive powers for certain matters while others (including personal status laws) may also be legislated at the local State level. Citizens may opt to be married under and governed by the provisions of the Matrimonial Causes Act 1970 (Cap 220) and Marriage Act 1990 (Cap 218). Cases under these laws are heard in separate civil courts.	In the former Northern Region, Muslims have long been able to approach state Muslim courts for the adjudication of personal status matters on the basis of uncodified Muslim laws, historically influenced by the Maliki School. Muslim laws are not available in any of the states in what used to be the Western and Eastern Regions. Since 2000, a number of states have passed Acts extending Muslim laws to criminal offences (in particular hudood offences). These are supposed to apply only to Muslims and those who choose to have Muslim laws applied to them, but it is not settled whether Muslims can choose to be governed by other laws.	Citizens throughout the country may opt to be governed by unwritten customary laws for family matters and some land issues. In dominantly Muslim areas, access to non-Muslim customary laws may be difficult. They are adjudicated through the state customary courts.	In customary law cases, case law has increasingly held that gender inequality is "repugnant to justice, good conscience and equity" and has also cited CEDAW (ratified by Nigeria without reservations) in justification.

pakistan

Constitution	Other Laws	Muslim Laws	Customary Laws	General Comment
The structure and principles of the 1973 Constitution have been subverted by repeated amendments during marital law, military governments and elected governments since the 1980s. The 1985 Eighth Amendment made the 'Objectives Resolution' preamble a substantive part of the Constitution. While the OR also talks of social justice, in the regressive political atmosphere since the 1980s it has been emphasized and used to attacks women's fundamental rights. The Constitution has inherent contradictions. A. 8 states that all laws and customs in violation of fundamental rights guaranteed in the Constitution are void yet, for example, amendments introducing the Federal Shariat Courts are discriminatory. Meanwhile several discriminatory laws and customs remain and have not been challenged on the basis of A.8.	Following the British colonial policy of leaving family law to be guided by personal laws, each religious community has separate laws, although all cases are heard by general Family Courts established under the 1964 Family Courts Act. To marry under the secular 1872 Special Marriages Act couples are required to renounce their faith, now effectively impossible for Muslims given restrictive blasphemy laws. Family Court judges do not have to be Muslim to hear cases of Muslims but increasingly non-Muslim judges declare themselves incompetent. Women may be judges. The Guardians & Wards Act 1890, Child Marriage Restraint Act 1929 and Dowry Restriction Act 1976 apply to all communities.	Promulgated following recommendations by the 1955 Rashid Commission, the Muslim Family Laws Ordinance 1961 gave substantial protection to women's rights within the family, but stopped short of many women's demands. The MFLO has remained a focus of attack by regressive politico-religious forces since its introduction. In 2000, although provisions relating to polygyny and to registration of marriage were upheld, certain provisions relating to registration of divorces were held 'repugnant to Islam' and to be amended by the legislature. The government has now gone in appeal.	Not justiciable for Muslims, and courts routinely reject recourse to custom in family law cases. Family laws for Hindus are largely uncodified and are heard on the basis of long-established custom.	Numerous cases under the Zina (Enforcement of Hadd) Ordinance 1979 involve family law matters such as registration of marriage and divorce. While attempting to save women from the extreme punishments provided under Ordinance, the courts have undermined the protective spirit of the MFLO. The MFLO has alo been the focus of a highly charged debate over whether the statute law or the injunctions of Islam are to be supreme, and whether the superior courts have the power to declare a law repugnant.

philippines

Constitution	Other Laws	Muslim Laws	Customary Laws	General Comment
The 1987 Constitution contains a gender equality provision and provides for a secular state. In 1989, four provinces in Mindanao with sizeable Muslim populations were granted autonomy.	In order to give effect to the 1987 Constitution's gender equality provision, a new Family Code applicable to all Filipinos who are not Muslims was introduced in 1988. This Code amended some of the discriminatory provisions of the 1949 Civil Code but it remains strongly influenced by Catholic conceptualiztions of marriage.	In 1977, in an attempt to appease Muslim separatists, a Code of Muslim Personal Laws was enacted under the unpopular Marcos regime. Muslim women were not consulted as women in the drafting of the Code. There are current efforts to lobby for a reformed Code through women parliamentarians. The CMPL does not codify all aspects of family laws and thus Sharia Court judges have considerable powers of interpretation. The Code applies to all Muslims but is generally less option-giving for women than the Family Code applied to other Filipino women. The Shari'a Courts which hear cases under the CMPL were only established in 1985. Appeal lies to the Shari'a Circuit Courts and thereafter on questions of law to the Supreme Court. There is a grave shortage of Shari'a Courts but Muslims may access the regular Civil Registry in areas where there is no Shari'a Court. There is only one woman Shari'a Court judge.	Under American colonial rule, the Moros of Mindanao and Sulu had resisted attempts at codification, preferring to remain governed by uncodified laws. Thus, until 1977, Muslims essentially remained governed by the 'Kitab', i.e., customary adat law and interpretations of Muslim laws. In interpreting the CMPL, Shari'a Court judges may only refer to adat law if it is not in contradiction with the Constitution, the CMPL, public order, public policy or interest.	There is an on-going armed struggle for independence/ autonomy for areas in Mindanao with a high proportion of Muslims. Although several peace accords have been signed, armed conflict continues between extremist politico-religious groups and the army, destabilizing development initiatives.

senegal

Constitution	Other Laws/Muslim Laws/Customary Laws	General Comment
Under Article 1 of the Constitution, Senegal is a secular democracy, guaranteeing equality of all citizens without distinction including gender. A. 5 prohibits discrimination including on the grounds of religion, while A. 24 protects freedom of religion.	The Code de la Famille, which applies to all communities, is largely based on the Napoleonic Code but is also influenced by Wolof customary laws and recognizes aspects of Muslim laws such as dower and the husband's duty of maintenance. Only marriages registered under the CF are recognized although mechanisms exist for the registration of marriages performed under customary and Muslim laws for up to 6 months after the ceremony. Muslim judges existed in the post-independence period but have not been replaced as they have retired, and the formal judicial system is now entirely secular.	

singapore

Constitution	Other Laws	Muslim Laws	Customary Laws	General Comment
Singapore is a unitary secular state, which separated from the federation of Malaysia in 1967, having earlier been under British colonial rule. There is no gender equality clause in the Constitution.	Singapore's laws and its legal system are inspired by English Common Law, although family laws of the indigenous Malay Muslims and Chinese peoples were left largely unchanged by the British. Family laws not based on Muslim laws include the Women's Charter, the Guardianship of Infants Act (which includes custody provisions), the Evidence Act (which deals with legitimacy), and the Adoption Act. These statutes apply irrespective of the parties' religion. Marriage between parties, of whom one is Muslim, is possible under the Charter.	The Administration of Muslim Law Act of 1957 contains the only substantive Muslim laws applied in Singapore. The AMLA established the Syariah Court to deal with matters of Muslim family laws.	Customary practices are not justiciable.	There is dual jurisdiction of the Civil Family Courts and the Syariah Court over matters involving Muslims that relate to child maintenance, custody, guardianship, paternity and inheritance. Muslims tend to take these matters to the civil courts which have appropriate powers of enforcement. Parties in the Syariah Court may also seek the enforcement of or appeal against judgments and amend orders relating to the above mentioned issues through the Civil Family Courts. There has been no real effort to streamline procedures for these two parallel court systems.

sri lanka

Constitution

The 1978 Constitution contains clauses on basic human rights, including non-discrimination on the grounds of sex. These rights are justiciable provided violation is by administrative/executive action. Right to equality can be restricted on the grounds of national security and in the interest of religious and racial harmony. All laws including gender discriminatory laws in existence before the 1978 Constitution cannot be challenged for non-conformity with constitutional provisions.

Article 9 of the Constitution gives Buddhism 'the foremost place' in the Republic, and requires the state to protect and foster Buddhism, subject to guarantees of freedom of belief for all religious communities.

Other Laws

Roman Dutch law, introduced by Dutch colonizers, is considered the residuary law although it also applies as an independent system of law in certain areas of civil law. Many statutes, such as the Penal Code, are based on English law, inherited from a subsequent period of British colonial rule.

Parallel personal status laws apply to different communities. The General Law, which is an amalgam of Roman Dutch and English Common Law principles applies to the general population, but Kandyan law and Thesevalami apply to certain sections of the population.

A Muslim can marry a non-Muslim under the General Law, but two Muslims cannot validly marry under the General Law.

Muslim Laws

Muslims (including Malays) are governed by Muslim laws. These were first codified in 1806 during Dutch colonial rule. The current Muslim Marriage and Divorce Act of 1951 draws heavily on the Shafi School. The Act contains both substantive and procedural law but is not comprehensive; wherever the Act is silent, the law of the sect to which the party belongs is to be used as the basis for decisions.

The Quazi Courts hear matters governed by Muslim laws; appeal lies to the Board of Quazis and ultimately to the Supreme Court. Only Muslim males can be Quazis.

A 1992 commission to examine reform of the MMDA included two women but the Board of Quazis did not accept their recommendations.

Customary Laws

Customary practices are not justiciable for Muslims.

General Comment

Muslim women and children have benefited from legal values in the General Law applicable to the majority non-Muslim community. Recent reform in favour of women (on child marriage, marital rape and abortion) has not been extended to Muslims because of the growing influence of identity politics and Muslim lobbyists within parliament. Sri Lanka has ratified CEDAW and has also formulated a Women's Charter to implement CEDAW locally.

Quazi Courts have few powers of enforcement. To have decrees in their favour enforced, women married under the MMDA have to approach the civil courts.

There have been instances of conflict of law. Muslims may adopt under the 1941 Adoption Ordinance, but under case law, inheritance matters will be governed by Muslim laws.

sudan

Constitution	Other Laws	Muslim Laws	Customary Laws	General Comment
The 1998 Constitution lists the sources of Sudanese law as: Islamic Law, results of Referenda, the Constitution, Social Customs. Under the Constitution it is the state's duty to emancipate women from exploitation and to encourage their role in public and family life. The Constitution guarantees gender equality and prohibits discrimination on the basis of sex. Sudan is a federation.	The legal system is influenced by Muslim laws, civil systems adopted in many Arab countries, and English common law, following a period of British colonization.	Muslims are subject to Muslim laws with regard to inheritance, divorce, family relationships, charitable trusts, and zakaat. Governments of the northern federal States attempted to institute Muslim laws as the national civil and criminal code. This has been the primary cause of a long-running civil war. The 1992 Muslim Personal Law Act governs family matters. Courts in the South do not formally apply Muslim laws.	Customary laws are applied in family matters involving non-Muslims.	In the early 20th century Sudan had some of the world's first female parliamentarians and was among the first countries to codify family laws. There is an on-going civil war between the Muslim-majority North and Christian-majority South.

tunisia

Constitution	Other Laws	Muslim Laws	Customary Laws	General Comment
A. 1 of the 1959 Constitution establishes Islam as the religion of the republic. Article 5 [Personal Integrity, Conscience, Belief] states, the Tunisian Republic guarantees the inviolability of the human person and freedom of conscience, and protects the free exercise of beliefs, provided they do not disturb the public order. Article 6 [Equality] states, all citizens have the same rights and the same duties. They are equal before the law.	The Tunisian Civil Code, which applies to all citizens, is largely inspired by French law following the colonization of Tunisia. In personal status matters, each community, including a Jewish minority, is governed by separate laws, and there is no option for marrying under any other laws.	The 1956 Code du Statut Personnel (also known as the Majalla) applies to Muslims. Although Tunisia is Maliki dominated, the CSP is inspired by various Schools, and contains notably progressive provisions in the areas of polygyny and talaq.	Customary practices are not justiciable.	

turkey

Constitution	Other Laws	Muslim Laws	Customary Laws	General Comment
The preamble to the Constitution emphasizes the secular principle of no interference of religious feeling in state affairs and politics. Article 2 includes secularism and respect for human rights as characteristics of the unitary Turkish state. Article 10 establishes that there shall be no discrimination on the basis of sex, among others. A.24 establishes the freedom of religious belief, but adds that religion cannot be exploited for personal or political gain.	The Turkish Civil Code governs family matters and applies to all citizens irrespective of their religious or ethnic identity. Following a major campaign by a coalition of women's groups, sweeping amendments were made to the CC which came into force in 2001. The amendments substantially altered many of the more patriarchal provisions of the CC which had been based on the Swiss Civil Code, inspired by the Napoleonic Code.	Not applicable. Provisions of Muslim laws such as mahr, talaq, etc are not recognized and polygyny is banned.	Customary practices are not justiciable.	Amendments to the CC were strongly opposed by powerful politico-religious parties and forces.

uzbekistan

Constitution	Other Laws	Muslim Laws	Customary Laws	General Comment
The 1992 Constitution, establishing Uzbekistan as a democratic republic, retains many elements influenced by decades of Soviet rule. A. 18 guarantees equality before the law regardless of differences including gender, while A. 46 establishes equality of rights between men and women. A. 31 guarantees the right to practice or not to practice any religion.	The legal system continues to be dominated by Soviet influence, even after independence in 1991. The Civil Code, which governs family matters, is almost identical to the previous Soviet Code and highlights the equality of men and women within marriage.	A recent law has permitted couples to append a negotiated marriage contract to the standard marriage registration procedure, possibly in recognition of the concept of Muslim marriage. It is however little known and its details are not available.	Customary laws are not recognized and some customary practices in family matters are criminalized.	There have been repeated debates in Parliament and the media regarding the possible legalization of polygyny, which continues to be practiced. The age of marriage has also been lowered following pressure from conservative Muslim groups.

3a MARRIAGE REQUISITES: AN OVERVIEW

In most Muslim communities represented in this Handbook, a valid marriage establishes certain essential rights and responsibilities such as mutual inheritance between spouses, maintenance rights for the wife and children, and legitimacy of children borne during the marriage[1]. These rights and responsibilities are established whether the law the couple were married under is based on Muslim laws of the various Schools or other sources, because at a very basic level marriage has the same effect in all societies.

For women, contracting an invalid marriage can result in any or all of the following outcomes, depending upon the legal and social context: that they become social outcasts; that the law does not recognise their rights in marriage; that they face destitution on desertion or the husband's death; that they face prosecution for zina (sex outside a valid marriage). These possible outcomes are the public consequences of an invalid marriage.

But the question of whether a marriage is legally and/or socially valid is also linked with deeply personal issues such as individual happiness, sexual fulfilment and reproductive rights. That these topics are rarely the subject of research into women's legal status should not be allowed to obscure the reality that laws and customs impact women's daily lives. If the law (as it does in some systems) recognizes the right of male guardians to compel a woman into marriage, that law also effectively sanctions marital rape and the likelihood that the woman will have little control over when and how many children she will have. If a woman's right to exercise choice in marriage is made impossible by social attitudes, those attitudes may in effect prevent her from ever experiencing love in marriage. Therefore, laws and customs concerning the requisites of a valid marriage are closely tied to women's emotional and physical well-being.

requisites are similar across all systems

Based on the concept of marriage as a contract, almost all Muslim communities share a list of basic requisites for a valid marriage which relate to:

- The legal capacity of the parties to contract a valid marriage (whether they possess mental and physical capacity, and are free from any impediment because of age, gender, personal status and/or religion);
- Consent of the parties; and
- The presence of witnesses.

Even in countries where marriage comes under laws not based on Muslim laws and where marriage is not seen as a contract, similar requisites apply.

- Muslim laws also regard mahr (dower) as an essential element of a valid Muslim marriage.

Mahr (dower, see glossary) is a payment made by the groom directly to the bride and is different from bride-price and dowry. Bride-price refers to a payment from the groom or his family to the family of the bride. Dowry refers to the goods that the bride brings to the marital home. The precise nature of mahr is controversial as it appears to fall in between a requisite and a consequence of valid Muslim marriage. Mahr is also referred to as a 'consideration' for marriage. In some systems mahr may be listed in the statute as an essential element of valid marriage. Even if it is not specified at the time of marriage, mahr is presumed to exist (mahr ul mithl or 'proper dower'); and even if the marriage is not consummated, half of the mahr may be due if the marriage is dissolved.

Even though laws tend to share similar requisites, the way these are interpreted and applied across Muslim countries and communities largely depends upon the source of the law: Muslim laws, customary laws, or laws based on other sources. What may be considered as valid in one system or community may not be in another. For example, under Fiji's Marriage Act, which is not based on Muslim laws, all marriages (including that of Fijian Muslims) can be validly witnessed by two women. Conversely, under Sudan's Muslim Personal Law Act a marriage witnessed by women only would be an invalid marriage. Even systems governed by laws derived from the same source may differ in their provisions. For example, Algeria's Code de la Famille and the Philippines Code of Muslim Personal Laws are both derived from Muslim laws, but each specifies a different minimum age for marriage. There is at the same time a vast gap between laws and practices, even within the same community. For example, if an aunt and a niece are polygynously married to the same man, the Pakistani courts (following Muslim laws) would declare the later of the marriages to be invalid, yet such marriages continue to be found among some communities in Pakistan.

the codification of requisites

Requisites for a valid marriage may be determined through statute law, case-law, or by reference to Muslim laws or local custom.

Where requisites are laid down in the statute law, some laws explicitly define only the requisites for a valid marriage while others also list the effects of and penalties for an invalid marriage. Still others instead define only the bars to a marriage. Muslim laws of the Sunni Schools distinguish between void and irregular marriage (most forms of irregular marriage being those where there is a temporary bar to the marriage that can be corrected, upon which the marriage becomes fully valid); the Shia Schools, on the other hand, only recognize the concepts of valid and void marriages. Laws not based on Muslim laws use only the categories valid and invalid. Interestingly, most codified laws based on Muslim laws also treat marriages as either valid or invalid. Tunisia's Code du Statut Personnel, for example, states that marriages failing to fulfil certain provisions concerning requisites are irregular, but the law then goes on to clarify that they "shall be void." Still, this law does recognize certain effects of an invalid marriage if it has been consummated. These include the woman's right to mahr and the paternity of any children. Thus, in general, when discussing provisions concerning validity as defined by codified laws, we have used terms as they appear in the statute.

Where the law fails to specify requisites, these may be regulated through standardized marriage contracts or determined by recourse to Muslim laws and local customs.

Generally, the more clearly the requisites for a valid marriage have been specified in a given context, the more option-giving this context is for women. Clear specifications protect women from litigation and from confusion concerning their status (and the rights that flow from that status). When specifications are unclear, women can be subject to attempts to disinherit them as wives and even attempts to prosecute them for zina[2]. As in all other aspects of laws and customs governing family matters, in situations where there is a lack of clarity, inevitably the confusion is resolved in favour of the more powerful party to the dispute. Accordingly, the vast majority of resolutions concerning marriage and dissolution will favour men. Thus, laws which specify the consequences of invalid marriage, the mechanisms for enforcement of requisites, and the means of redress in the event of violation (including penalties for violation and who is liable) usually offer more protection to women than do laws that do not. However, where the requisites are highly restrictive regarding women's autonomy, codification may reduce women's options. For example, laws which void a marriage if it is contracted without the consent of the father/grandfather acting as wali (marriage guardian) can limit a woman's ability to exercise choice in marriage.

Clearly one needs to cross-reference any laws and practices regarding validity with a wide range of other laws and practices in order to fully understand the possible impact on women's lives. For example, penal provisions concerning zina may lead to penalties (as a consequence of an invalid marriage) that are not mentioned in family laws.

Women's physical and emotional autonomy has been consistently and blatantly violated by laws and practices concerning the requisites of a valid marriage. These violations have been particularly grievous and frequent in the areas of consent and capacity.

capacity: age, gender and marital status

Muslim laws establish maturity (commonly defined as puberty) as the minimum age at which men and women have the capacity to marry. However, some Muslim communities are governed by laws that are not based on Muslim laws. Still others recognise Muslim personal laws while raising the minimum ages for marriage.

In some schools of Muslim laws, a woman may never have the right to contract her first marriage independently; she always requires the consent of a marriage guardian. An adult Muslim woman's social and legal capacity to take an autonomous decision to marry is analysed in the section on Capacity (p.65).

Capacity also relates to the issue of whether or not a person is free to marry because of their existing marital status. In all systems, a woman who is still married or who has not been divorced properly is considered to have no capacity to marry. In contrast, under similar circumstances men are considered to have the capacity to marry in systems which permit polygyny. Systems based on Muslim laws limit men to a maximum of four wives. However, often systems based on customary laws set no such limitations (see Polygyny, p.197).

whom can a woman marry: other aspects of capacity

Once capacity is established in terms of age, gender and marital status, any legal bars to a marriage must be addressed. Muslim laws, irrespective of which school of thought that they are based on, list three categories of relationships that stand in the way of a valid marriage: consanguinity (close blood relationship); affinity (relationships acquired through marriage); and fosterage. In the simplest terms, these laws bar incestuous relationships. However, what counts as 'incest' varies widely. In systems where family laws are not framed with reference to Muslim laws, or where there is a history of tribal exogamy, laws also may include first cousins among the consanguine while not barring marriage between foster siblings. Similarly, systems dominated by the Shafi and Hanafi schools have differing provisions about exactly what counts as 'fostering.' These provisions establish fosterage relationships based on how much milk two babies have shared from the same mother.

Muslim laws also establish prohibitions based on religious affiliation. These laws prohibit female Muslims from marrying non-Muslim males while permitting Muslim males to marry a Kitabia (see glossary). However, not all systems based on Muslim laws explicitly codify such provisions. The standard interpretation that Muslim women can validly marry only Muslim men is debated by some male scholars and has been widely challenged by feminist theologians and activists. In countries where there is no option to marry under a law not based on Muslim laws, women face an impossible 'choice' between urging their fiancés to convert to Islam, having to marry and settle in another country, or not marrying at all.

In many communities, it is equally impossible to marry across other boundaries: class, race, ethnicity, tribe or sect. These bars are culturally determined and may be equally significant. Women who contract legal marriages against social norms may experience severe social sanctions. A perfectly legal marriage that has been certified by a court of law often fails to acquire the status of a socially valid marriage.

The concept of kafa'a (the requirement of the social equality of spouses, see glossary) provides additional means for limiting women's choice in marriage. In systems where kafa'a is a legal grounds for contesting the validity of a marriage, it may be used to reinforce and legitimise social barriers for marriage. In addition, customary bars to marriage across boundaries may be reinforced by laws that in effect endorse 'honour crimes.' These laws and/or judicial interpretation can implicitly sanction 'honour killings' firstly, by distinguishing between killings perpetrated in the name of 'honour' and those where other motives are presented, and secondly, by stipulating that a lesser punishment be awarded to those convicted of 'honour crimes.'

consent

Although many systems state a woman should consent to her marriage, very few systems envisage the mechanisms that would make this a reality (e.g., ensuring the bride signs the marriage document or register, or providing for a public official to hear her consent). Some laws even explicitly state that 'silence is consent' (Indonesia as long as there is no clear rejection, Sudan). Ensuring a woman gives her free and informed consent to a marriage is not easy. It is not enough to insist that she is heard to say 'yes' loudly because physical or emotional duress may compel her to do so. At the same time, it cannot be presumed that failure to formally hear consent indicates a forced marriage. In some communities women are consulted about their choice of spouse while being apparently excluded from the wedding formalities. While men are forced into marriage as well, women's social positions and reproductive roles make them far more vulnerable to forced marriage. The section on Consent (p.77) provides a more detailed analysis.

witnesses and mahr (dower)

Systems following family laws based on Muslim laws and systems following family laws based on other sources often differ greatly regarding what constitutes a legally acceptable witness (especially whether or not women can act as witnesses to a marriage).

Mahr is covered extensively in Chapter 5: Marriage Contracts, in the sections on Registration and Validity (p.133), Marriage Contracts and Registers (p.147) and Mahr (p.179), as well as in the section, Financial Rights and Settlements on Dissolution (p.311). Therefore, in this section we discuss mahr only as it impacts the validity of a Muslim marriage.

when a marriage does not fulfil the requisites

Different systems vary widely in their approaches to marriages that do not meet the requisites of a valid marriage. Some of these differences arise from differences found in the various possible sources of law (for example, Sunni thought, Shia thought, or European common or civil law inherited from colonial rule, or a mixture of these). A confusing range of terms is used to describe these marriages, including 'irregular', 'void' and 'voidable'. In some instances no rights arise out of a marriage deemed invalid. In other instances the consequences of a marriage (e.g., the legal paternity of any children) remain intact. A variety of terms are also used to describe the relief available if a marriage is declared invalid, including 'nullity', 'annulment' and even 'dissolution of marriage'.

For the sake of clarity, this Handbook discusses the status and possible remedies for marriages that lack a particular requisite in the section on that requisite. For example, for provisions regarding marriages where mahr is not specified or remains unpaid, see Witnesses and Mahr (Dower), p.109 and Other Forms of Dissolution for Women, p.281. Provisions regarding marriages contracted within the prohibited degrees (see glossary) or without witnesses are also covered in their relevant sections (p.95 and p.109 respectively). However, because the issues of choice in marriage and forced marriage (which are closely linked with capacity and consent) are so interlinked and of such importance to women, legal and social trends concerning these issues (as well as the remedies available when marriages fail to fulfil requisites of capacity and consent) are discussed in a separate section, Forced Marriage and Choice in Marriage, p.87.

The forced marriage of minors and remedies for such marriages (such as, the option of puberty, see glossary) are discussed in Child Marriage, p.117. The option of puberty available in Muslim laws allows a woman who was given away in marriage as a minor by her guardian to reject the marriage on attaining maturity. In some systems based on Muslim laws, this option effectively allows her to override her guardian's wishes. However, where ijbar (the guardian's right to compel his ward, even an adult woman into marriage) is recognized, the option of puberty becomes effectively meaningless. Thus, to understand who is defined as a minor as well as to examine a wide range of issues concerning capacity and consent in child marriages, in addition to examining the chapter on Child Marriage, the reader will need to examine Chapter 3b on Capacity.

engagement and marriage rituals

Because WLUML has chosen to focus on a limited number of issues in this Handbook, engagement and marriage rituals have not been covered. The sources of Muslim laws do not make any specific religious requirements concerning these rituals, and both laws and practices vary widely. While breaking an engagement can result in severe social penalties in some communities (even leading to blood feuds), it is perfectly acceptable to break an engagement in others. Some systems provide for specific legal redress in the event that a broken engagement results in a loss of property or damage to the bride's 'honour' (Fiji). Tunisia's CSP specifies that either party may terminate an engagement and requires that the party breaking the engagement return engagement gifts to the other party. Other systems provide no explicit redress to the 'wronged party' in the event that a broken engagement causes damages. Accordingly, the only recourse would be a civil suit, or a suit for criminal defamation in the event that, for example, a malicious and unfounded allegation is made publicly against one party, and then the engagement is broken (Pakistan, Philippines).

States may require a marriage to be performed at a specific venue in front of state representatives (marriage registrars); such requirements are dealt with on p.134 under Registration and Validity. Beyond this, states do not legislate on marriage rituals, except occasionally to control excessive expenditure. However, communities often have strongly entrenched ideas about rituals without which a marriage is not socially recognized. For example, one young woman who was assisted by a networking group to leave her community in order to be able to marry the man of her choice was distraught because she felt that she could not be married 'properly' without the women of her community being present to knock her head together with her husband's head. She regarded this ritual as the essence of a valid marriage ceremony.

endnotes

[1] In systems not based on Muslim laws, inheritance rights of children are not an automatic consequence of valid marriage. Muslims governed by such systems therefore, have to make wills specifying how their estate is to be divided. In Fiji, for example, it would not be enough to simply state in the will that 'Muslim laws are to be followed' as there is no recognition of personal laws.

[2] Muslim laws do not regard a couple liable to zina if they believe themselves to be validly married. For example S. 5 of Pakistan's Offence of Zina (Enforcement of Hudood) Ordinance 1979, exempts men and women from charges of zina if they 'suspect themselves' to be married to the other person. However, this provision has failed to protect couples from being charged under the Zina Ordinance if a third party questions the validity of their marriage. While the courts have subsequently dismissed these cases, the social and emotional suffering caused by such charges should not be underestimated.

3b MARRIAGE REQUISITES: CAPACITY

introduction

To have capacity for marriage means that the bride and groom are free from any impediment to their marriage: they are not too young; they are not already married (unless polygyny is permitted); they are not closely related; where the spouses are of different religions, there is no bar to their inter-marriage; and they are capable of making a decision to marry without having to have permission from their parents, the courts or any third party.

Legal capacity may be quite different from social capacity. For example, a country's law may recognize that an adult Muslim woman has the capacity to contract a marriage independently, while society expects her to have the permission of her wali (guardian for marriage). Also, legal capacity in marriage may be treated differently from general legal capacity. Some laws may recognize an adult Muslim woman to be capable of entering into other contracts (such as employment contracts or business contracts) while still not recognizing her as having the capacity to enter into a marriage contract.

This section focuses on age and gender as the two major factors that determine capacity[1]. See Capacity to Marry – Other Prohibitions p.95 for coverage of issues concerning capacity relating to both forbidden degrees and marriages with non-Muslims, as well as p.97 for coverage of issues concerning capacity as it relates to polygyny.

Most capacity requisites are closely related to issues of bodily rights and freedom of choice. However, laws in Sudan additionally require that men (only) must be arshad (roughly translatable as someone morally and ethically mature), meaning capacity is determined by a man's conduct rather than his economic status. The bride has no role in deciding whether the proposed husband meets this requirement.

fixing a minimum age

It can be both protective and restrictive to fix an age below which a woman (and a man) cannot legally make an autonomous decision to marry - i.e., an age below which they lack the capacity to make such a decision. What may be helpful for a woman in one situation may be unhelpful for another woman in a different situation. For example, Fijians under 21 cannot marry without their parents' permission. This could be interpreted as protecting young Fijian women from making an unwise decision. However, the law also guarantees parental control of their children's choices for some years after they may have become sexually active. Iran's laws on the other hand, derived from an interpretation of Muslim laws, regard puberty as the signal of capacity. To understand how this works in practice, one must also examine provisions concerning walis and remedies against forced marriage (see p.87).

Currently, international consensus appears to define 18 years of age (for both women and men) as an appropriate minimum age for marriage, although clearly this is an average which cannot take into account individual variations in development. However, generally, laws setting a minimum age for marriage allow men and women to reach mental and physical maturity before they enter into marriage. The Child Rights Convention (Article 1), the 1964 Convention on Consent to Marriage, Minimum Age for Marriage and Registration of Marriage (Article 2), and the Convention on the Elimination of All Forms of Discrimination Against Women (Article 16) all contain provisions about capacity for marriage and the right to choice in marriage, and appear to agree that 18 is an appropriate minimum age for marriage (see Child Marriage, p.117).

However, many countries have a confusing mixture of laws in which the legal age of 'adulthood' may vary for different issues: voting, marriage, legal majority, criminal liability (including liability for zina). Such inconsistency creates problematic gray areas for young women and girls who seek to make independent choices in marriage.

Because many parents seek to control their daughters' sexuality or use it to their own financial or social advantage, a lower age of legal capacity may be more option-giving for females when it allows them to avoid this control and manipulation. However, this advantage must be weighed carefully against the dangers of child marriage. Where forced child marriages are commonly practiced, a lower age of capacity for marriage for females may benefit only the few who are able to make an autonomous decision while harming the majority who are at risk of forced child marriage.

The legal age of marriage for men and women in Muslim communities differs from system to system. For instance, in both Bangladesh and the Kyrgyz Republic, the legal age is 18, with no exceptions recognized by law. In other systems the minimum age ranges from 9 to 21 years, or is set at puberty (which may or may not be defined in law). Using puberty as the minimum age for marriage is problematic. In medical terms, 'puberty' is a process rather than a single, specific event, although most systems and customary practices appear to regard the onset of menstruation as the indication that females have attained puberty. However, the vagueness of the term 'puberty' can give the courts some discretion in deciding whether or not the appropriate age has been reached. For example, in Sudan, courts and guardians use personal value judgments to interpret 'puberty.' Socially, the onset of puberty is considered the ideal age for marriage and the flexibility used to determine the age of 'puberty' gives the wali the capacity to contract a girl's marriage whenever he determines that it would be 'for her own good.'

Finally, in some systems there is no minimum age at all (the Gambia under customary and Muslim laws, Sri Lanka for Muslims). This lack of minimum age does nothing to enable a woman's choice in marriage because of the prevalence of early and forced marriage. These laws also place women and girls from Muslim communities at a disadvantage compared with those of other religious communities.

Some laws permit exceptions to the minimum age of marriage with court permission. While these laws recognize the reality of sexual activity, they also undermine the protective element of minimum age legislation and leave loopholes that can be exploited by families. Whether such compromise laws work to women's advantage or disadvantage will therefore be determined by reference to practices.

uneven trends in age of marriage

There are uneven trends regarding the age of capacity. Generally, the age of capacity, in both law and practice, has been rising in most Muslim contexts. However, in Yemen (see box p.69), Uzbekistan, and Iran, the age of marriage has been lowered under the influence of retrogressive interpretations of Muslim laws or pressure from fundamentalists.

wali practice limits choice for women

In the context of marriage, walayat-al-jabr, or wali, refers to the marriage guardian. In both laws and practices a wali is always male (usually the father or grandfather). A comparison of laws that contain provisions regarding walis reveals considerable confusion about a wali's precise role.

In some systems, notably Sudan, the notion of wali merely implies an agent or representative, someone who contracts the marriage on a woman's behalf and conveys her consent. Indeed, the term commonly used in Sudan is wakeel (agent, or representative). In contexts where women are secluded and segregated from men, it could be positive for a woman to have a male to represent her interests at a very public event like a marriage.

In other systems, the wali must consent to the marriage or it is invalid (unless the bride has obtained court permission to marry because her wali has withheld his consent unreasonably) (Malaysia, Sri Lanka). Thus, whatever a woman's age, such a system regards her as lacking the capacity to make an independent decision to marry, simply because she is a woman.

In yet other systems the law appears confused as to whether the wali is merely the woman's agent or has real powers over her choices (Philippines, Indonesia). For example, Morocco's Moudawana states that the wali shall not contract a woman's marriage unless she authorizes him to do so, but in the very same clause it adds 'except in the case of ijbar.' Confusion over whether a wali is merely a representative or a guardian undermines any protective element implied in the notion of representation.

Changing social circumstances, such as migration and the breakdown of the extended family, have shown that courts are confused about the 'logic' behind wali practices. For example, with the breakdown of communities in Morocco, increasing numbers of adult women are approaching the courts to claim they have no father to act as their wali, and the courts have been permitting these women to contract their own marriages or to choose their own walis (made possible under a 1993 amendment to the Moudawana following women's demands). However, the courts have yet to offer an explanation as to why orphaned women should have greater capacity than other women. In Sudan, under similar circumstances, the court will appoint a wali for a virgin and this wali can be an unrelated man. Thereby, for some women, the role of the wali is reduced to a purely procedural matter of representation as he is given no social control over her.

Laws and practices that enforce the wali concept severely restrict a woman's physical and mental autonomy. Where these laws and practices are enforced, women from Muslim communities find themselves at a comparative disadvantage with women of other communities and with men from Muslim communities.

Walis enjoy a great deal of control over brides in countries and communities following the Maliki and Shafi schools. (North Africa, most West African Muslim communities and South East Asia; Tunisia is the exception as it has, in law at least, made the wali optional.) Conversely, in countries and communities where the Hanafi school dominates (South Asia with the exception of Sri Lanka), as well as in countries where secular laws govern marriage (Central Asian Republics, Fiji, Senegal, Turkey) or where 'civil marriage' is possible for Muslims (the Gambia, India, and some Nigerian States), no wali is required by law. Even if a wali is not required, laws may restrict a women's free choice by codifying the concept of kafa'a (the requirement that the spouses be of equal status, see below)(Egypt).

alternatives where the wali refuses consent

As we have seen, a wali may wield absolute control over the bride's choices or he may play a largely symbolic role. These differing levels of power conferred on walis by laws and the community greatly influence the level of autonomy enjoyed by brides in any given context.

For example, certain communities in northern Nigeria use walis, but they tend to intervene and persuade a wali to accept the woman's choice when a conflict of opinion arises.

Least option-giving are those contexts in which the woman's consent is seen as irrelevant and a wali can override her refusal through ijbar (a process by which a wali can compel an adult woman to marry a person of his choice by claiming that the marriage is in her best interest). Where ijbar has been invoked, a woman has few options to avoid the marriage. She can try to object to the wali's choice by accessing the concept of kafa'a (see p.88).

Slightly less restrictive are those contexts where laws allow women to approach the court when the wali withholds his permission on 'unreasonable' grounds. Unfortunately, few laws define 'unreasonable' so a woman's future is left in the hands of judges who may share the wali's restrictive norms. In Malaysia, judges now routinely assume the power of wali to authorize a woman's marriage, but in Sri Lanka such provisions are accessed less frequently. Whatever the judicial practice, where a woman must appeal to a court to override her wali's decision, the burden of proving that his decision was 'unreasonable' lies on the woman; it is not presumed that a woman has the right to choice in marriage.

Morocco's Moudawana is an example of laws that offer confusing options to women who do not have their wali's permission to marry. In practice, this confusion works to deny women their right to choice in marriage. The law permits ijbar, and under the law, the wali retains the right to object to a marriage on the grounds of the prospective groom's unsuitability. So while a woman may approach the court when her wali unreasonably refuses permission for her to marry, the judge will then grant permission to her only if he judges the prospective husband to be of equal status (applying the principle of kafa'a). In other contexts, where a wali's permission is unnecessary to contract a marriage, the wali may still have the power to annul the marriage by accessing the concept of kafa'a (Morocco). In such contexts, the state recognizes patriarchal control of a woman's choice in marriage but does not require that it be exercised.

Procedures for alternatives are important because if they are complex and unclear, women gain little from them. Obviously, the contexts where the courts themselves willingly act as the wali or waive the requirement are more option-giving.

No matter what the available alternatives to circumvent a wali's control, and no matter how little power a wali actually has, the wali concept still serves to ensure patriarchal control of a woman's choices. The wali concept implicitly supports the idea that women do not know what is best for themselves, as well as the idea that what is best for a woman's natal family's interests is somehow automatically best for her. Accordingly, questions concerning walis and capacity have been at the center of some of the most internationally publicized cases in recent years (see p.75 regarding cases in Pakistan).

capacity in the event of remarriage

While some systems do not require a divorced or widowed woman to obtain a wali's permission to remarry (Iran), other systems are silent on this (for example, in Sri Lanka, where there has been contradictory case law concerning walis and remarriage).

trends towards greater choice in marriage

There are positive trends in the interpretation of laws governing capacity in marriage and in many countries courts are increasingly willing to accept that parents should not have an exclusive right to make decisions for their daughters as well as for their sons. Economic issues may be partly responsible because families can no longer support daughters who have left their unhappy marriages. Also, women are becoming more aware of their right either to marry without parental permission or at least to approach the courts for an alternative permission. Thanks to empowerment and awareness-raising work among communities, the positive effects of support and solidarity through the process of networking, and fortuitous social changes brought about by other socio-economic forces; there has been an overall trend away from forced marriage and towards parents taking their children's choice into consideration. Therefore, problems concerning parental permission are generally declining, although in some communities there might at the same time be a contradictory rise in 'honour crimes' against women exercising free choice in marriage.

endnote

[1] The capacity of people of unsound mind to make an autonomous decision to marry is not dealt with here in depth. It is one of the few issues where all Muslim countries and communities have similar provisions (and where they match non-Muslim societies), which require a guardian's consent. An example is A. 7 of Tunisia's CSP.

Changing Trends

Socialist South Yemen's Family Law No. 1 of 1974, Articles 7 and 11 revoked the customary restriction on women testifying to their own marriage contract, and in 1984 the age of marriage was raised to 18 for women and 20 for men.

But on unification with North Yemen in 1990, and the introduction of the 1992 Law concerning Personal Status, the age of marriage was reduced to 15 for both females and males, and the wali requirement was reintroduced.

In Malaysia, until the introduction of new family laws in the 1980s, if a wali refused to give consent the right of couples to marry of their own choice was not clear. In some decided cases, the kadi merely applied the Hanafi ruling (in predominantly Shafi Malaysia) that when the parties have reached puberty, they may enter into marriage of their own free will. Other cases 'transferred' the role of granting consent to the kadi or court when the wali was more than two marhalah (about 70 km) away.

Although young couples continue to believe that the solution to a lack of consent from the wali is to run away and then seek the transfer of the wali's authority to the court, this is no longer necessary. Under the new Muslim family laws enforced in all 13 States of Malaysia, a wali's consent is a requisite but it can be dispensed with by the court if the wali unreasonably withholds consent, and most courts grant permission to marry when the couple is of or close to marriageable age.

NOTES

LAWS: Marriage Requisites - Capacity

Criteria: Minimum Age of Marriage

☺ More option-giving are those laws which:
- Fix 18 as the minimum age of marriage for both women and men.

😐 The middle ground is occupied by those laws which:
- Allow exceptions to the minimum age.

☹ Less option-giving are those laws which:
- Fix puberty as signal of capacity for the minimum age of marriage.

☺ 18 years for females; exceptions not permitted

Bangladesh: Under the CMRA, 1929 (amended in 1984), the minimum age for marriage is 18 for females and 21 for males.

Kyrgyz Republic: The minimum legal age of marriage is 18 for both males and females.

😐 17-18 years for females; exceptions are possible

Turkey: Under the amended CC, marriageable age has been raised from 15 to 18 for females. Under exceptional circumstances, the minimum marriageable age can be lowered to 16 with court permission.

Algeria: The minimum age of marriage is 18 for females and 21 for males. The judge can grant an exception to the minimum age of marriage for females and males on the grounds of benefit or necessity.

Tunisia: The minimum age of marriage is 17 for females and 20 for males. Below these ages, both females and males must have the consent of a male or female guardian (A. 6 of the CSP), or they may obtain court permission, but only 'for pressing reasons and for the obvious benefit of both spouses' (A. 5 of CSP).

Uzbekistan: The minimum age for marriage is 17 for females and 18 for males (a drop from the minimum of 18 years for both males and females under Soviet law). Under A. 15 of the FL, under special circumstances the local authorities may provide permission for the age to be reduced by a maximum of one year.

Tajikistan: Under A. 12 of the Family Code, the minimum legal age for marriage is 17 for both males and females, but this may be reduced by a maximum of one year in exceptional cases (for example, if the female is pregnant or the parents are missing).

21 years for females and males; exceptions are possible

Fiji: Marrying when below the age of 21 requires parental consent. If the female is over 16 and the male over 18, the spouses can seek written permission from the Magistrate if the parents unreasonably withhold consent. All parties are to be heard.

Gambia (marriages under the CMA and CiMA): Under S. 7(b) of the CiMA and S. 11 of the ChMA, the minimum age for both males and females to marry is 21. If one of the spouses is below 21, parental consent must be given.

Indonesia: Under the LM, the minimum age of marriage is 16 for females and 19 for males. Spouses under 21 require the consent of the parents.

Nigeria (marriages under the MCA): The MCA does not specify the age of marriage, and resort is to the English law that prevailed at the time of colonial incorporation to Nigeria (1960). Under this law, the minimum marriageable age is 21, or 18 with parental consent for both males and females.

16 years for females; exceptions are possible

Senegal: Under A. 111 of the CF, the minimum age for marriage is 16 for females and 20 for males. Only a judge may authorize a marriage below this age for 'grave reasons' (usually interpreted as pregnancy). An enquiry and parental consent are also required. Under A. 138, a parent can have an under-age marriage annulled. But under A. 140, the parent loses this right if the marriage was later approved expressly or tacitly or where, before the spouses reached majority, the parent failed to act for more than 1 year after knowing of the marriage, or where the spouses complete 19 years of age without a complaint being registered.

Pakistan: Under the CMRA, 1929 (amended through the Muslim Family Laws Ordinance, 1961), the minimum age of marriage is 16 for females and 18 for males. Above this age, a Muslim female's right to choice in marriage is clearly established through case law, although the lower courts occasionally give unfavourable judgments that are overturned on appeal. Case law has accepted that even females of 15 years have capacity to independently contract a marriage unless it is established that they lacked the mental capacity to understand the meaning of consent. The courts have argued that while the marriage of a female below 16 constitutes an offence, the marriage is valid if the female has attained puberty, as under principles of Muslim laws (Behram Khan v Mst. Akhtar Begum PLD 1952 Lahore 548; Allah Diwaya v Mst. Kammon Mai PLD 1957 Lahore 651; Bakhshi v Bashir Ahmed PLD 1970 SC 323; Zafar Khan v Muhammad Ashraf Bhatti and another in PLD 1975 Lahore 234).

Morocco: Under A.8 of the Moudawana, legal capacity for marriage is attained at 15 for females and 18 for males.

Egypt: The minimum age of marriage is 16 for females and 18 for males. Under A. 9 of the LMA, any marriage between spouses who are below the age of maturity needs a wali. If he refuses, the judge will decide if the objection is reasonable.

Malaysia (except Perak State, see below): The minimum age of marriage is 16 for females and 18 for males However, in certain circumstances (undefined and therefore discretionary), the Syar'iah Judge can give written permission for the marriage of minors.

15 years for females; exceptions are possible

Cameroon: Females younger than 15 and males younger than 18 can marry if they have permission from the President of the Republic and their parents. Lack of permission renders the marriage voidable, i.e., it can be rectified if permission is given later.

☹ Puberty for females

Iran: Under A. 1041, marriage before reaching the age of puberty is prohibited. Under A. 1210, the age of puberty is 15 full lunar years for males and 9 full lunar years for females. However, a marriage contracted before reaching puberty is valid if authorized by the natural guardian, provided it is in the ward's interests.

Nigeria: In Kano and Sokoto States (with Muslim majority populations), the minimum age of marriage is puberty. The Native Authority (Declaration of Idoma native marriage law and custom) Order S. 49(3) of 1959 (a colonial law in a Christian majority state) sets the minimum age at 12 years. The 1956 Bill of the former Eastern region (colonial era, dominantly Christian populations) set 16 years as the minimum marriageable age. The law is silent concerning the effects of marriages involving spouses below the minimum age.

Philippines: Under the CMPL, minimum marriageable age is defined as puberty for females and 15 for males. A female is presumed to have reached puberty at the age of 15. The Shari' a District Court may, upon petition of a proper wali, order the solemnization of a marriage in which the bride has reached puberty but is younger than 15, but not younger than 12. The proper wali's consent is sufficient for the validity of the marriage.

Sudan: Marriageable age for females is 10 years or attainment of puberty.

No fixed minimum age of marriage

Sri Lanka: There is no minimum age of marriage for Muslims but the marriage of a female below the age of 12 requires that a quazi give his permission. However, since intercourse between an adult and a child below the age of 12 is defined as statutory rape, the law effectively limits marriages of children below this age.

Gambia: The law is unclear. Under the 1997 Constitution, males and females of full age and capacity shall have the right to marry and form a family, but full age and capacity are not defined in law. The MCA 1986 (Cap. 43) is silent on the minimum age of marriage but renders a marriage void where the parties are not of marriageable age. Recognition of customary law adds further complications. Under S.7(e) of the 1997 Constitution, the laws of Gambia consist of both constitutional law and customary laws

Malaysia (Perak State): There is no minimum age for marriage.

LAWS: Women's Capacity for Marriage

Criteria

☺ More option-giving are those laws which:

- Do not require a wali.

😐 The middle ground is occupied by those laws which:

- Require a wali but offer women a means of challenging 'unreasonable refusal' or;
- Do not require a wali but nevertheless allow walis to access kafa'a.

☹ Less option-giving are those laws which:

- Regard marriage without a wali as invalid and do not offer any alternative.

☺ **No wali required**

Non-Muslim laws: **Cameroon** (marriages under CSO, Civil Code, 1981), **Fiji, Gambia** (marriages under CMA (Cap. 41:02), MCA (Cap. 43), Nigeria (marriages under MCA), **Turkey, Uzbekistan, Kyrgyz Republic.** In the Kyrgyz Republic under A. 155 of the CrC, it is a crime to obstruct a marriage.

Hanafi jurisprudence: **Sri Lanka** (a wali is not required for Hanafi women who have attained puberty), **Bangladesh, Pakistan.**

Tunisia: Under A. 9 of CSP, both husband and wife have the right to contract their marriage themselves or appoint proxies. A. 3 regarding validity does not require consent of the wali.

😐 **Wali is required; mechanisms exist for alternatives**

Egypt: Although a wali is required, a marriage can be authorized by the court if the wali refuses. The wali cannot prevent a marriage on account of the mahr amount or social status (an apparent reference to kafa'a).

Iran: Under A. 1043 of the CC, regardless of the bride's age, if she is a virgin she needs the consent of her father or grandfather to marry. For subsequent marriages, no wali is required.

Malaysia: Under S.37(b) of the federal territory law, it is an offence to prevent a woman of 16 or a man of 18 from contracting a valid marriage, punishable with a fine, imprisonment of 6 months, or both. S. 7 recognizes the wali's consent as a requisite of a valid marriage. However, the law in S. 13 allows dispensation of the wali's consent in favour of consent by the court if there are valid grounds for dispensation, "after due inquiry in the presence of all parties concerned".

Philippines: Under A. 15(c) of the CMPL, the proper guardian in marriage (wali) must give his consent, following which the offer and acceptance must be witnessed. The CMPL requires the consent of the contracting parties but consent is given through a wali. Under A. 18, the wali's authority is required for solemnisation, but the CMPL does not mention the effect of non-compliance. The CMPL recognises any of the four Sunni schools and therefore theoretically a Hanafi woman would not require a wali. As yet there have been no cases that have raised this issue in court.

Sri Lanka: Under the MMDA, Muslims are governed by the law of their sect. Under S.25(1) of the MMDA, marriage of a Shafi woman of any age in violation of the requirement of obtaining the wali's consent is not valid. But, S.47(2) allows a woman whose wali is unreasonably withholding consent to request a Quazi to authorise the marriage. Where an inquiry is held by the Quazi and an order is given in favour of the woman to marry without permission of the wali, a permit authorizing the registration of the marriage is issued after the lapse of 10 days from the order (to allow the wali to appeal).

Sudan: In Sudan, the wali is an agent rather than a guardian, and this agent is known as a 'wakeel'. Under S. 25 of the MPLA of 1991, marriage without a male agent (wakeel) is considered void. S. 32 of the MPLA 1991 ranks the guardians according to their blood relations. However, it is not obligatory for the agent to be a relative to the wife. Widows and divorcees do not require a wakeel. Virgins do require an agent but he does not need to be a relative.

Wali is required; mechanisms exist for alternatives; kafa'a is recognized

Algeria: A wali is a requisite for valid marriage and must be a male relative. A judge can act as guardian for women who do not have a wali. Under A.12, the wali cannot stop the woman from contracting a marriage if she so wishes and if it is in her interest. If there is an opposition, the judge can authorize the marriage. But under A. 12, a father can oppose the marriage of his daughter who is a virgin if it is against her interest.

Morocco: Under A.12 of the Moudawana, 'guardianship is the right of the woman' and she appoints the wali. But the wali's consent is always required for valid marriage. Under A. 5(1) the offer and acceptance is between the husband and wali (who acts with her consent). A 1993 amendment waived the wali requirement for women whose fathers are deceased, although the law remains silent on whether or not a non-virgin requires a wali. Under A. 13, if a wali obstructs a marriage, the judge will decide if the objection is reasonable or not and shall give her in marriage but only 'to a man of equal status'. Under A.14(1) the wali has the right to object to a marriage on the grounds of kafa'a.

Nigeria (marriages under Muslim laws): A wali is required (standard texts of Muslim jurisprudence used by Sharia courts). Texts do not specify the age or circumstances in which a woman no longer requires a wali and do not offer an alternative when the wali refuses permission. However, case law indicates that the notion of wali is closer to an agent rather than a guardian and other male relatives may act as the wali.

☹ **Indonesia**: Under A. 14 of the KHI, the presence of the wali of both parties is a requirement for marriage. The marriage certificate for Muslim marriages requires the signature of the wali or a proxy. There is no specified procedure if the wali refuses consent. There is no relaxation of the wali requirement for Hanafi women. However, case law reveals cases where women have successfully requested the court to act as wali where a father refused to permit an adult woman to marry of her own choice (Ruling No. 40/Pdt.P/1999/PA.Btl.).

IMPLEMENTATION

Waiver of age requirements

Algeria: Taking the social situation of the parties into consideration judges usually grant waiver of age restrictions in the event of pregnancy.

Capacity of 15-18 year old females to contract marriage

Bangladesh: There is contradictory case law over the capacity of Muslim females aged 15-18 to contract a valid marriage. Even in the event of clear consent and a valid marriage document, it is common judicial practice to forcibly send females who have married against their parents' wishes under the age of 18 to shelter homes or judicial custody, pending a decision in their cases or even until they have reached majority, rather than allowing them to remain with their husbands. The courts seem concerned primarily with the notion of the "minority" of women and girls and consequently of the need for them to be placed "in custody" whether with their parents (Sukhendra Chandra Das v Secretary, Home Ministry 42 DLR 1990 79) or neutral third parties, including, in the worst cases, the jail authorities (Khairunnessa v Illy Begum 48 DLR, AD, 1996, 67). Cases where 15-18 year old women have been permitted to marry without parental consent include Ananda Mohan Bannerjee v The State 35 DLR 1983, 315.

Parent's right to object to marriage

Fiji: In R. v Registrar General: ex-parte Abdul Hamid, Court of Appeal case 386/1985, the court held that the lower court's procedural failure to give the father a chance of a hearing (when he objected to a marriage) did not invalidate his Muslim son's marriage.

Capacity of adult Muslim women to contract marriage

Pakistan: Lower courts sometimes rule that a Muslim woman requires parental permission to marry, but higher courts consistently uphold an adult Muslim woman's right to choice in marriage (Mst. Humera Mehmood v The State and others PLD 1999 Lahore 494), even if the father claims to be Maliki (Hafiz Abdul Waheed v Miss Asma Jehangir and another PLD 1997 Lahore 301).

Waiver of wali requirements

Morocco: A.11 & 12(3) of the Moudawana are interpreted as allowing adult women with no father to contract their own marriage or choose their own wali. Algeria: courts usually grant a waiver of the wali requirement for widows and divorcees.

Sri Lanka: Case law is contradictory on whether or not non-Hanafi widows and divorcees require the wali's permission in the case of remarriage. In Rahuman v Yasin 1941 2 MMDR 128, it was held that for an adult female who is a thayyib, the wali bears only the notion of agency as opposed to guardianship. In Rhode Rhyde v Ibrahim 1951 3 MMDR 130, it was held that a thayyiba has to obtain the guardian's consent.

Malaysia: In Azizah v Mat (1976) 2 Jurnal Hukum 251, the father of a young woman refused to give his consent to her marriage, wanting her to earn a living first. On her application to the Registrar, he (the registrar) transferred the marriage guardianship to a wali raja (meaning the court). Her father was allowed to give evidence, and it transpired that his refusal to give consent was based on the fact that he wanted compensation for maintaining her. The consent to the marriage was given by the court.

PRACTICES

For trends on age of marriage, see Child Marriage p.117.

Wali has limited powers

Northern Nigeria: Although a wali is regarded as necessary, women seeking to marry against parental wishes can usually mobilize community pressure to convince the wali. Nigeria: Women have also been known to convince some other male relative (an older brother, or an uncle) to stand as wali for them.

Marriage requires parental approval

Gambia, Philippines, Sudan & Central Asia: In Muslim communities, marriage requires parental approval, which is seen to be the father's consent. Women's choice in marriage is particularly restricted by traditional socio-cultural attitudes that impose various limitations on a women's choice of husband. But increasingly, especially in urban communities, parents now allow daughters to choose their partners, with their guidance.

Central Asia: The socially accepted norm of women marrying as soon as they have reached the legal minimum age (18) strengthens parental control over their marriage choices. The legal possibility of marrying as young as 16 contradicts the requirement of 12 years compulsory education. Fathers for their own interests often arrange a match, and when the fathers part ways, the couple has to divorce.

Gambia: For females of all ages, parental consent is mandatory, but adult men may contract a valid marriage without parental consent. The reason given for this inequality is that the payment of bride price, a core element in any marriage ceremony, cannot be done properly without the consent of the bride's family.

Philippines: Although the law permits Hanafi women to marry without a wali, in practice, all marriages are done through a wali.

Extreme sanction against choice in marriage

India, Pakistan, Palestinian communities in Israel, Turkey: Couples use community and family pressure to create space for choice marriage. If parental opposition continues and the marriage goes ahead, honour crimes can happen (found across communities and classes).

Pakistan: Families who oppose their children's marriage choices use various penal provisions that are now part of the Zina (Enforcement of Hudood) Ordinance 1979 to obstruct them. In most cases, parents file a case of kidnapping against the husband and make the wife a witness against the man she married out of choice. Even if she states that she was not kidnapped and her husband takes the plea that he has married her, the couple has to prove that they are validly married, otherwise they risk serious criminal charges, as any sexual relation outside marriage is a serious crime. People contracting choice marriages face problems in registering their marriages. And although an unregistered marriage is not invalid, a lack of registration may raise doubts about the very existence of the marriage, which can make contesting a charge of kidnapping difficult.

Turkey: Honour crimes exist side by side with considerable independence in marriage choices. In a survey (see Canan, 1997), 54% of women had met and married independently from their families.

Shafi women change sect to avoid wali requirement

Sri Lanka: Shafi women resort to changing their sect to get married without a wali's permission. Many women are not aware that the law allows the Quazi to give permission in the event of the wali's opposition. Even when women are aware of the law, they may choose to change sect through an affidavit because this process is less time consuming and difficult than obtaining a Quazi's permission. MWRAF found that between 1989-1994, the Kandy Quazi received 100 wali applications, but issued only 25 permits. If a wali permit is refused, parties go before another Quazi and get a permit. Some Muslim couples have married under the General Law to avoid the wali requirement, but their marriages are not valid because Muslims must marry under the MMDA.

Friends acting as agents on behalf of the bride

Sudan: where the wali acts as an agent rather than guardian, and where the law permits a non-relative to act as the wakeel, a woman who chooses a spouse against the will of her proper wali's wishes can (and often does) get a friend or sympathetic relative to act as the representative for her marriage contract.

Social Forces Clash over the Right to Choice in Marriage

The question of women's right to exercise choice in marriage has been the focus of increasingly public clashes between two contradictory social forces in Pakistan. There has always been resistance to women contracting marriage out of choice, against the wishes of their families. However, in the last two decades, on the one hand, there has been an increase in the number of women contracting marriage out of choice; and on the other hand, the resistance by their families has also increased, facilitated by discriminatory laws and the anti-women approach of the law enforcement agencies.

These trends were visible in two highly publicized cases that took place in the 1990s, involving the daughters of powerful families, Saima Waheed and Humaira Butt. The full political and social weight of these families was pitted against their daughters who were supported by the women's and human rights groups to which they had turned. In the past, if the daughter of a powerful family contracted a choice marriage, the family would usually avoid public legal action. But today, increasing social conservatism has made the mobilization of the legal system and police agencies in their cause far easier and encouraged them to bring endless legal actions against their daughters. At the same time, organized resistance to women's oppression has increased. The result has been that, whereas in the past such cases would involve individuals pitted against one another, today such cases see powerful families not only attempting to undermine the credibility of human rights groups, manipulate the press, and vilify supportive lawyers, but even launching physical attacks upon the offices and shelters of such groups.

Before the introduction of the Zina (Enforcement of Hadd) Ordinance, 1979, families would either routinely file a kidnapping case against the woman's husband or file a petition for writ of habeas corpus, alleging illegal confinement by the man and/or denying the existence of a valid marriage. Prior to 1979 fornication was not a crime, but with the introduction of the Zina Ordinance, with its heavy penalties for all sex outside a valid marriage, the pressure upon couples contracting a choice marriage has undoubtedly increased. The seriousness of the offence of zina in the eyes of the law and the fact that it is now a crime against the state mean that state agencies such as the Police automatically become involved in pursuing the couple.

Saima Waheed contracted a marriage against the wishes of her prominent industrialist family, which also has strong links with conservative religious groups and madrassahs (religious schools). They contended that as a Muslim woman she did not have the right to contract a marriage against the wishes of her father and that she was duty bound to obey her family. Humaira Butt also contracted a marriage against the wishes of her father who was a member of the Provincial Assembly. In her case, however, her family contended that she was already married to a cousin and therefore her claimed marriage was invalid. In both cases, after lengthy legal battles, existing case law which accepted an adult Muslim woman's right to contract a marriage of her own choice was upheld (Hafiz Abdul Waheed v Miss Asma Jehangir and another PLD 1997 Lahore 301; Mst. Humera Mehmood v The State and others PLD 1999 Lahore 494).

The strong linkages and cooperation between local women's and human rights groups assisting Saima and Humaira was a major factor in the success of the cases. At one point, Humaira was in effect kidnapped by police from a well-respected charity shelter in another province where she had taken refuge. These police clearly hoped to take her back to her home province where the local administration could be more closely influenced by her father. There were serious concerns for her safety. But a rapid response from the groups, their ability to network across the country, and the strategy of making the attack on the shelter public ensured that no further harm came to her.

In Saima's case her family attempted to circumvent established law in Pakistan regarding the right of an adult Muslim woman to contract a marriage of her choice by claiming that as the father was Maliki and that as such, she was unable to marry without her wali's permission. It was perhaps the first time that a case was so publicly focused on the question of the different interpretations of Muslim laws by various sects rather than on established Pakistani law. Her lawyers were able to use their linkages with other groups to mobilize interpretations, opinions and judgments from around the world to support their response that Saima, as an adult Muslim woman, did not require her wali's permission.

3c MARRIAGE REQUISITES: CONSENT

introduction

Both Muslim laws and laws based on other sources regard consent as a requisite of a valid marriage. Because Muslim laws define a Muslim marriage as a contract between the spouses, they usually stipulate that there should be an offer and an acceptance of the contract's terms and condition by the parties in one sitting.

However, laws and customs often deny women an active role in the contract process and do not provide procedural mechanisms that ensure that the woman's free and informed consent is given. This passive role leaves women vulnerable to forced marriage. Indeed, some (but by no means all) systems based on Muslim laws directly permit a wali (guardian for marriage) to force his ward into marriage under the concept of ijbar (compulsion in marriage). Although the power of ijbar is limited by the general condition that the marriage must be 'for her own good,' the very fact that a law permits a woman's consent to be overridden and that it is not for her (but for the courts) to decide whether this is justified, undoubtedly strengthens social attitudes which presume that male relatives are all-powerful in deciding a woman's marriage options.

Although men can be forced into marriage, the implications of forced marriage are generally not as extreme for men as for women because they (men) often have greater access to divorce (especially where talaq is recognized), and they do not experience physical vulnerability in relation to their wife/wives (as they do not experience pregnancy or face the possibility of marital rape).

In order to be meaningful in practice, consent must be informed and not given under any form of mental or physical pressure. We must be careful to distinguish between arranged marriages, where a woman may consent to a choice made by her parents, and forced marriages, where a marriage has been contracted against the woman's will. The requirement of consent protects women against forced marriage. An adult woman must determine for herself whether or not her marriage has been forced upon her. This section does not deal with the issue of the forced marriage of minors because very different provisions and options apply to minors (see Child Marriage, p.121 & p.128).

A woman's claim to her individual right to consent is often perceived as a violation of the community's collective right to determine whom the community's women will marry. By transgressing boundaries in marriage, women may challenge the existing social order. Often the conflict between a woman who claims her rights and the authorities in her community who seek to deny her these rights is characterized in the community and the courts as a conflict between 'modern' or 'western' and 'traditional' or 'Muslim' values. Such a stereotypical characterization deliberately overlooks the fact that values change and that Muslim laws invalidate a marriage lacking consent. Strategies for challenging this labelling of 'east vs. west' have emphasized a human rights perspective in some contexts (occasionally referring to international human rights instruments) while in other contexts, they have emphasized social justice as a goal for Muslim societies. An additional strategy has been to point out the likely negative consequences suffered by a community or parents who force a marriage. These consequences include the economic burden of caring for a daughter who leaves an unhappy marriage.

laws requiring or facilitating the woman's consent

In countries where there are parallel laws, the provisions concerning consent often provide different rights to different women, depending upon which law they are married under. Laws not based on Muslim laws generally provide greater space for consent because they do not recognize the wali concept. Accordingly, such laws unambiguously require the woman herself to consent. Of course, a law which requires a woman's formal consent does not guarantee that forced marriage will not occur.

Those laws that both clearly invalidate marriages lacking consent from both spouses and specify penalties for those who force anyone into marriage are the most option-giving (Turkey, Tanzania and Tunisia). Tanzania has taken positive steps to strengthen such provisions by detailing in the text of the law what cannot be taken as consent and by specifying in the same law the punishment that will be awarded for violation. Also, laws can encourage the participation of the bride by including requirements that she indicate her consent in the standard marriage contract and/or registration forms. For example, the standard marriage contract in Bangladesh and Pakistan recognizes women's greater vulnerability to forced marriage by requiring the bride's signature while allowing a proxy to sign for the groom.

procedure is important

The way in which consent is expressed and to whom it is expressed indicates how seriously the issue of consent is taken in a given context. If a law or practice accepts silence as consent (Indonesia, Sudan) and does not require the woman to be present at the ceremony (Sudan), that law usually offers less protection than a law or practice that obliges the woman to say 'Yes' out loud before an official (Turkey's Civil Code and case law in Tunisia) (see also Registration and Validity, p.133).

But all such provisions still cannot prevent mental and physical coercion, and activists have found that 'protective' legal measures have limitations that only social activism can address.

Additionally, one must ask what it is that the bride is consenting to. Does the law or custom require that the terms and conditions of the marriage contract are read out to her so that she is aware of her rights and responsibilities and can offer her informed consent? Is she, for example, informed (where the system allows for it) that there is space in the contract where she could add in her own conditions (see Negotiated Rights and Responsibilities, p.167)? This information is particularly important in contexts where women may be excluded from negotiations concerning the conditions (financial and otherwise) of their marriage contracts.

resisting forced marriage

There are a number of factors that can make it especially difficult for younger women to resist forced marriage. These include issues of mobility, women's lack of economic and social support networks outside the family and immediate community, and the particular problems women may face in accessing formal and informal justice systems. For these reasons it is important to explore options under the formal law for preventing forced marriage or for ensuring that the marriage is subsequently declared invalid and the perpetrators punished.

In practice the strength of legal measures designed to ensure consent is often closely linked with the legal age of marriage. Although even older women with an income may find it difficult to resist a forced marriage, younger women have an especially difficult time asserting their right to consent.

where forced marriage continues

Many laws concerning consent and forced marriage are contradictory, or they are undermined by (predominantly male) judicial interpretation. This lack of legal protection reflects the persisting perception that women are the property of their families. For example, Morocco's Moudawana specifies that a wali cannot compel an adult woman to marry, but in the same clause, states that the court can compel her to be 'under the marital authority of a husband' if 'immorality' is feared. 'Immoral' actions by unmarried men apparently do not lead to their being forced into marriage.

For example, State Muslim family laws in Malaysia (which recognize ijbar) are clearly based on the assumption that the wali has a woman's best interest at heart. Such laws presuppose that women, especially when they are young, cannot know what is good for them. Compatibility (kafa'a) with the chosen groom does not depend on the wife's personal choice, but upon legal criteria. Nevertheless, forced marriage is not practiced in Malaysia and Singapore because other aspects of laws and social attitudes prevent it. The only circumstances under which a couple may be 'forced' into marriage are those in which the couple has had pre-marital sex and the woman is pregnant. In most cases, they are expected to marry unless the woman undergoes an abortion.

Customary violations of women's right to consent may take place in a wide variety of situations and with varying justifications. In some communities, ignoring a woman's consent may be justified on the grounds that the family is simply concerned about her economic security and is marrying her to a person judged to be economically secure. Activists have countered that such a justification overlooks the reality that many women are economically independent and are employed outside the home.

In other contexts, women may be sold into prostitution through false marriage contracts. Especially where feudal-tribal patterns still exist, the exchange of women may be used as a means of settling feuds. The Pakistan Supreme Court has rejected this practice. In one case brought to court in July 2002, eight women were given along with cash in compensation for an unspecified number of murders. The Supreme Court took suo moto action, and the administration returned the women to their families. In another case, Pakistan's Peshawar High Court held that giving a woman in marriage as part of a settlement in a feud (a practice known as swara) is illegal and, that the resulting marriages must be considered invalid (Jang newspaper, 30 November 2000).

Other social groups treat women as property by allowing a dead husband's brother to 'inherit' his widow (technically termed 'levirate'). This practice is found in parts of the Gambia, Nigeria, Palestinian communities, Pakistan, Senegal, and southern Sudan. While people in Nigeria are abandoning this tradition, there are still cases of levirate. If the wife refuses to marry her brother-in-law, she has to abandon her rights to maintenance and inheritance as well as to her children. Meanwhile, people in the Gambia are increasingly embracing this practice and justifying it with reference to religion and the idea that the family should 'stick together'. In Sudan a similar logic is applied when, after the wife's death, the family insists on marrying the dead woman's sister to the widowed man. In some cases this may even be forced.

Is Forced Marriage by Family Members an Offence?

In a number of countries both the kidnapping of women for the purposes of marriage and the trafficking of women are criminal offences.

In Bangladesh, India, and Pakistan, various sections of the pre-Independence 1860 Penal Code (S. 361, 363, 365, 366, 368) criminalize kidnapping "of a woman with intent to compel, or knowing it likely that she will be compelled, to marry against her will, or in order that she may be forced or seduced to illicit intercourse, or knowing it likely that she will be forced or seduced to illicit intercourse." Even importing into the country a woman/girl under 21 years is an offence if done with the intention that she will be forced to or seduced to illicit intercourse. In Pakistan S. 366 has been replaced by S. 11 of the Zina (Enforcement of Hudood) Ordinance, 1979 that uses virtually the same wording and specifically mentions the use of criminal intimidation or abuse of authority or any other method of compulsion. The penalties are severe in all three countries, including the possibility of life imprisonment and heavy fines.

To date, the courts have only regarded these provisions as applying to the kidnapping or abduction of women by strangers or non-family members (in fact often used when a woman leaves the family home voluntarily with a man of her choice). It is ironic that provisions supposedly protecting women against forced marriage by strangers - abduction - are in practice used by families to prevent choice marriage. In the event of the forced marriage of an adult woman, her only recourse is to file a case of illegal confinement against those who are holding her. Most commonly relief is pursued through a petition of habeas corpus. In many instances, the courts in Pakistan have accepted the petition and set the woman at liberty.

NOTES

LAWS: Marriage Requisites - Consent

Criteria

☺ More option-giving are those laws which:
- Regard a marriage without the bride's consent as invalid;
- Criminalize the act of forcing someone into marriage.

😐 The middle ground is occupied by those laws which:
- Require the bride's consent but undermine this requirement in other provisions; and/or
- Are unclear.

☹ Less option-giving are those laws which:
- Recognize ijbar.

☺ **Lack of bride's consent renders marriage invalid; force criminalized**

Tanzania: Under S. 16(1) of the Law of Marriage Act 1971, no marriage shall be contracted except with the consent, freely and voluntarily given, by each of the parties. S. 16(2) specifies that when free consent is assumed not to have been given: "For the purposes of this Act, consent shall not be held to have been freely and voluntarily given if the party who purported to give it (a) was influenced by coercion or fraud; or (b) was mistaken as to the nature of the ceremony; or (c) was suffering from any mental defect, whether permanent or temporary, or was intoxicated, so as not fully to appreciate the nature of the ceremony, and references in this Act to "consent" of an intended marriage shall be construed as meaning consent freely and voluntarily given." S. 151 provides for 3 years imprisonment (no option of fine) for anyone convicted of fraudulently inducing or forcing or intimidating someone into giving consent.

Kyrgyz Republic: Under A.155 of the CrC, it is a crime to force a woman into marriage and/or to kidnap a woman for the purposes of marriage.

Senegal: Under A.141 of the CF, a marriage without the consent of the spouses (which includes forced marriages) shall be declared null. Absolute nullity is considered a matter of public policy and anyone with an interest can seek such a declaration. The Senegalese Code Penal punishes forced marriage.

Tunisia: Under A.3 of the CSP, there is no marriage without the consent of the spouses. Under A.21 the marriage is declared null and void. A.3 is interpreted in case law to mean that consent should be manifested in an undisputable manner by saying "Yes" before the officiating officer.

Turkey: Under A.142 of the CC, both the woman and the man are required to openly declare their free will in front of the marriage official.

Uzbekistan: Under A.63 of the Constitution and the Family Law, marriage is based upon the free agreement of both spouses. Under A.136 of the Constitution, forcing a woman into marriage or preventing a marriage is forbidden.

Force is not permitted; no penalties

Fiji: Force invalidates a marriage but duress is not defined and no punishment is provided. In Nisha v Aziz 1981, the court (citing that she was financially independent of parents and could have therefore resisted forced marriage) rejected a woman's plea to have her marriage nullified on the grounds of duress. The court defined duress narrowly as occurring only under physical threat. The court did not recognize social pressures as sources of duress.

Algeria: Under A.13, it is forbidden for the wali, be he the father or any other person, to compel a woman to marry. Also, he may not give her in marriage without her consent. Only the Civil Status Registrar or a notary can ask for the consent when establishing the marriage certificate.

Bride is to sign marriage documents; forced marriage is not defined

Bangladesh & Pakistan: The standard marriage document is to be signed by the bride (whereas the groom may consent via a representative), signifying her consent. However, forced marriage is not defined and there is no criminalization of failure to obtain consent and no law specifies that forced marriages are invalid. In Mst. Humera Mehmood v The State and others PLD 1999 Lahore 494, the court used dictionary definitions to construct consent as the conscious expression of one's desire without any external intimidation or coercion.

Iran: The chief official of the marriage registry is obliged to read out the conditions of the marriage contract to both parties and have them separately sign each of the conditions to indicate acceptance of the conditions.

☹ Consent of bride is required but undermined by other provisions

Egypt: A.5(2) provides that two adults are required to testify that there has been some consent between the husband and the wali. Nothing is said about the consent of the bride.

Philippines: Under A.17 of the CMPL, the marriage document is signed or marked by the contracting parties. Consent obtained by violence, intimidation, fraud, deceit or misrepresentation vitiates the consent and renders the marriage voidable A.32(c). However, the low minimum age of marriage, combined with provisions which allow the marriage to be regularised after the circumstances vitiating the consent have ceased, weakens the protection against forced marriage.

Malaysia: Consent of both parties is mandatory for a marriage to be recognized and registered (S.13 of the federal territory law). Any person who uses any force or threat to compel a person to marry against his will commits an offence and shall be punished with a fine not exceeding RM 1,000 (approx. US$ 265) or with imprisonment not exceeding 6 months or with both such fine and imprisonment (S.37 of the federal territory law). Although this provision appears to be weakened by the statement 'unless permitted under Hukum Syariah' (which can be interpreted as opening the door to ijbar), the law also allows dispensation of consent in circumstances recognised by Hukum Syariah. The legal situation is thus confusing.

Nigeria: For Maliki communities (the majority of Nigerian Muslims), a biological father has the power of ijbar (courts may refer to Bulugul Marami, p.260 Fighus Sunnah Vol. II). However, the wali cannot compel his daughter to marry a man suffering from contagious diseases (such as leprosy), insanity, or reproductive problems. Case law is clear that ijbar cannot be enforced for adult women, and the courts generally accept a variety of circumstances which overrule the possibility of ijbar, including where the woman earns some money herself.

Sri Lanka: S.25(1)(b) requires the wali to obtain the bride's consent prior to the marriage. But the bride's signature is not required at the registration of the marriage, even if her sect's law permits marriage without a wali.

Indonesia: Under A.14 of the KHI, both bride and groom must be present at the marriage and there must be an exchange of ijab and qabul. Under A.6(1) of the MA: a marriage shall be founded upon an agreement between both the aspirant bride and the aspirant bridegroom. However, under A.16(2) of the KHI, consent "may also be in the form of silence meaning as long as there is no clear rejection."

Sudan: Virgins are to be consulted and the Ma'azoun and the two witnesses are obliged by law to verify the consent of the bride. However, the law considers silence 'a sign of consent.' Widows or divorcees have the right to ask the wakeel to marry them without prior consultation. Although there are no penalties for violating the virgin's right to consent, she can take the case to court, and the marriage may be considered invalid and automatically dissolved.

☹ Law is unclear

Gambia: The laws are contradictory. Under S. 27(2) of the 1997 Constitution, marriage shall be based on the free and full consent of the intended parties. Under Muslim laws a woman should not be given away in marriage without her due consent. However, constitutional protection for customary laws undermines efforts to prevent forced marriage.

Ijbar is recognized

Malaysia (Kelantan and Kedah States): Despite provisions requiring the bride's consent, if the woman is an unmarried virgin (anak dara), the father or paternal grandfather (wali mujbir) can marry her to anyone of his choice without her consent. Three conditions have to be satisfied: (a) the wali mujbir and the groom are not in enmity with each other; (b) the groom is of the same social status as the bride; (c) the groom is in the position to pay a reasonable maskahwin (mahr).

Morocco: Under A.5(1) and A.12(1) CSP, the wife must consent to the marriage. But under A.12(4), the judge may compel the woman to marry "if it is feared that the woman will fall into immorality."

IMPLEMENTATION

Officials do not always fulfill their responsibilities

Algeria: Although an official is supposed to hear the consent in order to validate a marriage; in practice, with a traditional marriage, it is difficult to demand that this provision be followed.

Bangladesh: To strengthen the role of Nikah Registrars in ensuring that requisites have been fulfilled, the qualifications for Nikah Registrar were tightened under the Muslim Marriages and Divorces (Registration) Rules, 1975. The Registrar must possess an Alim Certificate from a Madrasha Board established under law (i.e., a qualification indicating knowledge of Muslim laws), be between 21 and 40 years of age, and be a resident of the area. Despite these attempts to make sure Registrars are properly qualified, the registrars still fail to challenge forced marriages.

Pakistan: In Shah Din and Others v The State, PLD 1984 Lahore 137, the court held that "it is the duty of the Nikah Registrar, among other things to make proper inquiries as to whether or not the parties are acting of their free will and without any compulsion." The court said that if the Nikah Registrars fail to ensure the free consent of the parties, they are to be held responsible. But the 1997 Report of the Commission of Inquiry for Women noted that often lawyers, touts, and marriage registrars work together to deceive young women into contracting fraudulent marriages.

PRACTICES

Forced marriages exist; consent increasingly recognized

Central Asia: In big cities and highly educated families, women are given a limited say. Parents may force daughters into marriage. In Tajikistan, kidnapping for the purpose of marriage does occur. Women find it difficult to escape such situations because of unsupportive social attitudes. During the civil war and unrest of the early 1990s, thousands of women were abducted then subsequently abandoned by their families if they escaped. Local women's groups have established shelters to rehabilitate these survivors.

Fiji: Forced marriages are found among Indo-Fijians. They are rarely challenged in court both because many women do not know that forced marriage is unlawful and because they are unwilling to pay the social price of non-compliance.

Gambia: Marriages are often arranged without the consent of the woman, and betrothal at birth is common. Forced marriage is justified by explanations that women burden families economically. Traditionally, the wishes of the family are considered paramount and supersede those of the bride and groom. Practices of denying widows inheritance result in a widow having to choose between accepting her dead husband's brother as her new husband or not being able to access her dead husband's farm land which is her only means of survival. To make matters worse, a brother may choose not to inherit a poor woman or a woman with many young children and therefore leave her (and her children) to destitution.

Nigeria: City dwellers and educated parents tend to seek their children's consent before a marriage is arranged. In rural areas child marriage is more common. For adult women in rural areas, the consequences of forced marriage (marital breakdown and the woman's return to the natal home) can be cited as reasons to avoid forced marriage.

Pakistan: Arranged marriage rather than forced marriage is the norm. However, a woman's right to consent may be ignored even when the formality is rigorously observed. Consent may be beaten out of the bride, or her head may be nodded forcibly, or her silence may be taken as consent. Women are not aware that forced marriage is invalid; betrothal at birth or a young age is common. However, women are increasingly resisting forced marriage through social means (accessing community pressure or shelters and women's groups), and parents are more careful to obtain true consent.

Senegal: Wife 'inheritance' (levirate) is practiced, whereby after the husband's death the wife has to remarry his brother or a close male relative. Imams who were interviewed during the GREFELS research stated that under Muslim laws a virgin must consent to the marriage before its celebration. The father or guardian does not have the right to ignore her opinion, and compulsion is not permissible. However her silence is taken as consent.

Sri Lanka: Among most Malays consent is obtained orally. In rural areas, fathers choose the husband and the bride's choice is not considered. There is a positive trend among educated middle classes where parents are securing real consent from their daughters.

Sudan: Marriage formalities exclude women, and the bride's consent is usually certified by consulting her guardian(s) or male relatives. The wakeel (agent) of the woman may come to take her consent on the same day and time when the Ma'azoun is contracting the marriage. Often this is done as a nominal procedure where the wakeel goes inside to ask for her consent. Sometimes he may not even ask her. Moreover, as the bride cannot attend the ceremony, her consent is taken for granted.

Turkey: A WWHR survey found 54% of women had met men and married independently from their families and 41% had been married through arranged marriages. Amongst those who had arranged marriages, 39.7% had not been able to see their husbands before marriage; 28.6% were not asked whether or not they wanted to get married; and 28.6% did not marry willingly. Forced marriage is not on the women's movement agenda although it is widespread among some communities.

Lobbying to Change State Attitudes Towards Forced Marriage

Forced marriage is increasingly recognised as a problem among migrant communities in Europe, both by members of the communities themselves and by the local authorities.

In the UK, the Foreign & Commonwealth Office has set up a special Community Liaison Unit, which is responsible for providing information and support to citizens who contact the Foreign Office regarding forced marriages. In response to activism by NGOs and to increased awareness of the need to respond to forced marriages, various Police Forces around the country have worked with NGOs to develop guidelines for combating this problem. In addition, over the past two years activists have produced informational materials for both professionals (lawyers, teachers, health workers, immigration officials, etc.) who may come into contact with people being forced into marriage and at-risk youngsters.

Additionally, the British Government has changed its policy regarding the assistance provided to British Bangladeshis and British Pakistanis (dual nationality is possible) who have been coerced into marriage. In the past, when dual nationals (mostly women and girls, but some men) appealed for assistance from the British High Commission, they were told by officials that they could not be helped as they would have to abide by the rules of the country that they were currently located in. This weak response was given to dual citizens who had been coerced into marriage on 'family holidays' in Bangladesh, even though they were below the legal age of marriage in Bangladesh.

Activists in both Bangladesh and Pakistan began a concerted effort to meet government officials and provide them with briefing papers which informed them that the laws in all three countries do not permit forced and child marriage. In Bangladesh, when a child (under 18) is married, the father as well as the solemnizer of the marriage and the groom (if he is an adult) are all liable to punishment. Likewise, in Pakistan where the age of marriage for females is lower at 16, the forced marriage of anyone above that age can be declared invalid.

In the year 2000, after much work was done by local and UK-based NGOs as well as by sympathetic UK officials, the policy was changed. The British High Commission now assists all genuine cases of forced marriage, whether the person involved is a dual national or just British national.

However, UK-based groups continue to express concern that the forced marriage issue may be used as an excuse to introduce tighter immigration controls (for example, see http://news.bbc.co.uk/1/hi/uk_politics/2446875.stm, 12 November, 2002). In Norway and Denmark there has been considerable debate concerning the issue of minors from immigrant families marrying through arranged marriages abroad and then seeking to bring their spouse to Norway or Denmark. The Norwegian government has pledged to create shelters for those fleeing forced marriages, and there are calls for mandatory government prosecution in forced marriage cases so that an unwilling spouse would not have to initiate legal action against her own family. However, side by side with these positive developments, in both countries there have been calls for a higher age of marriage for migrants and second-generation nationals, which anti-racist groups are rejecting as discriminatory. In Denmark, spouses of immigrants are particularly liable to have entry refused when the Danish spouse is under the age of 24.

3d MARRIAGE REQUISITES: FORCED MARRIAGE & CHOICE IN MARRIAGE

introduction

This section discusses remedies that are available after a marriage has been contracted without a wali's permission (if this is required) or without an adult woman's consent. Since women are more vulnerable to forced marriage, and since divorce is often more accessible to men, these remedies are usually more important to women.

The status of marriages and the relief available when other requisites of marriage (unrelated to consent and capacity to consent) are lacking are discussed in Witnesses & Mahr, p.109, and Capacity to Marry – Other Prohibitions, p.95.

Remedies to a marriage obtained without proper consent can be accessed only once a 'marriage' has actually taken place, and one of the spouses (or in some cases a third party) seeks clarification about the status and effects of the 'marriage.' Is it a marriage at all? What happens to the inherent and any negotiated rights resulting from this marriage? Is the paternity of the children recognized? Does the wife have a right to inheritance?

Relief varies from a court declaration that the marriage was never a marriage (void ab initio) to allowing the wife to seek dissolution. Both these possibilities require the intervention of some recognized forum, usually a court or traditional council. Community pressure against a marriage and social sanctions may also prevent spouses from continuing an unacceptable marriage.

Laws in many countries are silent on the precise remedies and consequences of a marriage that lacks an adult woman's consent. They do not provide a clear mechanism for relief. In contrast, laws often emphasise a wali's right to obstruct a marriage or to compel his ward to marry.

systems not based on muslim laws

In systems not based on Muslim laws, a marriage lacking the consent of either of the spouses is considered defective. In Turkey, for example, the law allows the spouses to apply for dissolution in the event of forced consent.

In Cameroon the law distinguishes between a marriage lacking spousal consent ('void') and one where consent was forced ('voidable'). In this system, a 'void' marriage is considered never to have existed, whereas a 'voidable' marriage can be corrected and made valid if the bride later confirms that she accepts the marriage. The distinction is a subtle one, but it is important for women's rights. An example of a 'void' marriage is one where a woman can prove that she was never even present at her alleged marriage. In such a case, she obviously never consented to it. This concept protects women against harassment from men who falsely claim to be their husbands. An example of a voidable marriage is one where a woman was forced to consent. The law then grants her the power to accept or reject the marriage. Whatever she decides, the paternity of any children is recognized. This 'voidable' concept is useful in systems that otherwise give women only narrow grounds for divorce such as proven adultery.

Senegal also distinguishes between absolute nullity (where the woman's consent to the marriage was lacking) and relative nullity (where she was coerced or deceived into consenting to the marriage). In the latter case, she has the right to accept the marriage or to have it declared annulled. If she chooses the latter, she nevertheless retains all rights arising out of the marriage.

relief in systems based on muslim laws

In systems based on Muslim laws, there is a basic division between those that recognise the wali concept and those that do not.

In Pakistan, which does not require a wali, there is no explicit provision in the Muslim Family Laws Ordinance regarding the effect of a lack of consent. However, if a marriage never took place, a woman can approach the court to have a declaration that the marriage never existed (jactitation of marriage). In the event that she wishes to dissolve the marriage but not undo its results, e.g., protect the legal paternity of any children, she can apply for dissolution under the Dissolution of Muslim Marriages Act, 1939. Under the DMMA, consummation is taken to imply consent unless the woman can prove clearly that she was coerced, kidnapped, or confined, or that the marriage document was forged. In the case of a forced marriage where she is unable to prove such force, the woman would have to base the suit on other grounds for dissolution, such as non-maintenance or cruelty (see p.286 for the grounds under the DMMA).

There is limited relief available to women in systems that permit compulsion in marriage (ijbar). In Iran, for example, a woman may apply to the court to have a forced marriage declared void. But the guardian can obstruct the voiding process if he can prove that he contracted the marriage in her best interest. In some cases, a woman could try to access the concept of kafa'a (the requirement that spouses be equally matched) in order to have an unwelcome marriage annulled. Even if a claim to incompatibility could be made on the grounds of kafa'a, the laws do not provide a clear mechanism for women to make such a claim. Instead, the laws only discuss the wali's right to prevent a woman from seeking such remedies or the wali's right to ijbar.

The situation in systems that have a wali requirement but do not explicitly permit ijbar is more confused. For example, Sri Lanka does not have any explicit provisions regarding relief in the event of forced marriage. However, case law shows that women can appeal to the court using the concept of kafa'a (even if this is not acknowledged as kafa'a) as a basis for a claim that the groom chosen for them is unsuitable.

when third parties can interfere

Laws (and also customs) differ over who can seek relief in the event that a marriage is contracted without the fulfilment of the requisites relating to capacity to consent and consent.

Generally, the right of third parties (the guardian and/or the state) to interfere in a marriage is only recognized in systems where a wali is required. This provides a powerful tool to force the termination of marriages that do not meet the parent/guardian's personal or social approval or state requirements for a valid marriage. Even the threat of having a marriage declared void can be used as a means of forcing women to comply with social and traditional norms that violate their personal freedoms.

However, some systems allow any affected party to approach the court in the event of a suspected lack of consent (Senegal). This allows other family members or even concerned officials (where a matter of public policy is at stake) to assist women in situations of forced marriage when social pressures prevent them from bringing the case to court themselves. In some systems, a third party can also file for jactitation of marriage if they have a direct interest in the matter; for example, an existing husband can file a suit if some other man appears and claims to be married to the same woman.

the consequences of ending a defective marriage

Few laws are clear about the precise consequences of having a marriage declared defective or of having it dissolved because of some defect. This lack of clarity can lead to great confusion about many issues, including the status of the woman (is she considered never married, or does she have to observe a waiting period before remarrying?), the economic rights due to the woman because of the marriage (including the precise moment these rights, if any, terminate), the status of children, and whether or not the marriage established prohibitions on the basis of affinity between the spouses.

Tunisia's Code du Statut Personnel is perhaps the clearest as it spells out the consequences of ending defective marriages, both those that have been consummated and those that have not been. If an invalid marriage remains unconsummated, it is entirely without effect. However, if an invalid marriage has been consummated, the wife is entitled to mahr; the paternity of the children is recognized; the wife is obligated to observe idda; and a relationship of affinity is established. However, no maintenance or inheritance rights are due to the wife.

Senegal also provides exhaustive details regarding the effects of a marriage subsequently declared annulled. Provided the woman was acting in good faith and was forced or deceived into the subsequently annulled marriage, she retains all the rights due to a wife in a valid marriage

NOTES

LAWS: Forced Marriage and Choice in Marriage

Criteria

☺ More option-giving are those laws which:

- Do not recognize ijbar; and
- Provide a clear mechanism for declaring that a spouse's consent is lacking, and then specify the effects of such a declaration.

😐 The middle ground is occupied by those laws which:

- Are unclear about the relief possible and the effects of a defective marriage.

☹ Less option-giving are those laws which:

- Recognize ijbar and allow a wali's claim to ijbar to overrule a woman's complaint regarding her lack of consent.

☺ Ijbar is not recognized; clear mechanisms and effects in the event of a woman's lack of consent

Bangladesh & India (marriages under the SMA): Under S. 19 of the Divorce Act 1869, a suit for nullity may also be filed on the grounds that consent was obtained by force or fraud.

Senegal: Under A. 138 of the CF, a marriage lacking the consent of one of the spouses or based on the consent of a spouse that was obtained through force or error is liable to relative nullity. Under A. 140, such a claim must be made by the injured spouse and that spouse must act within 6 months of gaining her/his liberty or discovering the error. Thereafter the right is lost. Under A. 141, a lack of consent by one of the spouses is liable to absolute nullity, and the marriage can never be confirmed. Anyone with an interest can access this right. Under A. 144 a marriage declared null is considered dissolved from the date of the declaration. A. 144 & 145 permit acknowledgement of any retrospective effects of a nullified marriage. However, only the spouse acting in good faith can benefit.

Tunisia: Under A. 22, if the marriage is unconsummated, there are no consequences of the marriage if it is then declared invalid by a court. If the marriage is consummated and then declared invalid, the woman can claim her mahr; the paternity of the children is recognized; and the woman must observe idda before remarrying. These laws cover marriages celebrated without the required consent of spouses. No divorce proceedings are necessary, and either of the spouses or any of the parents or guardians or the state legal department can seek a declaration regarding the marriage.

Turkey: Under A. 151 of the CC, spouses forced into marriage may seek a declaration that they were coerced and have the marriage annulled.

Bangladesh & Pakistan: The MFLO, 1961 does not specify the requisites of valid marriage and the effects of irregular or void marriage. However, the standard marriage contract (kabinnama in Bangladesh and nikahnama in Pakistan) formulated under the MFLO Rules does reflect the requisites of a valid marriage (see p.150). A woman may file a suit for jactitation of marriage to establish the non-existence of a marriage without her consent.

Pakistan: Case law is clear that marriage without consent is void (Mst. Humera Mehmood v The State and others PLD 1999 Lahore 494). S. 23 of the Family Courts Act 1964 states that the validity of a registered marriage cannot be challenged, but case law has established that if a woman complains of fraud, deception, coercion, lack of consent, etc., then even a 'valid', registered marriage can be challenged. In Mohammad Azam v Mohammad Iqbal PLD 1984 SC 95, a five-member full bench held that S. 23 of the Family Courts Act assumes validity of marriage only if certain conditions have been satisfied, and this Section does not prevent any party from showing that the marriage has not taken place at all, that fraud has been committed, or that the nikahnama was a forgery and/or signatures to it were forged. Case law is clear that even if a husband has obtained a decree of conjugal rights but in that suit the validity of the marriage was not determined, the decree does not bar a wife from filing a subsequent suit for jactitation of marriage (Mohammad Rafiq v Family Court PLD 1985 Lahore 613). Case law also permits a woman to apply for dissolution under the DMMA, 1939 in the event that she is forced into marriage, meaning that she retains all rights arising out of the marriage.

Cameroon: Marriages can be annulled if they are 'void' (cannot be corrected) or 'voidable' (can be corrected if the vice is rectified). Marriage without the consent of the spouses is void and is treated as if the marriage never existed. Marriage under duress is considered voidable.

☺ The law is unclear about possible relief and effects in the event of a woman's lack of consent

Algeria: Under A. 32 of the CF, a marriage shall be declared void if one of the constituent elements is invalid. This implicitly includes marriages where the consent of the parents and/or spouses was lacking. The law is silent on the possible relief from and the effects of such a marriage.

Fiji: Marriages may be annulled due to a lack of consent of spouses or due to the marriage being contracted under duress. Case law has defined duress as physical threat to life only and does not include social pressures as a form of duress. Annulment requires an application to the court. Such marriages are then considered to have been void ab initio, i.e., never valid.

Malaysia: Under S. 37, the use of force or threat to compel a person into marriage against their will or to prevent the marriage of spouses who have attained the legal age is liable to a fine of up to RM 1,000 and/or to imprisonment of up to 6 months. Under S. 52(1)(j), a woman coerced into marriage may apply for faskh, meaning that the law does not differentiate between annulment and divorce.

Indonesia: A. 22 on dissolution of marriage does not recognise the concept of annulment. Marriages that are subsequently declared invalid, even if not consummated, are dissolved by divorce.

Sri Lanka: S. 25(1)(b) merely implies that a marriage without consent is not valid. The law does not provide for a specific procedure to challenge forced marriages or to have a marriage declared invalid. Case law reveals that a disparity of age can be grounds for some woman to obtain relief through annulment (rather than through divorce) (Sithi Umma v Aydroos (1949) 3 M.M.D.L.R. 96).

☹ Ijbar is recognized, but relief may be possible in the event of a woman's lack of consent

Morocco: Under A. 12(4) ijbar is recognized. A. 5 and 32 are not clear regarding the validity of marriages lacking the woman's consent whereas A. 5 (on validity) clearly specifies the requirement of the wali's consent. Under A. 37, a marriage whose validity is disputed shall be dissolved by talaq and idda; legitimacy and inheritance are confirmed. Under A. 14 kafa'a is available to both the woman and the wali, while under A. 15 relief on the grounds of incompatibility in age between the spouses is available to the wife alone (the nature of the relief is not mentioned).

Nigeria: A marriage contracted without the wali's consent is liable to be declared void among Malikis. However, since such dissolution is counted as a talaq, the couple are not liable for adultery; any children are considered legitimate; and the woman must observe idda. Case law in Muslim courts establishes that ijbar is not upheld for adult women and also that a woman can prevent herself from being forcibly married.

Sudan: The MPLA declares that a marriage may be declared void if the condition of the spouses' consent is not fulfilled. S. 62 renders such marriages void. However, ijbar is recognized. Weaknesses in provisions concerning the bride's consent make proving force difficult. Instead, courts usually focus on the validity of the procedures, i.e. what the wakeel has transferred to the Ma'azoun as the wife's opinion. Moreover, failure to follow procedures does not invalidate a marriage contract.

Iran: A court may declare a forced marriage void. However, guardians are given the opportunity to prove that they contracted the marriage in the best interests of an adult woman, and if they are successful, they can prevent the marriage from being declared void.

PRACTICES

Social attitudes and practices prevent women from seeking relief in the event of forced marriage

Egypt: Most women are unaware of legal provisions for declaring a marriage void. They often leave their husbands and wait out 5 years of separation in order to apply for a divorce. Additionally, women may fear that having their marriage declared void will result in the loss of their rights (including the right to maintenance) and a loss of the legal recognition of their children's paternity.

Fiji: Annulment on the grounds of forced consent is rarely accessed because of ignorance of the law and fear of social consequences.

Senegal: Custom does not acknowledge annulment as an option in the event of failure to respect any requisite of marriage. Women rarely access nullity even in the event that the husband fails to pay the agreed dower (where the dower has been stipulated as a condition of the marriage).

Women are able to seek relief in the event of forced marriage

Nigeria: Women and girls may find sympathetic relatives to assist and support them in cases against a father who forces them into marriage. Local newspapers also report such cases when they reach the courts. For example in September 2002, a 19-year old woman who was still studying in the northern town of Jos approached the Muslim court seeking an order to prevent her father from forcing her into marriage. Her father had already contracted the marriage on her behalf. She told the court that she would suffer psychological trauma, and her right to choose a husband would be infringed if she had to go through with the marriage (http://news.bbc.co.uk/1/hi/world/africa/224284.stm)

Negotiating Space in a Forced Marriage Case

Even when a woman is an adult in her early twenties, it may be difficult for her to resist parental pressure and instead make a marriage of her choice.

One such case involved a 22-year-old woman studying at Dhaka University. Her parents wished for her to marry her cousin in order to keep their property within the family (she had no brothers). She was placed under considerable emotional pressure, and she was made aware that she would be confined to the house and not allowed to attend her classes or go anywhere at all if she refused to go through with the proposed marriage.

Under these circumstances, the woman agreed to the marriage, provided she could have the option to divorce her husband (via talaq tafwid, the delegated right of divorce) if she was not 'happy,' All parties agreed to allow her this option, and she signed the marriage contract. The wedding ceremony was held the following week, and she was allowed to resume her classes. She attended her classes but then took shelter with a friend and got word to a human rights organization about her predicament. The organization took steps to file for divorce on her behalf.

In this case, the woman used her knowledge about the provision of talaq tafwid and her awareness that her parents, in order to avoid a public scandal, needed her to appear willing in order for them to go ahead with a big 'society' wedding.

Kafa'a is Applied – But Would Not Happen Today

Law schools in Singapore teach the following case as an example of a worst-case scenario in the application of kafa'a. The case also illustrates a conflict of laws between Penal Code provisions, which punish a man who entices a minor away from her lawful guardian, and Muslim laws, which regard a Hanafi female who has reached puberty as an adult (and therefore independent of her guardian). However, following reforms in the 1980s, the court's unfortunate decision would not be applied today.

In re Husseinah Banoo (1963, unreported decision), a 14 year old girl ran away from her wali in Singapore with her boyfriend, Abdul Rahman to the state of Negeri Sembilan in Malaysia where the kadi (registrar) married them. It was not clear as to why the power of wali was transferred to the court. There are two possibilities; the first being that the girl was Hanafi and had reached puberty; the other being that her wali mujbir (father) was more than two marhalah (about 70 km) away.

The father applied to the court to set aside the marriage, not on the grounds that his consent had not been given, but on the ground of kafa'a. The registrar who married them gave evidence that he married them because there was a danger that if he did not marry them, they would commit zina.

This case reflects the general position of the local courts that they give greater priority to preventing illegal sexual intercourse than to insisting on the consent of the wali. Under the local interpretations of Muslim laws, if the wali is two marhalah away (about 70 km), the court automatically has the right to assume the power of wali and marry the couple, and it does not matter to the registrar whether or not the ward has run away from the wali or the wali happened to reside at a distance from his ward or is temporarily away from his ward. Today, laws in the region accept this position of the courts, and codify the power of the court to act as the wali.

Unfortunately in the Husseinah Banoo case, the marriage was set aside on the ground of kafa'a (although she had already given birth to a child). According to local practice, the principle of kafa'a is strictly followed among Hanafis. This is the only case where it is known that a marriage was set aside even though it had been consummated. The father also had Abdul Rahman charged under the Penal Code for kidnapping a minor, and Abdul Rahman was found guilty.

3e MARRIAGE REQUISITES: CAPACITY TO MARRY - OTHER PROHIBITIONS

introduction

All societies place legal and social restrictions on both who may marry (that is, who has the capacity to marry) and whom that person may marry (that is, who is eligible to be a particular person's spouse). Restrictions may prohibit marriages within the forbidden degrees (consanguinity, affinity and fosterage), marriages where the spouses are not considered free to marry due to existing marital ties, and (in the case of Muslim laws) marriages that violate rules of religious affiliation.

All laws dealt with in this handbook agree that there is a permanent bar to marriages within the forbidden degrees and that such marriages can never be valid. But systems differ over whether marriages violating the remaining limitations are just temporarily barred (in which case the defect can later be rectified, making the marriage fully valid) or permanently barred.

Also, communities may impose limitations concerning a proposed spouse's economic and social status (see kafa'a, p.88) or limitations based on ethnicity, caste, tribe, etc. Often, but not always, community norms dictate a narrower range of suitable matches than do the laws governing the same community. Still, sometimes matches that fall within the legally forbidden degrees can be deemed socially 'suitable' by communities. Often everyone involved remains unaware that the marriage is void in the eyes of the law.

Many communities practice exchange marriage, first cousin marriage, and the pledging of children at birth. All of these practices variously constrict women, both because they fail to offer a choice of partner and because later during the subsistence of the marriage, such ties are considered by the community to be far more binding than 'ordinary' marriages.

Some codified systems have legislated a list of permanent and temporary bars to marriage and have specified within that legislation the effects of marriages that violate these bars (Algeria, Cameroon, Philippines, Senegal, Tunisia). Other codified systems apply bars to marriage without specifying these (or the consequences of violating them)(Bangladesh, Pakistan). In some systems the prohibitions may be listed but their effects are not listed (Morocco). Some laws clearly address certain prohibitions and their effects while only vaguely addressing other prohibitions. For example, Sri Lanka's Muslim Marriage and Divorce Act defines marriage within the forbidden degrees as an offence liable to 3 years imprisonment while a marriage contracted during a woman's idda merely cannot be registered, and the law remains silent as to the consequences of such a marriage.

When systems provide clear codification of provisions concerning the capacity to marry, they protect couples from contracting unions that are liable to being declared invalid. Additionally, unambiguous codification provides clear rules to assist the court in making a decision in the event that a union is challenged.

While women are, by and large, excluded from freely determining their marriage partner, they suffer more from the consequences of a void or irregular marriage. Their maintenance and inheritance rights, as well as the legal paternity of their children, are at risk. Thus, unclear and weak laws tend to work to women's disadvantage.

We draw a further distinction between those laws that base marriage prohibitions on interpretations of Muslim laws (Tunisia) and those that base prohibitions on other sources, such as the Napoleonic Code (Cameroon). Prohibitions drawn from these two types of sources differ most importantly in the area of inter-faith marriages.

Finally, laws defining other prohibitions concerning capacity for marriage for Muslims should be compared to laws within the same country that are applicable to other communities or that apply when a couple chooses to marry under a law not based on Muslim laws.

permanent bars to marriage

Certain kinds of marriage are forbidden because the parties are within what is termed the 'forbidden degrees' of relationship to each other.

These include three categories:

- **Consanguinity** relationships arising through blood;
- **Affinity** relationships arising through marriage;
- **Fosterage** (rada) relationship arising out of being suckled by the same woman.

Prohibitions rising out of consanguinity prevent marriages between a man and his daughter or mother (and by the same token a woman with her father or son), and all ascendants and descendants in the direct line (e.g., granddaughter and grandson). They also prevent brothers and sisters, full and half, from marrying. Laws express these prohibitions in various ways. While some focus on which women are forbidden to particular men, others express limitations in more gender neutral terms.

Laws also differ as to whether or not they define cousins to be within the forbidden degrees of consanguinity. Both Cameroon's Civil Code and the Philippines Code of Muslim Personal Law prohibit marriages between third cousins. Morocco's Moudawana only prohibits first cousin marriages. In Pakistan and among Muslims in Sudan, there are no prohibitions concerning cousin marriage; even first cousin marriages are permitted. It is hard to categorize any of these laws as more or less option-giving for women because much depends on other practices associated with cousin marriages.

However laws define consanguinity, they agree that couples defined as blood relatives can never be validly married. In the event that such a marriage is contracted and subsequently declared invalid, some laws recognize the paternity of children conceived during the invalid marriage (Morocco) while others do not (Cameroon).

Concerning prohibitions arising from affinity, most schools, Shia and Sunni, agree that affinity arises out of sexual intercourse between two parties whether it is lawful or not. Accordingly, individuals related through a valid marriage or through any other sexual relationship are not permitted to marry. However, the Shafi School holds that an unlawful sexual relationship does not create relationships of affinity. Accordingly, only individuals related through a valid marriage would be prohibited from marrying one another because of restrictions concerning affinity.

While the main Sunni and Shia schools apply the same or similar prohibitions concerning consanguinity and affinity, they differ dramatically in their treatment of fosterage. Shias apply the same rules to relationships resulting from fosterage that they apply to relationships resulting from consanguinity. On the other hand, Sunnis apply separate, more narrowly defined prohibitions, to relationships arising from fosterage.

In systems influenced by the Sunni Schools, the bar to marriage between foster siblings and children breast-fed by the same woman varies subtly from systems to system. Sunnis base the fosterage relationship, and any prohibitions arising from it, on the frequency and duration of a foster child's breast feedings. Morocco's Moudawana, for example, establishes a foster relationship between two children after the mother of one of the children provides five full breast feedings to the other child within the first two years of life.

Laws in Algeria, where the Maliki School dominates, offer perhaps the widest and most categorical fosterage prohibitions practiced by Sunnis. These laws establish a fosterage relationship after a single drop of milk has been provided by the same mother. However, since adoption is not recognized in Algeria, marriage between adoptive siblings is possible as long as they did not share their mother's milk. In contrast, Tunisian law recognizes adoption and accordingly, also prohibits marriage between adoptive parents and children, between adoptive parents and the child's spouse, and between adoptive siblings. Unusually, Lebanon's unsuccessful family law reform proposed to eliminate prohibitions based on fosterage.

While it is difficult to assess whether a wider or narrower prohibition is more option-giving, one can be certain that unclear laws create the greatest potential for problems because they may leave the validity of marriages in doubt. For example, laws in Pakistan and Bangladesh do not specifically legislate what is and is not a valid marriage. With various traditional schools of jurisprudence differing on the milk-fosterage issue, the validity of some marriages may be cast into doubt depending on who is judging that validity.

While all the legal systems examined in the handbook recognize marriage limitations based on 'forbidden degrees,' some systems contain additional prohibitions. For example, the Philippines stands out as the only country to have specifically legislated against marriages between a couple where both or either of the spouses have been found guilty of murdering the new partner's former spouse.

bars concerning existing marital ties

Systems based on Muslim laws may also list additional bars relating to existing marriage ties. Under these bars a man is prohibited from marrying a fifth wife, from marrying two sisters or close female relatives at the same time in a polygynous marriage, and from marrying a woman still observing idda. In Cameroon and Senegal, at the time of the marriage, the husband must specify whether the marriage is going to be monogamous or polygynous. In Senegal he must also specify whether he will limit himself to potentially two wives or to more. If the husband subsequently attempts to contract a marriage that violates these agreed specifications, the subsequent marriage will have no effect in the eyes of the law.

When a marriage violates prohibitions concerning existing marital ties, Sunni Muslim laws often refer to that marriage as an 'irregular' marriage. The term 'irregular' implies that in certain cases the marriage can become fully valid (for example if an earlier wife is divorced by a polygynous husband with 5 wives). However, under some codified laws marriages that violate these prohibitions are liable to being declared void through the courts (although some effects of the marriage may be recognized, see p.105, Senegal). Laws in Iran, which are based on Shia jurisprudence, do not recognize irregular marriages at all and consider such marriages void.

the validity of marriages contracted during idda

Like bars to marriages within the forbidden degrees, bars concerning existing marriage ties place women at a greater risk when they are unclear or unspecified.

As noted earlier, Pakistan's laws suffer from such a lack of specified prohibitions and their effects. Additionally, individuals who engage in sexual relations outside of a valid marriage are liable to prosecution for zina. Local case law has seen a discussion of the effects of void and irregular marriage in the context of zina cases, where women face harsh sentences for contracting another marriage during their idda. In other words, to assess the impact of an irregular marriage, one also has to examine any penal provisions concerning bigamy and zina. Such an assessment is equally necessary in systems not based on Muslim laws, such as in Senegal, where bigamy is an offence.

Pakistani case law distinguishes between marriages contracted during the idda that follows various forms of dissolution. Whether the idda follows talaq, talaq tafwid, or divorce by the wife through the courts determines the consequences of such a marriage. If a woman marries during idda after her husband has pronounced talaq, her new marriage is void because the authority to revoke the talaq lies with the husband during the period of idda; if he then revokes the talaq the woman would be married to two people at the same time and thus any subsequent marriage in existence of the earlier marriage is void. Here she would be liable to bigamy and also possibly to zina if the subsequent marriage had been consummated (see p.265 for how the courts have dealt with this problem).

However, if a woman has exercised talaq tafwid, any marriage that she contracts during her idda may fall in the category of 'irregular' because her contracting a subsequent marriage indicates that she does not intend to revoke the talaq, and her husband does not have the authority to revoke her talaq. Similarly, a marriage contracted by a woman during the idda that follows after she has obtained a court decree for dissolution also falls in the category of 'irregular' marriage because again the husband has no authority of revocation, and it is for the woman to decide whether or not to reconcile and render the dissolution decree ineffective. These issues were discussed in detail in Abdul Sattar v Mst. Zahida Parveen and 10 others in 1991 MLD 403.

marriage between muslims & non-muslims

Systems not based on Muslim laws usually do not prohibit marriages between spouses of different faiths.

Generally, Muslim laws do not recognize as valid a marriage between a Muslim woman and a non-Muslim man while they do allow Muslim men to marry Kitabia women. (Some laws even allow men to contract an irregular marriage with a woman outside these faiths, e.g., Hindu.) Jurists are divided as to whether a marriage between a Muslim woman and non-Muslim man is void or irregular. (For example, in the sub-continent Mulla's Principles of Mohammedan Law, S. 259(2) states that such a marriage is irregular, while Fyzee terms it void.)

However, in some systems men are also barred, either explicitly or in effect, from marrying non-Muslims. For example, in Malaysia the law defines a Kitabia so narrowly that inter-faith marriage is a virtual impossibility, and marriages contracted abroad cannot be subsequently registered in Malaysia if they do not match these legal requirements. In contrast, some systems based on Muslim laws do not explicitly codify such provisions. (Morocco's Moudawana and Malaysian laws do, Tunisia's Code du Statut Personnel does not.)

Even where Muslim laws specifically prohibit inter-faith marriages, couples may have the option of marrying under another law that would recognize their union (Bangladesh, Cameroon, India, Nigeria, Senegal, Singapore, Sri Lanka).

In Bangladesh, the Special Marriages Act of 1872 enables inter-faith marriages, but the law implies that both parties must make a profession of non-belief. On doing so, a Muslim woman loses her right to inheritance and her right to dower – not to mention any religious identity. There is an ongoing campaign by Ain o Salish Kendro (ASK) to do away with the renunciation provision (as has happened with India's Special Marriages Act 1954) and amend the Act so as to have a truly secular and civil option for citizens who wish to exercise their right to marry in a non-religious forum. Islamization in Pakistan has certainly narrowed women's options in this area. Since the 1970s, access to the Special Marriages Act 1872 has all but ceased because of strict penal provisions concerning blasphemy that make it impossible for someone to renounce Islam. In Sri Lanka, a Muslim woman can validly marry a non-Muslim under the General Law of Sri Lanka. Subsequent to such a marriage, the woman would be governed by General Law and not Muslim laws. General Law differs from Muslim laws in provisions concerning a number of issues, including divorce and inheritance. In Singapore, a Muslim can marry a non-Muslim under the Women's Charter (which recognizes marriage where one of the parties is Muslim). However, the state appears to discourage such marriages, and as a matter of practice, the Muslim party is usually told to seek advice from the Registrar of Muslim Marriages before he/she contracts a Charter marriage.

Equally, the validity of marriages with men from sects declared non-Muslims (in certain countries) has become uncertain. Ahmedis/Qadianis, for example, who face considerable persecution in Pakistan, no longer approach the regular courts for resolution of their family matters. Instead they have evolved their own parallel system. In Iran, on the other hand, new legislation requires registrars to automatically register the marriages of men over 20 years and women over 18, without asking their religion. This legislation seems to be easing some of the problems faced by Baha'is.

Whereas marriages between Muslim men and non-Muslim women may be more or less socially acceptable, marriages of Muslim women with non-Muslim men face far greater social restrictions. Regardless of available legal options, most such couples move abroad to marry. Their ability to return to their own countries depends on the prevailing social climate as well as on whether or not their marriage would be legally recognized.

However, some countries restrict even the possibility of a Muslim woman marrying a non-Muslim man abroad (under a system that apparently has no religious prohibitions). For example, the Sudanese Embassy in some European countries has forwarded notices to local municipal authorities listing two conditions that are to be applied when a Sudanese female citizen seeks to marry in the municipality. Firstly, she must provide a certificate from the Sudanese Embassy verifying that she is single. Such a certificate is not provided according to a set procedure. Instead, a certificate may be provided or withheld according to the ideological judgements of embassy personnel. Secondly, she must provide a letter verifying her father or guardian's consent to the marriage. This letter also must be certified by the Embassy.

Laws may also discriminate against women marrying foreigners. For example, Iranian women have to get official permission to marry non-Iranian citizens while Iranian men only require such permission if they are in sensitive official posts. The marriage also has to be contracted via a Muslim marriage ceremony because the status of civil marriages contracted abroad is unclear. (Civil marriages are not recognized officially. However, courts may arbitrarily recognize certain rights arising from the marriage any way. In one such case, the court upheld a husband's right to 'obedience' from his wife (from a foreign civil marriage).) Under Iranian law, all marriages of Iranian citizens abroad must be registered with the embassy. Such a registration requires that a couple present a Muslim marriage certificate and/or a conversion certificate. Obviously, when Iranian citizens live where there is an absence of diplomatic relations with Iran and, accordingly, there is no embassy, they encounter great difficulties contracting a valid marriage.

the effects of marriages that violate other prohibitions concerning capacity

In some cases marriages within forbidden degrees are dealt with by a decree of annulment. Thus in Senegal, an absolute annulment may be declared in the event that the marriage was (a) between persons of the same sex (b) between persons related by a forbidden degree of consanguinity or affinity (c) between a man and a woman who is in a existing union not yet properly dissolved. In these instances the spouses are obliged to automatically separate on discovery that their union is irregular. Although these marriages are liable to annulment, even by third parties, the effects of such marriages (up until the date of annulment) remain valid. Thus, the legal paternity of any children will be recognized, and any inheritance cannot be reclaimed by the deceased's family.

In contrast, some systems do not recognize any effects arising from prohibited marriages. Morocco's Moudawana prohibits marriage between two people who are related through consanguinity, affinity, or suckling, as well as prohibiting marriage between a man and a woman who is observing idda. (A marriage contracted during a women's idda remains invalid even after the idda is over.) The effects of marriages that are found to violate these prohibitions are merely implied under another article, and it appears that all such marriages are without legal effect.

Tunisia's CSP is clear that marriages violating the prohibitions are void and do not require divorce. However, the law entitles a woman to mahr, establishes paternity, and requires the woman to observe idda. Additionally, the law specifies that the void marriage did establish relationships of affinity.

Nigerian laws follow Muslim laws more closely than Tunisian laws. Accordingly, marriages within the forbidden degrees are treated as void ab initio and have no recognized effect; while irregular marriages, even if not consummated, are accorded some status.

Political Misuse of Annulment Provisions

In some countries (Algeria, Egypt), third parties have asked the court to void a marriage following the alleged apostasy of one of the spouses. This strategy has been used by politico-religious extremists to 'annul' the marriage of political opponents. Here we will discuss one such case that occurred in Egypt.

In 1993, the Arabic literature professor, Nasr Hamid Abu Zaid was charged with apostasy. The charges were brought by a lawyer and another man who were acting on behalf of politico-religious activists. The claimants argued for the compulsory separation of Prof Abu Zaid from his wife, based on his 'apostasy' as allegedly expressed in his writings and research.

Egyptian law does not have an explicit provision concerning apostasy. However, Egyptian family law leaves it open for judges to apply Hanafi law in cases that are not dealt with in the Egyptian Civil Code.

The charge was brought under the hisba principle. According to this principle, Muslims may interfere in the lives of those who have committed a crime against God or against the people, even if these individuals have no direct interest.

The Court of First Instance rejected the case in 1994. The court did not recognize the hisba principle and rejected the case on the basis that those who had filed it had no direct interest. This decision was overturned in 1995 by the Cairo Court of Appeal, which decided that Abu Zaid's marriage was void due to his 'apostasy'.

The Egyptian Public Prosecutor then took the case to the Supreme Court on the grounds that the decision represented a severe threat to social order and stability in Egypt. To no avail: the Supreme Court confirmed the judgment in 1996.

The Egyptian government, in an attempt to stop further such litigation by Islamists, passed a law in 1996 that prohibits any party from filing, directly to the court, any case that concerns personal matters and is based on the concept of hisba. From now on, charges brought to the court by an individual rather than the public prosecutor, are not admissible unless filed by a person with a direct and personal interest.

This legislation successfully thwarted a similar attempt by politico-religious groups in 2001 when a lawyer brought a charge of apostasy against the prominent feminist writer Nawal el-Saadawi. The judge dismissed the case against her, ruling that only Egypt's Prosecutor General could file an apostasy case and that the lawyer lacked the required legal status.

NOTES

LAWS: Marriage between Muslims and non-Muslims

Criteria

Due to the lack of information available on how case law treats the effects of unions violating permanent and other bars to marriage, we have not listed laws according to more or less option-giving criteria in this section. One exception is the sub-section on marriages with non-Muslims, where provisions are listed according to whether or not alternative marriage options exist for interfaith couples.

☺ **No bar exists**

Cameroon, Fiji, Senegal: There are no legal bars to marriage between people of different religious faiths.

Lebanon (1998 proposed uniform civil code, never passed): Does not mention the religion of the intending spouses and thereby indirectly allows a Muslim woman to marry a non-Muslim man.

😐 **Alternative laws exist**

Gambia & Nigeria: Muslims may marry under the MMDO and the MCA respectively which do not prohibit inter-faith marriages, or under those customary laws that do not prohibit inter-faith marriage.

India: The SMA, 1954 provides for a marriage between any two persons, regardless of religion provided the male is 21 years old and the female 18. If the marriage is solemnized outside India, both parties must be Indian citizens and domiciled in India. Following registration, succession to the spouses' property is regulated by the Indian Succession Act of 1925.

Sri Lanka: A Muslim woman can validly marry a non-Muslim under the General Law of Sri Lanka. Subsequent to the marriage, she will be governed by General Law and not Muslim laws. The two types of law differ greatly in their provisions concerning divorce and inheritance. Two Muslims may not marry under the General Law.

Bangladesh: Marriage between a Muslim woman and a non-Muslim man is dealt with under general principles of Muslim laws. Such a marriage is considered void and the legal paternity of the children is not recognized. However, these couples can marry under the colonial SMA, 1872, but both partners would be required to make a declaration of 'non-faith.' The Act's preamble states that, 'Whereas it is expedient to provide a form of marriage for persons who do not profess the Christian, Jewish, Hindu, Muslim, Parsi, Buddhist, Sikh or Jaina religion and to legalize certain marriages, the validity of which are doubtful....' Muslim men can contract a valid marriage with a Kitabia woman. Also, a Muslim man may marry a Hindu woman but the marriage would be considered irregular. In an irregular marriage, the legal paternity of the children is recognized but there are no rights of inheritance or maintenance established between the spouses.

Singapore: Under S. 3(4) of the WC, no marriage between Muslims shall be solemnized and registered under the Act, meaning that where one of the parties is a Muslim, solemnization and registration under the Act is possible. However, Singapore's laws are not clear as to how inheritance would be dealt with in such cases, and there has been no case law as yet to clarify the situation.

☹ **Marriage between Muslim women and non-Muslim men only possible if the man converts to Islam**

Pakistan: Since the 1970s, access to the SMA has all but ceased because of strict penal provisions concerning blasphemy that make it impossible for someone to renounce Islam. Since Ahmedis/Qadianis were declared non-Muslims in Pakistan in 1974, it has not been clear if the MFLO applies to marriages involving Ahmedis or if a Muslim woman can validly marry an Ahmedi man. The courts have preferred to avoid dealing directly with this controversial issue and have instead ruled on the immediate issue at hand (maintenance demand and validity of talaq). In the three known cases, it appeared that the husband was attempting to evade his legal responsibilities by claiming that the marriage was not valid, and in each the court ruled in the woman's favour without directly dealing with the issue of validity (Nasir Ahmed Shaikh v. Mrs. Nahid Ahmed Shaikh NLR 1986 Civil 659; LN 1986 Lahore 597; Muhammad Rashid v. Mst. Nusrat Jahan Begum 1986 MLD 1010 Lahore).

Algeria: The marriage of a Muslim woman to a non-Muslim man is defined as a temporary impediment, which may be rectified (i.e., if the husband converts to Islam).

Iran: Muslim women cannot validly marry non-Muslim men but such a marriage will be recognized if the man converts to Islam. Under new marriage registration provisions, if a man over 20 years and a woman over 18 go to a registry and say they are husband and wife, the registrar has to register their marriage without asking them their religion. While the law may have been intended to solve some of the problems faced by Baha'is in Iran, it could be used to facilitate inter-faith marriages also. (However, so far there is no evidence suggesting that it has been used for such purposes.) If a non-Muslim woman marrying an Iranian Muslim man does not convert, the marriage is registered as a temporary marriage with a duration of 99 years. Wives have limited rights in a temporary marriage.

Malaysia: Under S. 10 of the IFLA, 1984, a Muslim woman can marry only a Muslim man. A Muslim man may marry a non-Muslim woman, who is a Kitabiyah. However, the Act narrowly defines a Kitabiyah as a woman whose ancestors were from the Bani Ya'qub, a Christian woman whose ancestors were Christians before the prophethood of the Prophet Muhammad, or a Jewish woman whose ancestors were Jews before the prophethood of the Prophet 'Isa. Marriages contracted abroad, which do not conform to the requirements of Hukum Syr'iah, cannot be registered.

Sudan: A Muslim woman does not have the capacity to marry a non-Muslim man. A Muslim man may marry a Christian and/or a Jewish woman.

LAWS:
Prohibitions on the Basis of Consanguinity and Affinity

In **all the countries dealt with here** (exceptions and details are dealt with below) void marriages include those between **blood relatives** (ascendants and descendants, as well as maternal and paternal aunts and the daughters of a brother or sister), as well those contracted between persons related through **affinity** (father/grandfather's ex-wife or widow; son/grandson's ex-wife or widow).

Cameroon: Under the CSO and CC, there are additional prohibitions concerning consanguinity and affinity; persons so related cannot get married up to the fourth degree.

Gambia: Under S. 148 of the CrC, incest is a criminal offence. A man cannot have a sexual or marital relationship with his mother, sister, daughter, or granddaughter. A woman over 16 who consents to a sexual relationship with her grandfather, father, brother, or son is also guilty of a felony. Relationships through affinity are not prohibited.

Philippines: Under the CMPL, there are additional prohibitions concerning consanguinity and affinity; no marriage shall be contracted between any man or woman and his/her relatives by affinity in the ascending line and in the collateral line within the third degree.

Senegal: Under A. 141-145 of the CF, marriage within the forbidden degrees of consanguinity and affinity (not defined) is liable to annulment by any interested party or the state. The marriage is considered void as of the date of annulment, but the effects of the marriage remain valid (inheritance until the date of the decree and legal paternity of any children).

Sri Lanka: Under S. 80 of the MMDA, males and females over the age of 12 are liable to up to 3 years of imprisonment for knowingly having carnal relations with those related to them by consanguinity and affinity. Under S. 80(2) women can claim coercion as a valid defense. These constitute greater prohibitions than in the General Law.

Sudan: The law expressly prohibits marriage with stepdaughters.

LAWS:
Prohibitions on the Basis of Fosterage and Adoption

Systems based on Muslim laws generally follow the principle that fosterage (the relationship created by rada' - suckling) creates the same prohibitions as do consanguinity and affinity. However, the amount of milk (or number of breast feedings required to establish a relationship of fosterage differs (see details below).

In contrast, the following systems (not based on Muslim laws) do not have prohibitions based on suckling: Bangladesh (SMA, 1872), Cameroon, Central Asian Republics, Fiji, Gambia (MMDO, 1941), India (SMA, 1954), Nigeria (MCA, 1970), Senegal, and Turkey.

Tunisia: The law permits adoption; therefore, adoption creates the same prohibitions as do consanguinity and affinity. Under A. 17 of the CSP, suckling (no amount is defined) creates the same impediments to marriage as do consanguinity and affinity.

Lebanon: The unsuccessful 1998 uniform civil code proposed to permit marriage between spouses related by fosterage (suckling).

Algeria: Under S. 27-29 of the CF, fosterage is covered by prohibitions concerning consanguinity. Fosterage is established if the foster mother breastfeeds (regardless of the frequency) the foster child during the first two years of life.

Malaysia: Under S. 9(3), 'fosterage through 'some act of suckling' creates a relationship prohibiting marriage.

Morocco: Under A. 28 of the Moudawana, five full feedings establish a relationship of suckling.

Philippines: A relationship of fosterage is established by the child being breastfed at least 5 times within 2 years of birth.

LAWS:
Other Bars to Marriage

Algeria: Under A. 30 and 34 of the CF, the following marriages are void: marriage with a woman who is already married; marriage with a woman observing idda following divorce or widowhood, and marriage with a 5th wife. These marriages shall be declared void, whether they have been consummated or not. However, paternity is established, and the woman must observe idda.

Bangladesh & India (marriages under the SMA): Under S. 2 of the SMA, marriages may be declared void or dissolved where a condition to the marriage is lacking. These conditions include that neither party, at the time of marriage, have a husband or wife living.

Morocco: Under A. 29 of the Moudawana the following women are forbidden temporarily: two women related by consanguinity (although marriage with a woman and the mother of her former husband or daughter of her former husband at the same time is not prohibited), a 5th wife, or a woman completing the waiting period. No effects of marriages formed in violation of these prohibitions are mentioned.

Philippines: The CMPL prohibits marriage between persons one or both of whom have been found guilty of having killed the spouse or either of them.

Tunisia: Under A. 22 of the CSP, an irregular marriage is declared void, but dower, paternity, idda, and relationships of affinity are established. Under A. 21, a couple that continues to live togethor following a declaration that their marriage is irregular is liable to 6 months imprisonment.

Senegal: The CF provides for absolute annulment in the case that a marriage is solemnized during idda and in the case that a marriage violates the specified number of wives in the marriage option. The spouses are obliged to separate on discovery that their union is irregular and any interested party or the state can seek a declaration of annulment. However, the legal paternity of the children is recognized, and any inheritance received by the spouse cannot be reclaimed by the deceased spouse's relative following an annulment decree.

PRACTICES

Marriages outside the community

Central Asian Republics: Inter-ethnic marriages do occur, but these are mostly between Russian women and Central Asian men; vice versa is more rare. Uzbek women may marry Tatars, Armenians, Georgians, etc., (i.e. non-Slav European nationalities). Inter-ethnic marriage is more common among urbanized, Europeanized youth.

Fiji: There are strong attitudes against inter-faith marriage. These attitudes have strengthened with the political polarization of the communities along lines of communal identity.

Iran: Marriages between Muslim women and non-Muslim men are not socially acceptable but even marriages between Muslim men and non-Muslim women are not viewed favourably. Debates around these issues have been raised by women activists and taken up by some religious leaders.

Lebanon: There are 18 separate religious communities recognized in Lebanon, and despite the years of Civil War, intercommunity relationships have formed. These relationships influenced the 1998 proposal to permit inter-faith, inter-sect marriages. Currently, couples whose religions do not permit them to marry travel abroad to do so.

Nigeria: Inter-ethnic marriages are possible (and increasingly common, in the urban areas and amongst the young and/or formally educated) but are most easily accepted between those of the same religious faith. The possibility of social acceptance for inter-ethnic and inter-religious marriage increases with the woman's age.

Pakistan: In Syed families, especially in Shia Syed families, women are not permitted to marry non-Syeds. If there is no suitable match for a daughter, some feudal Syed families of Sindh province will ask her to forgo her right to marriage. She then makes a formal renunciation on the Qur'an. This tradition is known as 'marriage with the Qur'an,' or haq bakhshwana (literally, forgoing the right). The woman is thereby condemned to a life without a husband or children and may live as a recluse. Families inflict such a fate on their daughter to to avoid her marrying a person of lower social status, as well as to ensure that property remains within the family.

Marriage outside the tribe/caste/sect is heavily discouraged in Pakistan, especially in feudal areas where social hierarchy is determined by caste combined with other factors. However, such marriages are slowly becoming more accepted.

Sudan: Muslim men are permitted to marry non-Muslim women while Muslim women may not marry non-Muslim men. The inequity in prohibitions reflects both the belief that men are strong enough to resist and avoid conversion (and women are not) and the fact that children traditionally follow the father's religion.

Exchange marriages

Communities in a number of countries practice exchange marriage (often to avoid dowry practices and mahr). This is known as berdar in Turkey, badal in Jordan and Palestine, and watta satta or addo baddo in Pakistan. In exchange marriage, a man and woman from one family are married to a woman and man from another family. This exchange usually pairs brothers and sisters, but can skip generations so that an aunt and nephew, or even a father and daughter may marry into the same family. In Pakistan, even unborn children may be pledged in exchange marriages. The exchange may be 'equalized' by the addition of goods or cash if one of the pairs is uglier, older, etc. The fate of the two couples then becomes inextricably linked and if divorce or separation takes place between one couple, the other couple are forced by the community to divorce/separate even if they are happy together. Breaking an exchange marriage is extremely difficult because of the complex social relationships involved.

Marriages violating permanent and temporary bars

Gambia & Pakistan: Individuals from Muslim communities sometimes marry within the forbidden degrees due to ignorance of the provisions.

Philippines: The prohibition against marriage between relatives by affinity in the collateral line is often violated because it is said that the prohibition has no theological basis.

Sri Lanka: Case law on marriage within the forbidden degrees indicates that such marriages have been contracted. Religious authorities rarely intervene if they come to know of such a marriage.

Senegal: Qadis are aware of the prohibitions under Muslim laws and can annul the marriage if the violation comes to their attention.

A Marriage Between a Muslim and a Hindu: Can the Father Object?

A Hindu girl and a Muslim boy under 21 sought to marry without the consent of the boy's father (R v Registrar General: ex parte Abdul Hamid, Fij, Court of Appeal case 386/1985).

The couple obtained the consent of the Magistrate's Court on the ground that their parents were unreasonably withholding consent. Because of the Court's administrative mistake, the father did not receive notice of the hearing and therefore was not present to state his objections. The Registrar of Marriages married the couple, but the father sued the Registrar, saying the marriage was invalid without parental consent.

The question for the High Court was whether the father had a right to be heard before the Magistrate's Court decided to give consent to marry under S.13 of the Marriage Act.

The case went from the High Court to the Court of appeal, which said that the father was entitled to be heard and to make his objections. As the father had not been heard, the Magistrate's consent was not proper. However, the lack of notice was a mistake, not a deliberate act, and the fact that the proper procedures had not been followed did not make the marriage illegal.

Jalal, P. I. (1998), Law for Pacific Women: A Legal Rights Handbook, Fiji Women's Rights Movement, Suva, Fiji

3f MARRIAGE REQUISITES: WITNESSES AND MAHR (DOWER)

introduction

Laws and customs differ in whether or not they specify the number, sex, and qualifications of, as well as the duties of, those who may serve as witnesses to a marriage. This section examines these differences and their implications for women. For additional details regarding the involvement of witnesses in the procedure for marriage contracts and registration, see p.147.

This section also examines whether or not mahr is defined as a requisite of a valid Muslim marriage in law. Other aspects of mahr, including the possible benefits and problems associated with mahr and relevant practices are discussed on p.179. Also, mahr is mentioned briefly in Registration and Validity, p.133 and Marriage Contracts & Registers, p.147.

the role of witnesses

In general, systems that require witnesses to be present in order for a couple to contract a valid marriage are more beneficial to women. Ideally, the witnesses would be required to testify to the fulfilment of all other requisites: the age, capacity and consent of the parties, as well as the fixing of mahr and any other agreed conditions to the marriage (where this is applicable). Unfortunately, no existing laws specify such requirements. In essence the role of the witness is to protect against the violation of rights. Since women are generally the more vulnerable party in a marriage, witnesses are particularly important for them. For example, witnesses should act as a protection against forced marriage by attesting to the age and consent of the spouses. If there is any subsequent dispute about the existence of a marriage, witnesses can attest to the validity of the marriage (or at least to the good faith of one or both of the spouses) so that a woman would be able to retain her economic rights and ensure the legal paternity of her children.

However, particularly in communities where choice in marriage is strongly opposed, couples that are marrying against the wishes of their families may find it difficult to locate willing witnesses. In such situations, the requirement that witnesses be present for a couple to contract a valid marriage weakens the couple's ability to exercise choice. Also, laws that specify a particular qualification for witnesses may be used to reinforce traditional notions of power. For example, in Sudan laws require witnesses to be of 'good reputation and trustworthy.' In such contexts, witnesses offer little protection to women.

No known law provides for punishment of witnesses in cases where marriages violate legal requirements (for example, in the event of forced or child marriage). Only solemnizers are penalized.

Some laws specify what it is the witnesses are expected to attest to. They may witness the ijab (offer) and qabul (acceptance); or the payment of the mahr; or both mahr and consent. In terms of women's rights, the most important role of the witness is to attest to the woman's consent. Where the law enforces wali practices, only the wali's consent need be witnessed, which weakens any protection against forced marriage. Similarly, if the law considers 'silence to be consent' (Sudan), witnessing the bride's consent may become meaningless.

Laws are not always clear that the witnesses to a marriage must be the same witnesses who sign any separate registration documents. This lack of clarity leaves loopholes that can be exploited by those who seek to undermine a woman's rights in marriage.

witnesses and gender discrimination

Most laws require that two people (of unspecified gender) witness a marriage. In Fiji, where no personal laws are applied, a marriage witnessed by two women is valid, but in most systems based on Muslim laws, the presumption is that the two witnesses have to be male. However, the laws in Sudan and Yemen note that one man and two women may act as witnesses. Most laws do not expressly permit four women to witness a marriage. The lesser 'worth' of women as marriage witnesses is said to be based on Qur'anic provisions (2:282) regarding the witnessing of contracts involving future financial obligations. Since a Muslim marriage inherently involves the payment of mahr and maintenance to the wife, one could interpret marriage as a financial contract. The Tunisian Code of Civil Procedure is unique among laws based on Muslim sources in accepting that witnesses to marriage may be either male or female.

In almost all Muslim communities, the requirement of witnesses is upheld. However, these laws emphasize public acknowledgement of the marriage rather than ensuring that requisites are fulfilled and the spouses' rights are protected. Although they are closely involved in wedding ceremonies, women (and especially the bride) are often excluded from the contractual formalities and very rarely act as witnesses in unregistered, registered, oral or written marriages. Since the formalities are usually taken over by the more powerful figures in the two families, in practice, witnesses are unlikely to offer real protection against a violation of rights, such as forced or child marriage. Moreover, if the woman subsequently needs to prove the marriage or the conditions attached against the wishes of her family (for example, to get a divorce), she may find the witnesses are unwilling to help her access her rights.

the status of marriages lacking witnesses

Systems that require a marriage to be solemnized before an official or that do not recognize unregistered marriages tend to regard marriages without witnesses as invalid. Tunisia's law is clear that violation of any of the requisites of marriage (and it specifies precisely which Articles this relates to) renders a marriage void and without any effect if it remains unconsummated. If the marriage has been consummated, the couple are still required to separate without any dissolution proceedings. However, mahr becomes due; the legal paternity of any children is established; and idda must be observed.

Other laws, which do not clearly list the requisites for valid marriage (Bangladesh, Pakistan, Sri Lanka), can lead to litigation. In Pakistan, the consequences of such litigation have become entangled with the Zina Ordinance, 1979 (see p.63, footnote No.2).

However, in terms of practices, marriage is certainly regarded as a public, social event and therefore marriages without witnesses are extremely rare. Marriages without witnesses, in the sense that there has been no ceremony at all, are briefly discussed on p.215.

the status of marriages lacking mahr

Mahr is not a requisite for valid marriage in systems not based on Muslim laws. Therefore, among Muslims marrying under these laws, the presence or absence of a mahr only affects the social but not the legal validity of a marriage (see Mahr, p.179).

Senegal's Code de la Famille attempts to secularize family laws but recognizes some aspects of Muslim laws. Thus, the CF makes non-payment of prompt mahr grounds for nullity only if the couple agrees beforehand that mahr is a condition of valid marriage.

For those systems based on Muslim laws, the principle divide is between those laws based on Maliki jurisprudence and those laws based on other schools. For example, in Algeria and Tunisia where the Maliki School dominates, laws define a marriage without mahr as void if the marriage has not been consummated. If the marriage has been consummated, mahr ul mithl is due. In systems where other schools of law dominate Muslim laws (Bangladesh, Malaysia, India, Philippines, Sri Lanka), the failure to stipulate mahr in the marriage contract never renders the marriage void, and mahr ul mithl is always due (half before consummation and the whole after consummation). Most of these systems do not specify any provisions concerning mahr and the validity of marriage. (The Philippines Code of Muslim Personal Laws is an exception.) The implication is that mahr is an automatic element of a Muslim marriage.

NOTES

LAWS: Marriage Requisites – Witnesses

Criteria

☺ More option-giving are those laws which:
- Specify that witnesses are a requisite for valid marriage; and/or
- Specify that the witnesses must attest to the bride's consent; and
- Permit women and men to act equally as witnesses.

😐 The middle ground is occupied by those laws which:
- Require witnesses but only imply that they must attest to the bride's consent; and/or
- Are silent about women as witnesses.

☹ Less option-giving are those laws which:
- Require witnesses, but these witness only the wali's consent; and/or
- Prohibit women as witnesses or equate two women with one man as witnesses.

☺ Witnesses attest to the bride's consent

Senegal: For a marriage contracted by an Officer of the State, two adult witnesses are required, one for each spouse. Under A. 147(1) for marriages not attended by an Officer of the State, when registering the marriage, two adult witnesses, who attended the marriage and can attest to the offer and acceptance, are required for each spouse. The sex of witnesses is not specified.

Philippines: Under A. 15 of the CMPL, the ijab and qabul and stipulation of mahr must be duly witnessed by at least two competent persons. The gender of witnesses is not specified. A. 30-32 on void and irregular marriages do not specify the status of a marriage without witnesses.

Sudan: Under the MPLA, witnesses must be trustworthy and of good repute. They attend the writing of the marriage contract to certify – by their signatures – the wife's consent to the marriage and the mahr. Witnesses are to meet and talk to the wife before the writing of the contract. The two witnesses may be either two men, or a man and two women. [Note: However, Sudan's MPLA regards 'silence as consent'].

Yemen: Under A.9 of the post-reunification LPS, two male Muslims or one man and two women may act as witnesses.

😐 Witnessing of bride's consent is only implied

Tunisia: Under A. 3 of the CSP, two 'trustworthy' witnesses to the marriage are essential for validity. The requirement of witnesses is mentioned in the same Article as the requirement of the consent of both spouses and mahr. This placement implies that the consent and the agreements concerning mahr are what snould be witnessed. The sex of witnesses is not specified. Under A. 21 & 22, a marriage lacking witnesses is void; no divorce is required to terminate it; and the contract has no effect. If the marriage has been consummated, mahr becomes due to the wife; the paternity of the children is recognized; and idda must be observed upon separation.

Turkey: The Civil Code requires that marriages be conducted before an official and two witnesses. The code implies that these people will witness the consent. The sex of witnesses is not specified. Marriage without witnesses is void.

Cameroon: Under A. 49 of the CSO, the names of witnesses to a marriage are to be recorded on the marriage certificate. The sex of witnesses is not specified. Marriage without witnesses is void.

Bangladesh: The standard marriage contract form requires the signature of two witnesses. It is only implied that by signing the marriage contract they are witnessing its terms and conditions and the fulfillment of requisites, including hearing the bride's consent. The gender of witnesses is not specified.

Indonesia: Under A. 2(1) of the MA, the validity of marriage is determined with reference to Muslim laws. A. 14 of the KHI (requirements of marriage) does not specify the gender of witnesses and their function.

Algeria: Under A. 9 of the CF, marriage must be contracted in the presence of a wali and two witnesses. The requirement of witnesses is mentioned in the same Article as the requirement that both spouses consent and agree to the mahr, implying that the consent of both spouses and the establishing of the mahr are the events to be witnessed. The sex of witnesses is not specified. Under A. 33, marriage without two witnesses is void before consummation, and no mahr is due. After consummation, if only one requisite is lacking, the marriage is confirmed.

Pakistan: The standard marriage contract form requires the signature of two witnesses. It is only implied that by signing the marriage contract, they are witnessing its terms and conditions, as well as attesting to the fulfillment of requisites, including hearing the bride's consent. Pakistan's 1984 Qanun-e-Shahadat (Law of Evidence) states that women cannot witness equally with men the signing of documents relating to future financial obligations. There are no known cases where the validity of a marriage has been disputed because one man and two women witnessed the marriage. The validity of a marriage without witnesses (although the solemnizer did appear in court to attest to the marriage) has been upheld in a zina case (Arif Hussain & Azra Parveen v The State, PLD 1982 FSC 42).

☹ Witnessing of bride's consent is only implied; wali practice recognized

Egypt: Art 5(2) provides that two adults are required to testify that there has been some consent between the husband and the wali. Nothing is said about the consent of the bride.

Malaysia: Under S. 11 of the IFLA, a marriage is void if it does not fulfill "all conditions necessary according to Hukum Syara." S. 11 of the same law does not allow for registration of void marriages. Under S. 21 at least two witnesses must attest to the payment of mahr. Under S.22 the entry in the Marriage Register of the particulars of the marriage (implying consent of the wali) and any conditions is to be attested by two witnesses present at the solemnization of the marriage. The sex of witnesses is specified in the federal territory law. The Kelantan law specifies that witnesses must be male in the Schedule to the law. Most state laws on Muslim evidence specify that witnesses must be male except in specified circumstances that relate to evidence of childbirth and matters within women's 'exclusive' knowledge.

Morocco: Under A. 5(1) of the Moudawana, two witnesses 'of good character' must attend a marriage for it to be valid. They are only required to hear the offer and acceptance by the husband and by the guardian. Under A. 41, witnesses attest to all requisites with the notable exception of the bride's consent. Under A. 41, two men of good character must witness the marriage contract. Under A. 32, provided there has been an offer and acceptance, a marriage lacking witnesses is considered irregular. There is no further provision, except the general statement under A. 82 that where the law is silent, the Maliki School is to be followed.

Sri Lanka: Under S. 19(1)(d) of the MMDA, two witnesses who were present at the nikah ceremony must sign the marriage register. The law does not explicitly require that they witness the bride's consent. The sex of witnesses is not specified. The law is silent on the status of marriages lacking witnesses.

Nigeria: It is assumed that two male witnesses are required.

LAWS: Marriage Requisites – Mahr

Criteria

Given differences regarding the advantages and disadvantages of mahr for women, laws are only listed alphabetically here.

Algeria: Under A. 9 of the CF, fixing the mahr is a requisite of marriage. Under A. 15, it should be stated in the marriage contract, whether the mahr will be prompt or deferred. Under A. 33, a marriage without mahr is void before consummation. However, after consummation mahr ul mithl is due, providing that other requisites have been met.

Bangladesh & Pakistan: No law specifies the requisites of a valid Muslim marriage. The standard marriage contract under the MFLO Rules, 1961, requires that the amount of mahr be recorded, as should be the portions that are prompt and deferred; the amount paid at the time of marriage; and details and value of any property given in lieu of the whole or part of the mahr. If no mahr is fixed, the courts will rule on the amount of mahr ul mithl.

Cameroon: Mahr is not a requisite of marriage under the CSO. Under A. 49 the marriage certificate should mention if any separate marriage contract was made before the marriage.

Gambia (marriages under Muslim laws): For a marriage to be valid under Muslim laws, the mahr must be paid by the husband at the time that the marriage is contracted, or a promise must be made to pay the sum at a future date if the husband is financially constrained at the time of marriage.

Indonesia: A. 14 (requirements of marriage) specifies the husband's duty to provide mahr. Under A. 30, the groom is to pay the bride a mahr in the amount, form, and type agreed upon by both parties.

Iran: Under A. 1087 of the CC, if the mahr is not mentioned in a permanent marriage contract, the marriage is still valid, and the couple may fix a mahr by mutual agreement after the marriage contract.

Malaysia: Specification of mas kahwin is not an explicit requisite of a valid Muslim marriage. S. 21 of the IFLA merely requires the Marriage Registrar to record the value and other particulars of the mahr, including any portion not paid at the time of the marriage, the promised date of payment; and particulars of any security given for the payment of any mas kahwin. As mahr is not stipulated as a condition in the law, any marriage without payment of mahr is not considered void under S. 11 of the law.

Morocco: Under A. 5 of the Moudawana, a marriage contract is not permissible without the specification of mahr. Under A. 20 the portion, if any, of mahr to be deferred must also be specified.

Philippines: Under A. 15 mahr must be stipulated. However, failure to stipulate mahr does not render the marriage void. Under A. 20, the amount of mahr may be fixed by the contracting parties before, during, or after the celebration of the marriage. The court, upon petition of the wife, will determine the amount of the mahr if it has not been fixed.

Senegal: Mahr constitutes an essential condition for the validity of marriages contracted under custom and Muslim laws. Under A. 132 of the CF, the spouses may agree that mahr is a condition of the marriage. If the intending spouses make such an agreement, the marriage may not be solemnized unless the prompt portion is paid. Under A. 138, if the spouses have agreed on mahr as a condition, the wife can seek a decree for relative nullity in the event that the prompt portion is not paid at the time of marriage.

Sri Lanka: The law does not state that mahr is explicitly required for the validity of a marriage. If no mahr is specified or expressly agreed upon at the time of a marriage, the courts have recognized the wife's right to receive mahr ul mithl on divorce or separation.

Sudan: Under S.27 of the MPLA, mahr must be recorded at the time of marriage. Under S.62, mahr is a requisite of valid marriage and a marriage can be declared void if mahr is not appropriate.

Tunisia: Under A. 3 of the CSP, the specification of mahr is a requisite for valid marriage. Under A. 21, a marriage without mahr is void before consummation. Following consummation, the marriage is still irregular and the only consequences will be entitlement to mahr ul mithl, recognition of the paternity of any children, and the requirement of idda upon separation of the spouses.

Turkey: Mahr is not recognized under the CC.

4 CHILD MARRIAGE

introduction

As seen in Marriage Requisites: Capacity, on p.70, systems vary widely in their provisions regarding the minimum age of marriage, which for females ranges from 18 years to as low as 9 lunar years (Iran). While that earlier section discusses minimum age requirements in terms of capacity and choice (that is, at what age, if ever, and under what circumstances a female can make an independent decision to marry), this section discusses minimum age requirements in terms of their impact on children, their rights and well-being. We will discuss whether or not systems recognize that marriages involving a spouse younger than 18 years old ('child marriages') have a generally negative impact on the child's physical and mental development as well as on their ability to exercise their rights. In systems where these negative impacts are recognized, we discuss how child marriages are defined, and whether or not there are regulations in place or evidence of other efforts being made to eliminate child marriages.

In this section, we classify (in agreement with the definition of 'child' in international instruments) all systems that permit marriages involving spouses younger than 18 as systems that permit child marriage. Apart from Bangladesh and the Kyrgyz Republic, where no exceptions are possible to this age limit, and Fiji, the Gambia (marriages not under Muslim laws), and Nigeria (marriages not under Muslim and customary laws) where some exceptions are possible, all other systems discussed in this Handbook permit what we define as child marriages.

Although most codified systems have legislated minimum ages for marriage or other restrictions on child marriage, these laws often set a very low minimum age and/or are full of loopholes. Moreover, in many systems that have provisions aimed at preventing child marriages and punishing those who facilitate them, these provisions are rarely accessed. These weaknesses in the law and its implementation often result in a wide gap between the legal minimum age of marriage and the minimum age practiced by communities.

Moreover, many laws and practices regard 'puberty' as the minimum age for marriage. Defining 'puberty' as the minimum age for marriage is problematic. In medical terms, 'puberty' is a process that can take months or years rather than a single, specific event, and the vagueness of the term 'puberty' introduces an element of subjectivity in deciding whether the appropriate age has been reached. However, most systems and customary practices appear to regard the onset of menstruation as the indication that females have attained puberty. Although we recognize puberty as a process, for the purposes of this section, we generally discuss puberty as it is seen in laws and practices: as an apparently identifiable event.

Convention on the Rights of the Child (1990)

Article 1 - For the purposes of the present convention, a child means every human being below the age of eighteen years unless under the law applicable to the child, majority is attained earlier.

Convention on Consent to Marriage, Minimum Age for Marriage and Registration of Marriage (1964)

Article 2 – State parties to the present convention shall take legislative action to specify a minimum age for marriage. No marriage shall be legally entered into by any person under this age, except where a competent authority has granted a dispensation as to age for serious reasons, in the interests of the intending spouses.

Legislators face many challenges when crafting child marriage laws. The main dilemma facing them is whether they should provide punishment for violation of age limits while simultaneously recognizing the effects of such marriages (e.g., the child bride can still approach the courts to claim maintenance and inheritance); **or** impose an outright ban on marriages involving underage spouses and strengthen this ban by refusing to recognize the effects of such marriages. A similar question exists regarding the recognition of unregistered marriages (see p.140). With both issues, it is women and girls who face the main impact of negative practices.

One of the main obstructions to the enforcement of provisions against child marriage is the lack of proper birth registration, especially in rural areas.

While we acknowledge that child marriage is devastating both for girls and for boys, this section will focus primarily on the impact this practice has on the lives of girls.

child marriage as forced marriage and possible legal relief

Most marriages involving those under 18 have a strong element of compulsion because:

- Children generally lack the capacity to understand the consequences of marriage and to make an informed decision; and
- Children usually have limited options for resisting family and community pressures concerning marriage.

Forced child marriages involve several interrelated issues including: who is permitted, if at all, to arrange for a child (younger than the minimum marriageable age) to be married; whether or not ijbar (compulsion in marriage) is permitted; and whether or not the child has any means of rejecting such a marriage, such as the concept of the 'option of puberty'/khiyar al-bulugh (in systems based on Muslim laws). Although the option of puberty provides child brides with some relief, the fact that many systems based on Muslim laws also permit guardians to arrange for their wards to be married at a very young age, means that generally this is an area where girls in Muslim countries and communities are at a substantial disadvantage compared to girls in systems that do not recognize Muslim laws. For example, Muslim girls may be married as young as 12 in the Philippines, whereas under the Family Code applicable to other communities, the minimum age of marriage is 18 for females and males. For forced adult marriages see p.87; for marriages below the minimum age of marriage and against family consent see p.72.

rights implications

Child marriages are arranged by families and guardians, sometimes sincerely (if mistakenly) in the belief that this is in the child's interests and sometimes as a means of securing family, commercial or other ties. Wherever virginity is highly prized, girls are seen as an economic burden on their natal families, and/or women's social role is viewed solely in terms of their reproductive role, early marriage is commonplace. Clearly, change requires far more than merely reforming legislation. In Nigeria, for example, only after the government campaigned to inform people about the health hazards of early marriage and educational levels rose, did they see a decline in child marriages.

Child spouses are deprived of childhood experiences appropriate for their mental and psychological development and are exposed to adult responsibilities at an early age. They face these loses and challenges as a consequence of marriages that they (in almost every case) have not given their informed consent to. Yet, if upon reaching adulthood, child wives wish to free themselves from their marriages, they often have no viable way of doing so. Even where it would be theoretically possible to seek an annulment or divorce, women often find that social realities make it all but impossible for them to seek such options.

Additionally, being a child wife exacerbates many of the problems experienced by wives of all ages. Child wives remain at the lower end of the family power hierarchy. Under the authority of adults, including their possibly much older husbands, they may be abused and used as domestic labour to service the needs of older wives and relatives in their matrimonial home.

Moreover, gendered power imbalances within marriage are worsened by a child wife's greater inability to negotiate sexual interaction with her husband. Unable to negotiate contraception or ensure sexual satisfaction, she is often denied a safe and satisfying sexual experience. Her physical and sexual immaturity also leaves her at a greater risk of experiencing pregnancy and childbirth related health problems including maternal death, vasico-vaginal fistula (VVF), and anal fistula.

In areas where overall life expectancy is low, child marriages also result in the creation of very young widows. If social attitudes prevent widow remarriage, a widowed young wife may find herself condemned to a long life of celibacy and single parenthood. If she returns to her parents or guardians' home, she may be considered a social and economic burden, and given little or no control over her life and the lives of her children.

minimum age for marriage and gender discrimination

Although provisions concerning the minimum age for marriage have already been discussed in Capacity (p.65), they are discussed here again. Here we look specifically at whether or not solemnizing or consummating a marriage below the minimum age carries any punishments, and under what circumstances, if any, are marriages below the minimum age permitted?

All systems specify minimum ages for a variety of things including voting, working, criminal liability, legal majority and marriage. Because of the varying purposes for which these minimums have been set, there is rarely a single age limit which applies across the board. However, it is certainly less confusing (and therefore less liable to abuse) when one single age limit applies for most issues. It is not enough that the age of majority and age of marriage be the same because both of these can be too young. In Iran, for example, both the age of majority and the minimum age of marriage are set at puberty, which the law states (according to the Shia School) is at the age of 9 lunar years for females. Therefore, if a single age minimum is set for majority and marriage; it is preferable that it be 18 years of age. Similarly, provisions that make marriages involving spouses below a certain age illegal and/or invalid are meaningless if the age minimum is extremely low (Sudan).

In recognition of the problems caused by child marriages, most systems have legislated a minimum age for marriage or placed other restrictions on child marriage. However, where different laws apply to Muslims, girls from Muslim communities may have less protection from child marriage than do girls from other communities (Philippines, Sri Lanka). In other cases, regulations applying to the same communities may be confusing and contradictory. For example, in Nigeria, federal 'civil law' states that 21 years is the minimum age for marriage (or 18 years with parental consent). However, some Nigerian states have legislated minimum ages and these vary from puberty to 12 or 16 years; all of these minimums are lower than the federal minimum. Additional contradictions come about because some states have laws criminalizing statutory rape (the sexual assault of a minor), but these laws do not apply if the assault is committed by the victim's husband.

Some systems do not differentiate between girls and boys when setting minimum ages for marriage (Fiji, Kazakhstan, and marriages not under Muslim and customary laws in the Gambia and Nigeria). However, most systems apply a lower age minimum for girls than for boys. Yet, girls, more so than boys, bear the negative physical impact of child marriages and are more vulnerable to power imbalances in marital relationships.

When systems set lower legal minimum ages for girls than for boys, these minimums appear to be based on the same patriarchal concepts that, at the community level, encourage child marriage for females (see Rights Implications, above).

exceptions to the minimum age

Some systems set a minimum age for marriage, but also permit marriages between spouses under this minimum age in exceptional circumstances, if the court provides permission. These systems also set a lower age minimum, below which no such permission can be given (Central Asian Republics, Philippines). This type of system is more option giving for women than systems that merely make child marriage illegal (but recognize its effects) because this type of system requires the involvement of the state (and one presumes that the state policy is to discourage child marriage).

For example, Senegal's Code de la Famille requires that under-age marriages involve both exceptional circumstances and court permission. Furthermore, such permission may be granted only after the judge has conducted an inquiry into the circumstances of the case. This type of process may help prevent parents from arranging an oral unregistered marriage for their under-age daughter and then presenting the marriage for 'validation' once she is pregnant.

However, when assessing which laws are more or less option-giving, one must pay careful attention to the actual age limits involved. The lowest possible age of marriage, with court permission, in the Central Asian Republics is 16 years for females. In the Philippines, this age may be as low as 12 years, and in Iran it is even lower. Finally, regardless of whether or not 'exceptional circumstances' are defined in the law, there needs to be a clear state policy that such provisions are not to be used as loopholes through which parties can continue to practice child marriage.

minimum age for consummation

If a system has legislated against statutory rape (see glossary), defined a minimum age for consummating a marriage, and/or defined an age of consent in sexual relations; these provisions may offer clues as to the state's willingness to protect young girls from child marriage. For example, in Sudan the law sets puberty as the minimum age for both contracting and consummating a marriage. In contrast, laws in Sri Lanka allow a Quazi to grant permission for a girl below the age of 12 to be married, but local laws also make it clear that consummating a marriage with a wife who is younger than 12 is considered statutory rape. In Pakistan, since the 1979 Zina Ordinance repealed previous laws regarding statutory rape, the law sets no legal minimum age for consummating a marriage.

Often where there is no legal minimum age for consummating a marriage, the minimum age is determined by customary practice. Most customs allow consummation to take place when a wife is far too young to be physically and mentally ready for either the consummation itself or for such possible consequences as childbearing.

regulating child marriage: validity and penalties

In some systems, all marriages involving a spouse below the legal minimum age (in the absence of court permission under exceptional circumstances, where this is possible) are considered invalid and with no legal effect (Cameroon, Central Asian Republics, Fiji, Yemen). Where the marriage is not recognised by the legal system, married children (and their children) can find themselves without any legal protection of their rights arising from marriage. Further, very stringent laws, not backed by other forms of social reform, may serve to send child marriage practices underground. An alternative to stringent laws that may work well under the socio-economic conditions that prevail in many of the countries covered in this Handbook, is to consider a child marriage invalid and liable to be declared void while also recognizing some of the rights from the marriage, e.g., maintenance for the spouse, paternity of the children, and inheritance. Such a system is applied in Senegal, where there are also very strict penalties for consummating a marriage with a child less than 13 years of age.

In some systems, contracting a child marriage is against the law, and those who solemnize it, as well as any adult spouse, are liable to penalties; but the marriage itself is still recognized as legally valid. This type of system offers a weaker protection than does the alternative above and this protection is weakened further where the fines or prison sentences provided are minimal (Bangladesh, India, Pakistan).

who can have a child married?

Although more commonly permitted in systems based on Muslim and customary laws, some systems based on other laws also permit guardians to consent to the marriage of their female wards who are below the minimum age of marriage. The guardians who are awarded such privileges by the law are, in most cases, male. (In Tunisia, even when a mother has the right of guardianship of her child after the death of the father, only the father's brother may consent to the child's marriage.) Since, as argued above, child marriages are unlikely to be made with the child's informed consent, such provisions, in effect, permit parents/

guardians to arrange marriages for their daughters when they are still younger than the legal minimum age for marriage (Cameroon, Egypt, Iran, Philippines, Sudan, Turkey).

Systems differ principally in whether they require the court's permission (Cameroon, Philippines, Sudan, Tunisia, Turkey) or simply a guardian's permission (Egypt, Iran) for a person to be married below the legal minimum age. While most systems that require a court's permission also require parental permission, only the court's permission is required in Malaysia and Senegal. Even where the court's permission is required for an under-age marriage, this requirement may not offer much protection if the legal minimum age is already extremely low, as in Sudan.

Some systems also require the child's consent (Tunisia, Turkey). Though such a requirement may be intended to protect a child's rights, it may do little to prevent forced child marriage because It is unlikely that a child would be capable of giving informed consent to a marriage.

dissolution of child marriages & the option of puberty (khiyar al-bulugh)

Women who have been the victim of a forced child marriage (where such a marriage is valid) may have the possibility of rejecting the marriage when they reach adulthood. In some systems, such a possibility is achieved through annulment procedures (Senegal), and in others, it is covered by legislation on dissolution (Bangladesh, India marriages under Muslim laws, Pakistan).

In systems based on Muslim laws, such an opportunity to retroactively reject a child marriage is commonly known as the option of puberty, or khiyar al-bulugh. However, systems differ over whether or not such an option is available to women who were married under their father's or grandfather's authority. In Bangladesh, India, and Pakistan, this option is available regardless of who arranged the marriage. In Iran and the Philippines, it is denied to women whose child marriages were arranged by their male guardian.

Where the father or guardian has the right of ijbar, the option of puberty may not be available at all. The concept of ijbar, in some schools of Muslim laws, permits a father or other male guardian to compel a child or adult women under their guardianship into marriage. The only condition that limits the guardian in his exercise of ijbar is that the marriage must be in the best interests of the bride (for ijbar in the case of adult women, see p.84). In some systems only a biological father may compel his minor or adult daughter into marriage. In Iran, if the guardian can prove that the marriage is in the best interests of the child, the marriage cannot be challenged.

Although the option of subsequently rejecting a child marriage offers women some relief, this relief is limited both because it is available only after the fact of marriage and because it requires a court procedure.

In addition, in systems that offer an option of puberty, there is usually a time limit during which a wife can apply. After that time, it is presumed that the wife has consented to the marriage. In some instances, the option of puberty may be exercised only after the wife has reached puberty and before she has reached the age of majority (18, in the case of Pakistan). In other instances, such options must be accessed within 4 years after the wife reaches puberty (Philippines). In Bangladesh, where there is a higher minimum legal age of marriage (18 for females), the law allows wives to access the option of puberty before they reach 19 years of age. Other systems require that this option be exercised immediately upon puberty (Senegal). Whatever the time limits, if a girl does not act within them, she will be left to seek dissolution on other grounds.

The option of puberty may be further restricted by a condition that the marriage cannot have been consummated. However, the courts may consider any consummation occurring before the wife has reached the minimum age of marriage as forced consummation and disregard it accordingly (Pakistan). Courts may alternatively insist that the marriage must not have been consummated after the age at which the option of puberty can be exercised (Bangladesh).

Identity Politics and their Impact on Family Law Reform

Although the issue of child marriage has been long debated among Muslims in Sri Lanka (as among other communities), they still have not set a minimum marriageable age. There has been little progress in reforming any statutory provisions for Muslims, largely because of the rise of identity politics.

In September 1995, the minimum age of marriage for persons in other communities in Sri Lanka (i.e., those falling under the General Law and Kandyan Law) was raised to 18 years for both males and females. No corresponding change was made in laws governing Muslims. The Minister for Justice justified this exclusion in the name of protecting the cultural traditions and aspirations of the Muslim community. In parliamentary debates he stated:

> "We recognize that the Muslim community is entitled to be governed by their own laws, usages and customs and it would not be productive to aim at a level of uniformity which does not recognize adequately the different cultural traditions and aspirations of the Muslim community. It is through respect for a diversity of cultures for a whole plethora of cultural traditions which enrich our land that the government is making that exception.
>
> "...This is not a sign of weakness or prevarication. It embodies the essence of democratic traditions. These are very difficult questions, especially in a country like Sri Lanka where different segments of the population are governed by different laws. I think it is not something that detracts from the value of our legal system but rather something that enhances and augments the value of our legal system to recognize the different cultural values and to seek to incorporate them all in a comprehensive body of jurisprudence that we give effect to in our country."

Hansard, Vol.101, No. 2, 20th Sept, p.209-210.

Thus a very specific understanding of 'customs,' 'culture,' and 'tradition' was used by political forces to deny the extension of rights to women in the Muslim community.

NOTES

LAWS: Child Marriage

Criteria

It is extremely difficult to compare provisions concerning child marriage because of the complex range of issues that need to be taken into account when assessing which are more or less option-giving. These issues include:

- Whether or not there is a minimum age for marriage, and if so, what it is;
- Whether or not marriages involving spouses below this age are legal, and if so, with whose consent and under what conditions;
- Whether or not there is another minimum age below which permission for exceptions is not possible;
- Whether or not child marriage is illegal and subject to penalties, and if so, who is penalized;
- Whether a child marriage is illegal but nevertheless valid; or
- Illegal and invalid with its effects still recognized; or
- Illegal and invalid with its effects not recognized;
- Whether or not there are any additional provisions (possibly in penal codes) regarding the consummation of marriage, the age of consent for sexual relations, and/or the definition of and penalties for statutory rape;
- Whether or not ijbar (compulsion in marriage) is permissible, and if so, who is recognized as having this power; and finally,
- Whether or not there are any provisions for child wives to reject their marriages, and if so, under what circumstances.

For example, it may be difficult to clearly state which of the following two possibilities is more option-giving for girls: a law that does not recognize the effects of a marriage contracted without court permission where the bride was less than 16, but that does allow child marriage with court permission and the consummation of such a marriage provided the bride is 13 (Senegal); **or** a law which sets 18 as the minimum age for marriage, and punishes solemnizers and adult spouses, but regards the marriage as valid (Bangladesh).

An additional problem for the Handbook is that we do not always have information regarding related provisions, such as those that criminalize the consummation of a marriage with a wife who is under-age or those that specify if husbands are liable for statutory rape.

Finally, the socio-economic and developmental context is vital to determining which laws are more option-giving. For example, in some Central Asian Republics, Fiji and Indonesia, 16-17 years is set as the lowest possible age for marriage. Marriages involving spouses below these ages are invalid and without effect. Such laws may be option-giving where birth registration is accurate, female education levels are high and other factors discourage early marriage. However, they would certainly undermine the rights of women and girls in contexts where commonly girls marry at a very young age.

LAWS: Child Marriage

Criteria

Taking into account the conditions prevailing in most of our communities, ideal laws should:

- Discourage child marriage by rendering it illegal for children (below the age of 18 for females and males) to be married;
- Allow exceptions only with court permission, this being granted only after an inquiry; and also, set a minimum age below which even court permission cannot be granted;
- Impose very strict penalties on guardians, solemnizers and adult spouses who violate these age limits; and also
- Recognize the effects of child marriages once they have occurred, so as to guarantee the rights and legal claims of the child spouse.

No such law exists; therefore, in this section there will be no 'more option-giving' ranking. Within the middle-ground category we have attempted to indicate which provisions may offer women and girls more options, but these indications are only a provisional assessment, based on the limited information that we have at this time.

Marriages involving spouses younger than 15 are not recognized

Uzbekistan & Kyrgyz Republic: The minimum age of marriage is 18 for females, but the court may authorize marriages at 17 for exceptional reasons, with parental permission.

Gambia & Nigeria (marriages under the CiMA (S. 7b) and MCA): The minimum age of marriage is 21 for females and males, but marriage is possible at 18 with parental permission. The MCA is silent about a minimum age, but this can be presumed from the CiMA, which sets 18 as the age of consent. A marriage is void where the parties are not of marriageable age.

Fiji: The minimum age of marriage is 21 for females and males, but marriage is possible at 16 with parental permission.

Indonesia: Under the LM, the minimum age for marriage is 16 for females, and spouses under 21 require parental permission.

Turkey: Under the amended CC, marriageable age has been raised from 15 to 18 for females. Under exceptional circumstances, the minimum marriageable age can be lowered to 16 with court permission. Under A.151 of the CC, minors as well as adults may apply the court to have their marriage annulled on the grounds of coercion.

Yemen: On national unification the minimum age for marriage was reduced from 16 to 15 for females. Under A. 15 of the 1992 LPS, marriages between spouses who are under 15 are not valid.

Courts may grant permission for marriages involving spouses younger than 15 but not younger than 12

Senegal: Under A. 111 of the CF, the minimum age for marriage is 16 for females. A judge may grant permission for girls younger than 16 to marry for exceptional reasons (e.g. pregnancy) after the judge has made an inquiry. Marriages that do not have judicial authorization and are not registered are not valid. A. 111 was modified on 5 August 1999 by the National Assembly to recognise the practice of child marriage among certain communities, Peuhl, al Pulaar, Layene, etc. The minimum age for consummating a marriage is 13. Under A. 300 of the CP, the penalty for consummating a marriage with a spouse younger than 13 years of age is imprisonment for 2-5 years; if the act of consummating the marriage results in grave injuries, even temporary infirmity, or if the sexual relations led to the death of the child or if the act was accompanied by violence, the punishment shall be imprisonment of 5-10 years.

Bangladesh: Under the CMRA (as amended in 1984), the minimum age for marriage is 18 for females. Anyone solemnizing and contracting a child marriage, as well as any adult spouse, is liable to punishment (light imprisonment and/or a fine). However, marriages involving girls younger than 18 are valid and their effects recognized. Under S. 375 of the PC, sexual intercourse by a man with his own wife is considered rape if she is under 13 years of age. Under S. 376 sex with a wife under 12 years of age is liable to imprisonment for life, and shall also be liable to fine; if the woman raped is his own wife and is not under 12, he shall be punished with imprisonment of up to two years, or with a fine, or with both.

Cameroon: The minimum age for marriage is 15 for females. Marriages that involve girls younger than 15 are considered void. Marriages in which one or both spouses are younger than the marriageable age are possible only for serious reasons and with the authorization of the Head of State/ President. Under the Penal Code A. 356(4), arranging, solemnizing, or being an adult spouse in a marriage involving a girl less than 14 years old is punishable by imprisonment of at least 2 years, notwithstanding any mitigating circumstances.

Philippines: Under the CMPL, the minimum age for marriage is puberty for females and a female is presumed to have reached puberty at 15. The Shari' a District Court may, upon petition of a proper wali, order the solemnization of a marriage in which the bride has reached puberty but is younger than 15, but not younger than 12. The wali's consent is sufficient for the validity of the marriage.

Courts may grant permission for marriages involving spouses younger than marriageable age, but family laws are either silent regarding an absolute minimum age or specify a low absolute minimum age

Algeria: Under A. 7 of the CF, the minimum age for marriage is 18 for females. A judge may grant an exception on the grounds of benefit or necessity, provided that the spouses possess discernment.

Tunisia: The minimum age for marriage is 17 for females. Marriages involving girls younger than 17 require court permission.

Malaysia: Under S. 8 of the IFLA, the minimum age for marriage is 16 for females, and marriages involving girls younger than 16 require the permission of the Syar'iah court.

Egypt: Under A. 9 of the LMA, the minimum age of marriage is 18 years for men and 16 years for women. Parties who are below this age may marry with a wali's permission.

Sri Lanka: Under the MMDA there is no minimum age for marriage. Under S.23 the marriage of a girl younger than 12 requires the permission of a Quazi for the purposes of registration. Under S. 82, it is a punishable offence for a Registrar/abettors to register the marriage of a girl younger than 12 if they know that permission from a Quazi has not been obtained as required by S.23. Under S. 363 of the Penal Code 1883 as amended in 1995, sexual intercourse between a man and his wife, who is younger than 12, constitutes statutory rape. An unregistered marriage is nevertheless considered valid.

Sudan: Under the MPLA, the minimum age of marriage is 10 years. Marriages involving spouses younger than 10 require the approval of a judge. When girls younger than 10 are married without a judge's approval, the marriage is still valid. Under S. 34 of the MPLA, marital relations between spouses should not take place before the wife reaches puberty.

Morocco: Under A. 8 of the Moudawana, marriageable age is 15 for females. Under A. 9, marriage may be contracted by the guardian provided the female has reached the age of discernment.

A Minimum age of marriage exists, but regulation is weak

Pakistan: Under the CMRA (as amended by the MFLO, 1961), the minimum age for marriage is 16 for females. Anyone solemnizing and contracting a child marriage, as well as any adult spouse, is liable to punishment (light imprisonment and/or a fine). However, marriages involving girls younger than 16 are valid and their effects recognized. Prior to the 1979 Zina Ordinance, consummating a marriage with a wife younger than 13 (17 in NWFP) was not legal. Since 1979, there are no legal restrictions on consummating a marriage with a wife of any age.

Nigeria: In Kano and Sokoto States (with Muslim majority populations) the minimum age of marriage is puberty. The Native Authority (Declaration of Idoma native marriage law and custom) Order S. 49(3) of 1959 (a colonial law in a Christian majority state) sets the minimum marriageable age at 12 years. The 1956 Bill of the former Eastern region (colonial era, dominantly Christian populations) set 16 years as the minimum marriageable age. The law is silent concerning the effects of marriages involving spouses younger than the minimum ages.

☹ No minimum age of marriage; no restrictions on marriage consummation

Gambia (marriages under Muslim and customary laws), Malaysia Perak State, some States of Nigeria: There is no minimum age of marriage. (We are unsure if there are provisions restricting the consummation of marriage.) In Nigeria, where there is no codified minimum age of marriage, this age is generally presumed to be puberty. In the Gambia, the 1997 Constitution (Section 7 paragraph (e)) recognises the application of customary law without any modification, hence permitting customary child marriages.

Iran: Under A. 1041 of the CC, marrying before reaching the age of puberty is prohibited. Under A. 1210, the age of puberty is 15 full lunar years for males and 9 full lunar years for females. However, a marriage contracted before reaching puberty is valid if authorized by the natural guardian provided it is in the ward's interests. This overturned the earlier Family Protection Law, which, in A. 23, required that the court and a doctor had to agree that an under-age woman was physically and psychologically ready to marry before she could be permitted to do so.

LAWS: Option of Puberty

Criteria

☺ More option-giving are those laws which:

- Permit the option of puberty no matter who gives the minor female in marriage.

☹ Less option-giving are those laws which:

- Do not permit the option of puberty if the minor female was given in marriage by her father or paternal grandfather; or
- Recognize ijbar and require the woman to prove the marriage was not in her interests.

☺ **The option of puberty can be accessed even if the minor female's father or paternal grandfather gives her in marriage**

Bangladesh: A woman may approach the court to exercise the option of puberty within 1 year of attaining majority (18 years). Under S. 2(vii) of the DMMA, the option is available even if she was married by her father or other guardian, provided the marriage has not been consummated. However, the courts do not regard the consummation of a marriage as a voluntary confirmation of that marriage unless both spouses are at least 18 at the time that it takes place.

Pakistan: Under S. 2(vii) of the DMMA (as amended by the MFLO in 1961), any female married, when she is younger than 16, by her father or other guardian may exercise the option of puberty before she reaches 18 years of age, provided that the marriage has not been consummated. The courts regard any consummation taking place before the wife is 16 years as forced consummation.

Senegal: A minor has the option to reject her child marriage on reaching 18 years of age. This right is lost if it is not exercised immediately upon reaching majority. Under A. 142 of the CF, nullity cannot be invoked for minor spouses, until after they have reached the required age.

Nigeria: Although under uncodified Maliki laws, the father/grandfather's right of ijbar is acknowledged, in practice the courts do not accept ijbar. Instead, they permit females who have reached the age of maturity (generally regarded as puberty) to seek an end to a child marriage.

Sri Lanka: A female given in marriage before puberty can exercise the option of puberty, and can apply to the Quazi court to have the marriage repudiated. The law is silent about whether this right is available if the marriage was contracted by the father or grandfather but in case law the courts have nevertheless proceeded on the basis that a Muslim female may exercise the option of puberty if she was married as a minor.

☹ **Option of puberty available, but not if minor female's marriage was arranged by her father or paternal grandfather**

Philippines: Under A.16 (3) of the CMPL, marriages contracted through a wali that involve spouses younger than the prescribed age (puberty) are regarded as betrothal and may be annulled upon the petition of either party within four years after they have reached the age of puberty, provided no voluntary cohabitation takes place and the wali who contracted the marriage was not the father or paternal grandfather.

Iran: If a woman announces upon reaching puberty that she did not consent to a marriage contracted while pre-pubescent, the marriage remains valid provided the guardian is able to show that the marriage was contracted in her best interest.

Malaysia: In Kelantan and Kedah States, if a girl is an unmarried virgin (anak dara), the father or paternal grandfather (wali mujbir) can marry her to anyone of his choice without her consent.

Morocco: Under A. 12(4) of the Moudawana, the concept of ijbar is recognized and a married female has to prove that her forced child marriage was not in her interests in order to access relief.

PRACTICES

Trends away from child marriages

Overall, the general trend across Muslim countries and communities, as elsewhere, appears to be towards an older age of marriage for females, although in many communities this may still be well below 18. The growing need and opportunities for women to be formally employed or economically active in the informal sector is leading to delayed marriage (especially where women are not expected to continue to earn an income after marriage). Growing dowry practice may also delay marriage until the girl's family can afford her marriage. Rising female education and awareness raising efforts by women's groups are also factors.

Pakistan: According to the official Pakistan Demographic Survey, 86% of 15-19 year old females have never been married, compared with only 25% in the 1961 population census.

Senegal: Many men oppose the trend towards an increase in the age of marriage; they claim that this change is the result of negative 'western' or 'modern' influences. However, there is a growing recognition that forced marriages create future problems for families. In addition, changing employment patterns are also influencing marriage age. As more men are losing their employment and more women are gaining employment, families are motivated to keep daughters working.

Rising incidence of child marriage

Contradictions to the international trend away from child marriage can be seen wherever there is a growing influence of extremist politico-religious groups who promote a fear of female sexual transgression. Such trends are usually combined with growing poverty and a lack of alternatives (e.g., education, employment) for females. Examples include the Muslim community in Sri Lanka who have been displaced by the conflict over Tamil independence, as well as communities in Uzbekistan and Tajikistan. Among migrant Moroccan communities in Europe, fathers are being heavily pressured by mosques (often funded by the Moroccan government) to return their 14-15 year old daughters to Morocco to get married 'before they transgress.'

Continued negative practices concerning child marriage

Bangladesh: Child marriages still continue in rural areas. In extreme cases, child marriages have lead to the wife's murder for her 'failure to perform wifely duties,' i.e. she is killed because she cannot cope with having sexual relations. Problems also arise as a lack of proper documentation for birth registration can lead to falsification of the girl 's age in marriage documents. A WHO report on Bangladesh shows that in certain areas, 60% of female juveniles were married when they were under age because of rising poverty and fears concerning sexual transgression. Given the social reality of Bangladesh, including illiteracy and women's lack of agency over their sexuality, access to the option of puberty is very narrow, and though legally available, it is rarely exercised.

Egypt: It is common for girls aged 13 to be married, but the marriage is only registered when they reach 16. This practice results in problems for wives when trying to prove the legitimacy of their children and when trying to secure their inheritance if the husband dies before the marriage is registered.

Gambia, Turkmenistan, Pakistan: It is not uncommon for girls to be betrothed (breaking such an engagement is socially very difficult) at birth, and orally married very young. Families make such engagements to guarantee a particular match and to avoid practices that require excessive exchanges on marriage (dowry, mahr and other payments, see p.179 & p.189).

Gambia: Most girls are given away well before they reach the age of consent (18). Those responsible for legislating and enforcing any provisions regarding child marriage are often guilty of such practices and may be reluctant to set a positive precedent for women. Being a wife is regarded as the only socially desirable state for women. As a result, parents arrange early and forced marriages to prevent their daughter from remaining 'on the shelf'. According to the 1993 Gambian census, nearly one-third of girls age 13-19 had been married but only 1.6% of boys in the same age group had been married (rural areas: 35.3% girls/1.8% of boys; urban areas: 21% girls/ 1.1% boys) (UNDP, 1997: 46).

Nigeria: Throughout the country, child marriage is commonly practiced in many communities that are heavily influenced by conservative Muslim laws and/or customary laws. However, the highest rate of child marriage occurs in parts of the north, which is largely Muslim. There are no restrictions, in customary or Muslim practice, on the age when sexual relations may commence once a marriage is solemnized. Government and activist campaigns to educate people about the health hazards associated with child marriages (or rather early childbirth) have had some success, and there has been a decline in marriages involving girls who have either not reached puberty or have just reached puberty. Still, the figures are quite high.

Pakistan: There is a general trend away from early marriage in rural areas, with some exceptions. For example, among the urban and feudal middle class, the influence of Islamization in recent years has resulted in more marriage and engagement during college years (late teens and early twenties) whereas previously a girl was generally expected to complete her studies before marrying. Since cousin and exchange marriages are common, child marriages may be formed to avoid losing a suitable match when it is available. Families fear that they may not find such a match later. The consummation of such marriages is usually delayed until after the onset of menstruation, even if the couple live in the same compound. Sometimes the husband may rape his wife before sexual contact has been socially sanctioned. The community does not usually consider this a problem. Also, girls may be given away in 'marriage' as part of a settlement of a feud.

Child marriages are oral and not registered, and therefore, difficult to prove. This lack of proof obstructs a girl's ability to access the option of puberty, especially if the girl wishes to annul the marriage against her parents' wishes. The option of puberty is accessed generally only when the two families quarrel, or the natal family is interested in another match. The practice of pledging a child in marriage at her birth is on the decline.

Philippines: In rural Muslim towns and villages, both boys and girls usually become engaged at puberty with the approval of their parents. In contrast, in Marawi and in Davao City, families prefer to engage and marry their children much later, usually when they are in their 20s.

Sri Lanka: There is a steady trend towards marriages being contracted after both spouses have reached 18. However, research among Muslim communities displaced due to ethnic conflict has shown an increase in child marriage, mostly due to economic reasons.

Sudan: The MPLA's failure to restrict child marriage is seen as accelerating the phenomenon, especially in rural areas. Girls are married well before they reach 18, usually without their consent. The elder members of the families assign cousins or relatives to each other. In some cases actual marital life may not be initiated until the girl reaches puberty. However, the spouses need not have reached puberty for the marriage to be valid.

Turkey: A study in Ankara showed that although the average age of marriage for women is 22, many women were also married as young as 14, and 41% were married through arranged marriages.

Uzbekistan: Rural girls marry early, especially in the Ferghana Valley region, where they sometimes marry as early as 14 or 15.

Adda Bano Refuses to Accept Her Fate

Fourteen years old and brilliant, Adda Bano, one of 33 children in her family, was informed that as a result of her excellent performance in school, she was being transferred to the best Federal Government College in Nigeria (Queen's College Lagos). With excitement, she boarded the flight to Lagos on Friday afternoon. Meanwhile, unbeknownst to her, her maternal brother was sent off on an errand ...

At the same time that her flight was taking off, Adda Bano's wedding fatiha was being said elsewhere, and while she was still in the air, she became a wife... When she arrived in Lagos and began behaving in her normal exuberant way, her mother admonished her and then added that since she was now a wife, she should behave like one. Adda Bano had been married off to a cousin who was 56 years old! Boldly, she told her mother that this could not be, for she had been told nothing of a marriage.

Later when she was asked to dress up for her nuptial night, she did so, not knowing what that meant. Then she was told to go into the man's room... There she waited and when the groom came in, she knew by instinct that something was terribly wrong, and she ran from the room. Outside, she was greeted by angry attempts to get her to go back into the room so that her marriage could be consummated. During the struggle she was severely beaten. Still she did not cower and allow herself to succumb. She threatened to commit suicide and was left alone for the rest of the evening.

escape

The next morning, she waited for her mother to become distracted, and then she left the house with her stepsister, who was also eager to escape the same fate. She had been brought to Lagos for the groom's friend.

The two sisters went to a house in the neighbourhood, and Adda Bano tried to sell her jewellery to the woman who lived there. Suspecting Adda's reasons for wanting to sell, the woman was at first unwilling to purchase anything, and she told the girls that she had no money. So the girls asked her to pay whatever she could, and she did. Then they found their way to the airport but were disappointed to discover that they didn't have enough money to fly back home. Some young boys at the airport suggested that they try the motor park. From there they made their way home, with Adda Bano having to pawn her shoes to make the last leg of the journey!

When they finally arrived home, they found that a search was on. Adda Bano overheard that she was to be returned to the man. She made two further attempts to leave her parents home. On each occasion her siblings and other relatives gave her shelter. Each time, the man she had been married to brought charges of kidnapping against her hosts, and they were arrested. Finally, her brother reported her situation to Social Welfare and a friend brought the case to the Centre for Women and Adolescent Empowerment.

The Centre immediately went in search of Adda Bano and found her already in the house of the Juvenile Judge. The social welfare agent had taken her there because the law provided that no one could remove her from there. The judge was cooperative and agreed to assist the staff of the Centre by going to see the Youth Officer in the Ministry for Social Development and getting the charges ready to present in court as soon as it opened the next day. In addition, he agreed to hold discussions with the Social Welfare Department and the Chief Magistrate to develop a legal strategy for Bano.

The case for adda bano's human rights

The following morning in the Upper Area Court, two cases were filed on Adda Bano's behalf. The first was a plea for annulment, and this was based on the belief that there can be no Muslim marriage without the consent of the bride. And, the second case was filed alleging that Adda Bano's human rights had been violated.

Her father was subpoenaed to come to court, but he refused to appear. In such cases it is customary to invite the accused and if he doesn't appear to defend himself, to pronounce judgment without the accused. At midday on that same day, the courts signed the annulment.

Though she was free, Adda Bano still had many obstacles to overcome. She went back home as any little girl would. The Centre assured her that they would support her. When she got home, her father told her that since she wanted to go to school so badly, she should go ahead; but, he would not pay her fees or buy her books or uniform. She shared her situation with the Centre and was given the necessary assistance to facilitate her schooling. For a while she seemed settled. But within days, her father called her just as she was about to go to school and told her that he wanted to talk to her. To her surprise, she was beaten and bundled into a vehicle and once again taken to the "groom's" house. When they got there she was left with an elderly Aunt. She promptly left; probably with the Aunt's tacit approval; and went to the Centre to seek shelter. She thus became a ward of the Centre.

Her school was changed after discussions with her principal. Even though the principal had supported Adda all along. She still felt that Adda should be moved to boarding school because a day school couldn't offer a girl protection from being kidnapped after school or on her way home. It was agreed that an attempt should be made to take her to a boarding school, which was just outside the town. The school has strict rules and procedures and it would be very difficult to take an unwilling girl out of the school. Above all, the principal was generally respected and accepted as being strict about the movements of her students. This principal accepted Adda Bano and assured the Centre that she would take responsibility for looking after her.

Eventually, Adda Bano's father gave up and said that he trusted the Coordinator of the Centre with his child. Meanwhile, the 'groom' decided to marry another wife. His new wife was 18 years old and he took pleasure in announcing this fact in the local newspaper. Such an announcement is quite unusual in the community, so it was taken to be his way of saying, "I have given up, and anyway I now have 4 wives!"

Annulling a Forced Child Marriage

A young woman in Edinburgh, Scotland won a court battle to have her forced marriage annulled. The judge said Aneeka Sohrab had been "deceived and then frightened into a marriage," at the age of 16. Miss Sohrab, 19, from the Pollokshields area of Glasgow, was married in a mosque in the city in 1998. She told the court that she was informed of the wedding the week before it was to take place and refused to go through with it. She was told she would bring disgrace to her family and would have to be sent to Pakistan. Her mother also threatened to commit suicide. The groom, Raja Khan, had arrived in Britain three months before the wedding. The court heard that Miss Sohrab's parents met those of Mr Khan, from Bury in Lancashire, weeks before the marriage and agreed a wedding should take place. The marriage broke down, and Miss Sohrab left her husband within months. The judge said that though the parents had thought they were doing the best for their children, he was very sorry for both the bride and groom and feared their lives had been blighted. He hoped their youth would allow them to recover. Bashir Maan, the Scottish representative on the Muslim Council of Great Britain, said: "If it hasn't been working and one of the parties isn't happy, there's no harm in annulling the marriage. ... The Shariah does not force the parties to live together."

Reported on the BBC website http://news.bbc.co.uk/1/hi/uk/scotland/1946135.stm - Tuesday, 23 April, 2002,

5a MARRIAGE CONTRACTS: REGISTRATION AND VALIDITY

introduction

This section deals with marriage registration requirements. Registration requirements may apply to both written and oral marriages.

One must be careful to note the distinction between fulfilling registration requirements and fulfilling the requisites of a valid marriage (see p.59). Couples will need to fulfill the requisites of a valid marriage before they can complete the compulsory clauses included in a marriage contract and/or registration form (see p.147). However, the process of fulfilling those requisites is separate from the process of actually registering the marriage with the state or some other authority. While failure to fulfill the requisites or conditions of a valid marriage affects the validity of that marriage, failure to fulfill the registration requirements may or may not affect the validity of a marriage.

Valid marriage contracts or documents ensure that the terms and conditions of a marriage are publicly known. Overall, the greater the level of documentation of a marriage, the lesser the chances of a dispute over its terms and conditions, and the easier it should be for a woman to access both her inherent rights and her negotiated rights from the marriage (see p.153 & p.167).

Systems range widely in the rigorousness of their registration requirements. Some systems require that couples follow a two-step permission and registration procedure (Malaysia). Others recognize oral, unregistered marriages as valid (Nigeria, marriages under Muslim and customary laws). Countries also differ as to the validity of marriages that have failed to follow the required registration procedures. While some systems declare the marriages unrecognized and invalid (South, Africa, Fiji), others require registration but do not allow a faulty registration to affect the validity or non-validity of the marriage (Malaysia).

Often when the law defines a marriage as invalid because it has not been properly registered, customs will recognize that same marriage as valid. Such contradictions rarely work to women's advantage.

For women who are individually empowered, or for women in communities where women's inherent and negotiated rights in marriage are protected somewhat equitably, the flexibility offered by oral contracts can be beneficial.

However, the vast majority of women live in situations where women's marital rights are not as well protected as men's. As the more vulnerable party in a marriage, a woman benefits from documentation of the marriage because it increases her chances of being able to access her inherent and negotiated rights. As social change penetrates even isolated villages and breaks down earlier mechanisms of social control, women who lack marriage documents become even more vulnerable because oral contracts may become unenforceable. Thus formal laws, despite all their weaknesses, generally prove more option-giving than do practices.

Communities often also take a hypocritical attitude towards marriage registration. On the one hand, communities may resist registering marriages because a demand for registration by one party may be viewed as an insulting indication that they do not 'trust' the other party. On the other hand, communities may choose to register marriages when they receive some official benefit as a result (state pensions, passports, visas, etc.). Often community representatives will use traditions selectively to justify their avoidance of administrative measures that protect women's rights.

In systems where there are severe penalties for being convicted of engaging in extra-marital sex (Iran, Pakistan), couples need proper marriage documentation to protect them from prosecution. This protection is especially important when families (and others) are allowed to file zina charges against couples that have married against their families' wishes.

In some cases, registration can impose controls on society that have negative consequences for women. For example, in Indonesia marriages between Muslims and non-Muslims are customarily quite common but face problems in registration. The state is attempting to reinforce identity boundaries by raising these obstacles.

The relationship between registration and validity is not always established exclusively by family laws. Relevant provisions may be found in general civil laws; or in rules, directives, and forms as well. Therefore, one must consult a wide range of materials to understand the relationship between marriage validity and marriage registration in any particular community. For example, the law may be silent about the status of unregistered marriages, while also stipulating that only spouses in registered marriages can claim state social security benefits.

registration and validity of marriage

In countries where the laws are based entirely on sources other than Muslim laws (Cameroon, Central Asian Republics, Fiji, South Africa, Turkey), those laws tend to recognize only marriages that have been both conducted through a civil procedure and registered with the state. The legislation of such provisions may have been motivated by one or more of the following: the colonial need to regulate the population, the state's desire to protect women's rights in marriage, and/or the state's desire to reduce the social power of imams.

The consequences that couples face for contracting an unrecognized marriage vary according to the level of state control in a given context. In a highly centralized state, every aspect of the couple's daily life could be challenged. On the other hand, in a community that has little interaction with the state and formal law, the couple may note little, if any, impact.

Couples continue to contract 'religious' marriages (e.g., nikah ceremony at the mosque), even if these marriages are not recognized by the state if their communities view these marriages as socially valid. In many communities, couples may get 'married' twice – once through a religious ceremony and once through a state-recognized ceremony.

Sometimes communities use 'religious' marriage procedures (outside the civil process) as a means of contracting illegal child or polygynous marriages. If the law declares such an unregistered religious marriages to be invalid, the wife has no means of accessing her inherent and/or negotiated rights through the courts. Instead, she must rely on her community to resolve any disputes.

On the other hand, there are many systems where validity is determined by the fulfillment of the requisites and conditions of marriage. Thus, validity is not dependent upon registration, although an unregistered marriage may be questioned if there are other doubts about its validity. Registration may be seen in such systems as merely an administrative measure. Nevertheless, the registration procedures ought to require that the registrar verify the fulfillment of the requisites for validity.

Overall, systems that recognize unregistered marriages as valid (even though they may have penalties for failing to register) undermine the protective element of registration (Egypt, Malaysia, Pakistan Sri Lanka). However, refusing to recognize unregistered marriages at all may prove too harsh a solution in many contexts.

two-step procedures

Some systems have a two-step procedure for validating a marriage. Firstly, the intending spouses have to give notice of their intention to marry (or apply for permission to marry), and then they must wait a specified period until the marriage can take place. Secondly, they have to register the marriage once it has been concluded. A variety of systems have this kind of two-step procedure (Fiji, Cameroon, Senegal, Malaysia, Sri Lanka).

The two-step approach has merits. By requiring prior permission/notice to marry, such systems theoretically allow time for a thorough investigation into whether or not the requisites for marriage have been fulfilled. If the law were to require that any failure to fulfill requisites be corrected before the ceremony could begin, women would enjoy greater protection from violations, such as early and forced marriage.

However, few advantages have been gained from most two-step procedures. In Senegal, for example, we found that the poor state of official records and the possibility of falsifying these records have resulted in the notification procedures being ineffective. Indeed, a two-step system could obstruct a woman's exercise of choice (where such choice is not already subject to her wali's approval) by providing those who oppose her choice of husband more time to take action. Our research does not point to any clear advantage or disadvantage to the two-step system in practice.

registration, proof of marriage and penalties

Many systems that require registration provide for penalties for failure to register. These may include light prison sentences and/or fines.

The question of who is responsible for registration and what penalties they face for failure to register the marriage is important. Obviously, in systems where the marriage has to be conducted by or in front of a Registrar, or similar state official, this question does not arise. If registration is purely the responsibility of the husband, the law may prove very weak since it may be in a man's interest to obstruct his wife from accessing her inherent and negotiated rights. More effective provisions are those that allow both women and men to take their marriage documents for registration and those that hold the person solemnizing the marriage responsible for registration (Bangladesh, Pakistan).

The customary exclusion of women, especially brides, from registration procedures often weakens any protections provided to them by registration requirements. Systems that do not require the bride to sign the marriage register (Sri Lanka) are particularly weak in this regard.

Systems where registration does not affect validity may allow for late registration (still subject, of course, to fulfillment of the requisites and conditions of marriage). A time limitation may or may not be specified. In Malaysia, for example, married couples who have not registered their marriage are given a limited period of time after the marriage date to make a late registration. Still they are required to pay a fine for registering late. Where late registrations are possible, it may be undesirable to increase the associated penalties because such an increase could backfire and cause couples who would have registered late never to register at all.

In some systems unregistered marriages remain permanently unrecognized (Central Asian Republics, Turkey). But in other systems where unregistered marriages are unrecognized, individuals in an unregistered marriage can gain access to marriage-related benefits through mechanisms (often lengthy) that prove unregistered marriages before the court or another authority (Algeria, Indonesia, Morocco, Senegal). Similar mechanisms are often available in systems that recognize oral, unregistered marriages as valid. Because women may have difficulty producing the necessary evidence to prove their marriages, such after-the-fact recognition mechanisms offer only limited assistance when women try to access their rights through the courts. Still, laws that include such an option at least offer women the possibility of accessing their rights through the courts. Usually, once a marriage is thus proved, it is treated as if it has been registered.

Senegal's Code de la Famille combines state sanctions against unregistered marriages (unregistered couples cannot access state medical benefits) with provisions that allow oral customary and religious marriages to be registered up to six months after their solemnization. While the Code does not declare unregistered marriages to be invalid, courts do require that parties bringing a marital case to court produce a marriage certificate before they can have a hearing. Accordingly, a woman seeking assistance from the court would have to go through the legal process of establishing the existence of her marriage before her actual complaint could be heard. Thus, the law discourages many from seeking justice.

In contrast, for marriages under Muslim laws, Nigerian laws do not require couples to provide evidence of their marriage in order to access state benefits or to get a court hearing regarding a marital claim. Proof of marriage is only required in the case that some party contests the marriage (for instance, in-laws in an inheritance claim).

marriage certificates and registered contracts

Where marriages are registered and couples receive a marriage certificate or registered contract as proof of the marriage and its registration, it is important that the bride receives a copy of any issued documents. It is also important that rules permit wives to easily acquire duplicate copies of these documents in the event that their own copies are destroyed. Laws or rules that explicitly require both that women receive a copy of marriage documents and that women will have access to additional copies of these are, therefore, more option-giving. Less option-giving laws (Senegal) require only one copy of the 'marriage book' to be issued to the couple, and this is invariably given to the man.

In some systems a marriage is certified simply by an entry in the official marriage register. In other systems, marriage contracts are filled out in multiple copies, and one is kept by the registering authority; another is filed with a central record; and, the remaining copy/ies are given to the couple. By whichever method marriages are certified, the associated documents constitute a public record, and any person can apply for copies of these records. Although marriage certificates and/or registered marriage contracts are usually sufficient proof of a valid marriage, additional evidence may be needed to prove a valid marriage if the truth of a certificate or entry is contested in court (see p.85)

solemnization

Different systems have varying requirements regarding solemnization. In some systems, the marriage ceremony and registration are to take place as one event (a one-stop process) at a recognized or designated place such as a mosque or town hall (Algeria, Central Asian Republics, Fiji, Turkey). In other systems, an official who registers marriages may be permitted to solemnize a marriage in a place other than the designated place (home of the bride, for example)(Malaysia, Iran, Sudan). Still other systems do not have any requirements concerning either the location where the marriage is to be solemnized or the person who is to solemnize it, provided that the marriage is subsequently registered before a state authority (Bangladesh, Sri Lanka, Pakistan). In Senegal, oral marriages contracted under customary laws or Muslim laws are permitted as long as they are registered within six months.

Registration procedures vary greatly because states vary in their level of regulation as well as in their recognition of community practices. In addition, Muslim laws (unlike Christian laws, for example) do not require the involvement of religious authorities in marriage ceremonies. In some systems, parties are increasingly choosing a one-stop process (Singapore). In others, parties continue to conduct marriage ceremonies outside the formal system because there is a shortage of state recognized marriage officers (Senegal, Sudan).

Whatever the system that is enforced, the registering state official's qualifications and sensitivity to women's rights are important. In Bangladesh the state has recognized the important role that officials play in protecting women's rights and has accordingly strengthened the requirements for Nikah Registrars. These measures have been taken to ensure that marriage requisites are upheld, particularly requisites that prevent child marriages.

Additionally, the requisites of a valid marriage are more likely to be met where registering authorities are liable to be penalized for their negligence in the event that they register a marriage in which requisites have not been fulfilled.

foreign marriages

As the global trends of increasing migration and emigration continue, marriages contracted abroad are becoming more common. Laws and community practices may differ greatly in their recognition of these marriages.

Some systems provide for the registration of marriages contracted by citizens abroad. Usually, such foreign marriages are subject to the same requisites or conditions of marriage as are marriages contracted domestically (Malaysia). While some systems provide clear rules governing the recognition of marriages solemnized abroad (Malaysia), others do not.

People who are governed by two systems, such as Bangladeshi British and Pakistani British dual nationals in the UK, are particularly vulnerable to ambiguities in the law. In the UK, these dual nationals must go through a civil ('Registry') marriage because British law only recognizes civil marriage under the Marriage Act of 1949 (as amended to date). However, the Muslim Family Laws Ordinance, 1961 also applies to them wherever they may be because it is an extra-territorial law. Accordingly, dual nationals who have their marriages solemnised abroad must fill in the standard marriage contract form (kabinnama/nikahnama) provided by the Consular Officer of the Bangladesh/Pakistan mission in the country where marriage is solemnized. After the marriage, the form must be returned to the mission where it is attested to and returned so that it can be forwarded to a Nikah Registrar in Bangladesh/Pakistan. Sending the contract to the proper Nikah Registrar (that being the registrar for the area where the wife is a resident, or in the case that the wife is not a Bangladesh/Pakistan national, the registrar for the area where the groom is a resident) is the responsibility of the person who solemnises the marriage. (If that person is not a citizen of Bangladesh or Pakistan, then the groom takes on this responsibility. If the groom is not a citizen the wife is responsible.)

Even though the MFLO requires that dual nationals follow the above procedures, Bangladeshi and Pakistani courts have nevertheless recognized civil marriages that have been solemnized before a Registrar in the UK as valid Muslim marriages as long as these marriages did not violate Muslim laws (by, for example, forming a union between a Muslim woman and a non-Muslim man) (Ali Nawaz Gardezi v Lt. Col. Mohammad Yusuf PLD 1963 SC 51; Marina Jatoi v Nuruddin K. Jatoi PLD 1967 SC 580).

The State Recognizes the Importance of Marriage Registration

Most states recognize that a woman suffers severe consequences when the status of her marriage is unclear. When states regulate marriage registration, even in systems where registration does not affect validity, they are acting to protect women from those who might otherwise take advantage of any ambiguity in a woman's status.

The Muslim Family Laws Ordinance, which introduced the compulsory registration of marriages in Pakistan (and Bangladesh when it gained independence from Pakistan), is an example of a regulation that was designed to protect women. This ordinance has faced opposition from extreme right politico-religious groups ever since it was introduced in 1961. In 1974, Bangladesh replaced the MFLO S.5 with the even more protective Muslim Marriages and Divorces Registration Act. This act strengthened the marriage registration provisions.

In Pakistan, in the 1990s there was a concerted effort by extreme right politico-religious elements to have the MFLO declared 'unIslamic' by the courts. Although they were partly successful (in 2000 certain sections of the MFLO were struck down), S. 5, relating to the registration of marriages, was upheld (Allah Rakha and another v Federation of Pakistan and others PLD 2000 FSC 1).

In Iran, marriage registration was mandated decades before the 1967 Family Protection Act. However, the view that registration was not a requirement under Muslim laws continued to be widespread, and many couples continued to marry without obtaining any documentary evidence. In post-Revolution Iran, this view spread when the Family Protection Law was cancelled in 1980. However, the old registration law was never cancelled. Women protested the lack of protection that they faced because so few marriages were being registered. As a result, the authorities reaffirmed that the registration law was valid and that registration of marriage is compulsory.

NOTES

LAWS: Marriage Contracts - Registration and Validity

Criteria

We found it difficult to develop criteria for assessing whether or not the provisions discussed in this section are option-giving for women. In our debates, it became clear that the same provisions have different effects in different contexts. Several factors seem to influence the effects of such provisions, including the manner in which the provisions are administered; the developmental conditions present where they are applied (for example, the accessibility of forums for registration); and the social attitudes that prevail in the context where they are applied.

While we agreed on the criteria for the more option-giving provisions, we debated as to whether systems that invalidate unregistered marriages should be in the middle-ground category or in the less option-giving category. It appears that in contexts where education levels are high, there is social support for protecting women's rights in marriage, and registration facilities are easily accessible; weak registration requirements (i.e., a provision that recognizes unregistered marriages as valid) are less option-giving because they undermine the necessity of registration. Accordingly, in the same type of context, laws that invalidate unregistered marriages serve to motivate parties to comply with registration requirements and should, therefore, be placed in the middle ground category.

However, in most of our contexts, the above-mentioned conditions do not exist and accordingly, women have little control over the registration of their marriages. Therefore, in most contexts, laws that penalize women for contracting an unregistered marriage by declaring that marriage invalid are unfair and should be in the less option-giving category.

While we have chosen to go ahead and categorize laws in this section, we recognize that the following categorizations will require further discussion.

☺ More option giving laws are those which:

- Make registration compulsory while holding solemnizers responsible for meeting registration requirements; and
- Give access to state benefits and/or certain citizenship rights pertaining to married persons only to persons in registered marriages;. and
- Provide mechanisms for late registration.

😐 The middle-ground is occupied by those laws which:

- Declare unregistered marriages to be invalid; or
- Give the same access to rights and benefits, whether or not marriages are registered.

☹ Less option-giving are those laws which:

- Have no registration requirements; or
- Have no mechanism for late registration and/or recognizing unregistered marriages.

☺ Unregistered marriages are not valid

Cameroon, Central Asian Republics, & Fiji: Only a registered marriage, celebrated before a civil status registrar is legal. If a marriage is unregistered, the law does not recognize any rights arising from that marriage.

Indonesia: Under A. 2(2) of the MA and A. 5(1) of the KHI, all marriages are to be registered as a matter of public order. Under A. 6 of the KHI, an unregistered marriage does not acquire legal power, and under A. 7 a marriage can only be proven through a Marriage Certificate. However, under A. 7(2) couples can apply to the Religious Court for marriage isbat (statement). Registration requires that both spouses, their parents, the registrar who was present during the ceremony, and two witnesses be present to sign the marriage certificate. Violations by the registrar are 'misdemeanours,' liable to imprisonment of up to 3 months or a fine not to exceed Rp. 7,500 (less than US$1). Others found guilty (including bride) are liable to a fine not to exceed Rp 7,500.

Senegal: Under A. 125 of the CF, one month's notice must be given before marriages can be solemnized in areas where there is a civic centre. These marriages must be celebrated publicly at the civic centre in the area of the couple's domicile or residence. Under A. 114, marriages, whether solemnized at the civic center by the Officier de l'Etat Civil or solemnized otherwise, are to be registered, and a marriage book is given to the husband while the first copy of the certificate is given to the wife. Although under A. 130(3), the state recognizes only written marriages, the law implicitly tolerates verbal marriages that have been solemnized under customary or religious laws, provided that they are registered within 6 months (A. 147(1)). For registration both spouses and the witnesses to the marriage must appear before the OEC.

Tunisia: Under A. 4 of the CSP, a marriage shall be proved only by an official document prescribed by law. A marriage that takes place in the home of one of the spouses or at any other private venue must be conducted before two notaries public. Alternatively, a marriage may be conducted publicly before a civil status registrar in a Municipal Council office (or before a consular or diplomatic officer if the couple marries abroad). Marriages not conducted before a civil status registrar or before two notaries public are null and void.

Turkey: Under the CC, only civil, registered marriages are legal. A religious marriage ceremony confers no legally binding rights. A religious marriage ceremony can be held only after a civil ceremony. Violation of registration requirements renders the couple and the religious authority liable to criminal penalties. Marriages are legalized by the mayor of a relevant district or by a civil servant acting with the mayor's authority. Under A. 137, in villages the council of village elders has to be notified of the couple's intention to marry, and then the village headman must legalize the marriage. If both the bride and groom are Turkish citizens and they marry in a foreign country, the relevant Turkish consulate must legalize the marriage. If either the bride or groom is a citizen of the country where the marriage is taking place, the marriage is legalized according to the procedures of that country. Such a marriage is valid in Turkey as long as it does not contravene Turkish law.

😐 Registration is compulsory but is not a condition for validity

Algeria: Under A. 18 of the CF, marriage must be conducted before a notary or another official who is legally competent. Under A. 21, provisions in the Code of Civil Status apply to registration procedures. Under A. 21, an unregistered marriage may be made valid through court judgment, provided other requisites have been fulfilled. It is then entered in the Register of Civil Status.

Bangladesh: Under S. 3 of the MMDRA, all marriages under Muslim laws shall be registered 'notwithstanding anything contained in any law, custom or usage' (wording which is stronger than the repealed S. 5 of the MFLO – see Pakistan below). Under S. 5(2), violation is punishable with imprisonment of up to 3 months and/or a fine of up to 500 taka (approx. US$ 9).

Egypt: The contract is drawn (notarized) before the official authorized to perform the marriage ceremony (the Mazoum) and registered in the official registrar of the state. A contract is valid even if it is not notarized. However, a wife in an unofficial marriage does not have access to the same state benefits as does a wife in a notarized marriage.

Iran: Registration was introduced in the pre-World War II period via legislation that remains separate from the Civil Code. It was reaffirmed in the 1980s, following apparent public confusion. The Chief official of the Marriage Registry is obliged to read out the conditions of the marriage contract to both parties and to have them sign the contract if they accept the conditions. Unregistered marriages remain valid although failure to register can result in a fine. Oral marriages are technically valid if the husband acknowledges the marriage. However, if the validity of the marriage is disputed, women have difficulty proving the marriage because they have to produce two male Muslim witnesses that will attest to the existence of the marriage.

Malaysia: Under S. 16 of the IFLA, each party must apply for permission to marry from the Registrar. This application must be submitted at least 7 days before the marriage is due to take place (exceptions are possible). Under S. 17, the Registrar is to examine the requisites, including whether or not the husband has obtained permission to marry in the case of polygyny. In certain instances permission to marry can be granted only by a Syar'iah Judge. However, under S.6 and 32, non-registration does not invalidate a Muslim marriage that is valid under Hukum Syar'iah. Only the solemnizer (authorized or otherwise) who solemnizes an 'unauthorised' marriage is penalized. The validity of such a marriage can be proved in a court by the presentation of evidence, and if so validated, the marriage is then registered. The law also sets out the procedures for and formalities of contracting a marriage. Included are provisions concerning places for marriage, forms of marriage, application for marriage, permission to marry, solemnization, ta'liq, attestation of witnesses, registration of marriages, entry in the marriage register, copies to be made available for both parties, and voluntary registration of marriages contracted before the passing of the Muslim marriage law. Under S. 31, Muslim marriages contracted abroad (provided they fulfill Hukum Syar'iah) must be registered within 6 months of return to Malaysia or within 6 months of the date of marriage; late registration is possible on payment of a fine.

Morocco: Under A. 43 of the Moudawana, the text of a marriage contract shall be entered into the register of marriages at the court, and a copy is to be sent to the Directorate of Civil Status. No penalties for non-registration are mentioned in the Moudawana. The wife or her representative is to be given possession of the original document within 15 days, and the husband has the right to obtain a copy. Under A. 5(3), in exceptional circumstances a judge may hear a claim of marriage and accept lawful evidence in confirming the marriage.

Pakistan: The standard marriage contract (nikahnama) is formulated under Rules 8 and 10 of the MFLO. Under S.5 of the MFLO, registration is compulsory (with the Nikah Registrar of the area where the wife resides), and there are light penalties if the solemnizer does not have the marriage registered; there is no time limit for registration. The procedure for registration is outlined in Rule 11 for marriages solemnized in Pakistan and Rule 12 if this is abroad. The law does not require any form of religious ceremony for a valid nikah, nor does it require the presence of a religious figure. The law does not specify that an unregistered marriage is invalid. Courts recognize unregistered marriages if they are proved through other evidence (Arif Hussain & Azra Parveen v The State PLD 1982 FSC 42, a zina case). There have been cases where the courts do not accept an unregistered marriage because of other doubts and a lack of clear evidence, especially when one party claims the marriage and the other denies it.

Philippines: A.17 of the CMPL requires a written marriage contract, which is defined as a public declaration instrument to be signed in triplicate by the contracting parties and witnesses and attested to by the solemnizing officer. One copy is to be given to the parties, one to the Circuit Registrar and another kept by the solemnizing officer. While there is no penalty for failing to register a marriage or for late registration, unregistered oral customary marriages are not recognized. Marriage certificates are required for claiming social security benefits, passports, etc.

Sri Lanka: Under S.17 of the MMDA, marriages are to be registered immediately after solemnization. This is the duty of the groom, wali (where required), and solemnizer; all of whom are required to invite the Registrar to the nikah ceremony. There is no separate marriage contract, and instead, an entry into a marriage register (established under the MMDA) is made and attested to. Under S.81, 83, and 85, there are light penalties (maximum of 6 months imprisonment) for failure to register and for registration by an unauthorized Registrar; but under S. 16 non-registration does not render the marriage invalid.

Sudan: Registration is required and state-recognized. Ma'azouns are to attend the marriage and attest to the information in the marriage contract. Any adult Muslim male may solemnize the marriage. Women without registered marriage contracts face difficulty in accessing their rights through the courts.

☹ Registration is not required

Gambia (marriages under Muslim laws): Under the MMDO, registration is an optional administrative procedure with no penalties for failure to register. Thus, oral unregistered marriages are recognized as valid. However, only women with registered marriages are able to claim benefits such as maternity leave with salary or other conjugal benefits. Registration does not need the presence of both spouses. The Muslim Court is the statutory office mandated to register marriages and issue marriage certificates involving Muslim parties within their jurisdictions in the Gambia.

India (marriages under Muslim laws): Although there is no code that requires registration, many communities recognize the benefits of registration or, at least, keeping a public record of marriage documents. In Bengal, for example, official procedures exist for voluntary centralized registration of Muslim marriages. In other communities, a copy of the marriage contract may be kept with the local mosque or jamaat.

Nigeria (marriages under Muslim and customary laws): There is no registration requirement.

IMPLEMENTATION

The state recognizes social preference

Fiji: Many religious leaders are also certified marriage officers and can therefore perform the two ceremonies – one required by law and the other by community practices.

Administrative problems obstruct registration

Senegal and Sudan: There is a shortage of officials who are authorized by the state to certify marriages. As a result, marriage contracts are often oral and unregistered.

PRACTICES

Oral, unregistered marriages remain common

Gambia: Most marriages are conducted under customary law with some element of Islamic principles. Usually, the imam or Kadi presides over a Muslim marriage. Most marriages in both urban and rural areas are not registered and can therefore be dissolved only by the Kadi (or by a chief in some of the provincial communities). Most women are not aware of the option for registration and may be denied certain rights, such as paid maternity leave, as a result. Even where marriages are registered, records are poorly kept (especially in the rural areas), and often the registering authorities appear unconcerned about the low rate of registration.

In contrast, when a Muslim man marries a non-Muslim woman who does not convert to Islam, registration of the marriage is considered almost compulsory. Likewise, Gambian women of higher social and educational status are increasingly likely to have their marriages registered.

Sudan: Often unqualified Ma'azouns conduct oral marriages, and in such cases no document is registered in a Personal Law Court. Men avoid registering their marriages in order to avoid at least two financial disadvantages. Firstly, marriage registration requires that fees be paid (that are tied to the amount of mahr). Secondly, the registration documents the amount of mahr, and this documentation could be used in a claim against the husband. The groom's family may avoid these disadvantages by using the pretext that they prefer an agreement based on 'traditional trust.'

Trends favour registration, especially where there are state benefits

Cameroon: Men who have contracted oral marriages may subsequently have them legalized in order to receive state benefits.

Malaysia: Marriages are generally registered unless a couple is migrating (although a nikah is performed to satisfy the families), or marrying quickly (the couple may accept the fine and register it later); or when a non-Muslim has been married abroad.

Philippines: Most contracts are oral and conducted at a public ceremony. However, since the late 80's, most women are undergoing late registration of marriages so that they can travel, receive social security benefits, apply to jobs abroad, etc. In places where there are no Sharia courts, like in Davao City, women are registering their marriage with the local Civil Registrar, with the help of the Office of Muslim Affairs.

Sri Lanka: Unregistered customary marriages are very rare. Due to social norms of gender segregation, women are not involved in the registration process.

Trends are mixed

Algeria: For a marriage to be socially valid, it needs only to be celebrated in the presence of witnesses. Registration in urban areas is more common.

Pakistan: Oral, unregistered marriages remain common; however, in urban Sindh and Punjab, there is a high rate of registration. There is a positive trend towards couples filing their nikahnama and registering their marriage, due to an increased awareness of benefits. Marriages are registered where benefits accrue (e.g., men in the armed forces who then get family benefits, or couples seeking to emigrate). In some communities marriages are written on 'stamp paper' (but not official nikahnama forms), and registered with the local imam or local revenue official. In most communities an imam masjid or some other religious figure solemnizes the marriage. Solemnization by a family elder or some other respected figure is also accepted and practiced.

Senegal: Customary and religious marriages are solemnized at the mosque or at home by an adult Muslim male in the presence of witnesses and spouses. Oral customary and religious marriages often are not registered. However, some mosques now keep unofficial marriage registers and, although these have no legal value, these are acceptable as evidence in the event of litigation. Women (in the event that they take a case to court) often find that their husbands have registered their marriages, though they (the wives) were not present at the registration because another woman was used as a substitute. While the identity of witnesses is systematically verified, the bride's identity is not. Since women are then unaware of where the marriage was registered, they have no means of securing a copy of the marriage certificate. Many women know their husbands have a marriage certificate but do not dare demand it (needed, for example, to claim state medical benefits) for fear of arguments. Most women who initiate formal procedures for delayed registration abandon them because these procedures are difficult and lengthy, and officials are obstructive and demand that the husband be present.

Cameroon, Central Asian Republics & Fiji: Muslims usually have two ceremonies: a 'court marriage' (i.e., legal marriage) and a religious ceremony (nikah). Unregistered marriages are common in polygynous situations because polygyny is illegal. Inheritance and paternity suits tend to arise out of oral marriage.

A Powerful Man Attempts to Evade Marriage Recognition

A now notorious case concerning the recognition of an unregistered marriage has been followed by many Indonesian women's groups and is being used as an example of the problems women face in trying to have their marriages recognized, especially when their husbands are powerful men.

In 1996, Rina married Mandra, one of Jakarta's most famous celebrities. The marriage, which was widely attended by the local community and covered in the media, was conducted in accordance with the general legal requirements: both bride and groom were present, as were their parents; the ijab and qabul were witnessed, and a mahr was fixed. However, since Mandra could not produce documentary evidence before the Marriage Record Official that he was divorced as he claimed, the marriage was not recorded, although he (the husband) promised to record it as soon as possible.

However, by the time their son Ratan was born, the marriage had still not been recorded. After the child's birth Mandra refused to acknowledge Rina as his legitimate wife and Ratan as his son; he also claimed to be still married to another woman.

Assisted by the legal organization LBH-APIK Jakarta, Rina applied for marriage isbat (a statement declaring the marriage) before the Religious Court, with the aim of both clarifying the status of her marriage and establishing the status of her child, who still did not have a birth certificate.

The Court ignored the testimony of witnesses who confirmed the marriage was valid according to Muslim laws, and criticized Rina for not delaying the marriage until Mandra produced documentary evidence of his status. The Court further argued, on a technicality, that the provisions of Article 7 of the KHI concerning marriage isbat do not apply in Rina's case because the isbat proceedings were not part of a divorce suit. Although Article 7 permits marriage isbat in a wide range of circumstances, in practice, the courts only accept it as part of divorce proceedings. This is apparently in an attempt to prevent the isbat process from being used as a means of regularizing 'under-hand' marriages (those conducted outside the law). But it leaves little legal option for women who want to establish the status of their marriage but do not want a divorce.

Women's groups are now advocating a change in judicial attitudes. They are additionally demanding that wherever couples or a spouse is able to prove a marriage was valid under Muslim laws, marriage isbat should be accepted by the courts.

Provisions papers No.2/Pdt.P/1997/PA.Bgr., documentation of LBH-APIK Jakarta, quoted at Sisters in Islam Regional Workshop on Islamic Family Law and Justice for Muslim Women, June 8-10, 2001, Kuala Lumpur, Malaysia.

5b MARRIAGE CONTRACTS: MARRIAGE CONTRACTS AND REGISTERS

introduction

For marriages to be valid and/or registered, most systems require certain information to be recorded with the recognized authorities. As noted in Registration and Validity (p.133), registration of a marriage may be necessary for validity in some countries, while in others it is not.

However, even if the state does not recognize Muslim marriages (Fiji, South Africa), they may be registered with the mosque or written down. Even where oral marriages are the norm, aspects relating to property (mainly mahr) may be recorded (under other civil procedures).

This section focuses on written marriage contracts/documents and systems that do require registration. We do not discuss the registration process itself (see Registration and Validity, p.133), but rather the content of standardized forms and documents used in the registration process. Discussed are standardized state-enforced forms, written contracts recognized under parallel judicial systems such as Quazi courts, entries in official documents, and particulars contained in marriage certificates and other similar documents.

Since marriage documentation is essentially a procedural matter, family laws themselves do not always state what has to be recorded (although Morocco and Sudan's laws do). In such cases requirements are found either in other civil code rules or simply in the official forms themselves (Bangladesh, Pakistan).

The clauses that a particular state or community chooses to form their standard marriage contract indicate the extent to which that state or community enforces the requisites of a valid marriage, as well as the extent to which they protect the spouses' rights. The compulsory aspects of a marriage contract establish a baseline of associated rights and responsibilities. Where there are few compulsory clauses, the state or community effectively leaves enforcement of marriage requisites, rights, and responsibilities unregulated. The protections (or lack thereof) offered in a standard marriage contract are particularly important for women who are often the more vulnerable party in a marriage.

Theoretically, there should be no contradiction between the provisions contained in a marriage contract and those contained in the same marriage's registration forms. However, in practice, corruption and general state inefficiency can create mismatches between the details recorded in the marriage contract and the marriage registration forms. In other cases the details recorded in the various copies of the marriage documents issued to each spouse do not match. More option-giving are those laws which clarify which copy of each document is to be considered the final version. Furthermore, this final copy should be the one kept with an 'impartial' authority, such as the local government centre.

Whether or not the registering authority actually checks all the details that are to be recorded depends largely on social attitudes and the state's willingness to enforce penalties if the forms have not been filled in properly. In many cases the names of the groom and bride may be misspelled, or, where marriages of related couples take place at the same time, the 'wrong' couple may be recorded as 'married.' Out of ignorance or inappropriate advice based on narrow social attitudes, divorced/widowed women may not write their correct status, which can cause subsequent problems (e.g., the wife loses her ability to claim maintenance for children from a previous marriage).

The various standardized forms that are required for validity and/or registration of marriages in different systems have many elements in common. Accordingly, we have not listed these in terms of more or less option-giving. Generally, however, the greater the level of detail required, the greater the level of protection the forms offer.

recording the requisites to marriage

Typically, the name, address, and age of each spouse is recorded. Requiring that the age be listed acts as a basic protection against child marriage. However, since most child marriages are oral and certainly unregistered (to avoid any penalties for child marriage), the protection provided is limited. Often the bride's age is falsified if she is near to the legal minimum age.

In addition to recording basic personal information, forms commonly contain a clause establishing provisions concerning mahr (see p.110 regarding the validity of marriages where no mahr is stated). Contracts or registration forms that require detailed information about the mahr agreement usually save women from problems in litigation if they subsequently need to recover their mahr. Because mahr is a requisite of a valid Muslim marriage, its existence is assumed. However, contracts may stipulate details including: how much of the mahr will be prompt; how much of the mahr, if any, will be deferred; how much of the mahr has been paid already at the time of the marriage; and, what form the mahr will take (such as moveable or immovable property or cash).

As witnesses are also a requisite of a valid marriage (see p.110), it is standard for marriage documents to provide fields for their signatures as well as for the stamp or signature of any regulating authority.

In addition, documents must record the date that the marriage is contracted in order to establish the legal paternity of any children conceived during the marriage, as well as to establish the point at which maintenance and inheritance rights become due. Similarly, recording the existing status of the intended spouses (whether unmarried, divorced, widowed, or already married, in the case of the man) prevents a number of possible confusions. Firstly, such records help establish the validity of the marriage (clarifying that the woman is not undergoing a waiting period, or that the man is not violating any limitations on polygyny). Secondly, such records make it clear if there are already children from a previous marriage who will continue to have certain economic rights from their fathers. Unfortunately, many systems only require the woman to record her status. Such a discriminatory requirement could facilitate evasion of regulations concerning polygyny or could assist a man in concealing a history of multiple divorces.

Whether or not a bride must sign the contract and/or registration forms indicates whether or not she is considered a primary actor, or simply a bystander, in the process of contracting the marriage. In addition, not requiring the bride's signature facilitates forced marriages. In Sri Lanka there is no space provided for the bride's signature on the registration form, and in Algeria only the wali's signature is compulsory. Both of these systems undermine a woman's agency as an independent contracting party. Where the bride is not required to sign the marriage contract, and there are stipulations that prevent women from marrying without parental permission or allow compulsion in marriage, women's marriage choices are further restricted.

additional standard clauses

Additional standard clauses are those clauses, not already mentioned, that must be included in any given marriage contract, and if they are not, the violating parties and/or the registering authority could suffer consequences under the penal code. Where polygyny is regulated, marriage contracts and registration forms may require the husband to state whether or not he already has a wife/wives and/or whether or not he has secured her/their permission(s) for a subsequent marriage (Bangladesh, Malaysia, Pakistan). Laws in Senegal and Cameroon also require that the husband record in the contract his marriage option (that is whether or not the marriage will be and/or remain monogamous or polygynous). However, contracts that do not record the husband's marriage option are still valid. When this option has been recorded, the document can then serve as evidence in any subsequent litigation concerning polygyny.

Where the law requires a couple to choose the property regime that will apply to their marriage, the choice of property regime is recorded. (Cameroon, Senegal).

In Malaysia and Iran, reforms have introduced standardized forms that place certain conditions on the marriage. The groom must indicate his acceptance of these conditions in order to contract the marriage. If the husband subsequently breaks one or more of the conditions, the wife has an automatic right to seek dissolution through the courts.

In Bangladesh and Pakistan, the standardized marriage contract, introduced under the Muslim Family Laws Ordinance 1961, has a range of clauses in addition to those concerning requisites. Leaving these blank does not invalidate the contract but can lead to disputes over what rights and conditions have been negotiated. Unfortunately, the option-giving nature of these additional clauses is defeated by the common practice of automatically striking them out (see Negotiated Rights and Responsibilities, p.167).

Contractual Obligations – Never to be Understood!

Written marriage contracts and registration forms are undoubtedly useful in terms of proving the existence of a marriage and its conditions. However, the vast majority of women do not know what is written in these documents, simply because they cannot read or because it is written in a language they do not know.

One highly educated networker from the Gambia had no knowledge of the contents of her marriage contract because it was written, as is traditional, in Arabic. She was able to find out what it contained only when she applied for a scholarship in the UK, and the British Council required her to show evidence of her marriage in a translated copy. She had to go through a Public Notary to the High Court of the Gambia to get a translated copy. This process took three months. Her experience illustrates the difficulties that woman can face when trying to determine the provisions contained in their marriage documents.

NOTES

. . . .

LAWS: Marriage Contracts and Registers

Algeria: Under A. 15 CF, the marriage contract must stipulate whether the dower is prompt or deferred. Details regarding the information that is to be recorded when registering the marriage are found in the Code of Civil Status.

Bangladesh & Pakistan: In addition to various optional clauses, the following must be recorded in the standard marriage contract form: a) Place of marriage; b) Names, addresses, age of spouses; c) Status of wife; d) Names of witnesses to marriage; e) Date that the marriage is contracted; f) Amount of dower, and whether prompt and/or deferred; how much paid at the time of marriage; g) Details of whether or not the groom is already married and of polygamy permission documents; h) Name and address of solemnizer; i) Registration fee; j) Signatures of bride, groom or his vakil (agent), witnesses to marriage, and solemnizer; and Nikah Registrar's official seal.

Cameroon: Under A. 49 of the CSO, the marriage certificate should include: a) the name of the civil status registry; b) the surname, first name, date & place of birth, residence, and profession of each spouse; c) the consent of each spouse; d) the consent of parents in the case of a minor; e) the surname and first name of witnesses; f) the date & place of the celebration of marriage; g) mention of any separate marriage contract concluded before the marriage; h) a statement as to whether the spouses have opted for joint or separate property; i) mention of the matrimonial regime (monogamy or polygyny); j) the surname & first name of the civil status registrar; k) and the signatures of each of the spouses, the witnesses, and the civil status registrar.

Gambia (marriages under Muslim laws): Under the MMDO, the standard registration of marriage form has the following 23 clauses in Arabic: a) Consecutive number; b) Name of bridegroom and father of bridegroom; c) Residence of bridegroom; d) Name of bride and father of bride; e) Residence of bride; f) Whether or not the bride has ever married, and if so, whether she was widowed or divorced by former husband; g) Whether bride is an adult or otherwise; h) Name and address of guardian of bride; i) Date on which marriage was contracted; j) Amount of dower; k) Amount of dower which is prompt; l) Amount of dower which is deferred; m) Amount of dower which was paid before or at the time of marriage; n) Whether or not any property was given in lieu of the whole or any part of the dower with particulars of the same; o) Special conditions (if any); p) Place at which marriage took place; q) Name of person who hosted the marriage ceremony; r) Signature of bridegroom; s) Signature of bride; t) Signature of bride's guardian; u) Signatures and residences of witnesses of the marriage (two witnesses required); v) Date of registration; w) Signature and residence of Registrar.

Malaysia: S. 21 of the IFLA requires the details of the mas kahwin to be recorded in the marriage register, while S. 22 mentions the recording of 'prescribed particulars,' as well as the prescribed or other ta'liq pronounced after the marriage has been solemnized by the husband (see Other Forms of Dissolution for Women, p.285). The ta'liq differs from State to State.

Morocco: Under A. 5 of the Moudawana, the dower must be specified or the marriage contract is not permissible. A. 41 and 42 provide a list of the details that must be recorded in the marriage document, including the amount of the dower, specifying that which is payable immediately and that which is deferred and whether it was seen to be received or was acknowledged.

Philippines: The marriage contract for Muslims is similar to the standard contract applicable to citizens of other communities under general law. While the law does not define any compulsory clauses that must be written in the marriage contract (apart from the required stipulation of mahr), a ruling from the Sharia Court requires that the order of marriage (whether first or second, etc.) and the amount and particulars of mahr (whether cash or other) must be recorded.

Senegal: The marriage contract must include the amount and form of mahr (if the parties have agreed that mahr is a condition for the validity of the marriage), a statement as to the matrimonial property regime (joint, total separation, or 'regime dotal,' whereby the husband manages wife's dower during the marriage, but it remains hers and is to be returned to her on dissolution), and a declaration as to whether the marriage will be monogamous or (limitedly) polygynous (this being entirely the husband's decision).

Sudan: The text of the marriage contract consists of: (a) administrative information; (b) the name of the husband (no specification of his age or marital status); (c) information on the wife: name, marital and puberty status (implying whether she is a virgin, widow, or divorcee); (d) el mahr, mokadam and mokar; (e) approval of the husband signed by his proxy; (f) approval of the wife's guardian; (g) certification of two witnesses.

Tunisia: Marriage contracts are civil contracts and must include: (a) the exact identity of spouses; (b) the mutual consent of spouses; (c) in the case of minors (persons below 17 years), the guardian's authorisation; (d) the names and signatures of witnesses;(e) the mahr.

5C MARRIAGE CONTRACTS: INHERENT RIGHTS AND RESPONSIBILITIES

introduction

Inherent rights are those rights that, according to the relevant law, arise automatically from registering a marriage or contracting a valid marriage (written or oral). The inherent rights and responsibilities arising out of marriage in any particular context largely determine the power relationship that will exist between husbands and wives in that context. Regardless of the source of laws, most systems distinguish between husbands and wives when assigning inherent rights and responsibilities, and almost always these distinctions establish a power dynamic that favours the husband.

Systems governed by customary laws most often do not use written contracts. Hence, such systems establish the inherent rights and responsibilities arising from marriage through oral agreements made between parties, as well as through unspoken agreements arising from common practice (see p.213 for the rights arising out of mut'a marriages).

Systems influenced by the patriarchal Napoleonic Code (often through a history of colonization, even though the existing laws may be based on Muslim laws) appear to provide particularly limiting definitions of women's rights and responsibilities in marriage. Interestingly, uncodified systems, or systems in which laws do not specify the rights and responsibilities of wives, are sometimes more open to change and liberal interpretation than codified ones.

Whether or not a woman can access her inherent rights through any formal forum (civil, religious or customary) will depend upon whether or not the state recognises her marriage as valid. Where states regard marriages under religious and customary laws as invalid, rights in marriage can be claimed only by those who register their marriages under the civil law (see Registration, p.134).

The inherent rights arising from marriages that are oral, unregistered, and unrecognised under the law may be enforceable through non-formal community forums. However, given the general tendency of such forums to be dominated by patriarchal ideologies, women attempting to access their rights through these forums face severe constraints.

Mahr, while much like an inherent right, is actually an essential element of a valid marriage, rather than an inherent right, and is discussed in a separate section on p.179.

Certain rights, which are presumed to be inherent, are, in fact, negotiable. For example, the presumed 'right' of husbands to practice polygyny and talaq, or to determine the mobility of their wife(s) can sometimes be modified by negotiated clauses (if these are possible under the law, see p.172-174). This section, therefore, deals with the 'default' inherent rights that arise from a marriage if no negotiated clauses are amended to a marriage contract (see Negotiated Rights and Responsibilities, p.167).

different rights for different communities

Where couples may choose which set of laws will govern their marriage, the inherent rights may differ substantially under each set of laws. However, in most contexts where multiple systems apply, women do not have the option of choosing which system they want to be governed by. Where various religious and ethnic affiliations determine which set of laws will apply to a particular person, Muslim women may find themselves at a disadvantage when they compare their inherent rights and responsibilities in marriage with those of women from other communities. For example, if one compares the rights and responsibilities of women married under the Philippines Code of Muslim Personal Law with those of women married under the Philippines general law Family Code, one will find that the provisions set out in the CMPL are far more restrictive for women than are those set out in the Family Code.

Under the CMPL:

- The wife shall be entitled to support during the marriage;
- The husband shall fix the residence of the family (A. 35);
- The wife shall dutifully manage the affairs of the household (A. 36(1));
- The wife may, with her husband consent, exercise any profession or occupation or engage in any business, provided that these activities are in keeping with Islamic modesty and virtue (A. 36(3)).

Under the Family Code (not based on Muslim laws):

- The spouses are jointly responsible for the support of the family;
- The husband and the wife shall fix the family domicile;
- The husband and the wife shall jointly manage the household;
- The husband's consent is not required for the wife to exercise her profession, nor is it required for her to engage in an occupation or business.

the gender imbalance in inherent rights

Some systems have codified all or some of the inherent rights arising from a valid marriage. Laws specifying inherent rights may be based on Muslim laws, customary laws, or other sources. Inherent rights are usually claimable upon the registration of a marriage. However, some systems recognize inherent rights that arise from unregistered marriages as well (if the marriage can be proved through other evidence)(Bangladesh, Pakistan, Sri Lanka, Tunisia).

Where rights are codified, men are often allotted rights, and women responsibilities. This appears to be the case particularly in laws based upon Maliki jurisprudence or the Napoleonic Code (Algeria, Morocco, Tunisia, Senegal).

There may be a contradiction in the law between the rights of the husband and the rights of the wife. For example, a woman trying to exercise her right to control her own property may be severely constrained in doing so if the same law recognizes her husband's right to control her mobility. Case law often indicates how such conflicts are resolved in practice. In addition, one spouse's exercise of his/her inherent rights arising from marriage may contradict the fundamental rights guaranteed to the other spouse under the country's constitution. For example, a husband's right to determine the family home may violate a wife's right (as a citizen) to freedom of movement. Again, case law reveals how such conflicts are resolved in a particular context. In Sri Lanka, the debate continues as to how the right to mobility should be categorized. If this right were to be categorized as a personal law issue, then it would be excluded from purview under the constitution. However, if it were to be categorized as a fundamental right, it would be guaranteed under the constitution.

While rarely addressed by the laws or customs that define inherent rights, shifting social situations and class origins may alter the impact of inherent rights and responsibilities. For example, a wife's right to maintenance from her husband is often rendered meaningless by economic realities. Many poor and middle class families need women to earn money, just so that the family can survive.

mutual rights

Inherent rights and responsibilities may or may not be reciprocal. Examples of reciprocal rights include the right to fidelity (Cameroon), the right to maintain a joint household (Fiji), and the right to mutual maintenance (Central Asian Republics). Examples of reciprocal responsibilities include the duty of mutual support (Cameroon, Indonesia), and the duties of equally shared consortium (where consortium includes housework, child care, love, affection and sexual services) (Fiji). In Indonesia the law states that the rights and responsibilities of the wife and husband are 'equivalent ...in the life of the household and in the social intercourse in society.'

Reciprocal rights are more likely than nonreciprocal rights to ensure an even balance of power in a marriage and are less likely to encroach unequally on the other rights of each spouse. However, mutual rights must be evaluated with reference to other inherent rights and responsibilities, as well as with reference to the reality of women's lives in each context. Women's capacity to fulfil their obligations is frequently limited by their unequal socio-economic status. Consequently, a theoretically mutual responsibility can be, in practice, more burdensome for women.

In Bangladesh, India, and Pakistan, the law permits spouses to file for restitution of conjugal rights. While this provision is equally available to both spouses, it is almost always used by husbands to harass wives who have left the marital home following domestic violence or disputes, rather than by wives to ensure sexual fulfillment. In a well-publicized case in Bangladesh, Nellie Zaman's husband countered her suit for divorce with a suit for restitution of conjugal rights. The court rejected his petition as being against the equality provisions of the constitution (34 DLR 1982 p.221).

inherent rights recognized in all systems

There are certain inherent rights presumed to arise out of marriage (whether it is conceived as a contract or sacrament), which are common to all the systems examined here. These rights can be circumscribed, expanded or limited through negotiations, but they can never be negotiated away. These include maintenance, sexual rights/co-habitation, and rights relating to children (guardianship, maintenance and paternity). In systems based on Muslim laws, inheritance is also a presumed right that cannot be negotiated away.

The legally recognized paternity of children conceived during a marriage is assumed by most systems to be an inherent consequence of marriage. However, various time limits may be applied in order to determine recognized paternity. These limits are discussed in Status of Children, p.231.

Maintenance is most often stipulated in terms of food, clothing, and accommodation (see Maintenance, p.217). Some laws specify the level of maintenance required, with many stipulating that the level of maintenance should be in keeping with the husband's financial means. Some laws also stipulate that the level of maintenance should not be less than that which the wife is normally accustomed to.

In Egypt, the wife loses her right to maintenance if she is convicted of apostasy. However, her marriage remains valid.

co-habitation and sexual rights

Joint residence is established as a consequence of marriage in all the systems dealt with here. Furthermore, sexual availability and access are presumed to be extensions of joint residence. Where a husband has a right to practice polygyny, a wife's right to cohabitation and sexual access is severely restricted. (Her maintenance and inheritance rights are likewise restricted.)

In many systems couples have a duty to cohabit and unreasonable refusal to do so is grounds for divorce. However, in some of these systems, courts are permitted to consider potential physical or moral danger as a reasonable basis for granting permission to a woman to live with her children apart from her husband (Cameroon).

In systems influenced by the Maliki School and/or the Napoleonic Code, the husband has the right to determine where the couple will live. In other contexts where the law stipulates that rights are mutual, the courts may recognize inequitable customary practices that allow the husband to determine the residence. For example, in Fiji the lower courts have accepted the Indo-Fijian custom, wherein the wife lives with her in-laws, as a valid basis for granting husbands the right to compel their wives to live in the husband's natal family home.

One spouse's refusal to live with the other spouse without reasonable cause (which may be variously interpreted) can lead to a denial of maintenance (in the case that the refusing spouse is a woman), divorce, or a suit for the restitution of conjugal rights. Because women also have a right to cohabitation with their spouse, they have the presumed right to sexual access as well. Indeed, a husband's failure to provide sexual fulfillment constitutes a valid grounds for dissolution in most systems. However, taboos against women claiming sexual fulfillment can limit women's ability to claim this inherent right. Nevertheless, a wife's threat to hold a husband publicly accountable for his failure to fulfill her sexually can increase her power to resolve other disputes. Women in working-class neighbourhoods of Cairo, as well as in Sudan, have been known to use this threat to counter domestic violence.

Various laws reflect diverging positions concerning a wife's right to refuse sexual relations (and cohabitation) on the grounds that prompt mahr has not been paid. In some systems, the wife cannot refuse sexual relations on these grounds if the marriage has been consummated (Iran), but in others the husband's refusal to pay prompt mahr is a valid defence to a suit for restitution of conjugal rights (Bangladesh, Pakistan, Sri Lanka).

No matter what laws state about sexual access, social practice often demands that the wife make herself available to the husband upon his request. Indeed, by failing to recognize marital rape, most systems implicitly deny a wife the right to refuse sexual intercourse. Fiji is an exception since the UK House of Lords decision R v R [1991] 1 WLR 767, which held that the offence of rape does apply within a marriage if, in the circumstances of the case, the wife does not consent to sexual intercourse.

negotiable 'inherent' rights

Most systems based on Muslim laws presume that men have an inherent right to divorce while women do not. The resultant power imbalance between spouses impacts the exercise of any other rights in such a marriage. Similarly, in most systems based on Muslim and customary laws, the husband is presumed to have the right to contract polygynous marriages, while the wife has no such parallel right. However, these 'inherent' rights can be subject to negotiated conditions in a marriage contract (see Negotiated Rights and Responsibilities, p.167).

But in some systems based on Muslim laws, these apparently 'inherent' rights are no longer recognized. A reassessment of public policy has resulted in reforms in several countries. Indonesia and Tunisia, for example, do not recognize the man's right to exercise unilateral talaq. In addition, Tunisia has prohibited polygyny altogether, and Indonesia has made it illegal for government officers to contract polygynous marriages (see Polygyny, p.197, and Talaq, p.255).

'obedience'

In many systems based on Muslim laws, it is the wife's duty to be 'obedient' to her husband (Iran, Malaysia, Morocco, Sudan). However, there are exceptions (Bangladesh, Pakistan).

Socially, as well as in some laws, obedience may be defined as an inherent duty. However, even in systems that codify 'obedience,' the terms of that obedience can be negotiated. For example, negotiated clauses in a marriage contract may give a wife the right to choose her work or the right to refuse to relocate when her husband takes a job in another area (see Negotiated Rights and Responsibilities, p169).

Systems that legislate the wife's duty to 'obey' her husband have different provisions concerning 'disobedience.' In Malaysia a women who wilfully disobeys an order from her husband is liable to a fine (although this is hardly implemented today). Other systems make disobedience grounds for withholding maintenance (Egypt). Still others make disobedience grounds for divorce. In Sudan the nashiz (disobedient) wife is considered neither divorced nor married. She is deprived of the right to maintenance, matrimonial residence, and custody of her children. In extreme cases, restrictions are imposed on her freedom of movement within and outside the country.

Of course, social attitudes and traditions may differ from the law. In Pakistan, the superior courts recognize that a wife may live separately from her husband and still be entitled to maintenance, if she has 'reasonable cause' to do so. Reasonable causes include cruel conduct of the husband, the husband's interference with the wife's property (including non payment of mahr), and the husband's interference with the wife's religious belief. Still, because of community beliefs and practices, many women that leave their marital homes under such circumstances no longer receive maintenance once they have returned to their natal families.

fidelity and chastity

Many laws, either in their texts or in their interaction with other laws, apply different standards to husbands and wives concerning the right to fidelity.

Morocco's Moudawana lists amongst the rights of the husband, 'the preservation of the wife's body and chastity,' and Iran stipulates that wives are to be loyal and faithful. Neither system provides wives with similar rights over husbands. In Fiji and Sudan, husbands are only considered to have violated the law if they are adulterous in their own homes. Women are considered adulterous if they engage in any extramarital sexual act, regardless of the location.

Above all, where polygyny is a legal possibility, the husband is, by definition, excused from fidelity to his existing wife. She is nevertheless obligated to remain faithful. However, laws may place restrictions on a husband's adulterous activities. For example, in Cameroon a husband can be held liable for adultery if he has sexual intercourse with his fiancée in his marital home (Cameroon). In other cases the courts may not permit a polygynous union between a man and a woman with whom the he had an earlier affair (Singapore).

husband as 'head of household'

Because of the husband's obligation to financially maintain the household, many systems define him as the head of the household. In some systems, this definition is codified (Cameroon, Indonesia, Iran, Senegal) and in others it is presumed. Even where the law does not codify a husband's position as the head of the household, other administrative procedures or requirements can have a similar effect. In addition, many communities regard the husband as the 'head of household,' regardless of how he is defined by state laws and procedures.

Such laws, procedures, and attitudes often do not reflect the realities of women's lives (see Maintenance, p.217-218). International and national labour migration trends have resulted in large numbers of wives operating as heads of households when migrant husbands are absent. There have been few legal changes to reflect this new reality. Such a gap in law and reality can create real logistical problems for families. For example, if a wife in such a family is not recognized as a head of household, how is she to access provisions requiring the signature of the absent 'head of household?'

The status of 'head of household' brings a wide range of possible powers. In some systems, a husband's position as 'head of household' gives him the right to restrict the wife's mobility. For example, in both Iran and Egypt, a wife must have her husband's authorization to travel and to obtain a passport. Also, husbands may be given the right to determine whether or not (and under what conditions) wives may work or study, what they may study, and what type of work they may do (Cameroon). States may further reinforce such rights by requiring women to obtain their husband's permission to work in government jobs (the Sudan).

The husband's powers as 'head of household" often extend to controlling marital property. Unless the couple clearly negotiates how marital property will be controlled (and by whom) in their marriage contract, the husband's right to control the marital property may be presumed or even directly provided for in laws (Philippines, Senegal). Such laws undermine a wife's right (under Muslims laws) to control any wealth that she has or creates.

Not all systems give the husband such sweeping powers. Several systems based on Muslim laws, as well as on other sources, have enacted legislation designed to strengthen the wife's position in marriage. The Fiji courts follow British common law, and after changes to common law in the 1980s, 'equal right of consortium over each other' has been interpreted to mean that the husband cannot prevent his wife from leaving the matrimonial home; cannot kidnap her and keep her locked away; and cannot demand love, affection and sexual services unless he reciprocally offers these same.

In other systems, the courts have interpreted existing laws in such a way as to strengthen women's position in marriage. In Pakistan, for example, social attitudes grant men superior status in the family. This superior status is reinforced by the state in numerous ways, including the use of administrative forms that require the husband's signature (even when the wife is the sole applicant for a service), as well as laws that presume the wife's domicile follows that of her husband. However, whenever women have challenged their husband's right to control their mobility, the superior courts have affirmed a woman's right to autonomy.

While administrative measures that confirm the husband as 'head of household' can be as limiting as similar laws, they are often easier to change. Reforming family laws can be extremely difficult, especially where related issues have become politicized by extreme right wing politico-religious groups. Changes in administrative procedures may be less controversial.

sharing of household responsibilities

Where laws codify household responsibilities, these are most commonly assigned to the wife as a duty. In most such systems, the husband is charged with financial maintenance and the wife with the physical maintenance or supervision of the household (Iran, Indonesia). But this apparently equitable sharing of responsibilities does not bring equal status. For example, Indonesia laws define the husband as 'head of household' and the wife as 'mother of the household,' giving the wife equal responsibility but not equal status.

Such provisions ignore the reality that women may either contribute to family income through labour on the family farm or business, or through paid employment outside the home. In an interesting twist, Iranian laws recognize that the domestic services rendered by the wife do have a financial value. In the event that the husband divorces the wife, the husband may owe the wife payment for all domestic services rendered (see p.165).

Some systems assign household responsibilities to husbands as well. Laws in Fiji, for example, require that household responsibilities, including childcare, be shared equally amongst both spouses.

Amended Turkish Civil Code Removes Husband's Position as 'Head of Household'

Following widespread campaigning by a united platform of 126 women's groups in 2000-2001, the Turkish Civil Code was drastically amended, overcoming resistance from conservative religious groups and nationalists.

The new Civil Code has taken a new approach to the family and women's role in the family. The old legal approach, which assigned women a legislatively subordinate position in the family, with rights and duties defined in respect to the husband, has been abandoned in favour of an approach that defines the family as a union based on equal partnership. This new approach is reflected in the language of the new Code. The terms 'the wife' and 'the husband' are replaced by 'the spouses.' The new approach to the family is reflected in several other changes as well:

- The husband is no longer the head of the family; spouses are equal partners, jointly running the matrimonial union with equal decision-making powers;
- Spouses have equal rights over the family residence;
- Spouses have equal rights over property acquired during the marriage;
- Spouses have equal powers to represent the family.

The *New* Legal Status of Women in Turkey, Women for Women's Human Rights – New Ways, Istanbul, 2002

NOTES

LAWS: Marriage Contracts - Inherent Rights and Responsibilities

Criteria

☺ More option-giving are those laws which:
- Specify equal rights of the spouses over each other.

😐 The middle ground is occupied by those laws which:
- Do not codify obedience; and/or
- Do not codify the husband as head of household.

The lower middle ground is occupied by those laws which:
- Do not codify obedience, or do not define the husband as 'head of household' but confer other powers to the husband, which are not shared by the wife.

☹ Less option-giving are those laws which:
- Codify obedience and give the husband powers of control over the wife.

☺ **Rights and responsibilities of spouses are equal**

Turkey: Under A. 41 of the CC amended in 2001, the family is based on equality between spouses. Under the new A. 186, the spouses have joint decision-making powers regarding the family. They contribute towards family expenditures through their labour and possessions, in accordance with their capabilities. Under the new A. 186, the spouses jointly decide the place of the marital residence. Under A. 185 the spouses must cohabit (repealing the old provision that the wife had to live where the husband lived). Under the new A. 194, the spouses have equal rights over all matters relating to the family home, and neither can independently change a rental agreement or sell the family home. Under the new A. 189, the husband is no longer the sole representative of the union, nor does he have sole control over the family savings. Under A. 187, the wife can retain her own name after marriage. Under the new A. 192, neither spouse requires the other's permission to work or to choose a profession. (However, A. 192(2) requires that the harmony and welfare of the marriage union should be borne in mind when choosing and performing a job or profession.) No law can force a wife to return to live with her husband; if she leaves the marital home, the husband's only option is to apply for divorce.

Fiji: Following changes to British common law in the 1980s, spouses have equal rights of consortium over each other (includes housework & child care, love, affection and sexual services). The husband cannot prevent his wife from leaving the matrimonial home or restrict her mobility. Provisions for restitution of conjugal rights are gender neutral, but are used by men to pre-empt the wife's demand for maintenance after she leaves due to cruelty. If the wife refuses to obey an order for restitution, any divorce suit by the husband is likely to be granted, and he will not have to pay maintenance for the period that she was not in the marital home.

Central Asian Republics: Provisions in the Soviet Family Code, which stipulated a mutual obligation of spousal maintenance, have not been changed following independence in the early 1990s. For example, under A. 22 of the Family Code of the Kyrgyz Republic, women and men have the same rights and duties in marriage, and spouses should care for each other and develop their own abilities. Similarly, A. 1 of the Uzbekistan Family Law envisages family relations based on mutual affection, trust and respect, cooperation, mutual support and responsibility of all family members and the unhindered enjoyment by family members of their rights.

Indonesia: The rights and responsibilities of the wife are equivalent to the rights and responsibilities of the husband in the life of the household and in the social intercourse in society. Under A. 31 of the MA, the husband and wife shall bear the lofty responsibility of maintaining a household. The husband is head of the family, and the wife is the mother of the household. Under A. 30, both parents are responsible for the maintenance and education of children. Under A. 31(3), the husband shall protect the wife and provide her with all the necessities of life in accordance with his capabilities, while under A. 34 the wife shall take care of the household to the best of her ability.

Tunisia: Under A. 23 of the CSP, amended by Law No. 93-74 of July 12, 1993, the spouses are to treat each other with kindness, make their conjugal life pleasant, and refrain from causing each other harm. The spouses are to fulfil their conjugal duties in accordance with custom and usage. They are to cooperate in running the affairs of the household and in ensuring the proper upbringing of children. This amendment replaces the original A. 23, which required the wife to obey the husband and did not envisage mutual responsibilities. However, the husband remains head of the family and as such is responsible for the needs of the wife and children according to his means and their status. The wife is to participate in supporting the family if she has money. Under A. 24 the husband has no right over the wife's money.

'Obedience' is not codified; the law does not state the husband is head of household

Bangladesh & Pakistan: Under S. 9 of the MFLO, inherent rights and responsibilities include the husband's responsibility to maintain his wife 'adequately' (and 'equitably' if more than 1 wife). Mutual inheritance follows the principles of Muslim laws. Other inherent rights are understood from the DMMA, including the wife's right to control her own property and follow her own religion. Case law further interprets the DMMA to reject any right of the husband to control the wife's mobility and profession. In both countries until 2000, provisions for restitution of conjugal rights were gender neutral, and the superior courts generally rejected attempts by husbands to use this provision to harass wives who have left the marital home due to the husband's unreasonable behaviour (Nellie Zaman case, 34 DLR 1982 p.221). However, since an amendment to the Family Courts Act in **Pakistan**, husbands have a statutory option to file for conjugal rights in the event that the wife files for maintenance or dissolution.

Pakistan: While the law does not codify any requirement that the wife has to take the husband's name or have his permission for work or travel, laws in other areas appear to grant men superior status in the family. Under domicile provisions, a woman who had joined government service before marrying retains her domicile after marriage, but a woman who joins government service after marrying looses her original domicile and acquires the domicile of her husband. These provisions affect a woman's access to government jobs (which often require candidates to be domiciled in a specific area of the country); they have been unsuccessfully challenged in court. On marrying, a woman has to have her national identity card revised to replace her father/guardian's name with her husband's name. If she is applying for a passport and does not change the names, she can have a passport issued for only one year; the passport is extendable for a further four years provided she has her national identity card revised. Case law establishes that a husband cannot restrict his wife's mobility (Muhammad Tufail v Muhammad Hanif 1984 MLD 1489; Haji Hafiz Ali v Noor Muhammad & Others 1983 PCrLJ 204; Muhammad Qasim v Haji Saleh 1997 PCrLJ 1014).

India (marriages under Muslim laws): Mutual inheritance follows the principles of Muslim laws. Other inherent rights are understood from the DMMA, including the wife's right to control her own property and follow her own religion.

Sri Lanka: Under S. 98 of the MMDA, the mutual rights and obligations of the parties are determined by the law of the sect to which the parties belong. There is no indication of how rights and obligations are to be determined in the event that parties belong to different sects. The PC does not recognize the husband's right of reasonable chastisement as defence to assault. Under S. 47(1)(b) of the MMDA, the husband is to maintain the wife. In case of non-payment of prompt mahr, domestic violence, or failure to provide separate accommodations (for more than one wife), the wife may refuse sexual access as well as refuse to live with the husband.

Obedience is not codified, but the husband is head of household or has other powers of control over the wife

Philippines: The spouses have the right to cohabit, to have mutual respect and fidelity, to render mutual help and support, to inherit from one another, and to initiate divorce. Under A. 67(1) of the CMPL, the wife has a right to maintenance, and under A. 36(1) she must dutifully manage the affairs of the house and purchase things necessary for the maintenance of the family, for which purchases the husband is bound to reimburse the wife. Under A. 35, the husband has the right to decide the marital residence unless the mahr has not been paid or the dwelling is not in keeping with the wife's social status. The wife controls any property she brings into the marriage, but the CMPL presumes a community of property regime and, therefore, she cannot acquire property without the husband's permission. Under A. 36(3), a wife's right to engage in any profession or business is conditional upon the husband's consent as well as upon the job being 'in keeping with Islamic modesty and virtue.' Under the general law applicable to other communities, husbands do not have such powers, and all rights and responsibilities are joint.

Senegal: The spouses are obliged to cohabit, to be mutually faithful, to provide support and care, to share a communal life, to show each other respect and affection, and to offer moral and material assistance when needed. However, under A. 277 of the CF, the husband is the head of the family, and he has primary authority over the children during the marriage. Accordingly, his decision overrides his wife's in the event that they disagree— that is, provided his decision is based on the interests of the family (A.287). Under A. 153, the husband has the right to choose the marital home; the wife has to live there with him (and he has to accept her there), provided doing so does not bring physical or moral danger to the family. The wife can, as an exception in the event of physical or moral danger, be authorized by the departmental judge to have a separate residence for herself and her children. Under A. 375, the husband has primary responsibility for family expenses, but the spouses contribute according to their respective capacity. Each of the spouses has the power to enter into contracts regarding the household expenses, and spouses are liable for debts contracted by the other spouse. Under A. 371 and 374, the wife may follow any profession, and both partners may independently open and operate bank accounts.

Cameroon: The husband is the head of the family. The wife is obliged to live with him and he to receive her. Married couples have a duty to cohabit, and unreasonable refusal by one party is grounds for divorce. Under A. 212 of the CSO, the spouses have a duty to remain faithful. Spouses have a duty of mutual assistance, which includes supplying each other's needs and necessities for existence and attending to each other. The court may permit the wife to live apart with her child, if the residence chosen by the husband is proven to pose physical and moral danger. The husband has full powers of administration over the family property. The husband has the right to object to his wife's professional or commercial activity.

☹ 'Obedience' is codified

Malaysia: Under S. 129 of the IFLA, any woman who wilfully disobeys any order that was given by her husband and lawful according to Hukum Syariah' commits an offence and shall be punished with a fine not exceeding RM 100 (approx US$ 26) or in the case of a second or subsequent offence, with a fine not exceeding RM 500 (approx US$ 130). This broad provision is contrasted with the specific responsibilities allocated to the husband under sections 126-128 requiring him to cohabit, not to ill-treat the wife, and to give 'proper justice' to her. The husband is liable to the same fines as the wife if he fails to fulfill his responsibilities. Under Section 59, the husband is to maintain the wife, but she is not entitled to maintenance when she is nushyuz (unreasonably refuses to obey the lawful wishes or commands of her husband). She will be considered nushyuz for such acts of 'disobedience' as refusing to have sex, leaving the husband's home against his will, or refusing to move with him to another home or place without valid reason.

Iran: The husband is to provide economically for the wife, and she is to be loyal and faithful. Both husband and wife are to be respectful of each other and perform their Islamic responsibilities. The husband is the head and manager of the household. Under A. 1105 of the CC, a wife is not to leave the house without her husband's permission, and, if she does so, she can be declared 'nashezeh', depriving her of economic rights. Under A. 1105 and 1114, a wife requires her husband's written, certified permission to obtain a passport and to travel abroad. A wife is to reside in the husband's home (that is, she is to be a state of tamkin, which presumes sexual availability) to qualify for maintenance. She can keep her own family name. Women in mut'a marriages have more mobility rights than women in permanent marriages, but they have fewer rights to maintenance and inheritance.

Egypt: The wife has a right to maintenance if she submits herself to her husband and does not leave the matrimonial home without his permission (permission may be unnecessary under special circumstances). Maintenance cannot be forfeited if the wife goes out for lawful work, provided she does not abuse her right to work and also provided that her working is not contrary to the interests of the family. A husband reserves the right to determine if a wife's work is contrary to the interests of the family, and he is, therefore, not obligated to provide maintenance in the event that he has asked her to refrain from working, and she continues to do so.

Morocco: Under A. 34 of the Moudawana, spouses have mutual duties and rights, including cohabitation, good companionship, mutual respect and affection, the preservation of the interests of the family, mutual inheritance, and the legitimacy of children. However, A. 35 and 36 specify different rights of the husband and wife with regard to each other. The husband is to provide maintenance (food, clothing, medical care, accommodation); treat wives with equity and equality; allow the wife to visit her family and receive them in accordance with custom; and not interfere in her property. The wife is to preserve her body and chastity, obey her husband according to custom, breastfeed the children if she is able to do so, supervise the household and its affairs, and respect her husband's parents and relatives according to custom.

Sudan: Under S. 51 of the MPLA, the wife's rights include maintenance, permission to visit her family and relatives, good and fair treatment that does not violate any of her material and non-material rights, and equal treatment with her co-wives in the event of polygyny. Under S. 52, the wife is to serve and obey the husband (except in committing a sin) and to maintain her husband and herself with her husband's money. Obedience to the husband is an obligation on the wife that starts at the time the husband pays mahr and provides the matrimonial home. Breach in obedience gives the husband the right to withdraw maintenance. Under S. 75, 'disobedience' includes leaving the matrimonial home without a legal justification, working outside the home without the husband's permission and approval, or refusing to travel with the husband without a legally justified reason. Under S. 92, 'disobedience' renders a wife 'nashiz,' and she is declared neither divorced nor married. She is deprived of maintenance (including matrimonial residence) and custody of the children. The MPLA cancelled the compulsory restoration of the wife to the matrimonial home. Using peaceful means, the husband may attempt to restore the wife twice. The wife has the right to initiate a legal claim to negate the obedience lawsuit. The 1977 amendments gave a wife who has deserted her matrimonial home and been declared 'nashiz' by a court order, the right to apply for divorce if certain conditions have been met. These include: the passage of two years since the declaration and her willingness to pay compensation to the husband.

IMPLEMENTATION

Positive interpretations of inherent rights

Cameroon: A husband was held liable for adultery for having sexual intercourse with his fiancee in his marital home, even though he was in a polygamous marriage (S.C. order n.181 of 19th November 1979).

Fiji: While lower courts have cited a wife's refusal to follow Indo-Fijian custom (which requires a wife to live with her in-laws) as grounds for refusing maintenance, higher courts have not supported the view that the wife must live with in-laws.

Negative interpretations of inherent rights

Fiji: Provisions for the restitution of conjugal rights are gender neutral. However, when a wife leaves the marital home to escape abuse, sometimes her husband will use these provisions to pre-empt her demand for maintenance. If the wife refuses to obey the order, the courts usually grant the husband a divorce and do not order him to pay maintenance for the period after she left the home.

Iran: The law requires the wife to respect her husband. What constitutes a lack of respect is left to the interpretation of judges. Most judges are extremely conservative in their background and training. Consequently, often their interpretations of respect require that the wife must be tamkin (remain in her husband's house, also implying sexual availability).

The husband has rights that are conditional upon his fulfillment of responsibilities

Nigeria: The husband is considered the head of the household to whom obedience is due from the wife. There is acceptance that such obedience is conditional upon the husband fulfilling his responsibilities. These include providing maintenance, permitting reasonable visits to family and friends, and not interfering with his wife's religious duties. However, a wife's only recourse, in the event that the husband fails to fulfill these responsibilities, is to ask her family to pressure him and, if that fails, seek a divorce.

Negative practices concerning inherent rights

Cameroon: Husbands frequently abuse their legal powers of administration over family property.

Morocco: Husbands are assumed to be economically dominant, and this dominance is presumed to require the wife submission and obedience. However, in Morocco today many wives provide all or some of the family's support because the husband is unemployed. Even in such cases, the husband retains his right to submission and obedience.

Senegal: Neither customs nor local interpretations of religion provide for equal gender relations. While wives and husbands are given equal rights to engage in their religious observations and to have access to conjugal relations, these rights do little to offset the usually assumed right of husbands to demand obedience and submission. One imam's interpretation of custom and Muslim laws led him to state (when questioned by the GREFELS Women & Law research team) that the wife owes obedience and submission to the husband within the prescribed limits: she must not go out of the house without her husband's permission, and her visits to relatives must not harm the husband's interests. In addition, according to this imam, the wife must supervise the education of the children and manage the household without being wasteful. If she fails to adhere to these rules, her husband is permitted to verbally correct her, refuse sexual relations, and also physically punish her (in that order, clearly paraphrasing an interpretation of the Qur'anic verse, Surah Al-Nisa:34).

Sudan: The practice of declaring women 'nushuz' forces women in unhappy marriages to depend on their male relatives and also to refrain from demanding their rights.

PRACTICES

Positive practices concerning inherent rights

Iran: Although in conservative areas a wife is not socially permitted to reject her husband sexually, wives in urban areas may refuse conjugal relations in order to pressure their husbands. Women's open acknowledgement of this tactic has led to a conservative media backlash that has worked to the detriment of women's bargaining power.

Pakistan: In certain areas of Makran Division (Baluchistan), the bride remains in her natal home, and her husband moves in to join her (a practice known as (ghar damad). Any future change of residence requires the permission of the wife's parents, and the upholding of this practice can be made part of the marriage agreement. In Punjabi there are idioms clearly indicating that such a practice is distained, but the very existence of an idiom indicates that the practice does occur. This ghar damad condition can be and is made part of a marriage agreement in various communities.

Wages for Housework: Strategizing for Change in Iran

Men's arbitrary right to divorce and polygynous marriage in Iran has created financial and emotional havoc for women and their children, becoming a major source of dissatisfaction among women, even among religious and traditional social groups, which normally support the regime. It has also encouraged alternative interpretations of Muslim laws and legal texts by local Islamic women activists and also by more liberal religious and political leaders.

These reinterpretations led to the amendment of the divorce laws in 1993. The most significant aspect of this amendment was the introduction of wages for housework. However, demanding wages for one's work is not new in Iran's Civil Code. Article 336 states, "Anytime a person, according to the request of others, performs activities that are outside religious or customary responsibilities, he or she is entitled to receive fair wages for what she or he has done, unless it is known that the person has done this in order to have other benefits." Hence, it would be possible for a wife to receive wages for work performed in the home based on this law, assuming that a sympathetic judge heard the case. However, since this possibility was not explicit, women often did not know that they had this right. The introduction of the new law has made it easier for judges to see the demands of women. Moreover, because of the publicity, which has surrounded this subject, women are increasingly conscious of their rights in this context.

This law has been very controversial. Many conservative religious leaders, including members of the Assembly of Religious Experts (majlis-i-khobragan), who ratify all laws passed by the parliament, disagree with the amendment. They believe that according to the law, women have a duty to educate the children, maintain good relations with their husbands; and do domestic chores. Accordingly, the performance of these tasks does not entitle the wife to wages. While the law was passed by the parliament, which has tended to be sensitive to public opinion, it was rejected by the Assembly of Religious Experts. Using special powers foreseen by the constitution (under Article 112), however, the government bypassed the Assembly of Experts, and the wages for housework provision became law.

The implementation of this law remains difficult. Neither women nor the courts are sure of the conditions under which women can apply to be paid for housework. On many occasions, it was assumed that women could only apply for the wages after the divorce was registered. To reduce the confusion, in 1995 the parliament made it compulsory for men to pay the wages for housework along with the wife's other rights, such as mahr and nafaqa, before the divorce could be registered.

According to Article 1 of the amendment of the Divorce Law, the wife may request payment for work she has performed that has been outside her religious responsibility. If the divorce was at the husband's request and the wife is not at fault, the sum is based on the length of time the couple lived together and the activities the wife performed, as well as the husband's financial situation. If the husband has no money, then it appears that the wife will not be paid.

In the four years that have passed since the law came into effect, the legislators have neither provided clarification nor ensured consistent interpretation of the law in the courts. Different courts frequently come to different conclusions. It is also doubtful that this law has made a substantial difference in the financial situation of women who are divorced, because of so few husbands are able to pay. However, the law has symbolic significance because it recognizes women's economic contribution through their unpaid work. This law has opened the way for other unconventional interpretations of Muslim laws and statutory laws. Moreover, it demonstrates that, under public pressure, the regime acknowledges the unfair state of the legal position of women in marriage and divorce.

While the wages for housework law discriminates in favour of women, it is clear that its intent was to compensate for the disadvantages that women face in marriage. Even so, it is a corrective move and not a total compensation for women's rights, which are currently denied in marriage (as marriage is defined by the current laws). The women based their demand for legal reform on alternative interpretations of Muslim laws and legal texts. These laws have opened the way for other progressive interpretations of Muslim laws and statutory laws in an environment where women have suffered from the many retrogressive changes introduced after the 1979 Revolution.

Hoodfar, H. (ed.) (1996), WLUML Special Dossier: Shifting Boundaries in Marriage and Divorce in Muslim Communities, WLUML, Grabels

5d MARRIAGE CONTRACTS: NEGOTIATED RIGHTS AND RESPONSIBILITIES

introduction

Negotiated rights are those rights or conditions that can be negotiated and made part of a marriage agreement. These can expand or limit the presumed rights and duties of both spouses, as well as allow for additional rights.

Generally, negotiated rights are applicable only in systems that regard marriage as a contract, i.e., those based on Muslim laws. However, systems based on other laws may or may not recognize 'pre-nuptial' agreements appended to a marriage certificate.

Local customs frequently determine the social possibility of negotiating the terms of marriage. Thus, in Saudi Arabia parties negotiate most aspects of the agreement while in Sri Lanka the concept of negotiating conditions to a marriage contract does not exist. Where negotiations do take place, these can be facilitated through standard marriage contracts or through registration forms that either have spaces to write in additional negotiated clauses or ask if specific conditions have been negotiated (for example, asking if the right of talaq has been delegated to the wife).

Negotiated clauses are crucial to determining the balance of power between spouses; they can offer women an important means of addressing gender inequalities. These clauses clarify the mutual obligations amongst spouses, and such clarity can prevent the intrusion of undesirable customs. They also facilitate mechanisms for relief (which otherwise may not be available) to be used in the event that obligations are not met. For example, clauses may grant access to divorce if certain contractual obligations are not met.

The range of issues negotiated may be rather wide, including levels of maintenance, place of residence, employment options, educational options, access to mobility, access to travel, division of household responsibilities, standards of living, breastfeeding options, control of property, polygyny restrictions, access to divorce, and standards for the husband's emotional treatment of the wife. Just as local custom often determines whether or not negotiation will take place, it likewise determines what issues can be negotiated. Mahr is an essential element of Muslim marriage, but its quantity and form can be negotiated and recorded in the contract. Mahr is discussed in greater detail on p.179.

That the ability to negotiate some rights exists at all is encouraging. However, lack of access to such provisions and social stigmas that discourage women – and their families - from asserting their rights limit the use and effectiveness of negotiation possibilities.

agency

Where women's agency is greater, women (either the bride or other women in the two families) may be involved in negotiating marriage contracts. However, in many communities, men from the two families conduct the negotiations amongst themselves. In Saudi Arabia negotiations occur amongst the men, but there is significant room for the mothers and the bride to intervene, and negotiations are vigorously and seriously attended to. In Egypt the bride is party to the negotiations and can give significant input into the process.

In contexts where negotiations take place long before the wedding, rather than actually at the time of the marriage ceremony, there may be more space for negotiators to address controversial conditions and convince any unwilling party. This does not, however, prevent others from obstructing the agreed conditions at the last moment. It is not uncommon for imams who are solemnizing a marriage to ignore or object to conditions that the couple and their families have agreed to.

Most negotiations occur prior to a marriage. However, it is socially or legally possible for new conditions to be attached to an existing marriage contract, provided these are written (as opposed to oral) and attested to by witnesses.

marriage as a contract

European and related systems of law view marriage as a sacrament and not as a contract. Where marriage laws do not recognize that Muslim marriage functions as a contract, the options for negotiation may also be curtailed. However, much depends upon whether the law recognizes additional documents drawn up at the time of marriage. (Laws in Cameroon and South Africa do recognize separate agreements as civil contracts, provided they are registered as such.) Even if the law recognizes such agreements, women may not be aware of their right to make such contracts.

While Senegal's Code de la Famille considers marriage a contract, it does not mention the possibility of negotiating conditions, apart from pre-agreed financial provisions, such as the amount of mahr (non-payment becomes a grounds for dissolution). This omission may have occurred because, in Senegal grounds for dissolution are very wide (including incompatibility), and the presumption is that negotiated conditions address only disputes and divorce. But negotiated conditions, if clear and genuinely mutually agreed upon, can pre-empt such disputes. The option of polygyny/monogamy is to be stated by the husband, and his decision on this issue is not conceived to be a mutually negotiated one (although this may be the case in practice).

Women's rights activists have focused considerable effort on increasing the possibilities for negotiated clauses in marriage contracts. They have worked as well to improve the wording of other optional clauses in order to maximize the rights-promoting and rights-protecting potential of these clauses.

Whether systems based on Muslim laws provide space for the insertion of additional conditions to standardized marriage contracts or not, they generally permit negotiated conditions only if these do 'not go against the principles of marriage.' Moreover, certain rights are regarded as inherent (see p.153) and so, theoretically at least, cannot be completely negotiated away. For example, the wife's right to maintenance and the husband's power of talaq are often defined as inherent rights. However, the couple can agree that they will share household expenses and that, if the husband pronounces talaq, he will pay the wife a certain sum in addition to any mahr due. While such an agreement does not eliminate a husband's right to pronounce talaq, it may prevent him from being able to afford to do so. In some systems, the rights of third parties cannot be negotiated, e.g. the child (or children's) right to maintenance is not subject to negotiated conditions.

women's right to divorce

A women's right to initiate divorce may be negotiated as well. This right can take the form of unconditional or conditional talaq tafwid (see p.267), or a ta'liq (see p.285). Commonly negotiated conditions, under which a wife may resort to talaq tafwid or a ta'liq, include if the husband renders the marriage polygynous, if he fails to maintain her, if he is unable to engage in conjugal relations or is impotent, if he does not treat her appropriately or treats her with cruelty, if he is or becomes insane, or if he does not meet other terms of the marriage contract. Most option-giving are those contexts where standard marriage contracts include these automatically (Iran, Malaysia) or, at least, ask whether or not there has been such an agreement made (Bangladesh, Pakistan).

Other aspects of divorce that can be negotiated include property settlements and post-divorce maintenance. Sometimes, child custody arrangements (in the event of divorce) are negotiated as well. Whether or not these arrangements are legally recognized depends upon local laws. Still, even if not recognized, such an agreements may serve as evidence in court.

Nevertheless, negotiating the terms and conditions of the husband's power of talaq can have complications. If the husband faces a heavy penalty for talaq, he may use violence to force the wife to seek dissolution herself. The burden will then be on the wife to prove this violence, and providing proof of violence is not always possible (see Other Forms of Dissolution for Women, p.281). Also, unless settlement of talaq-related penalties takes place before a divorce certificate is issued (Iran), women may have to enter into lengthy court proceedings to recover any financial settlement (Pakistan).

negotiating other rights and responsibilities

Even where standard contracts or marriage registration forms do not include space for negotiated rights and responsibilities, spouses can agree on the conditions of their marriage. Here we only discuss some of the more common conditions, but many others are possible, depending upon the couple's specific concerns.

Many women include a provision that restricts the husband's ability to take an additional wife (Egypt, Iran, Morocco). Where this is included in the contract, the wife will not have to show damage in requesting a judicial divorce.

Women may negotiate where they will live to ensure that they will not have to live far away from their families. They can also ensure that the couple will live separately from the husband's family (Saudi Arabia). If such an agreement is added to a wife's marriage contract, she cannot be denied maintenance on the grounds of 'disobedience' (see Maintenance, p.218) in the event that she leaves the marital home because of continuing conflict with her in-laws, and her husband refuses to move out of his parents' home.

Particularly in contexts where husbands have a legal and/or social power to control their wife's right to go out of the house, it can be useful to negotiate the freedom to travel and own a passport, to work outside the house, and to study without having to have the husband's permission.

Negotiated conditions can be simple or extremely detailed. For example, spouses may negotiate the terms of study for both partners and include in these further conditions to accommodate the time and resources required for their studies (Egypt, Jordan).

Negotiating household responsibilities can help to ensure an equitable sharing when both partners are employed. Negotiations on this issue may also serve to address and challenge assumptions regarding gender roles in the household. Where women are fully responsible for household duties, it may be possible for women to claim payment for household work (in Iran this has become an inherent right of women who are not 'at fault' in divorce).

Negotiated maintenance guarantees the wife a specific quality and quantity of maintenance and does not leave her at the mercy of invariably low maintenance decrees (see Maintenance, p.217).

In addition to negotiating basic maintenance, a woman may negotiate that her husband shall provide higher maintenance during the breastfeeding period or that he shall provide her with pocket money. Although such payments are not mentioned in Malaysia's law, the courts will recognize these agreements. While compensation for breast-feeding may be welcomed by mothers, it nevertheless reinforces the view that the children are the 'property' of their father, and the mother is merely a 'service-provider' for the father.

Some systems provide for couples to negotiate property regimes as well. These range from joint ownership of all property brought into and created during the marriage to completely separate ownership of property. Some systems the statutory law distinguishes between property and wealth earned during the subsistence of the marriage and property and wealth brought into the marriage (Turkey, Morocco, Philippines). In other systems, the property regime has to be specified in the marriage documents (Cameroon, Senegal). Negotiating a property regime allows a couple to work out a property arrangement that suits their specific circumstances and ensures that neither party suffers economically in the event of dissolution.

Although Muslim laws emphasising separate property regimes protect women's individual wealth, this protection may be unhelpful to women without any independent income or wealth. Separate property regimes also fail to address how the property and wealth created during a marriage will be distributed. They are likewise silent concerning how the financial losses incurred during the period that an employed woman takes time off from her job for child rearing will be shared. Thus, negotiating these matters in the marriage contract(s) can secure a woman's financial status.

accessing negotiated rights

Adding negotiated rights to a marriage contract corrects certain power imbalances between spouses and facilitates access to redress in the event of disputes by making the terms and conditions of the marriage clear. However, access to negotiated rights is not automatic in most systems. Moreover, even when women have added negotiated rights to their marriage agreements, they still may have to go before a forum and prove that a negotiated right has been violated before they can access any redress. Systems, and even individual judges, often differ over how much of the burden of proof they place on each party. For example, case law will show whether it is the husband who has to prove he has maintained the wife or the wife who has to provide proof of non-maintenance. Occasionally, the text of laws actually specifies whose word is to be taken as proof depending upon the nature of the dispute.

Nevertheless, certain negotiated rights require little proof to become accessible, for example, an unconditional talaq tafwid or a specific sum to be paid upon talaq by the husband. All that would be required to access such rights would be a copy of the marriage contract.

NOTES

LAWS: Negotiated Rights and Responsibilities

Criteria

☺ More option-giving are those laws which:

- Both explicitly recognize the possibility of negotiating rights and responsibilities; and
- Facilitate negotiation by having marriage contracts/registration forms that provide for specified and/or additional negotiated clauses.

😐 The middle ground is occupied by those laws which:

- Explicitly recognize the possibility of negotiating rights and responsibilities but do not facilitate negotiation through standard marriage contracts/registration forms.

The lower middle ground is occupied by laws which:

- Are silent about the possibility of negotiating conditions; or
- Do not see marriage as a negotiable contract but recognize 'nuptial agreements'.

☹ Less option-giving are those laws which:

- Explicitly prohibit additional agreements to a marriage.

☺ **Marriage contracts/registration forms include specified negotiated clauses and/or leave space for additional conditions**

Bangladesh & Pakistan: The standard marriage contract under the Rules of the MFLO carries provisions for talaq tafwid and restrictions on the husband's right of divorce (columns 18 & 19). There is no restriction on including any additional conditions, provided there is mutual agreement between the two parties. Column 17 allows for any special conditions. Column 20 allows for recording the details of any other documented stipulations relating to dower, maintenance, wife's pocket money, etc. Case law establishes which conditions can be negotiated. Custody of children may be negotiated, but no such negotiation will have legal effect, as the court will decide custody on the basis of the child's welfare (rather than on the basis of contractual conditions). Conditions stipulating exchange marriage also have no legal validity. Even where contractual clauses have been struck out, any subsequent agreement concerning negotiated rights holds legally valid.

Iran: A. 1119 of the CC allows either spouse to negotiate conditions to the marriage contract, provided the conditions do not go against the principles of marriage, and the standard marriage contract has room for additional conditions such as unconditional talaq tafwid. It is not legally valid to impose conditions that the law assumes encroach on the rights of third parties. For example, custody of children is thought to be the right of paternal grandfathers, as well as parents, and therefore, a wife cannot validly negotiate custody (in the event of dissolution) through her marriage contract. The standard marriage contract form introduced in 1987 contains 11 conditions under which the wife has access to talaq tafwid. These conditions are all related to some failure of or defect in the husband and include: his failure to pay maintenance; his failure to perform sexual obligations, his failure to reproduce, his failure to behave morally, his becoming insane, his developing a life-threatening disease, his imprisonment, his disappearance, and his failure to treat his wife justly. Both spouses sign each clause of the contract, signifying their acceptance of the agreed terms and conditions. The contract also offers the option that wealth accumulated during the marriage may be divided in half in the event of divorce. The wife benefits from these conditions only if she is not found to have failed in observing her obligations, specifically her obligation to 'obey' her husband.

Malaysia: Although the IFLA does not explicitly recognise the possibility of negotiating the terms and conditions of a marriage contract, it does recognize ta'liq, a suspended talaq available to the wife in the event that the husband fails certain obligations. Each state has a standard ta'liq agreement (which varies from state to state), and additional conditions may be entered into this document, which is signed separately from the marriage contract. Both the contract and the ta'liq are recorded with the Marriage Registrar.

☺ Uncodified law and no standard marriage contract, but negotiated conditions are recognized (see also practice)

India (marriages under Muslim laws): There is no standard marriage contract for those marrying under Muslim laws. However, informal adjudication forums, such as jamaat or mosque committees, as well as case law in the civil courts, recognize valid conditions to a Muslim marriage contract.

Nigeria (marriages under Muslim and customary laws): Negotiated conditions are usually verbal but will be upheld if proven in the Muslim and customary courts.

Saudi Arabia: Conditions to marriage are commonly negotiated in detail, and the conditions are upheld, provided they do not contradict the purpose of marriage.

The law explicitly recognizes the possibility of negotiating terms and conditions to the marriage contract

Morocco: Under A. 38 of the Moudawana, a condition that is in conflict with the lawful essence of marriage or its aim shall be void, but the marriage contract will remain valid. Case law recognizes stipulations that the wife may work, provided her working serves the general interest of the country. A. 30 recognizes the possibility of limiting the husband's right to polygyny. A. 44 recognizes the possibility of talaq tafwid. Under A. 43 the text of the contract is officially recorded.

Algeria: Under A. 19 of the CF, the parties may specify any conditions that do not conflict with the provisions of the Code itself.

Sudan: Under S. 42 of the MPLA, women have the right to stipulate any condition that neither prohibits a legitimate right nor legitimises a prohibited right. Conditions that are stipulated in the contract are obligatory on the husband.

Tunisia: Under A. 11 of the CSP, conditions can be stipulated in the notarized contract, and contravention of or failure to meet these conditions allows both spouses to apply for dissolution. Conditions can relate to persons or property.

Egypt: The law recognizes the wife's right to have an unconditional talaq tafwid inserted in the marriage contract. Doing so frees her from having to prove damages in the event of divorce. The right to work outside the home may also be negotiated. By decree of the Minister of Justice in 1931, ownership of the conjugal home and other assets cannot be incorporated in the marriage contract.

Cameroon: Under A. 49 of the CSO, the Marriage Certificate has to state the polygyny/monogamy option; joint or separate property regime; and whether or not a separate marriage contract has been drawn up.

Indonesia: The marriage certificate records whether or not there was any marriage contract, but the certificate does not record the details of any contract.

Turkey: Under A. 186-237 of the CC, a couple has the option of choosing between three different property regimes upon marriage: separation of goods (each party owns the goods and property that are registered in his/her name prior to and throughout the course of the marriage), union of goods (all goods and property owned by each party prior to and during the marriage are considered joint property of the couple); aggregation of goods (through a prenuptial agreement both parties decide upon which goods will constitute the joint property of the couple). Under A. 170, where a couple has not specified a property regime applicable to their marriage union, they are automatically considered to have accepted the separation of goods property regime.

☹ **The law is silent about the possibility of negotiating conditions to the marriage**

Sri Lanka: The MMDA does not mention the possibility of negotiated conditions. The marriage register does not provide space for recording negotiated conditions or additional documents.

Senegal: The CF only mentions pre-agreed financial payments. The option of polygyny/monogamy is the husband's right and is not viewed by the law as a mutually negotiable issue. However, grounds for dissolution are wide and include incompatibility.

The law does not view marriage as a contract

Fiji, South Africa: 'Nuptial agreements' may be registered under contract law.

Turkey: Under A. 202, 203, and 205 of the new CC, couples may choose an alternative to the default property regime by jointly signing a contract before a notary or declaring their decision in writing while applying for authorization to marry. The default property regime established by the new CC provides for equal division of marital property, while Under A. 220 property brought into the marriage remains the sole property of the original owner.

The law does not recognize additional agreements to a marriage

Central Asian Republics

IMPLEMENTATION

Pakistan: In certain cases courts accept contractual stipulations, even when these deviate from traditional Muslim jurisprudence. For example, where lifelong maintenance for a divorced wife has been incorporated as a stipulation in the marriage contract, courts have supported the wife's right to such maintenance. In one pre-Independence case (which would then be applicable in Bangladesh, India, and Pakistan), it was held that 'the marital rights ended with the divorce, but the contract subsists until the plaintiff dies or breaks it' (Muhammad Muinuddin v Jamal Fatima, 1921, 43 All.650).

Sudan: Other factors obstruct access to the possibility of negotiating conditions. If the wife intends to stipulate any marital condition(s), the husband's proxy must have a legally certified power of attorney; otherwise, he cannot sign the husband's approval in the contract. In contrast, if the wife does not stipulate any special marriage conditions, the proxy may sign on behalf of the husband, without a need for a certified power of attorney.

PRACTICES

Option-giving practices concerning negotiated conditions

Gambia: If a woman gives birth to many male children, the bride price and gifts due to the wife may be renegotiated. GAMCOTRAP research found that among Mandinka Muslims (49% of the Gambian population), many women with lots of sons have their own land because of these renegotiations. Negotiations are usually verbal between the two families; and it is understood that the woman must be fed, clothed, and not subjected to insults or any form of abuse. The negotiations are witnessed. Sometimes this process takes place publicly in the presence of the bride and groom. Most women are unaware that rights can be negotiated, and if agreements about rights have been made, usually women are unaware of their existence.

Egypt: The law prohibiting the negotiation of marital assets is in contradiction with the cultural belief that furniture and other movable assets belong to the wife.

Iran: Socially accepted conditions include the right to study and to work.

Nigeria: In Yoruba areas, there is an increasing demand for the inclusion of verbal conditions, including talaq tafwid. This increase has resulted from awareness-raising programs conducted by women's groups. Couples make verbal agreements, settled before both families, concerning such issues as the right to continue education after marriage. Educated families also negotiate terms, such as the number of children, regardless of sex, or that the 'husband will pay attention to his wife.' (This latter requirement acts as a form of protection in polygynous unions.) There is little awareness among women that such negotiations are a legitimate part of Muslim marriage laws.

Philippines: Families can negotiate the conditions under which the wife can seek a socially acceptable divorce.

Pakistan: In the Seraiki-speaking urban areas and in other parts of Punjab, a provision that the husband must provide the wife with pocket money (jeb kharch) is written into the nikahnama. In the rural areas such an agreement is not recorded, but there is a verbal understanding on the matter. This right to pocket money is considered quite separate from the right to maintenance (which covers food and clothing, etc.). Jeb kharch is entirely a wife's own money, to do with as she pleases.

In some communities, especially among Shias, a wife may receive a monthly payment during the time that she is breastfeeding; and the terms of this payment may be written into the nikahnama. In NWFP and parts of northern Punjab, the wife's parents sometimes demand that it be written into the nikahnama that their daughter is entitled to claim a fixed monthly maintenance amount in the event of divorce or separation. This maintenance is often paid, upholding the contract. It is also considered possible for women to stipulate the maximum number of children that they want to have and/or when they want to have them. This practice is particularly found among Shia families and is usually upheld.

In Mianwali, Jhang, rural Sargodha, and Kalabagh, conditions of the marriage are sometimes recorded on stamp paper (an official printed paper, which anyone can buy from the state; the document is then written, signed, and attested to by a notary public). These conditions on stamp paper are separate from the nikahnama form and are sometimes used instead of the standard nikahnama. One common condition that is often stipulated in these areas is that the husband must pay a fine if he contracts a second marriage or pronounces talaq without a valid reason. In the Kalabagh area, these kinds of contracts are strictly upheld by the community. Since these are contracts duly written on stamp paper and signed by witnesses, they become legal documents, which courts have upheld in the few instances where their validity has been challenged.

Saudi Arabia: Negotiated clauses are taken seriously and recognised as a means for women to ensure their rights are protected within the family. However, they are taken more seriously by the bride's family than by the bride herself (who often has little knowledge of the options). Usually, the bride's mother is the actual force behind the negotiated rights (acting through the father). Conditions commonly written into contracts among the middle and upper classes include: the right to continue education without the burden of domestic responsibilities, and the right to work outside the home. Sometimes women also specify that they want to live in a nuclear family and not with the husband's relatives, that the family will live in a certain city (to prevent the wife from being uprooted from friends and family support base if the husband's job is transferred), and/or that she will have a personal driver to ensure mobility (important given the law preventing women from driving). The contract can also stipulate that the wife, should her husband marry another woman, be granted a divorce, be paid a certain amount of money, or be given a separate house for her and her children. Generally, the stipulation and implementation of negotiated rights depends entirely on the bride's own family's willingness to protect her rights.

Less option-giving practices concerning negotiated conditions

Gambia: Since most Muslim marriages are verbal and not registered, there are no contractual stipulations to be enforced or negotiated. However, negotiations do take place between families, and these usually address financial exchange, the terms of maintenance, and the husband's treatment of the wife. According to Maliki precepts (the dominant school in the Gambia), a marriage should not be conditional upon the performance or non-performance of certain acts. Therefore, Muslims in the Gambia do not seek to negotiate conditions to any marriage contract. Most women are not aware that any agreements relating to rights within a marriage should be recorded.

Iran: Contractual conditions can be crossed out at the time of a marriage negotiation if both sides agree. In practice, an agreement to divide marital wealth can be ineffective if the husband takes more than one wife because under such conditions, marital wealth will be divided among both of/ all of the wives. In many parts of Iran, formal negotiations take place between the fathers of the groom and bride, leaving little opportunity for the bride or her mother to intervene. Custom prevents discussion of divorce rights at the time of marriage.

Nigeria: In Northern Nigeria verbal contracts address conditions within the marriage, not provisions regarding divorce. There is little demand for a written contract because the need for a contract is taken to mean that the marriage will end up in arbitration before a court. The enforcement of verbal agreements depends upon the relative social power of the parties.

Pakistan: Usually the optional clauses in a marriage contract are struck out, especially talaq tafwid. If a maulvi (religious figure) is solemnizing the marriage, often he will bring a nikahnama form, on which he has already crossed out the optional clauses.

Philippines: Women are not aware of the possibility of negotiating talaq tafwid.

Saudi Arabia: Conditions stipulating monogamy are considered haram and not possible.

Sudan: Contractual conditions are rare and usually made only when women are marrying for the second time. The most common condition added to a marriage contract stipulates that a separate matrimonial residency be provided to the wife in the event of polygyny. In very limited cases, women may stipulate the right to a job or profession, an education, or talaq tafwid ('esma). Conditions that limit the number of co-wives or children or establish freedom of movement are not added because there are contradictory views regarding the legitimacy of stipulating such conditions.

Strengthening Women's Access to Negotiated Rights in Marriage

The PILIPINA Legal Resources Center is currently working with the National Network for Muslim Women's Rights to promote a "Revised Code of Muslim Personal Laws". The proposed "Revised CMPL" has officially been presented to the House of Congress through Rep. Abdulgani Salappudin, the Vice Chair of the Committee on Muslim Affairs and through Rep. Patricia Sarenas, Chair of the Committee on Women.

The process of developing the proposals started with a research in 1988 by the PILIPINA Legal Resources Center (PLRC) on the aspirations of Muslim women in Mindanao. The next steps were legal literacy work for many years to popularize the Code and to discuss the provisions in the context of gender issues. In 1998, when our political party Abanse! Pinay (a women's political party with the goal of advancing the women's agenda in Congress through the election of three women sectoral representatives under the party-list system) won a seat in Congress and our party's Representative became the Chair of the Committee on Women in the House of Representatives, PLRC regarded this as a methodological and political chance to work for legal reform. In 1999, PLRC started to facilitate the process of reviewing and changing some provisions of the Code of Muslim Personal Laws.

One of the current hurdles faced by the network is the labelling of the CMPL as "Islamic" which has essentially put it beyond the reach of justice. Animating a legal reform process with the Muslim community was bound to take issue with ethnic identity, i.e. non-recognition of ethnic identity and cultural ethnocentrism. But, as advocates of justice, we cannot be champions of political and civil rights if we are loathe to address many of the issues most critical to women, ostensibly for fear of trampling on religious freedom and ethnic identity. This is not to say that religious freedom, identity, or even the right to follow cultural traditions are false issues. For the National Network of Muslim Women Advocates, they are among the most pressing and difficult issues we face. But, the difficulty of such issues is not justification for abandoning the aspirations of Muslim women; rather it is precisely the reason why legal reform is especially crucial. We are acutely aware that, on the questions of how and whether and when to pursue legal change, we who work as feminists advocating for legal and structural changes must take our lead from the women who live and work and struggle in the grassroots, and not vice versa.

These efforts of the National Network for Muslim Women's Rights to draft reform of the Code are based on progressive legislation in other Muslim countries, some of which has been accessed through the network Women Living Under Muslim Laws.

The gaps in the substantive law and actual implementation have shown that Muslim personal laws are often practiced to the detriment of Muslim women. Filipina Muslim women have the same status problems in the private and public spheres of life as experienced by their fellow Filipina Christian counterparts but as members of a religious community, for Muslim women there seems to be another level of inequality which has found its way into some provisions of the Code of Muslim Personal Laws.

Most ustajes are men and scholarships in Islamic studies are the preserve of men. The autonomous regions of Muslim Mindanao have the lowest literacy rates even as Filipino women are among the world's most highly educated, with literacy levels of 94.3%. The task of demystifying the sources of these customary laws which reduce the autonomy of women must involve the training of many Muslim women scholars who will have the authority and confidence to claim the entitlements of women by searching for space within these customs or interpretations to reformulate laws based on social justice.

There is consensus in the network that the following discriminatory provisions are found in the following areas of the Code of Muslim Personal Laws:

a) The provision on hereditary rights which is different for both sexes;

b) The provision on oral divorce which is the unilateral prerogative of Muslim men;

c) The provision on domicile;

d) The provision on the right to work or practice one's profession;

e) The provision on the management of the household;

f) The provision on child marriage which violate the rights of a child;

g) The operational definition of just treatment in subsequent marriage/s.

In the area of negotiated rights and responsibilities within marriage, the following has been proposed:

1. Pre-Nuptial Agreement - It is suggested that a pre-nuptial or ante-nuptial agreement be entered into by the contracting parties immediately before the celebration of the marriage, stipulating among others; the property relations of the spouses; the amount, schedule and mode of payment of dower (mahr); agreement on support after idda in case of divorce; whether talaq be delegated to the wife; and the type of marital relations that will govern the marriage - whether monogamy or polygamy. It shall also be stipulated that violation of any of the agreements will be a ground for divorce. This pre-nuptial agreement will be made a formal requisite of marriage.
2. Mahr - There has to be a new provision specifying that the agreed amount or value of mahr, its schedule and mode of payment should be stipulated in the pre-nuptial agreement and the marriage contract.
3. Rights and Obligations Between Spouses
   a. This provision on the rights and obligations between spouses has to be amended to include a provision requiring mutual consultation between the spouses as regards the fixing of the residence of the family. It should be part of the pre-nuptial agreement.
   b. Article 36, paragraph (1) has to be amended to emphasize the sharing of responsibility between spouses in managing the affairs of household
   c. Paragraph (2) of the above-mentioned article has to be amended too. This provision prohibits the wife from acquiring properties by gratuitous title without the consent of the husband, except from her relatives who are within the prohibited degrees in marriage. Apparently, the purpose of this provision is to avoid conflict in the family by reason of loss of trust. However, it will not be fair to the wife if such prohibition will not be applied to the husband. Hence, this provision should be amended such that both spouses should be prohibited to receive gifts or acquire properties by gratuitous title without the consent of the other.
   d. Paragraph (3) of the same article should also be amended. The spouses should consult each other and mutually agree on the exercise of their profession or occupation or in the engagement of their lawful business.

Extracts from a paper presented by Isabelita Solamo-Antonio, October 2002, see bibliography.

5e MARRIAGE CONTRACTS: MAHR (DOWER)

introduction

The precise nature of mahr is controversial because it may be variously defined as a consequence of, a requisite to, or a consideration of a valid Muslim marriage. However defined, mahr is considered essential and often listed as an essential part of valid marriage that must be mentioned in the marriage contract. Even if not specified at the time of marriage, it is presumed to exist (mahr ul mithl or 'proper dower'). Even if the marriage has not been consummated, half of the mahr may be due in the event that the marriage is dissolved. (For the legal effects of mahr, see p.110.)

To add to the confusion, there are two almost completely opposing opinions on the social implications of mahr and its affect on women's lives. Some women see mahr as a useful financial resource for women who are otherwise customarily denied control over assets. These women also value mahr as a potential bargaining tool in the event of a conflict in a marriage or on divorce (Palestinian community in Israel, Iran). In contrast, others view mahr as conceptually similar to a payment for sexual services or a price for virginity. These women see the abolition of mahr as an essential step in the battle to define women as agents in a marriage partnership, rather than as resources or property to be exchanged between families (e.g., activists in former South Yemen and Indonesia). (For other exchanges on marriage, including bride-price and dowry, see p.<>.)

Mahr may consist of money, land, clothing, jewellery, or even the recital of a Qur'anic ayat (verse). Mahr can also range in financial value from vast sums (so vast as to prevent young men from being able to marry) to purely symbolic amounts.

The dominant legal understanding of mahr is that it is a payment from the groom to the bride to be kept as her exclusive property and used at her discretion. However, practices differ considerably. Difficulties in the conceptual definition of mahr are evident in that few legal codes have attempted to provide a concise definition (Morocco is an exception). At most, systems specify what mahr can consist of and what it cannot (Sudan, Tunisia). However, most systems are clear that various amounts of cash or goods given by the husband to the wife during the marriage cannot be presumed to be mahr, unless this has been clearly expressed. (The issue of whose word is accepted by the courts regarding disputed mahr is discussed in Financial Rights and Settlements, p.314.)

laws and practices regarding the form of mahr

Mahr may be prompt (payable on the demand of the bride/wife and usually paid in full at the time of contracting the marriage), or deferred (payable in the event of death of the husband or divorce or after a specified time period), or partly prompt and partly deferred. Many systems require this information to be recorded in the marriage contract and/or at the time of registration (see p.150-151).

Agreeing to a deferred mahr may be the only means by which a woman can have the promise of a sizeable sum, which could secure her financial status in the event she is divorced or becomes a widow. However, deferring payment of part or all of her mahr means a woman runs the risk of losing it if her husband should become destitute or if he is never able to afford it. Women may also find themselves deprived of a deferred mahr at the end of a marriage. Difficult divorce proceedings may compel women to exchange their deferred mahr for custody of their children or for other rights. Substantial deferred mahr has even been identified as a cause of low-level domestic violence because husbands try to force their wives to seek khul' so as to avoid having to pay mahr. However, prompt mahr offers its own challenges. If mahr is customarily paid in full at the time of marriage (and is substantial), women's access to khul' may be obstructed because they do not have the means to repay the mahr.

Where mahr is not specified, most systems (whether this is codified or not) will recognize the principle of mahr ul mithl (proper dower); mahr ul mithl is considered prompt. If a woman seeks to recover an unspecified mahr under the mahr ul mithl principle, the court will assess the mahr due to her. The court bases this amount on the mahr received by the other woman in her family, or on the mahr due to another woman of her social status (Bangladesh, Iran, Pakistan, Sri Lanka). In some systems the status of the husband is also taken into account (Philippines).

Communities vary widely as to whether mahr is customarily prompt, deferred, or a combination of the two. Often the expected worth and form of the mahr will influence when it will be paid. For example, where the payment of mahr involves the transfer of land into the wife's name (practiced among some Pukhtuns of Pakistan), mahr is very rarely prompt. However, in Saudi Arabia and other Gulf communities, mahr is usually a substantial sum of cash and is paid in full at the wedding. In Iran mahr is also substantial; however, it is usually deferred. Prompt mahr payments are more likely in contexts where mahr is linked to the consummation of a marriage (Gambia, Nigeria - marriages under Muslim laws, and among some Shia communities in Pakistan).

laws and practices regarding the amount of mahr

Some systems set a maximum or minimum amount of mahr, and such provisions vary greatly. Tunisian law, for example, does not permit the customary recitation of a Qur'anic ayat as recognized mahr, whereas Sudan's code of personal law explicitly recognizes this as valid mahr.

In socialist South Yemen, the problems caused by customs that demand exorbitant mahr amounts have led the government to legally restrict mahr to 100 YD (about twice the average white collar monthly salary). The declared aim of setting these limits was to remove the class control over marriage that resulted from costly mahr and to make khul' easier for women by making it more likely that they would be able to repay the mahr themselves. The legal limit was backed by substantial fines and prison sentences but was still largely ignored by rural and wealthy families. This lack of compliance led women to push for the complete abolition of mahr to mark the 10th anniversary of the Family Law in 1984; they were unsuccessful.

Other systems are silent on the amount of mahr, and communities are free to practice local customs regarding acceptable amounts. Even within countries there is a wide variation in mahr practices; and the amount of mahr will depend upon local customs and the class, social status, education level, and even the beauty of the bride.

A number of communities base their practices on assumptions about the mahr that was given at the time of the marriage of the Prophet's daughter Fatima. Mahr based on this example may be called either mahr fatima or shara'i mehr. However, assumptions about this example vary so widely that using this standard does not ensure any uniformity. Communities variously interpret this mahr fatima to entail substantial sums or merely symbolic amounts. In the latter case, women can be constrained from demanding higher amounts by the feeling that they are going against the Prophet's own practice.

Where mahr is deferred, even substantial amounts can lose considerable value due to the passage of years and the impact of inflation, especially in economically unstable regions. To avoid this some women ask for mahr to be paid in more stable currencies i.e., US dollars, or in the form of gold. Following women's pressure, courts in Iran now link mahr settlements (on divorce) with inflation. This adjustment policy allows women to realize the full value of their mahr as it was intended at the time of its agreement.

Under Muslim laws, it is possible to raise the mahr amount during the marriage. Some communities may practice such increasing of mahr as a condition to the reconciliation of husband and wife following severe disputes. In some systems, to be legally valid any lowering or waiver of mahr requires the written and witnessed consent of the wife (Pakistan).

the rights implications of mahr

Most systems recognize the wife's right to refuse to consummate the marriage until prompt mahr is paid. However, if the marriage has been consummated but the mahr is still unpaid, systems differ over the wife's right to refuse sexual relations. In Pakistan, for example, if the husband has not paid prompt mahr and files for restitution of conjugal rights before consummating his marriage, his suit will be dismissed straight away. However, after consummation has taken place with the wife's free consent, his suit may be made subject to the payment of the mahr. In contrast, in Iran the wife can be ordered to return to her husband even if the mahr has not been paid if she has already consummated the marriage.

In some communities, wives may use their mahr to invest or trade and assure themselves of a degree of social independence from their husbands (Palestinian communities in Israel). In such communities, clearly a substantial mahr has some benefits for wives. In contrast, in contexts where mahr is basically symbolic, it offers little financial benefit to wives and may allow men to marry and divorce easily without fear of financial repercussions. However, larger mahr amounts are not necessarily beneficial. Where khul' is the most easily accessible form of divorce for women, smaller mahr amounts may work to their advantage. In addition, customarily substantial prompt mahr may make marriage less likely for both men and women.

Muslim laws (as reflected in many codes) stipulate that mahr is intended purely for the benefit of a wife and is to be controlled by her. However, in many communities, a wife is expected to spend much of her mahr on the wedding ceremony itself, or she may have little practical decision-making power over how it is to be used. In some communities the line between mahr and bride price becomes extremely blurred as the mahr is given to the bride's father. Morocco's Moudawana addresses this problem by explicitly prohibiting, in the chapter on mahr, the guardian from accepting anything in return for his daughter's hand in marriage.

Where women have been promised a substantial mahr in their marriage contracts, they may subsequently face considerable pressure to waive it (especially on the death of their husband in return for the right to remain in the marital home). In Pakistan, courts have been careful to ensure that such a waiver is not made under any compulsion but is done of the wife's free will.

recovery of mahr during marriage

Although mahr is theoretically the property of the wife, an attempt to recover prompt mahr (except where it is paid in full at the time of the wedding or soon after) is often interpreted as a sign of problems in the marriage. This implication socially obstructs recovery.

Where a marriage is annulled or dissolved before consummation, systems differ on whether or not mahr is due. In some systems mahr is due if the marriage ends because of a defect in the husband, but it is not due if the marriage ends because of a defect in the wife (Morocco). In other systems, half is due regardless of the reason that the marriage has ended (Bangladesh, India and Pakistan).

Procedural problems concerning the recovery of mahr are also discussed in Financial Rights and Settlements (p.314).

LAWS: Marriage Contracts – Mahr

Criteria

As a result of the conflicting analysis of mahr and its rights implications for women, we have not listed the provisions concerning mahr according to more option-giving and less option-giving criteria. Instead, provisions have been listed alphabetically.

Algeria: Mahr is defined as that which is paid to the future wife in cash, or any other benefit that is legally permissible. The amount is not specified; neither is there a maximum, and the mahr also may be symbolic. It is her property and it is to be freely disposed of by her. The form and amount of mahr should be stated in the marriage contract, be it immediate or deferred. A woman is entitled to full mahr after her marriage has been consummated or on the death of her husband. If there are disputes regarding mahr between the spouses or heirs before the marriage has been consummated, and none of them has proof of the original agreement, the dispute will be settled in favour of the wife. If the dispute occurs after the marriage has been consummated, it will be settled in favour of the husband and his heirs upon their oath. The Supreme Court ruled that gifts and acquired movables do not replace mahr when it is due. If the mahr is not paid, the marriage becomes void (S.C. decision, April 1990).

Bangladesh: Mahr amount and terms of payment must be recorded in the standard marriage contract. Under S. 10 of the MFLO, where mahr is not stipulated, mahr ul mithl is presumed; if the kabinnama fails to mention whether the mahr is prompt or deferred, it is presumed prompt. Bangladesh's Dowry Prohibition Act 1983 explicitly exempts mahr settled on a Muslim bride from any penalties and limits under the Act.

Central Asian Republics: Mahr is not recognized by the law.

Egypt: The parties may agree to the form of mahr. Under A. 19 of the LMPS (as amended in 1985), disagreement about the amount of mahr requires the wife to provide proof of their original agreement. If she cannot, the husband's oath is taken as valid. Where he swears to an amount not in keeping with mahr ul mithl, the courts will determine mahr according to mahr ul mithl.

Gambia (marriages under Muslim laws): According to Cadis, a fixed minimum for mahr is D189.25 (equivalent to US$8.40). Under custom the mahr is D4.50 (equivalent to US$ 20 cents), but it can be more depending on the capacity of the groom and the demands of the bride's family. The mahr must be paid before a marriage can take place and is necessary for a marriage contract to be recognized.

Iran: If mahr is left unmentioned in the marriage contract, the court may decide the amount according to the class and social status of the bride's family. Mahr can be claimed immediately after the contract is signed, and a wife can refuse to consummate the marriage until paid in full.

Malaysia: Under S. 21 of the IFLA, mahr (mas kahwin) shall ordinarily be paid by the man or his representative to the woman or her representative in the presence of the person solemnizing the marriage and at least two other witnesses. The Registrar shall ascertain and record the value and other particulars of the mas kahwin, as well as their terms of payment, including the promised date of payment and the particulars of any security given for the payment.

Morocco: Under A. 16 of the Moudawana, Morocco defines mahr as, "that money which the husband offers freely to show his desire to make a contract of marriage to establish a family and to confirm the foundation of affection and the community of husband and wife." Mahr is a legal obligation, and may take the form of anything that is a valid subject of contract. There is no lower or upper limit specified, and it may be prompt or deferred. Under A. 3, it is illegal to suppress the giving of mahr. Under A. 17-18, mahr is the property of the wife, and the husband has no right to demand that the wife should provide household goods, furniture, or clothing in return for the mahr. Under A. 21, the husband is not permitted to make consummation a condition for payment of prompt mahr. Under A. 19, a guardian may not accept anything in return for his ward's marriage. Depending on the agreement, all or part of the mahr shall be due upon consummation, and full payment of mahr becomes due on the death of the husband. The consummation of a marriage before the payment of mahr makes mahr a debt owing to the wife. Inability to pay the debt cannot be grounds for divorce. A wife is entitled to one half of the mahr if the husband pronounces talaq before the marriage is consummated. Under A. 22, a marriage annulled on the grounds of a 'defect' in the wife deprives the wife of mahr. A marriage annulled on the grounds of a 'defect' in the husband entitles the wife to full mahr.

Nigeria (marriages under Muslim laws): Mahr is compulsory and is considered necessary for marriage. The minimum amount is determined according to the equivalent of 1/4 Dinar, depending on the current exchange rate.

Pakistan: The mahr amount and the terms of payment must be recorded in the standard marriage contract. Under S. 10 of the MFLO, where mahr is not stipulated, mahr ul mithl is presumed; if the nikahnama fails to mention whether the mahr is prompt or deferred, it is presumed prompt. Prompt mahr is payable on demand and in full, and even may be demanded before the consummation of the marriage (PLD 1988 Karachi 625). In a case concerning exchange marriage where no mahr was fixed, the court held that "An exchange marriage may be a consideration for the parents of the spouses, but in order to constitute a valid marriage the dower amount or any other valid consideration in lieu of marriage has to be fixed, offered, and accepted by the spouses. Marriage of a relative of a spouse with some other, is by itself not a valid consideration for his or her own marriage" (Bashir Ahmad v Usman alias Chara and others 1995 P Cr L J 1909 Lahore). The courts have a legal duty to ensure that relinquishment of mahr is not due to compulsion or coercion but out of the woman's free consent (Mst. Jamila Bibi v Mian Khan PLD 1997 Lahore 417). If a husband does not pay dower for a considerable period of time, the wife can apply for dissolution of marriage under the DMMA on the grounds of interference in her property (Muhammad Mumtaz v Mst. Parveen Akhtar and another 1985 CLC 415, Lahore).

Philippines: Under A. 20-21 of the CMPL, there is no stipulated amount or form for mahr. Where no mahr has been fixed, the courts will determine mahr according to social status of the parties. The husband or his estate becomes liable for mahr. Mahr is the property of the wife.

Saudi Arabia: Mahr is always prompt and paid in full. The bride is at liberty to spend it as she chooses, although it may be spent in part on wedding expenses.

Senegal: Under A. 132 of the CF, the intending spouses can agree that an amount of money or goods to be paid in part or in totality by the future husband to the future wife will be a condition of the marriage. This amount cannot surpass the maximum value fixed by the law. A. 6(2) and (3) of the Law 67-04 of 24 February 1967, designed to limit excessive wedding expenditures, fixes mahr at 3,000 f CFA (approximately US$ 4.50), which amount is to be given exclusively to the wife. In the event that the wife refuses to join the marital home, judges tend to order her to return the legal maximum even if more was given. Mahr can be paid, either in full or in part, at the time of marriage. In a civil marriage the OEC must mention the amount of mahr the wife says that she has received, and the marriage is only valid if the prompt portion has been paid. At the time of contracting a marriage, parties also must choose a matrimonial property regime (joint, total separation, or 'regime dotal,' whereby the husband manages the wife's dower during the marriage, but it remains hers and is to be returned to her on dissolution). The non-payment of dower is grounds for nullity if the spouses have made any portion prompt.

Sri Lanka: At the point of registration, the amount of mahr, as well as the terms of its payment (including payments already made), are to be recorded. Where the amount is not recorded, mahr ul mithl applies; and under S. 18(2) of the MMDA, where the terms of payment are not recorded, mahr is assumed to be prompt. The wife's refusal to live with the husband is not a valid reason for denying her right to claim mahr, and where mahr is deferred, it will be valued at the rate operative on the date of demand of mahr (Sherifdeen versus Rahuma Beebi (1958) 4 MMDLR 160).

Sudan: Under S. 27 of the MPL, mahr need not be a monetary amount or asset. The emphasis is on the obligation rather than the financial value. Token gifts, such as Qur'anic verses, are legally valid forms of mahr. Where mahr has a monetary value, it should not be less than two thousand

Sudanese Pounds (approximately US$1). Where mahr is divided into prompt and deferred portions, both are to be stipulated in the contract. Women have the right to determine the value of the mahr. The first portion (mukaddam) is paid before the actual beginning of marital relations between the spouses. The code gives the wife the right to refuse conjugal relations until she receives the agreed upon amount of the mukaddam.

Tunisia: Under A. 3 of the CSP, mahr is a necessary condition for validity of marriage. There is no maximum or minimum limit for mahr, but it must not be 'worthless.' Mahr may consist of any licit good that has a value in financial terms. Under A. 12, mahr is considered the property of the wife, to be disposed of as she wishes. If mahr is not paid, there is no obligation on the wife to consummate the marriage. If consummation occurs before mahr is paid, it is considered a debt, for which the wife may demand payment. Under A. 12 and 13, a husband's financial inability to pay the mahr debt is not grounds for divorce. Courts have accepted that when couples decide not to mention the mahr in the marriage contract, it remains valid.

Turkey: Mahr is not recognized by the law. However, the wife may ask the husband to reimburse her for some of the wedding expenses if the marriage fails for reasons not attributed to her.

PRACTICES

Practices and trends are generally negative

Algeria: If the wife is young, her mahr may be given to her wali who then manages it for her. The giving of mahr is considered to deter the husband from repudiating or divorcing the wife. In addition, mahr provides some security for widows.

Bangladesh: It has become customary for the wedding gifts (given to both sides) to be listed as part of the prompt dower. This occurs even when the gifts will be repossessed by others after the wedding. This new trend undermines mahr and can be seen as an attempt to sidestep provisions restricting dowry.

Gambia: Husbands from different communities pay different amounts of mahr. While among the Sarahule mahr is very high, among the Mandinka it is low (about D4.5, equivalent to US$ 20 cents). Negotiations regarding mahr exclude women, and the money is exchanged between senior men. It is then distributed to senior women who apply customary distribution, leaving only leftovers for the bride. Because of the economic crisis, men are now less willing to endorse the practice of high dower amounts and have appropriated the women's activist argument that such exchanges amount to the selling of daughters. However, such arguments are not premised on the rights of daughters. Educated women are refusing mahr money, rejecting it because 'it is a way of controlling them as property.' The decision to utilise or dispose of the mahr is not the wife's. It is usually shared among relatives, including extended relatives. Each relative who receives a share of the 'badommoro' (Mandinka) or 'lekindye' (Wolof) is supposed to then contribute towards the dowry: pots, pans, household items, etc. In practice, usually only the women contribute and the men do not. However, among the Fulas, the father provides some utensils to the daughter.

Indonesia: Activists are pushing for lower mahr because they see it as the sale of a wife's services.

Iran: Mahr is usually a large sum that, in most cases, the groom cannot afford to pay. In the past, mahr was in the form of gold coins, land, or cash. However, due to the inflation over the past 20 years, authorities now try to encourage women and the families to record the mahr as gold or real estate in order to preserve its value.

Nigeria: Some communities determine a fixed sum to be paid as dower. For example, in the Gwandu Emirate Council in Kebbi State, husbands usually pay the prescribed sum (1/4 Dinar) or more. In some areas, mahr is often confused with bride price (Oyo and Osun). The mahr is usually given to the bride, but sometimes it is given to her parents who then use it for her. Mahr is invariably prompt. Payment of mahr is confused with marriage gifts in customary laws. For example, among the Hausa it may be counted as part of kayan sadauki (marriage gifts), some of which goes to the bride, but some of which goes to other (mostly female) relatives. Or, in some parts of Yorubaland, the groom's father may 'pay the mahr' instead of the groom – on the grounds that the groom should not think that he has 'bought' his bride.

Pakistan: There is a lack of awareness of the purpose of mahr. Practices vary quite widely, from common symbolic 'sharai mahr' (Rs 32.50, equivalent to US$ 40 cents) to the transfer of valuable immovable property (in parts of NWFP) to promised cash amounts of up to Rs 600,000 (equivalent to US$10,700) (among the professional urban elite). Shias tend to practice prompt but generally lower mahr. Mahr is rarely fixed in exchange marriages.

Philippines: Newlyweds feel that the giving of mahr is onerous because, in practice, it is given to the bride's family and relatives. Maranao marriages are more elaborate, and brides are usually given the full mahr just before or during the ceremony.

Saudi Arabia: Mahr is always prompt and paid in full. It is the bride's property to do with as she wishes. However, customarily she will spend part of it on wedding expenses.

Senegal: Custom differs regarding the requirement of mahr, and some communities do not regard it as obligatory. It is difficult to distinguish between mahr and bride price because mahr is commonly distributed among the bride's relatives. According to a district judge in the largest suburb of Dakar, families rarely respect the legal limit, and mahr varies from 2,500 f CFA (approximately US$ 3.70) to much larger sums, depending upon the social status of the parties. Higher amounts are normally required for younger women. Many blame mothers for demanding increasingly larger sums. Customarily, a marriage is valid only when the following have been paid: a) the 'tian' (by the groom to the bride at the time of celebration of the marriage); b) the lekku ndeye (a portion of the dower to be given to the mother to share with her relatives and friends); c) the beyu baay (a portion of the dower to be given to the father or guardian); and d) the nient ak transu (amount of money given by the husband at the time of the marriage celebration to seal the contract).

Sri Lanka: In the past mahr was calculated in kalanjees of gold (1 kalangee = 72g). Among the poorer classes, traditionally the groom paid 19½ kalanjees of gold (11.7 sovereigns) and among the wealthy, around 100 kalanjees (= 58 ½ sovereigns of pure gold). Today, mahr is usually only a very small token amount amounting to Rs. 101 (US $1) or Rs. 1001 (US $10). However, in areas where dowry is given by the family of the bride, the groom may pay mahr that is equivalent to 5% of the value of dowry. Although the marriage registration form contains a column to record the amount of mahr, both prompt and deferred portions, typically the amount of mahr is not entered.

Sudan: Traditionally, the prompt mahr (mukadam) is used for the wedding preparations. Consequently, the wife loses the right to use the mukadam money as she likes, and her family will receive, own, and decide upon the use of el mukadam. Often where the mahr is high, its promised amount is not correctly recorded in the marriage contract.

Tunisia: In practice, especially in towns, a symbolic dower of one dinar (equivalent to less than US$ 1) is mentioned.

Protecting Women's Rights Through Payment of Mahr

The primary economic consideration in premarital negotiations in Saudi Arabia is the amount of the mahr that will be provided to the bride. Because of the country's wealth, Saudi marriages involve a substantial mahr being offered to the bride, who generally keeps this for her personal use.

In Saudi Arabia, mahr consists of a sum of money, jewelry, and other precious items and is paid up front, at the time of the wedding ceremony. The mahr goes directly to the bride, who may spend it as she wishes. The jewelry and other tangible items of the mahr (such as silver platters, crystal ornaments, and the like) are displayed at the wedding ceremony for the guests to admire. Often the mahr is spent immediately on clothes or other personal items for the bride, distinct from her bridal clothes. However, this is not the rule, and the bride may spend the mahr however she wishes. One woman in Jeddah used it to pay for foreign relatives on her mother's side of the family to come visit her and attend the wedding. (However, it is said that in many villages in Saudi Arabia, the bride's family keeps the money, and the bride is deprived of it.)

Saudi women emphatically assert that the mahr does not reflect an economic exchange in which the woman's worth is measured by the amount of money that she receives. In fact, the amount of mahr is determined by the financial status of the groom or by local standards, not by any estimation of the worth of the bride. The mahr represents an important source of financial independence for the future bride, who in all other financial matters must rely on her husband for her support (unless she is independently wealthy through inheritance or possesses earnings from a job).

In addition, the mahr is said to protect against divorce (at least divorce initiated by the husband). While it is easy for a husband to angrily divorce his wife in the heat of an argument, remarrying her requires the payment of an entirely new mahr. In one case, a Saudi man divorced his wife and then immediately regretted the decision. However, when the Islamic judge in his town heard of the incident, he demanded that the man negotiate a new marriage contract - mahr and all - to demonstrate that divorce is not to be taken lightly.

Most women appear not to favour the lowering of mahr as a strategy to reduce the costs of marriage, as they usually do not have much interest in the economic stability of the future marriage, which is not considered a joint economic enterprise.

In Egypt mahr has not always been substantial. However, social and economic factors have had a tremendous impact on local marriage patterns, especially in urban areas where the high rate of rural-urban migration from diverse regions has resulted in the development of culturally diverse neighbourhoods. Nowadays, marriage partners may be from different walks of life and regions with diverse practices and traditions. Moreover, the material and emotional expectations of young men and women regarding their marriage and marriage partners have also changed. Hence there are many things up for negotiation, although mahr has emerged as the most important issue. Once there is an agreement on that, it is most likely that the parties will reach agreement on other matters.

Today in Egypt mahr is a considerable sum, varying with the social status of the bride's family. Mahr is considered the foundation of a secure marriage, especially as far as women are concerned. In Egypt, the mahr is customarily divided in two parts. The first, called the muqaddama (the beginning) is paid by the groom to the bride before the marriage and is spent on furniture for the couple. Sometimes the groom buys the furniture that the bride's side has requested, and this is then registered in the bride's name at the time of the signing of the official marriage contract. The second part, called mu'akhkhara, may be demanded at any time after the signing of the contract, but in most cases is used as a deterrent for divorce; if a man wishes to divorce his wife, he would first have to pay her this remaining sum. Therefore, the larger the sum of the mahr is, the more effective the wife's leverage.

Extracted from Wynn, L., Marriage Contracts and Women's Rights in Saudi Arabia, and Hoodfar, H., Circumventing Legal Limitation: Mahr and Marriage Negotiation in Egyptian Low-Income Communities, in Hoodfar, H. (ed.) (1996), WLUML Special Dossier: Shifting Boundaries in Marriage and Divorce in Muslim Communities, WLUML, Grabels

5f MARRIAGE CONTRACTS: OTHER PAYMENTS AND EXCHANGES

introduction

There are a number of practices that entail the exchange of goods and money between spouses' families. Communities may have an entire range of precisely defined gifts and exchange patterns associated with marriage, all of which have to be given and received in order for the marriage to become socially valid.

Practices vary within and across communities, depending upon a host of factors such as geographical region, ethnic community, and social standing.

Other payments and exchanges in marriage are not sanctioned by religion, and are instead seen as an immutable part of community custom and identity. Whatever the practice, marriage-related exchanges tend to reflect the view of women as a commodity. Morocco's Moudawana appears to address this by prohibiting the bride's guardian from accepting anything from the groom in exchange for his ward's hand in marriage. Other payments and exchanges in marriage also reflect the view of marriage as a social institution that brings together not just the spouses but whole families and communities. Such payments, therefore, bind couples together in such a way that dissolution becomes very difficult. Because entire families have a stake in the marriage, dissolution carries huge social costs for spouses.

While laws may attempt to limit or completely ban these exchanges in order to eliminate the heavy social and financial burden they place on families, the practices continue (Bangladesh, Central Asian Republics, India, Morocco, Pakistan, Senegal, Turkey). In general, cases are only brought under these laws when there is a dispute in the marriage. The police hardly ever apply the laws at the time of a marriage ceremony because the major violators are often those with power and influence in the community and because the practices are so ingrained.

In Bangladesh, policies for preventing dowry deaths (wives murdered by husbands and in-laws, apparently due to their failure to bring an 'appropriate' dowry to the marriage) have become a matter of public debate. However, due to an immense backlog of cases in the lower courts, very few cases brought under the Dowry Prohibition Act have been heard in the High Court. In India, pressure from women's groups and negative publicity concerning dowry deaths has led to the establishment of state level Anti-Dowry Cells in certain Indian states. However, as a result of scarce resources, these cells have tended to concentrate on dowry deaths rather than on preventing the practice of dowry and/or prosecuting those who make dowry demands.

types of payments

The most common forms of exchanges are bride price (given by the groom's family to the bride's family) and dowry (usually goods given by the bride's family to the groom's family or to the groom himself, although supposedly regarded as the wife's property). In some countries, different regions follow only one of these customs, while in others both practices are applied to the same marriage. However, these broad categories obscure the diverse range of payments that may be involved in the contracting of a marriage as well as obscuring the specific character of certain gift practices, such as kaikuli (Sri Lanka), pemberian (Malaysia), and the giving of marriage gifts to the bride and her relatives (Bangladesh, Nigeria, Pakistan).

Whatever the practice, brides are seldom themselves negotiators, beneficiaries, or even recipients of these payments. Families (usually fathers rather than mothers) often use such customary payments as a means of enriching themselves, acquiring goods they may otherwise not be able to afford, or facilitating the marriages of other family members. With changing economic conditions and high male unemployment in some communities, young women must find income-generating work to build up the dowry for their own marriage.

It would, however, be wrong to take a simplistic view of customary payments on marriage. In some instances, women may benefit.

In wealthy South Asian communities, a bride with brothers may receive a substantial dowry (including a house and a car) in a presumed agreement that she will not claim her share of inheritance when the parents die. The amount may even exceed her due share of inheritance. Given the problems associated with women's mobility and the difficulties they may face in managing immovable property, such a dowry may prove practical, even though it reinforces traditional notions of land ownership. In some communities, the groom gives the mother of the bride money, in recognition of her efforts in raising his bride (Iran, where it is called sheer baha - 'money for the milk,' Senegal).

consequences and trends

There are currently conflicting trends in payments and exchanges on marriage. On the one hand, growing materialism and poverty are encouraging families to demand increasingly higher amounts for dowries and bride-price. On the other hand, there is growing awareness of the negative aspects of such practices. In many communities families enter into life-long debt due to the marriages of their children, and marriage may be delayed due to its high cost. Moreover, both bride-price and dowry have been factors in domestic violence (see Volume II Violence Against Women). Husbands may be unwilling to surrender wives for whom they or their families have paid a high bride-price, or they may beat wives in order to extract a higher dowry. Whether the woman's family has received money for her hand in marriage or has had to buy expensive goods for her to take into the marriage, they are sometimes unwilling to accept her return (in the event that the marriage is unhappy) as a result.

Other forms of payment that occur at the time of contracting a marriage may undermine the practice of mahr and relegate it to a token practice. As a result mahr practice may continue, but it becomes purely symbolic, offering no financial benefits to wives.

Finally, such practices may encourage parents and guardians to arrange otherwise inappropriate matches and may also make material gain the primary social motive behind contracting a marriage. This can result in a host of unscrupulous practices.

For laws and practices concerning the recovery of other payments and exchanges on dissolution of marriage, see p.317).

NOTES

LAWS: Marriage Contracts – Other Payments & Exchanges

Criteria

☺ More option-giving are those laws which:
- Explicitly ban other payments and exchanges and impose strict penalties for violation of this ban.

😐 The middle ground is occupied by those laws which:
- Place a limit on other payments and provide penalties for contravention but do not penalize brides for violation.

The lower middle ground is occupied by those laws which:
- Regulate other payments through registration requirements but do not place any limits to their value and do not penalize the practice.

☹ Less option-giving are those laws which:
- Do not regulate other payments and exchanges on marriage.

☺ **Other payments are banned**

Bangladesh: S. 3,4, and 5 of the Dowry Prohibition Act of 1980 make the promising, giving, receiving, and demanding of money or other property, in consideration of a marriage, a non-bailable offence that is liable to imprisonment and/or fine. 'Dowry' is defined in the Act as property or valuable security given, or agreed to be given, as consideration in the marriage of the parties. In one case, the husband demanded a dowry of Taka 50,000 (approx US$ 1,000 at that time) in January 1991, even though the couple had been married in 1987. Because his wife was unable to come up with the money, he beat her and their minor daughter and sent them to her natal home. The High Court held that the defendant had committed an offence under the Dowry Prohibition Act 1980 (Salam Mollik v The State, DLR (1996) 329 Vol. 43; see also Rezaul Karim v Mst. Taslima Begum DLR (1988) 360 Vol.40).

Also, according to the PC, 'whoever intentionally puts any person in fear of any injury to that person, or to any other, and thereby dishonestly induces the person (to give) any property or valuable security or anything signed or sealed which may be converted into valuable security, commits extortion.' Indeed, the lines between extortion and demanding dowry have been blurred by the decision given in 1991 case of Rezaul Karim v Mst. Taslima Begum where the High Court Division of the Supreme Court held that marriage was not only a ceremony but also a 'creator of status' and that the subsequent demand of money or valuable security by the husband in consideration of giving the woman the status of a wife during the continuation of the marriage would amount to dowry, and, therefore, someone making such demands would be liable to the provisions applying to dowry.

Central Asian Republics: The giving and receiving of kalym (bride-price) was banned under Soviet rule and remains illegal.

India (all marriages): Demanding dowry is a cognizable, non-bailable offence.

Morocco: **Under** A. 19, the guardian is forbidden to accept anything for himself from a suitor in return for the marriage of his ward.

😐 **Other payments are limited and regulated by law**

Pakistan: Under S. 3 of the Dowry and Bridal Gifts (Restriction) Act, 1976 and relevant Rules 1976, the value of a bride's dowry and the presents given to her by her parents may not exceed Rs 5,000 in value; neundra and salami (money received by the bride from guests at the wedding) are excluded from this calculation. The law also states that all property given to the bride as dowry or as bridal gifts is absolutely hers; that the groom has no rights over this property; and that there can be no restrictions, conditions, or limits placed on her ownership. Husbands have sought to evade the obligation to return a wife's dowry on divorce by claiming that the dowry was illegal because it exceeded this limit. The courts have, however, taken the view that the husband cannot take advantage of any breach of law by the parents of the bride in order to deprive her of her property (Anisur Rehman v. Shahla Fatima 1988 CLC 1888; PLJ 1988 Lahore 378).

Senegal: Under A. 6 of the Loi 67-04 du fevrier 1967, limits are set to curb excessive expenditures on family ceremonies, mahr, and wedding expenses and engagement gifts for the wife; these expenses are not to exceed a maximum of 3,000 fCFA (approximately US$ 4.50), 15,000 fCFA (approximately US$ 22) and 5,000 fCFA (approximately US$ 7.30) respectively. The courts have limited the wife's obligation to return such payments to within the legal amount (Diop v Fall TPI Dakar 20-12-1977 RJS, Credila 1982 Vol III p.188).

Other payments are regulated by law

Malaysia: Under S. 21 of the ILFA, the pemberian (gifts) given or promised at the time of marriage must be recorded during marriage registration. However, the law is silent regarding the customary practice of hantaran.

Sri Lanka: The MMDA recognizes kaikuli, but not marriage gifts. Kaikuli is defined in S. 97 as any sum of money paid, or other movable property given, or any sum of money or any movable property promised to be paid or given, before or at the time of marriage by a relative of the bride or by any other person, to the groom for the bride's use. Kaikuli is to be held in trust by the groom on behalf of the bride and should be returned at any time on demand or on dissolution of marriage (Sawdoona v Abdul Munees 57 NLR 75). The husband cannot refuse to return the kaikuli on the plea that it was spent on the wedding. Case law has established that even if kaikuli money is used to pay for a gift to the wife, the gift becomes her property irrevocably.

Turkey: The law does not recognize the traditional bride-price paid by the groom to the bride's father.

☹ The law is silent regarding other payments and exchanges

Algeria, Cameroon, Egypt, Fiji, Gambia, Indonesia, Iran, Nigeria, Philippines, Sudan

PRACTICES

Paid by groom/his family to bride's family and paid by bride's family to groom

Malaysia & Singapore: Both parties exchange gifts, mostly of special foods, apparel, watches, and pieces of jewellery. This custom of the Malays is given effect in the Muslim family law. At times, the value of the gifts may be more than the mahr. Hantaran (handaran in Singapore) literally means 'sending over' in the Malay language. It is seldom in the form of cash unless it is to go towards the wedding ceremony expenses. Hantaran includes hantar belanja if sent to the bride's side which is the cost of hosting the reception. It also includes some gifts like clothes, shoes, jewellery (sometimes one of each — earrings, necklace, ring, bracelet), food (crafted intricately in all shapes, etc). The belanja money is normally origami'ed into some shape like a mosque, swan, etc., in ringgit bills in blue (RM50) and red (RM10) folded. Hantaran to the boys side is basically some clothes possibly songket (cloth with gold threads), shoes, food, etc. The groom's family has to spend more, and amounts can rise to RM10,000 (approximately US$ 2,600).

Nigeria: The Hausa give kayan sadauki (gifts which may be partly negotiated) to the bride and her family (parts of which go to her mother, aunts, sisters, etc.). There is a reciprocal practice of the bride's family then giving gifts to the marital couple (and therefore, to the husband since maintenance is his responsibility). Often the bride's family gives the new couple foodstuffs (sometimes grains, in amounts large enough to last a year). The amounts of these gifts are sometimes considered during the negotiations of compensation in khul' (see p.275).

Paid by a groom/his family to the bride's family

Central Asian Republics: The kalym is a large amount of money and/or goods given by the groom's parents to the brides' parents. The money is spent on the wedding itself and customary gifts; little is left for the young couple to spend or save. Kalym practice has been re-emerging following the collapse of Soviet rule and the growing influence of conservative political groups.

Iran: The groom pays the bride's mother sheer baha ('money for the milk').

North Yemen: The shart is paid by the groom to the bride's wali. It is at least double the mahr amount and may be up to 10 times the mahr amount.

Pakistan: Bride price (valvar, ser paisay, lab) is practiced widely among the tribal communities of the Pukhtun, Baluch, and some areas of Sindh and Punjab. In practice, either money and/or goods are given. The amount is determined by the bride's age, beauty, and her family's/tribe's status. Among the Pukhtun who practice valvar, the wife effectively becomes the property of her in-laws. Among the Baluch practising lab, a woman may return to her natal family in the event of divorce or the death of the husband. The practice of bride-price appears to be declining among all communities as families increasingly regard this custom as 'selling off' their daughters.

Philippines: Household goods are given by the groom's family, and the worth of these is fixed in pre-wedding negotiations, depending on the capacity of the bridegroom's family, wealth, and position in society. Marital gifts are also customary.

Turkey: The bride price paid by the groom to the bride's father/or family is supposedly in recognition of the cost of raising her and in compensation for the deprivation of her services following her marriage. The tradition has been dying out in the last decade, especially following extensive publicity given to tragic bride-price related cases and changing socio-economic conditions.

Senegal: For a marriage to be socially valid, a variety of customary payments must be made before the marriage can be finalized. The husband must pay the lekku ndeye (money given to the mother to share with her family and friends). He must also pay the beyu baay (money given to the bride's father or godfather) and the niente ak trensu (this payment is similar to dower and paid at the time of the wedding ceremony to seal the contract).

Paid by the bride's family

Bangladesh: Demanding joutuk (dowry) is a relatively new social evil, and some 50 years ago this practice did not exist as a problem among Muslim communities. Despite the Dowry Prohibition Act, dowry demands are now a common part of marriage negotiations, especially in rural areas and lower income brackets. Dowry may be in the form of goods and/or cash. A majority of domestic violence cases are blamed on the wife's inability to meet the husband and in-laws's dowry demands, which persist long after the marriage ceremony.

Due to the rising unemployment among young males in rural Bangladesh, marriage and dowry are seen as sources of income for them. If a son has some education, it increases the bargaining power of his family. Slightly affluent families in rural and middle class communities may demand the dowry of a ticket to the Middle East so that the groom can find a job, or they may demand investment capital for a business.

Egypt: The quayma is a list that the husband signs at the time of the marriage, which enumerates the belongings brought into the marriage by the bride. It also lists their cash value, which is usually inflated and acts as a potentially powerful protection for the bride in the event that there are problems in the marriage. The wife's family can threaten the husband by demanding that he give back all the goods in the quayma or pay their inflated value, failing which, they will sue him for breach of trust or misappropriation.

India: Muslim communities are strongly influenced by Hindu customs and among Muslim families in Hyderabad, the bride's family has to pay jode ki raqam (as a certain amount of cash) to the groom. A rickshaw (scooter) driver can demand Rs 5,000 to 10,000 (approximately US$ 100-200) while an engineer or doctor can demand Rs 100,000 – 300,000. If the bride's age and beauty is in question, the amount demanded can be higher. The groom's parents justify their demand by referring to the financial investment they have made in his upbringing. In many cases where the amount is high, the bride's parents then do not give her any share in inherited property. Since the jode ki reqam is not recorded, it cannot be recovered in the event of talaq. Rights activists see the practice of jode ki raqam as the main reason for the marriage of poor, young Muslim girls to wealthy Arabs from the Gulf States because no such payment is then required and indeed such brides then send part of their customarily large mahr back to their parents in India.

But among the Daudi and Sunni Bohras, the practice of jehez (dowry) had been prohibited by the community's clerics. Among other Muslim communities, the custom is also looked down upon as a negative influence of Hindu custom but has been increasing over the past 100 years, especially in Orissa and patrilineal Calicut families.

Pakistan: Jehez (dowry) is widely practiced in Punjab and among Urdu-speaking communities in other provinces. It is seen as securing the daughter's status with her in-laws. Conspicuous consumption, especially due to the influx of money from migrant workers in the Gulf area has led to lavish dowries. This is spreading to rural communities and to areas where dowry is not traditional (e.g., Baluchistan). Younger urban professional men and women are resisting the practice and preferring to buy household equipment together after marriage.

Sri-Lanka: Kaikuli, which is a Tamil/Hindu custom now practiced by Sri Lankan Muslims, is always a significant amount (except among the Malays where it is not commonly practiced). However, the amount is understated in the marriage registration form, leading to problems of recovery. Kaikuli is now paid in cash and/or movable property. As kaikuli amounts have risen in recent decades, mahr amounts have fallen correspondingly.

Turkey: The bride is responsible for furnishing the bedroom. In the event of divorce, she can recover all that she brought to the marriage as her dowry (provided that she can supply the necessary proof).

Who Can Afford to Get Married!

In Saudi Arabia, the husband is expected to provide not only a very substantial mahr but also all of the household goods and the payment of the often considerable wedding expenses. Saudi women interviewed in the mid-1990s insisted that a wedding cannot take place until the entire household - which includes a completely furnished apartment or villa - is ready for the married couple to live in, and this is the sole responsibility of the groom and his family.

This is expected of the husband regardless of his current financial situation. In one case, the husband had no money to lease and furnish an apartment, so he bought an expensive car on credit and immediately sold it to use the money for his marriage. His aunt, the bride's mother, helped him furnish and decorate the flat and would not allow him to marry her daughter until the apartment was completely furnished. Several years later, he was still paying off the debt of the long-gone car that was used to pay for their home. Any contributions from the bride or her family to the household are strictly voluntary and are not expected.

In Egypt, the bride's trousseau, which is purchased by her family, includes many nightgowns and enough clothing and personal items to assure that she will not need to ask her husband for personal items for at least five years. The greatest expense incurred in setting up a household is the key money needed to rent a small flat, which even in the most inexpensive neighbourhoods can be the equivalent of one or two years' salary for an unskilled or semiskilled worker.

The high costs of a wedding and setting up a new household result in the groom having to work hard for a few years before he can get married. Even though the husband is responsible for providing all these items, often the bride's family helps as much as they can. After becoming engaged, many young men migrate for a couple of years to the Arab oil-producing countries in order earn the money necessary to get married.

The increased expense of marriage has meant that the average age of marriage has risen considerably for women and men. The state, family planners, and some feminists may consider this a positive indicator for population control or women's increased status. However, in the low-income communities, the reality was more complex.

Some women, particularly those who are neither students nor employed, are resentful of having to postpone building a family. They are torn between wanting to have most of the basic household goods before marriage and not wanting to wait so long to marry, particularly since many engagements are broken after a couple of years. Women bear no stigma for a broken engagement and often break off an engagement when they assess that the prospective husband is not working hard enough to save the necessary money. Women are very conscious that a long engagement results in missing out on other potential grooms. Some women say that, fair or not, the reality of the society is that men can always find someone to marry, while a woman's possibilities diminish with age, particularly since men prefer to marry younger women. So women and their families must strike a balance between their demands from potential grooms and their desire to start a family. Many women, not wanting to wait so long, agree to marry older grooms who have worked and saved up enough to be able to marry.

Extracted from Wynn, L., Marriage Contracts and Women's Rights in Saudi Arabia, and Hoodfar, H., Circumventing Legal Limitation: Mahr and Marriage Negotiation in Egyptian Low-Income Communities, in Hoodfar, H. (ed.) (1996), WLUML Special Dossier: Shifting Boundaries in Marriage and Divorce in Muslim Communities, WLUML, Grabels

6a TYPES OF MARRIAGES: POLYGYNY

introduction

The term 'polygyny' refers to a form of marriage in which one husband is married to two or more wives simultaneously. Often it is used interchangeably with the term 'polygamy,' which refers to a form of marriage in which either a husband or a wife has multiple spouses at the same time. Because marriages involving one wife and more than one husband are not permitted in systems based on Muslim laws, or in most systems based on other sources; we use the term 'polygyny' in order to be more precise. However, we recognize that where the more general term 'polygamy' is used, it is most often understood to refer to one man married to two or more women.

Statute law regarding polygyny varies considerably, ranging from an outright ban (Central Asian Republics, Fiji, Indonesia for government servants, Tunisia, Turkey); to permitted but regulated (Bangladesh, Cameroon, Indonesia, Malaysia, Morocco, Pakistan, Philippines, Senegal, Singapore); to weakly or largely unregulated (Iran, Sri Lanka, Sudan).Countries with multiple systems may ban polygyny under laws which are not based on Muslim laws, but permit it under customary and Muslim laws (Gambia, India, Nigeria).

In practice, polygyny occurs to different extents across and within countries. Some communities practice polygyny as a norm (justified by custom or religion), while others appear to discourage it. The number of permitted wives generally depends on whether the source of the law is custom (unlimited) or Muslim laws (maximum of four). Prevalence depends upon community custom, class dynamics, and other factors such as rural-urban divisions. However, there are no hard and fast rules. While in the Gambia polygyny is more common in the rural areas, in some South Asian communities, it is more common among the urban lower-middle class.

Class often determines the form polygyny takes, especially whether it is secret or open. Where polygyny is the norm, wives are more likely to be aware of each other's existence; but in communities where it is not widely practiced, men's greater mobility outside the community may result in their contracting marriages in different areas, without the knowledge of their wives. Often polygyny is closely tied to cousin marriage and inequitable practices such as exchange marriage[1] and child marriage.

power imbalances

Whether open or secret, actually practiced or merely an option available to the husband, polygynous marriage reflects severe power imbalances between spouses. If practiced, polygyny undermines a wife's right to maintenance, inheritance, and sexual and emotional fulfillment; all of which must be shared with other co-wives. Privacy may be severely compromised in polygynous households. While sharing bedrooms may not be common, often kitchen and other household facilities must be shared amongst co-wives. Power imbalances between a husband and a particular wife are sometimes replicated in relationships amongst co-wives, giving rise to potential conflicts amongst them. Husbands often manipulate such conflicts.

Where polygyny is banned by law but the practice continues, subsequent wives find themselves unable to access any rights arising from their marriages. Even if polygyny is not practiced, the mere threat of polygyny, especially where men can access unilateral divorce, can be used to control a wife and limit her ability to assert her rights within the relationship.

The rights of first wives and subsequent wives are affected by polygyny. But the status of co-wives within the family and the community depends on the particular circumstances of the union. In some instances first wives are relegated to the background of family life, all but abandoned or left with no role but to provide domestic services for new wives. Alternatively, older wives may be able to use their seniority as a means of controlling subsequent wives. Indeed, if an older wife is a relative of her husband and she has land, her status within the extended family may ensure continued respect and security.

In both Cameroon and Senegal, the law requires that the matrimonial property regime be stated in the marriage certificate. This requirement rarely works to women's advantage (see Financial Rights and Settlements p.316 & p.326). While laws based on Muslim laws permit the wife to control her own property, any presumption that marital property is joint can cause hardship for co-wives since it then has to be shared among many. However, in Malaysia and Singapore, Shari'ah judges have the authority to order, as a part of an order granting permission for polygyny, that existing marital assets be distributed between the first wife and her husband prior to the second marriage. Among Nigerian Muslim communities, each spouse comes to the marriage with his or her own property and that property remains their own. Property acquired during the course of the marriage continues to be earmarked as belonging to this or that spouse depending on who bought or was given it or (more rarely) in whose name ownership is registered. However, there is no recognition of the non-monetary contribution made through domestic labour to the acquisition of marital assets. Given that women generally have less access to resources than men (especially when in seclusion or responsible for childcare), such a property regime usually benefits men in the division of marital assets and may result in a polygynous wife's creation of wealth benefiting other co-wives.

Where the state and/or society frown upon polygyny, women generally bear the greater burden of any consequences; men may face minor punishments, but women face issues such as pregnancy.

factors behind polygyny

In most societies, polygyny can be found across classes. This distribution reflects overall gender inequalities in society.

While there are a host of reasons that men use to allow themselves polygynous marriages, there are a few common reasons, some of which are supported by legislation. Customarily, these include the wife's failure to conceive (whether or not medically the 'fault' lies with her), the wife's 'failure' to produce male children, the wife's long-term illness, or the wife's distant location. In contrast, in many communities (Nigeria marriages under customary laws are an example of an exception), similar complaints about a husband are customarily not usually regarded as acceptable grounds for a wife to divorce her husband. In some cases polygyny may serve as a means of asserting a man's virility. In other cases, the compulsion to marry cousins or others chosen by parents, accompanied by the social impossibility of divorce, motivates men to choose polygynous marriages (Pakistan, among feudal families, South Africa).

On the other hand, women rarely 'choose' to enter into a polygynous marriage— that is, if they are aware or have any 'choice' at all, which is not the case when a child is married or when wives find themselves in secretly polygamous unions. First wives may accept polygyny for fear of being divorced by their husbands. If they refused and were divorced, they would have to face the social stigma and economic consequences of divorce. Older wives in cousin marriages may arrange a new wife for their husbands in order to release themselves from his physical demands. Subsequent wives (when they are aware that there is a first wife) may find the financial security and social standing offered by the status of wife preferable to remaining single. This is especially true where women suffer a reduction in marriage options that results from advanced education or age. In rare instances, women may opt for polygyny to avoid being a 'full-time' wife. By being a co-wife, they gain the consequent opportunities for personal independence. Men sometimes seek widowed and divorced mothers for polygynous marriages, as they are less likely to complain about the associated inequalities.

But even where women appear to be exercising an 'option' when they enter into a polygynous marriage, the attractiveness of such an option implies that equitable 'fulltime' relationships, sexual relationships outside marriage, or remaining unmarried (whether single, divorced or widowed) are not possible. Likewise, when a wife consents to another wife joining the marriage, she can hardly be described as having 'chosen' a polygynous marriage. The social consequences of any other option may be unbearable. A refusal could not only put a woman at risk of being divorced, but it could also bring pressure to bear from those invoking the 'religious right' of men to marry more than one woman. Women who refuse to give their consent can face the threat of being socially condemned as violators of 'divine' law.

In some instances traditional and cultural norms, accompanied by the conditioning effect of social/ community scrutiny, may be effective in ensuring a measure of equity in polygynous marriages. More frequently, communities are aware that Islam 'permits' polygyny, but the Qur'anic condition restricting polygyny to those rare circumstances where wives can be treated equitably is conveniently ignored.

complete prohibition of polygyny

A few countries have completely outlawed polygyny (and this has occurred only in countries with no parallel legal systems); these include: Turkey, Uzbekistan, and Fiji. The source of law in most instances is a colonial-Christian prohibition, such as British common law or the Napoleonic Code. Tunisia is unique in that its ban on polygyny is based on an interpretation of Muslim laws, inspired by Qur'anic verses stating that it is impossible to treat wives equitably.

Penalties for practicing polygyny in such systems can be serious (up to 5 years in the Kyrgyz Republic, Art 153 CrC). In Tunisia, the husband and subsequent wife are liable to one year imprisonment and/or a heavy fine. However, they are not liable for the crime of bigamy, which carries other penalties.

Legislation prohibiting polygyny may protect the rights of first wives. However, if the practice continues under unrecognized religious and customary systems, subsequent wives are unable to register their marriages and find themselves outside the protection of the law, with no access to the rights and state benefits available to women in registered monogamous marriages (see Registration and Validity, p.134).

The limitations of legal reforms that are not accompanied by other social reform policies are illustrated clearly by the realities of social practice. Even in systems that completely prohibit polygyny and provide criminal penalties for those convicted of practicing it, polygynous marriages are still performed under religious ceremonies and subsequently not registered with the state (Fiji, Uzbekistan).

polygyny in parallel judicial systems

In a number of countries, the state may recognize secular, religious and customary laws; and couples can opt to be governed by any of them, usually depending upon the form of the marriage (Gambia, India, Nigeria). In these countries, polygyny is usually recognized under Muslim and/ or customary laws, but penalized if the marriage is solemnized under other laws (Gambia).

Systems that allow couples to opt to be governed by customary, or Muslim, or non-Muslim laws seem to offer women a range of options (monogamy or recognition of their rights as polygynous wives). But since women often have little say in determining which law they will be married under, or whether their marriage will be monogamous or not, these advantages are limited.

In addition, men may purposely exploit parallel judicial systems to their advantage. In Malaysia's federal system, where each State has separate family laws and court systems, men have avoided regulation of polygyny by contracting a polygynous marriage in another state. However, a uniform Islamic Family Law was recently passed on to the 13 State governments by the Federal Government which is attempting to remove such discrepancies. Women's groups are nevertheless concerned that the new law, following pressure from conservatives, may introduce a uniform text that is the lowest common denominator, i.e., relax the tighter conditions imposed in some States.

In countries where polygyny is banned under laws applicable to other communities or civil marriage laws, men have converted to Islam in order to facilitate a polygynous marriage (Sri Lanka, Malaysia, Gambia). In Nigeria, men married under the Marriage Act (under which marriage is monogamous, and bigamy is illegal) may have previously married or may subsequently marry under customary or Muslim laws, and they can do so with impunity.

In Tanzania laws recognize different types of marriage (including Muslim and customary). However, they attempt to prevent men from exploiting these systems to their advantage by prohibiting them from combining monogamous forms of marriage with polygynous forms.

permission required for polygyny

Sometimes policy-makers have responded to women's call for a ban on polygyny by arguing that the regulation of – but not the banning of - polygyny is a preferable alternative to divorce. Such an argument ignores the option that the law could instead make unilateral and baseless divorce impossible.

In some systems, a husband is required to obtain the permission of a governmental authority, court or quasi-judicial body, or other forum to contract a polygynous marriage (Indonesia, Pakistan, Bangladesh, Malaysia, Singapore). The conditions for granting permission may focus on the permission of existing wife/wives and/or depend on 'defects' on the part of the existing wife/wives, e.g., inability to perform 'marital duties,' infertility, physical defects or incurable disease, absence from the country, or insanity. Systems that permit polygyny on the basis of such grounds, but do not permit women to divorce on parallel grounds, reveal a very biased view of gender relationships. In Singapore during the permission process, both the existing and proposed wives are consulted in order to solicit their views on the proposed marriage.

Some laws may alternatively, or also, focus on the conditions that the husband must fulfill, e.g., his financial capacity to maintain all the wives (Indonesia, Malaysia, Morocco). Conditions relating to the husband, such as requirements that he be able to provide 'equitable treatment,' usually focus on economic support and do not take into account women's sexual and emotional needs. This oversight has led some activists to call polygyny 'enforced menopause.'

There are subtle differences in the way that conditions are expressed ('polygyny is only permissible if...', 'polygyny is not permissible unless...'), but most authorities interpret the conditions for polygyny very loosely. The condition that a subsequent marriage be 'just and necessary' (Bangladesh, Malaysia and Pakistan) could be a powerful tool for regulation, but it is instead used to justify polygyny on the slightest grounds. In some instances, the authorities may even accept the wife's 'failure' to produce a male heir as sufficient grounds for granting permission for polygyny (Bangladesh, Pakistan). Interestingly, courts in Singapore encourage adoption rather than a second marriage. Where states require the existing wife/wives' consent for subsequent marriages, this requirement is seldom enforced, and wives are either ignored or coerced to consent.

Rarely do laws make separate dwellings a pre-condition for polygyny (Sudan). Other systems permit a wife to approach the court to ensure separate dwellings. In both types of laws, the definitions of equitable treatment and separate dwellings are not always clear. Separate dwellings may refer to either separate residences in completely separate locations; to different homes in a single residential complex/compound; or even to separate kitchens or separate bedrooms with shared facilities.

Where polygyny is permitted but regulated, penalties for failing to follow the required procedure are light (minor fines and/or prison sentences, and payment of prompt or deferred mahr), and in some systems the subsequent marriage remains valid (Bangladesh, Malaysia, Pakistan, Sri Lanka). In Cameroon and Senegal, a man who has chosen the monogamy option but marries polygynously is liable to imprisonment if the wife files a complaint; the subsequent marriage cannot be registered and is, therefore, invalid in the eyes of the law. In many systems that permit polygyny, the wife may be given automatic access to divorce, but usually divorce offers little consolation.

It is also important to note who can seek relief when procedures are violated. More option-giving are laws which permit first wives, as well as subsequent wives, to approach the courts in such instances. Most laws that attempt to regulate polygyny focus on men's right to polygyny, rather than on women's rights within marriage. In practice, these laws fail to ensure that men who exert the 'right' to polygyny reciprocate by respecting the rights of those they marry.

minimal regulation of polygyny

Other systems do not place any conditions on polygyny. Instead, they have procedures that must be followed in order to contract a polygynous marriage (e.g., giving notice to a court and/or the existing wife/wives). In Sri Lanka the husband is required to give notice of his intention to contract a polygamous marriage to the Quazi in the area where he lives, to the Quazi in the area where his wife/wives lives, and also to the Quazi in the area where his intended wife lives. These Quazis are then expected to display these notices in all the Jumma Mosques within their area, as well as in other public places.

Finally, some systems do not provide any regulation of polygynous marriages, thus leaving it to custom and tradition (customary laws recognized in West Africa, or uncodified Muslim laws in India).

polygyny and marriage contracts

In some systems, the type of marriage (polygynous/monogamous) must be stipulated in the initial marriage contract, and where monogamy is chosen, the type cannot be subsequently changed (Cameroon and Senegal). Senegal's Code de la Famille also requires the number of wives to be specified (one, two, or more than two). Although the law allows the husband to determine how many wives he will be limited to, the wife's opinion is important in practice.

Almost all laws framed under Muslim laws explicitly or implicitly permit wives to add conditions to the marriage contract, and these conditions can include a prohibition on polygyny. Women in Bangladesh, Morocco, Egypt, and Pakistan have successfully added such conditions to their marriage contracts. In Morocco, even if a woman does not limit her husband's right to polygyny in the marriage contract, she can sue him for 'harm' in the event that he marries again.

However, laws differ in the options that they give a wife in the event that her husband violates any contractual prohibition on polygyny. It is not always clear that the wife can actually prevent a subsequent marriage; she may merely have the right to divorce her husband after he has already contracted a subsequent marriage. In Senegal and Cameroon, any subsequent marriage that violates the agreed maximum is invalid, at least in law. In contrast, in Bangladesh, Iran, and Morocco, the subsequent marriage is nevertheless valid; and the first wife's only 'option' is to seek divorce and/ or demand any unpaid mahr.

Contractual options are additionally limited by women's lack of control over the marriage process. Few women have the social power to determine which system they will be married under, much less what conditions, if any, will be amended to their marriage contracts.

trends

Overall, polygyny appears to be declining in response to both socio-economic pressures and women's activism. However, in some countries where polygyny has been outlawed, the emergence of strong religious lobbies has opened up local debates about polygyny and its possible benefits. Those who advocate a revival of polygyny argue that it is a legitimately helpful means of providing socio-economic security for women (Uzbekistan, Tajikistan and Malaysia). In pre-Revolution Iran, a 1975 amendment attempted to regulate polygyny by requiring that a polygynous marriage have the existing wife/wives consent and providing punishments for those who contracted such marriages without consent (up to 6 months imprisonment). During that period, polygyny was considered relatively socially unacceptable. In the post-Revolution period, polygyny continues to be regulated, but changes in the overall social atmosphere have made polygyny more acceptable.

Polygyny is a focus of conflict between progressive and retrogressive political forces in Egypt. In May 1985, the Egyptian High Constitutional Court struck down a 1979 emergency law that had included provisions affecting women's rights within the family. When the government enacted the Personal Status (Amendment) Law (Law no. 100/ 1985) to revise the 1920 and 1929 Laws on Personal Status, many of the beneficial 1979 provisions were included in the new law. However, the 1979 provision that had allowed Egyptian women automatic access to divorce (on the grounds of harm) if their husband married polygynously was dropped, apparently as a concession to religious conservatives.

endnote

[1] Exchange marriage involves marriage of a brother and a sister of one family to a sister and a brother of another family. In extreme cases, a man may pledge any future daughter to his in-laws in exchange for his own wife. Exchange marriages imply that the fate of one couple is tied to the fate of the other couple, so that if one couple divorces, the other couple automatically has to divorce even if they are happy together. Exchange marriages are often among relatives, compounding the associated problems.

Trends in South East Asia

Some states in Malaysia require that consent of the existing wives be obtained for a polygynous marriage application to be accepted. In one of the 13 States (Selangor), this requirement was deleted in 1990, despite protests from women's groups. The deletion was based on the argument that the consent of the court should not be conditional upon the consent of the wife. At the same time, another state (the federal territory of Kuala Lumpur) amended its polygyny provisions to allow recognition of polygynous marriages that have been contracted without obtaining permission/s. This amendment allows the recognition of marriages contracted in South Thailand and Indonesia and marriages that have been solemnized in the state but not through the official channels. This recognition, while giving recourse to second wives and their children, eats away at any protective element found in regulations restricting or regulating polygyny.

Some Muslim based groups like the Malaysian Muslim Youth Movement (ABIM) in Malaysia organize periodic match-making projects for women-headed households. One official of the Islamic party (PAS), which runs the government in the state of Terengganu, proposed in 2000 that men be encouraged to marry women who headed households. In his proposal, monogamous and polygynous marriages (with women heads of household) would be encouraged by the state by the awarding of stipends to the new couples. His plan was abandoned after a public furor.

In Singapore the court solicits the views of the existing and the potential wife in a permission to marry (polygynous marriage) application. This 'consent' is one of many factors that the court would take into consideration when deciding whether or not the husband is capable of being just and fair to his existing and future wives. If they determine that he is capable, they will grant him permission. However, often when the potential wife discovers her future husband's previous marriage(s), she refuses to marry him.

In recent years, with the establishment of ferry services and the flow of Singaporean investments to the Indonesian islands south of Singapore, Muslim men are marrying Indonesian Muslim women polygynously. The women continue to live in Indonesia while their affluent Singapore husbands commute. The authorities in Singapore have done nothing to restrict this practice.

NOTES

LAWS: Polygyny

Criteria

☺ More option-giving are those laws which:

- Ban polygyny and penalize polygynous husbands and those who solemnize and/or register polygynous marriages

😐 The middle ground is occupied by those laws which:

- Declare invalid any marriage in violation of a contractual agreement on monogamy or limited polygyny; or
- Make polygyny conditional upon a formal procedure for permission and penalize failure to follow procedure; and
- Specify grounds for permission.

The lower middle-ground is occupied by those laws which:

- Require a formal procedure to obtain permission but do not specify any grounds on which the marriage may be prevented; or
- Specify grounds on which the marriage may be prevented, but do not provide any procedural mechanism; or
- Recognize contractual agreements on monogamy but only offer dissolution of marriage as the relief.

☹ Less option-giving are those laws which:

- Do not have any codified procedure or clear mechanism for relief for first and subsequent wives.

☺ **Polygyny is banned**

Tunisia: Under A. 18 of the CSP, any man who contracts a polygynous marriage is punishable with one year of imprisonment or a fine of 240,000 Tunisian francs or both. These provisions apply even if the new marriage is registered and even if the man continues to live with the first wife. A wife who knowingly enters a polygynous marriage is liable to the same punishments. But penalties for bigamy do not apply to marriages violating the ban on polygyny (and instead only apply if a wife has two husbands). Under A. 21 a polygynous marriage is considered irregular and can be nullified either by spouses, guardians, mothers, or the legal department. The effect is that the marriage is considered never to have existed, but the woman can claim her mahr; the legal paternity of the children is recognized; and the woman must fulfill idda before remarrying. Under A. 21, spouses who continue to live together after their marriage has been declared null and void are liable to 6 months imprisonment.

Fiji, India (Special Marriages Act 1954), Gambia (Civil Marriage Act 1938), Nigeria (marriages under the MCA, and Marriage Act 1990), Turkey, Uzbekistan, Kyrgyz Republic, Tajikistan: These laws have been influenced by British colonial laws, Soviet laws, and/or the Napoleonic Code. Subsequent marriages cannot be registered and additional wives have no legal rights. Polygyny is seen as bigamy, is illegal, and may attract heavy penalties. In the Gambia, bigamy is a felony liable to 5 years imprisonment. Under A.153 of the CrC of the Kyrgyz Republic, polygyny is punishable by imprisonment for up to 5 years. While A. 8 of Uzbekistan's Family Law does not define polygyny, it is nevertheless punishable under A. 126, Chapter V of the CrC. Under this provision, polygamy, or cohabitation with two and more women on the basis of one common household, is punishable with a fine of 50-150 times the minimum monthly wage, or correctional labour of up to three years, or by imprisonment of up to three years. Turkey's High Court stated that "relationships outside of marriage are illegal," and men must face the consequences of illegal affairs (YHGK 1864/ 1962-4-8/46). The High Court based this opinion on Contract Law, Article 65.

NOTE: In India, the Gambia, and Nigeria, polygyny is legal under other laws (customary and/or Muslim), and women in polygynous marriages may access their rights through the courts.

Lebanon: According to the 1948 Law Pertaining to Personal Status for the Druze Sect (Article 10), polygyny is prohibited. Article 9 of the 1998 Civil Marriage Law, proposed by activists but never passed, would have outlawed polygyny. Article 61 of the proposed law also stated that the paternity of children born from an illegal second marriage would not be recognized.

Polygyny is conditional upon formal permission, and this permission is granted on specified grounds; failure to follow procedure is penalized

Indonesia: A 1983 policy (PP No.10/83) requires public servants and members of the armed forces to request permission from their superior in addition to the regular permission procedures for polygyny. These restrictions were expressly intended to set an example for the rest of the population. Under PP No.45 of 1990, women public servants are not allowed to become second, third, or fourth wives. Under A. 4 and 5 of the MA, and A. 56 and 57 of the KHI, polygyny is permitted through an application to the court. The court may grant permission if the wife is unable to fulfil sexual obligations of marriage (duties as a wife); suffers from physical defects or an incurable disease ; or is infertile. A. 5 requires (a) approval of wife/wives; (b) assurance that husband will guarantee necessities of life for wives and their children; and (c) a guarantee that husband shall act justly in regard to wives and children. These requirements do not apply if a wife's opinion cannot be solicited or she has been absent for at least 2 years. Under A. 13 a marriage violating procedures can be prevented. There are no provisions for divorce on demand should the wife not agree with the court's decision.

Malaysia: Contracting a polygynous marriage requires the permission of a Syariah court. Conditions that must be met in order to obtain permission to contract a polygynous marriage vary slightly among the 13 States. The husband must justify in writing why the proposed marriage is just and necessary, which may include existing wife's sterility, physical infirmity, physical unfitness for conjugal relation, willful avoidance of an order for restitution of conjugal rights, or insanity. The husband must also provide details of income, financial obligations, and dependants, including those he will become responsible for after the proposed marriage. The husband must indicate whether or not the existing wife has consented. The court hears both the husband and existing wife/wives. Conditions include that the husband must be able to treat all wives equally and that the proposed marriage will not cause darar syarie (harm or danger in respect of religion, life, body, mind or property) to the existing wife/wives. Under S. 23 (7) of the federal territory law, the husband is liable to pay immediately the entire amount of the mahr and gifts due to the existing wife/wives, recoverable as a debt. Polygynous marriages in violation of required procedures can be registered after payment of a fine for failing to get court permission (amendment intended to protect new wife). Failure to follow required procedures is liable to 6 months imprisonment and a fine.

Bangladesh & Pakistan: S.6 of the MFLO regulates but does not ban polygyny. It requires that the husband obtain the written permission of the local government authorities (of the existing wife's residence and not the husband's) to contract a polygynous marriage. The husband has to satisfy the Union Council that he has obtained his wife's consent, but it may give permission even if the wife refuses. Under rule 14 of the MFLO Rules, a polygynous marriage must be 'just and necessary,' and it may be determined to be so on the basis of the existing wife's failure to have children; her insanity; her physical disability; her inability to have sex; or her refusal to live with her husband following a decree for restitution of conjugal rights against her. Injunctions may be sought to prevent marriages that violate MFLO S.6 from taking place. The DMMA, 1939 allows a woman to seek a dissolution if her polygynous husband either fails to treat her equitably [S. 2(viii)(f)] or fails to follow the required procedure [S.2 (ii-a)]. Under S. 2(ii-a), the first or subsequent wife must be the one to ask the Council to take legal action against the husband. Under S. 6(5) of the MFLO, failure to follow required procedure is liable to immediate payment of the entire mahr (deferred or prompt) that is due to the existing wife/wives and imprisonment of up to 1 year and/or a fine. Marriages in violation of procedure remain valid.

Singapore: In order to contract a polygynous marriage, the husband is required to apply to a shariah court. The court is to conduct an inquiry to determine the husband's financial position, his potential for treating his wives equitably, and if there are lawful benefits to the union. The court usually solicits the consent of the existing wife and of the future wife as a matter of practice. The existing wife is required to attend the proceedings. The court's decision may be appealed by either of the existing spouses.

Philippines: Under A. 27 of the CMPL, a Muslim male is permitted to have more than one wife, only if he can provide them with equal companionship and just treatment as enjoined by Islamic law and only then in exceptional cases. Under A. 162 CMPL, the husband is required to file written notification of his planned polygynous marriage in the Shariah Circuit Courts; a copy of this notice is served to all existing wives. The body, which is convened to adjudicate the application (the religious arbitration council), has wide discretion to decide whether or not to "sustain her (the wife's) objections" should there be an objection to the application. Only first wives can bring the matter to the Shariah Circuit Court. The husband is liable for offences if he violates the required procedure.

A statement of the husband's choice between monogamy and polygyny is required in the marriage contract; subsequent marriages in violation of this statement are void

Senegal: Under A. 134 and 130(3) of the CF, at the time of contracting a marriage, the husband must determine if the marriage will be monogamous or polygynous, and if polygynous whether he will have 2 or more than 2 wives. A monogamy option or polygynous option limited to two wives cannot be changed subsequently. The husband remains obliged to follow this option for his lifetime, even after the dissolution of the marriage for which he chose a specific option. Under A. 133, if the husband fails to indicate his option, it is presumed polygynous. He is not required to inform the wife of his decision. Under A. 141(6) & (7), a subsequent marriage violating the monogamy option or exceeding the maximum is to be declared annulled by the court. Under A. 333 of the CP, bigamy is punishable by imprisonment and a fine. However, the law is weak because the court can act only if the existing wife can prove the registration of the new marriage, and there is no relief for the new wife.

Cameroon: The laws concerning polygyny are similar to laws in Senegal. However, if the polygyny option is chosen, there is no possibility of stating a specified number of wives in the certificate. Where the choice is not stated, the courts have presumed the marriage to be polygynous.

Polygyny is conditional; dissolution is the only relief for the existing wife

Algeria: The reasons for a polygynous marriage must be justified and the existing wife must be informed. Any co-wife may petition for dissolution on the grounds of harm if her consent was not obtained.

Morocco: Under A. 30 of the Moudawana, polygyny will not be permitted if it is feared that the wives will not be treated equitably. Husbands are required to inform subsequent wives of their existing marriage, but they are not required to obtain the existing wife's permission. The existing wife may ask the court to look into the harm that has been done to her. Under A. 31, if a husband violates a contractual restriction on polygyny, the existing wife has the right to demand dissolution.

Yemen: Under Article 12 of the LPS, polygyny is permitted, provided that the husband is able to treat all wives equitably; that there is some lawful benefit to the subsequent union; that the husband can support more than one wife, and that the prospective wife and existing wife are both informed. Under A. 42(2), the husband is not permitted to require that the wives share accommodation, unless they consent, and they have the right to change their minds on this issue at any time.

☹ Minimal regulation of polygyny

Iran: The husband has to ask permission from the court or his first wife. The universal marriage contract recognizes the wife's right to talaq tafwid in situations where a husband takes a second wife without the consent of the first wife, or because of his failure to treat co-wives equally. Subsequent wives can also access divorce if the husband fails to inform them of his correct status.

Sri-Lanka: Under S. 24 MMDA, the husband must give notice to the Quazis of the areas where he, the existing wife, and the prospective wife reside. The notice must contain his name and address, and the names and addresses of the women. The Quazi must display copies of the notice in the Jumma Mosques and at other prominent public places in their areas. Failure to follow this procedure creates an obligation on the Registrar to refuse to register the subsequent marriage. A Registrar (and every other person who aids and abets the registrar) who registers a second marriage in violation of this procedure is liable to a fine not exceeding Rs.100, or to imprisonment for a period not exceeding 6 months, or both (S.82). Failure to follow the procedure does not affect the validity of the subsequent marriage. Even if the first wife receives notice of a subsequent marriage, there is nothing that she can do to prevent it.

Sudan: S. 10 of the MPLA, confirms the right of men to contract polygynous marriages with up to 4 wives. The husband may not accommodate his co-wives in the same dwelling, except when no objection is raised by the first wife/wives. The husband does not have to seek court permission. However, polygyny may be explicitly prohibited in the marriage contract, and if the wife has this right in the contract and subsequently gives permission, it would be presumed she gave this under pressure, and the subsequent marriage may be prohibited. But there have been no known cases accessing this.

Tanzania: Under S. 10 of the Law of Marriage Act, 1971, a marriage under Muslim laws is presumed polygynous or potentially polygynous (unless restricted by conditions added to the marriage contract). Under S. 15 no man married under the monogamous form of marriage can contract another marriage, and no man married under Muslim laws can subsequently contract a monogamous form of marriage. For polygyny the consent of existing wives must be sought. The form of marriage chosen at the time of the husband's first marriage cannot be changed.

Nigeria: Polygyny is permitted under Muslim laws (with a maximum of four wives) and customary laws (with no limit). There are no codified regulations concerning polygynous marriage.

Gambia: Customary marriages are considered potentially polygamous in nature and recognized by virtue of S. 5(1) of the Laws of England (Application Act), as well as the 1997 constitution of the Gambia. These laws permit a man to marry as many wives as he chooses. Marriages under Muslim laws are considered intrinsically polygynous and allow a man to marry a maximum of four wives with no regulation of conditions for polygyny or procedural requirements. Women who marry a married man under customary or Islamic law may approach the court to have their marriages validated. Doing so enables them to claim their rights in marriage.

IMPLEMENTATION

Where the state applies firm regulation

Bangladesh: A 1999 judgment by the High Court Division strongly discouraged polygyny and ordered that a recommendation be sent to the Law Ministry so that they could scrutinize whether or not polygyny could be banned. The recommendation suggested that the same line of reasoning used in Tunisia to ban polygyny could be used in Bangladesh (Elias v Jesmin Sultana, 51 DLR (AD) (1999).

Cameroon: In Che Maabo v. Che Maabo HCF/7mc/2m/98, a female judge refused to admit the precedent that a marriage certificate with no option stated is presumed polygynous. She declared the marriage monogamous, even though it had been celebrated according to native law and custom, and therefore, no option had been stated.

Malaysia: An Appeal Board ruling in Aisha bte Abdul Rauff v Wan Moh'd Yusof (1990) 7 Jurnal Hukum JH 152 highlighted that all conditions for polygyny are equally important and should be considered separately. Shari'ah judges have the authority to distribute marital assets to the first wife in the event of polygyny.

Nigeria: Courts uphold co-wives' rights to equal material treatment and sexual access (at least in terms of two nights each in rotation).

Palestinian community in Israel: The Israeli authorities do not want to be seen to interfere in polygamy. Although criminalized, the courts rarely apply the penal provisions.

Singapore: Scrutiny of financial conditions is applied rigorously. Men are required to produce income tax statements and salary slips. If income criteria fail, the application is dismissed. The courts consider equitable treatment the next most significant issue. If a wife proves her husband has been having an extra-marital affair with another woman, the husband's application to marry that woman can be rejected on the grounds of the prohibition against zina. The courts interpret 'lawful need' to mean the potential wife is a widow with children, an aged spinster, or a convert to Islam. If the wife is known to be barren, this is not a reason to allow permission. Where the wife has been ill, the applicant may be chastised for not caring for her, especially if they have been married for some time. The restrictions on polygyny are rigorously applied because the state does not support large families. These policies have a political dimension in Singapore because most Muslims are not ethnic Chinese.

Sri Lanka: A MWRAF survey found 83% of Quazis felt there should be a law requiring the permission of a Quazi for polygyny. The courts generally uphold a wife's right to separate residence, but 'separate residence' is not clearly defined. Earlier case law accepted a man's conversion to Islam as a legitimate means of contracting a polygynous marriage (AG v Reid (1964) 4 MMDR 195). However, in Abeysundara v Abeysundara (1997) SC Appn. No70/96, the second marriage of a man who converted to Islam in order to side-step problematic divorce procedures in the General Law was ruled to be invalid.

The state does not apply regulation strictly

Cameroon: When marriage certificates do not state a 'marriage option,' the courts have traditionally decided that the marriage should be considered polygamous. Monogamy is presumed to be the exception. The presence of female judges is helping to change this.

Indonesia: The court can decide whether or not the existing wife's permission is necessary, and her refusal to give her permission is sometimes seen as grounds for granting court permission for polygyny. A wife's absence abroad for work is also accepted as grounds for granting polygyny permission. Equality of treatment is only measured in monetary terms.

Malaysia: Courts assume that financial support is enough to ensure that the marriage would be just and fair. There are no cases to date where men are jailed for failing to follow the required procedure. Many have been fined, but the law permits both fines and jail terms.

Nigeria: Even when men who marry under the Marriage Act (i.e. monogamous marriage) have previously been married or they contract subsequent marriages (usually under Muslim laws or customary laws, if Christian), they are not prosecuted for bigamy.

Philippines: The law does not define 'just treatment.' The conditions for polygyny are not clearly laid out; there have been cases of mastectomy being accepted as just grounds. Though the husband is required to file written notification in Sharia Courts, implementation is weak because these courts are too far away or husbands choose not to inform wives.

PRACTICES

Polygyny continues despite regulation or an outright ban

Gambia: Polygyny is widespread. The 1993 Population and Housing Census, produced by the Gambian government Central Statistics Department (CSD), found 42.3% of ever-married persons (48% of women and 33.3% of men) aged 15 and over in polygynous marriages. Polygyny is more common in rural areas (53.3% women and 38.3% men) than in the urban areas (37.8% women and 25.3% men) (CSD 1993, 26-27). There seems to exist an inverse relationship between polygyny and education, especially amongst women. Slightly over half of women with no education are in polygynous relationships; 35.1% of women with primary education, 23.9% of women with secondary education, and 16.3% of women with post-secondary education are in polygynous unions (CSD 1993, 29). This trend is the same for both rural and urban areas (CSD 1993, 29). The only exception can be seen amongst men and women with post-secondary education in rural areas (both groups' levels rise from the steadily lowering rate with no primary and secondary education) (CSD 1993, 31). Possibly women with post-secondary education in rural areas have become 'unmarriageable' and so must compromise and accept a polygynous union. There seems to be a negative correlation between polygyny and high level or professional occupation, particularly in the case of women. Almost 5% of women and 9.1% of men who are in monogamous unions are in managerial and professional occupations, with only 1.3% of women and 7.4% of men in polygynous unions in these occupations. These findings suggest that women with socio-economic options mostly choose not to engage in or remain in polygynous marriages.

Most Gambian men in polygynous unions are not economically and financially able to keep more than one wife. However, men justify the practice by saying that "Islam gives me the right to keep up to four wives." Christian men circumvent prosecution for bigamy by converting to Islam. Bigamy is otherwise hardly prosecuted. Although generally wives are not consulted about polygyny, husbands may give the first wife gifts to make her accept the situation. Where there is objection from a wife, this objection could lead to a divorce initiated by her husband. Where a wife refuses to live with a second wife, she can move out of the husband's residence and negotiation will take place. GAMCOTRAP quotes research estimating that 20% of women are in polygynous unions where they are responsible for their own maintenance and that of their children.

Malaysia & Singapore: In many instances, where the court refuses to grant permission for a polygynous marriage, men go to another State (where restrictions are more lax) to get married or go to South Thailand or Indonesia to marry polygynously there. Marriages outside jurisdiction are not usually registered. First wives in Singapore have informed the court that their husbands threatened to divorce them if they did not consent to a subsequent marriage.

Morocco: Given that 86% of women are illiterate, few are able to exercise their contractual right to insist on a monogamous marriage.

Nigeria: Polygynous marriages appear to be higher amongst the well to do, in the rural areas, and in Muslim communities. However, polygyny is widespread in all parts of Nigeria and amongst all strata of wealth. Many men (regardless of religious affiliation) assume that men are 'naturally' polygynous and, therefore, have a right to practice polygynous marriages or liaisons. Amongst some sectors of Muslim communities, the right to marry polygynously is seen as virtually mandatory for a 'good Muslim man,' especially if he is also a member of the sarauta (the pre-colonial Hausa ruling class). The consent of existing wife(s) is irrelevant. Although it is considered courteous to inform existing wives, this is not mandatory, and wives may not realize they have a new co-wife until she arrives at the marital home (or when rooms are being built or renovated).

Senegal: When men violate their marriage option, the subsequent marriage is not celebrated or registered before the state authorities. Commonly, a monogamy option is violated by a second marriage contracted at the mosque (i.e., an unregistered marriage). In the eyes of the Muslim community, this second marriage is given as much, if not greater recognition than the first, civil marriage.

South Africa: Polygyny is practiced across class barriers. For many working class women, participating in a polygynous union is a means of some financial support. Among the upper middle class, men sometimes render their marriages polygynous on the pretext that ending the first marriage might bring about undue hardship to the first wife. Often they do this without informing the first wife or subsequent wives. (This is possible when wives live in different parts of the country and is made easier because the state does not officially recognize Muslim marriages.)

Sudan: Husbands rarely seek their wife's permission.

Tajikistan: Despite the legal ban, since the civil war and unrest of 1992, polygyny has become more widespread. In addition to the influence of the economic crisis, the growing influence of politico-religious extremism on public opinion (concerning the roles of women) has led to a general acceptance that rich men may marry more than one wife. However, there is no official data because the practice is still illegal. The parliament debated recognizing polygyny while considering the 1999 draft Family Code. Women in polygynous unions support the recognition of polygyny as a form of protection for themselves and their children, allowing them to access their rights under the law.

Uzbekistan: Despite the legal ban, polygyny continues (and continued even under Soviet rule), remains socially acceptable, and does not result in punishment. Polygyny receives some public support and has been widely discussed in the media as a solution to the 'problem of single women.' This refers to the phenomenon of women remaining unmarried because they have higher education or are pursuing careers and are then unable to find a man willing to marry them. The social acceptance of polygyny is, therefore, based on the view that it is not appropriate for women to remain 'without a man.'

Monogamy is NOT against Islam: Coalition on Women's Rights in Islam

On 18 March 2003 the Coalition on Women's Rights in Islam issued the following Press Statement. The Coalition includes: Sisters in Islam (SIS), All Women's Action Society (AWAM), Persatuan Isteri dan Keluarga Polis (Perkep), Persatuan Suri dan Anggota Wanita Perkhidmatan Awam (Puspanita), Perseketuan Pertubuhan-Pertubuhan Wanita Malaysia (NCWO), Persatuan Pekerja Wanita (PERWANIS), Wanita Perkim Kebangsaan, Wanita Inovatif Jayadiri (WIJADI), Women's Aid Organisation (WAO), Women's Candidacy Initiative (WCI), Women's Centre for Change (WCC) and Wanita Ikram.

The Coalition on Women's Rights in Islam regrets the reaction of the Muftis and others in opposing our Monogamy Campaign [launched 16 March 2003]. They have misunderstood and misconceived our effort. Let us clarify our position:

- We believe the practice of monogamy is according to *hukum syarak* [Sharia].
- We believe polygamy is allowed only in very exceptional circumstances.
- We believe monogamy is the ideal state of marriage in Islam. Surah an-Nisa 4:3 states: "If you fear you shall not be able to deal justly (with your wives) then marry only ONE."
- We are not calling for a ban on polygamy.
- We are asking that women who cannot live in a polygamous marriage be given the choice to leave that marriage. In an authentic hadith, the Prophet Muhammad (s.a.w.) forbade his son-in-law Ali ibn Abi Talib (r.a.) from marrying another woman unless Ali first divorced the Prophet's daughter, Fatimah. A great-granddaughter of the Prophet (s.a.w), Sakinah binti Hussein, a granddaughter of Ali and Fatimah, put various conditions in her marriage contract, including the condition that her husband would have no right to take another wife during their marriage.

We ask that the Religious Departments and the Syariah Courts establish procedures to ensure that the practice of polygamy in this country meets the demands of justice in Islam. These include:

- The establishment of a computerised national register of Muslim marriages and divorces to enable women to know the marital status of the men they are about to marry;
- The wife who chooses to stay in the polygamous marriage be given her share of the matrimonial property and to make fair and enforceable arrangements for the maintenance of the wife and children before permission for a polygamous marriage is given or is registered.
- The standard ta'liq agreement should include the option to give the wife the right to a divorce should her husband take another wife. The procedures for claiming mut'ah, harta sepencarian and maintenance for the children should also be facilitated to prevent undue delays that would cause hardship to the ex-wife and children.
- The court to establish clear procedure to strictly enforce the four conditions for polygamy under the existing Islamic Family Law. There must be concrete documentary and other evidence to prove that the application for a polygamous marriage meet all four conditions:

- the proposed marriage is just and necessary;
- the financial ability to support existing and future dependents;
- the ability to accord equal treatment to all wives;
- the proposed marriage will not cause *darar syarie* or harm to the existing wife in respect of religion, life, body, mind, moral or property.

- The court to ensure no application for polygamy or registration of an illegal polygamous marriage can be carried out without the knowledge of the existing wife.
- The application form for polygamy should be amended to reflect this is an application for polygamy and not an application for marriage as it is now.

Since 1996, Sisters in Islam and other women's groups have submitted four lengthy memorandums to the Government on reform of the Islamic Family Law to ensure that justice is done to Muslim women. Unfortunately, seven years have passed without much positive response.

The time has come for the Government to sit down with the women's groups to find solutions to the long standing problems women face in the syariah system.

all's well that ends well

The following are extracts from a message circulated by Sisters in Islam on 31 March 2003:

The newly formed Coalition on Women's Rights in Islam Monogamy Campaign was hit by scud missiles from some key people in religious authority and some women Islamic scholars and women's wings of Islamist groups, including Wanita JIM and Wanita Keadilan. A police report was also lodged against SIS and the Coalition, accusing us of insulting Islam.

They demanded that we stopped the campaign as it is against Hukum Syarak and it would undermine the faith of Muslims.

We all worked hard to get information out to key people, including all the Muftis, the Chief Ministers and cabinet ministers, so that they understood the objectives of our campaign and realise that nothing we have said and asked for is new or radical in Islam, and that it is all within a clearly documented Islamic tradition. Lost as well in all these attacks against us and the Coalition on Women's Rights in Islam was the widespread support we received from key women's groups, including the National Council of Women's Organisations and all the major political parties, except for PAS and Keadilan. 29 organisations went on stage to receive our campaign car stickers (1 Husband = 1 Wife; Monogamy is my Choice; If you fear you cannot do justice, marry only ONE) from Datin Seri Endon Mahmood (wife of the Dy Prime Minister). It was a very successful launch. Also, after the banner headlines demanding a stop to our campaign, many individuals, including first wives, phoned and emailed us to express solidarity.

We had an excellent meeting on Monday, 24 March with the Federal Religious Department, JAKIM and its DG, Datuk Shahir Abdullah. We gave them five presentations on aspects of the Monogamy campaign and Datuk Shahir in the end declared that the Monogamy Campaign was not against Hukum Syarak. On Tuesday, he appeared on TV3 s Wanita Hari Ini (Women Today) to clarify the practice of polygamy in Islam: that it is not the right of men, but a practice allowed in very special circumstances!!! He also said men who take second wives cannot use the excuse of helping these women if the polygamous marriage causes injustice and pain to the first wives! He was brilliant.

More importantly, on a longer term basis, we hope to work closely with JAKIM on women's issues and gender sensitising Religious Department officials and other government agencies on women's rights in Islam.

They have also agreed to study our proposal for polygamy to be included as a ground for divorce in the ta'liq certificate. They called us on March 25, requesting for the laws in the different Arab countries which allow for this and also for reading materials on the subject. We have forwarded all materials to them. We don't expect cvernight change. But this is a great beginning. We pointed out to them that even the Sheikh of al-Azhar (at that time he was the Mufti of Egypt) had supported the Egyptian women's groups campaign for a marriage contract which included the right to divorce should the husband take a second wife.

Needless to say, we are very pleased with these outcomes. This is a turning point in the struggle for the rights of Muslim women in Malaysia. We hope and pray that these announcements reflect a seeming change in mindset in the federal government religious authority towards a conscious commitment to develop a more progressive Islam in Malaysia.

6b TYPES OF MARRIAGES: MUT'A, CONCUBINAGE AND COMMON LAW MARRIAGE

introduction

Mut'a marriages are marriages that are contracted for a pre-determined time period, which may be from 1 day to 99 years, and are therefore sometimes known as 'temporary marriage.' This type of marriage is not recognized by the Sunni schools. Under the Shia schools, mut'a marriages require the fixing of mahr; and the wife's right to maintenance, legal paternity and inheritance rights of any children are recognized. However, the spouses may not mutually inherit; either party may break the contract at will; and the wife does not need to observe idda.

Historically, mut'a marriage has been restricted to Shia communities. But the practice has recently expanded to other communities, particularly under the influence of politico-religious extremists (for example in Algeria) and among the urban middle-class young in some countries (South Africa).

Women may enter mut'a marriages as a means of gaining the status of wife, to obtain economic support, as a means of legitimating a sexual relationship not intended to lead to permanent marriage, or serially as a means of sex work. Mut'a marriage is often considered to be preferable to sexual relations outside of marriage. Also, Mut'a can be used, in areas where there is strict segregation of the sexes, as a means of legitimizing and facilitating social interaction (Iran). When used in this manner, it reinforces segregation and the associated limitations placed on women's access to public life. The social stigma attached to mut'a, combined with state non-recognition of the practice (with the exception of Iran), has forced those practicing it to do so informally and without regulation.

rights implications

The possible benefits and/or disadvantages to women, as well as the rights implications, of mut'a are the subject of considerable controversy.

Some argue that where women are in a relatively strong social position, the possibility of determining the length of the relationship and having equal rights to dissolution may be appealing. This is particularly true if there is at the same time strong social or even legal condemnation of relationships outside marriage. Still, while some may argue that mut'a marriages serve to recognize both male and female sexuality and provide an outlet for its realization, others argue that mut'a simply reinforces the view that all sexual conduct must be regulated through marriage (whether permanent or temporary).

On the other hand, mut'a marriage has been criticized for legitimizing 'illicit' sexual relationships that would not otherwise be sanctioned by the law. It also reinforces notions of women's limited agency where women are compelled to use mut'a to facilitate their travel abroad, particularly for Hajj (women are not allowed to travel unaccompanied to perform Hajj).

Finally, some argue that mut'a is basically a rental agreement on a woman's sexual services (mahr given for a relationship of specified length). In such an analysis, mut'a reinforces patriarchal notions of women's bodies and sexuality. Indeed, because there is no minimum time period for which a mut'a marriage may be contracted, and this aspect of mut'a may be used to give religious sanction to sex work, many women find mut'a to be morally repugnant.

LAWS: Mut'a

Criteria

As a result of the conflicting analysis of mut'a and its rights implications for women, we have not listed the provisions concerning mut'a according to more option-giving and less option-giving criteria.

Recognized by law

Iran: Iran is the only country to recognize mut'a marriages as valid. Mut'a marriage was outlawed in 1932, but legalized again following the 1979 Revolution as a measure to reduce 'moral corruption.' In 1990, President Rafsanjani stated that couples need not register mut'a, i.e., a private ceremony without witnesses is valid. A standard contract does exist, but couples are not legally obliged to register mut'a marriages.

Explicitly prohibited in law

Senegal: Marriages that are specified for a limited time period are not valid.

The statute law is silent

Algeria, Malaysia, Morocco, Singapore, Philippines, Sri Lanka, Tunisia, Yemen: There are no provisions in the statutory law on mut'a.

Bangladesh: Any marriage registered under the MFLO is regarded as a permanent contract. Case law is firm that in order to be enforceable in the eyes of the law, a marriage should be registered. However, courts do recognize an oral marriage where there is other evidence to support its existence.

Pakistan: The statute law does not recognize mut'a. Since Islamization (post-1970s) and the introduction of the Zina Ordinance, 1979, all unions not recognized as valid render both partners liable to prosecution and heavy penalties. In some rare instances, the courts have accepted the validity of unwritten, unregistered, unwitnessed marriages in order to save a couple from penalties.

PRACTICES

Iran: Under the Shah, the 1967 Family Protection Law failed to mention mut'a and the practice was popularly perceived to have been banned. This perception resulted in an overall decline in its practice. However, mut'a continued to be practiced among religious traditionalists. Since 1979, there has been some revival, but it remains socially marginalized and stigmatized. In most cases, only young divorced women of lower classes (and some women of the middle-class) participate in mut'a. Often they contract mut'a marriages as a means to escape from their lack of a social support and/or their lack of shelter. Research has found that women often initiate mut'a unions. Still, most women seem to perceive mut'a as a male prerogative.

Despite strong official sanction (framed in terms of acknowledging both male, as well as female sexuality, and the need for its gratification), social disapproval results in mut'a rarely being registered. Few women choose to sign temporary marriage contracts. Contracts are used most commonly in cities and by middle-class men.

Even though the law recognizes the legal paternity of children from a mut'a union, the children's actual social status depends on how the father treats them.

Additionally, families may arrange for non-sexual mut'a marriages to facilitate easier social interaction amongst close friends and families, inside the home and outside.

Gambia & Nigeria (Muslim communities): Marriages of convenience are being entered into based on individual discretion. Women may participate in such unions for the purpose of obtaining a visa or to enable themselves to perform Hajj. (Saudi Arabia requires women Hajjis to be accompanied by husbands or family members.)

Pakistan: Mut'a is very rare among the Shia community (approx 12% of Pakistan's population).

Indonesia: Mut'a marriage is growing in the northern and central parts of Java where there are many foreign men working. They marry local women temporarily because, as foreigners, they are not allowed to possess land.

CONCUBINAGE

introduction

The term 'concubine' historically referred to a slave woman who was used for sexual purposes. Today, the term may be used to describe a mistress who is maintained by a man without there being any pretence that she and the man form a couple. The difference between historical concubines and today's mistresses perhaps lies in the fact that historically, concubines were a public status symbol and today mistresses tend to be less openly acknowledged.

Mistresses are universally frowned upon and not accepted by society. Still, wives have little actual power to prevent their husbands from taking a mistress.

In the **Gambia and Nigeria**, for example, most classes of men are known to keep mistresses. This practice is more common among Christian men and traditionalists. Perhaps, Muslim men satisfy similar desires through the option of polygyny.

In **Nigeria**, the emirs (descendants of the pre-colonial ruling class) still keep concubines in their homes. Some of these women are given more formal power then is given to legal wives. Indeed, sometimes they are given power over legal wives (in controlling access to the Emir, for instance). However, due to the combined (and in this case, mutually reinforcing) influences of 'westernisation' or modernisation and Islamization, this practice is dying out.

Sri Lanka's old 1806 Mohammedan Code recognized the legality of 'concubinage,' i.e. owning women for sexual purposes. The current MMDA does not recognize sexual relations outside of marriage, including what is today referred to as a relationship with a mistress.

COMMON LAW MARRIAGES

introduction

Common law marriages are relationships where individuals live together without any marriage ceremony for an extended period of time in what effectively amounts to a shared household and gives rise to marriage related rights and obligations between the 'spouses.' Sometimes the community and the law recognize the rights and obligations arising from these relationships, and sometimes they do not.

Systems with laws based on Muslim laws have varying provisions regarding the validity of unregistered marriages (see Registration and Validity, p.133). However, few would recognize a marriage where the couple was unable to provide any substantial evidence of their union or formal solemnization of some kind, or being so recognized by the families of the individuals concerned.

Common law marriages exist in some non-Muslim communities in **Sudan**. In the Philippines, while the Code of Muslim Personal Laws is silent, under the Civil Code, the property regime of unions without marriage are protected provided the man and woman have the capacity to marry each other.

De facto wives in **Fiji** (including those who have gone through unregistered marriage) do not have access to maintenance, matrimonial property, or the husband's pension, nor can they seek non-molestation orders under the law.

Prior to Islamization in the 1970s, couples in **Pakistan** could live together without a formal wedding ceremony, although this was not socially approved of. Since the 1979 ZO, couples living in such a relationship risk being reported to the police by third parties and consequently, suffering severe criminal penalties.

7 MAINTENANCE

introduction

All the legal systems covered in this Handbook (those based on Muslim laws, as well as those based on other sources) have provisions that oblige husbands to provide maintenance for their wives during marriage. In some systems both spouses may share equally the obligation to maintain each other (Turkey). In others the wife may share the duty of maintaining the family, but have a lesser obligation (Senegal).

In Muslim laws maintenance is referred to as nafaqa, and some laws define it specifically to include food, clothing, shelter, and other necessities (which in some cases includes domestic help). Some laws require that the husband provide 'adequate' (Bangladesh, Pakistan) or 'reasonable' (Malaysia) maintenance for the wife; what is included in maintenance is then subject to interpretation by the courts. In some contexts a husband may be less able to evade his basic responsibilities where the law specifically defines what is included in maintenance. At the same time, an open-ended law may allow courts greater flexibility to include additional costs such as those associated with childbirth, lying-in, and even the cost of providing any items that are necessary for a wife's mental well-being.

The amount of maintenance is generally determined by the husband's means or earning capacity, regardless of the wife's personal wealth or means. However, in some systems factors such as the social status and wealth of the wife may also be taken into account (Iraq, Malaysia).

All the codified laws dealt with here recognize a husband's failure to provide maintenance as a grounds for a wife to seek dissolution; many uncodified systems also recognize this in practice (see Other Forms of Dissolution for Women, p286-289). Some communities and laws allow a bride (or her family) to include in her marriage contract specific conditions regarding maintenance (see Inherent Rights and Responsibilities, p.153, and Negotiated Rights and Responsibilities, p.167). For information concerning maintenance following dissolution of marriage, see p.311.

theory vs. reality and women's rights

Community practices and codified laws concerning maintenance most often reflect very patriarchal interpretations of the marital union. When examining issues pertaining to maintenance, we see a particularly disturbing confluence of historical influences including restrictive interpretations of Muslim laws, Christian-colonial concepts of women's subordination, and negative customary practices (which indeed the Qur'an sought to address).

Under these influences, most systems conceptualize men as the sole maintainers of the family. Indeed, in Saudi Arabia it is considered almost deviant for a wife to be seen to contribute to the household expenditures. Although we recognize that in certain situations the husband's obligation of maintenance is beneficial to women, overall we see this conceptualization as disempowering women and perpetuating their lower status. This is because it is used both to justify a man's position as the 'head of household' and to give him the right to control his wife/wives. It is even used to excuse domestic violence. Additionally, in systems based on Muslim laws, these patriarchal interpretations of the marital union have been used to water down Qur'anic concepts regarding a woman's right to own property autonomously.

While such patriarchal perspectives continue to dominate laws and practices today, they do not reflect current social realities. Across communities and countries, husbands routinely violate their duty to maintain their wives, and women are often obliged to maintain the family. This is especially so where alcoholism, drug addiction, or male unemployment have become common, or in the case of polygyny.

In many communities, economic crises, as well as positive changes, such as increased educational and skill-building opportunities for women, have resulted in more women earning an income and contributing that income to the maintenance of the family. Laws that define men as the sole providers of maintenance, and consequently, give them powers over their wives and families, do not recognize these realities. Finally, such laws also ignore the real value of women's non-monetary contributions, such as their work on family land and/or their domestic labour.

In Senegal the Code de la Famille defines the responsibility of maintaining the family as a responsibility that is shared between husband and wife, with the wife having a lesser responsibility. The code does not clarify how each is expected to contribute. This omission allows the courts to interpret the law in such a way that in most cases a woman who is earning, or who has wealth, is required to use these resources to contribute to the family's maintenance. However, the courts do not acknowledge, and therefore do not factor in, the value of a woman's domestic labor contributions when calculating each spouse's contribution towards maintenance (when, for example, calculating the division of marital property).

While many women do, in reality, contribute to the financial maintenance of the family, many others find themselves financially dependent, and therefore vulnerable, for a number of reasons. For example, if a couple has children and the mother is the primary care giver (which is most often the case), there will be long periods when the wife is economically dependent on her husband; this also applies to women who are employed in contexts where there are no state maternity benefits or maternity pay from employers. Even if a wife is not too burdened with domestic duties to contribute additionally through paid work, often she has neither the skills needed nor the opportunity to obtain paid employment.

Under the 2001 amendments to the Turkish Civil Code, brought about by a unified campaign by women's groups, the previous principle that the husband was responsible for maintaining his wife and children was replaced by provisions that both spouses are to contribute towards the expenditures of the household with their labour and possessions in accordance with their capabilities. This change to shared responsibility reflects a move away from regarding the husband (as codified in the old Code) as 'head of household.' The new formulation both recognizes the reality of women's economic contributions (and the rights this should bring in terms of decision-making), and affirms the belief that women's equal decision-making within the family should not be purely dependent upon wage earning.

grounds for denying maintenance

Most systems, whether or not they are based upon Muslim laws, provide for situations where a wife can become disentitled to maintenance, even during the subsistence of a marriage. Thus, a wife's right to maintenance becomes conditional upon her fulfilling certain reciprocal obligations, e.g., residing in the same house as her husband, allowing him sexual access, housekeeping, child rearing, etc. (see Inherent Rights and Responsibilities p.153). Some systems mistakenly assume that as long as a wife is living with her husband, he is providing her with maintenance (Fiji, Sri Lanka).

Many systems based on Muslim laws attach a woman's right of maintenance to her duty to obey. Accordingly, these systems allow a husband to withhold maintenance if the wife is 'disobedient' (nushuz). A conditional relationship between maintenance and obedience may be codified in the law or established through case law.

The definition of 'disobedience' varies from one system to another. Some statutory laws clearly specify what actions are considered to constitute 'disobedience.' These may include committing apostasy, failing to submit to her husband without justification, leaving the matrimonial home without her husband's permission, and being employed against her husband's will (Egypt, Sudan). Disobedience is also inherent in the concept of tamkin, where the wife is expected to remain in the marital home and is 'disobedient' if she violates this expectation (Iran). In the case that a woman leaves the matrimonial home to escape violence, she customarily returns to her natal home. If her natal family can provide for her, she is usually willing to be declared disobedient, and thereby forfeit her right to maintenance in order to escape from brutality.

In other contexts 'disobedience' is more narrowly interpreted so that its use is limited to describing those situations where a wife leaves the matrimonial home without justifiable reason (Sri Lanka, Malaysia, Singapore). Laws also differ as to whether or not a husband's cruelty can cancel his right to 'obedience.' In Morocco the concept of a husband's right to his wife's 'obedience' has been codified, but these provisions stand apart from provisions concerning maintenance. Therefore, it is unclear if a husband's duty to provide maintenance is dependent upon his wife's 'obedience.'

Laws that both restrict a wife's right to sue for maintenance to situations where she is living separately from her husband and excuse a husband from maintenance duties if the wife commits the disobedient act of leaving the marital home, effectively offer a wife no recourse in the event that her husband does not provide maintenance.

In other contexts, the concept of a wife's 'obedience' to her husband is not codified. For example, Pakistan's Muslim Family Laws Ordinance does not mention such a concept, and Pakistan's case law very rarely applies any such concept. Indeed, the courts have routinely rejected a husband's attempts to control his wife's mobility (see p.161). However, a husband has a statutory option to file for the restitution of conjugal rights if his wife files for maintenance.

It is important to note whether or not laws utilize concepts of 'obedience' to grant Muslim women lesser maintenance rights than are granted to women of other communities (Sri Lanka). In Singapore, where the civil court has power to order maintenance for Muslim wives under a law not based on Muslim laws, the question of 'disobedience' as grounds for disentitlement to maintenance does not arise.

Whatever the codified laws on maintenance, community practices frequently link maintenance to 'obedience,' and obedience is often defined in such a way as to include the husband's right to determine when, and under what circumstances, the wife may leave the marital home.

situations where maintenance cannot be denied

It is a general principle, recognized in all countries where Muslim laws apply, that if a husband fails to pay his wife prompt mahr, she is entitled to maintenance, even when she is living separately from him. Generally, she is also entitled to maintenance from her husband even if she has her own property (Pakistan: Muhammad Younus v Farooq Ahmed and five others, 1988 SCMR 1346; Sri Lanka: Jiffri v Ummu Ayesha, 1958, 4 MMDR 154).

Some systems recognize additional circumstances under which a wife will be entitled to maintenance, even while living separately from her husband. These may include where the husband has been cruel to his wife, where the husband has failed to treat his wives equally (in a polygynous marriage), and/or where the husband has failed to provide separate accommodations for each wife (in a polygynous marriage). Regardless of how 'disobedience' is understood, if a wife is legally bound to obey her husband, her right to maintenance becomes a conditional right (as opposed to an inherent right of a married woman). In such contexts a husband can use the threat of withdrawing maintenance to increase his control over his wife. Because such injustices occur regularly, women have come to debate how they can correct the uneven power dynamics that are supported by laws and practices that give the husband the exclusive responsibility of maintaining his wife and family.

recovery of maintenance

Most systems have established mechanisms for the wife to recover unpaid maintenance from her husband. The process by which one initiates proceedings to recover maintenance is governed by certain rules and regulations, which may be found either in family laws or other procedural laws (which may or may not apply exclusively to

Muslim women). In uncodified Muslim laws and customary laws, provisions for recovery depend upon established practice. Only some of the research done by the Women & Law in the Muslim World Programme has examined these codified and uncodified procedures.

The length of time for which wives are entitled to claim past maintenance differs from country to country. In Tunisia it appears that wives have a right to claim maintenance that was unpaid for an indefinite period of time prior to their application. In many systems, the right to claim past maintenance is limited. In Pakistan for instance, according to case law, it is possible for wives to claim past maintenance for up to 6 years prior to the application. Egypt, Yemen, and Algeria limit claims to 1 year of past maintenance before the application while in Sri Lanka a maintenance order will only have effect from the date of application.

Some systems provide for interim maintenance while an application for maintenance is pending before the court (Malaysia). Such provisions are extremely important for women who suddenly find themselves with the entire responsibility of maintaining the family. Interim maintenance can make the difference between destitution and survival while courts cases drag on for months.

Most often the courts place the burden of proving a husband's income on the woman applying for maintenance. However, proof of income may not be easy to produce in situations where the husband is self-employed or there is little documentation of income in both the formal and informal sectors. Also, social attitudes can make it easy for a husband to seek the assistance of family members, and even employers, when hiding the extent of his wealth. Court settlements characteristically award very low levels of maintenance, regardless of the husband's financial status. Some systems allow wives to apply for an increase of maintenance, but they often also allow husbands to apply for a reduction of maintenance (Malaysia, Pakistan, Sri Lanka). These applications are often granted.

Enforcing maintenance orders is notoriously difficult even in the most developed legal systems. For many families, the strength of enforcement mechanisms means the difference between a useless piece of paper and economic survival. In some countries the maintenance award may be directly attached to the salary of the husband and recovered through the employer (Singapore). But such a solution requires a well-documented economy and the cooperation of employers. In other situations procedures for recovery and enforcement of decrees may not be clear or may be complicated. For example, Quazis in Sri Lanka have the jurisdiction to issue a decree of maintenance for Muslim wives, but the execution of that decree is dependent upon some other court or authority. In such systems a wife is left with the difficult task of coordinating different court systems.

Furthermore, even where the law provides for the imprisonment of a defaulting husband, implementation of such punishments may not be strict, or wives may be unwilling to (or under social pressure not to) send their husbands to jail. Thus, although the law may seem effective in theory, women have to undergo numerous difficulties to actually obtain their maintenance. Protracted court proceedings, the cost of legal action, and social attitudes are likely to prevent women from launching or following through with legal action against defaulting husbands.

Finally, husbands have other weapons they may use to frustrate maintenance claims. In some systems where there is no explicit link between 'obedience'/living with the husband and maintenance, a woman who is living separately from her husband and who makes an application for maintenance may be faced with a counter suit for the restitution of conjugal rights or a suit for custody of the children.

Amendments Limit Women's Access to Maintenance

Until an amendment to Pakistan's Family Courts Act, which came into effect in October 2002, the courts tended to insist that when a husband filed a suit for restitution of conjugal rights, he should 'come to court with clean hands,' in other words that his suit should not be mala fide. This was particularly so if the couple had been separated, and the husband had been refusing to appear in his wife's suit for maintenance, but then had filed a suit for restitution as a tactic to frustrate her maintenance suit. Unfortunately, the amended law grants husbands a statutory option that, in replying to a claim for maintenance, they can now claim for restitution of conjugal rights.

It is difficult to understand the intent of such a provision. It is possible that the aim was to address an issue long raised by rights activists: that if the husband files a separate counter suit (which may be filed in a separate court in another area), the wife had to respond and this increased the social and economic costs of trying to recover maintenance. Under the amendment the two matters (maintenance and restitution) are now consolidated into one suit, implying a linkage between the wife's sexual availability and her right to maintenance. Whereas previously the two issues could be settled separately, now a woman either wins her maintenance or finds herself ordered to return to her husband. If she fails to accept the restitution order, she in effect loses both her right to past maintenance and her right to future maintenance.

In sharp contrast to the reforms advocated by women's campaigns (under which the restitution of conjugal rights would be removed from the schedule of the FCA and would, therefore, no longer be a matter that the courts could hear), the new law encourages the harassment of wives through court action and curtails their right to maintenance.

NOTES

LAWS: Maintenance

Criteria

☺ More option giving are those laws which:

- Do not link a wife's right to receive maintenance to her 'obedience;'
- Recognize a wife's right to past due maintenance;
- Recognize a wife's right to file an application for recovery of maintenance while she is living with her husband;
- Provide for effective enforcement mechanisms;
- Recognize non-maintenance as grounds for divorce.

😐 The middle-ground is occupied by those laws which:

- Have certain limitations on the circumstances under which maintenance can be claimed; or
- Are unclear about the circumstances under which maintenance is not required.

☹ Less option-giving are those laws which:

- Explicitly link a wife's right to receive maintenance to her 'obedience.'

☺ **Maintenance is not linked to 'obedience'**

Turkey: Under A. 196 of the CC, either of the spouses has the right to ask a judge to specify the amount of financial contribution each should make. In establishing the amount of the contribution, the judge takes into account housework and childcare and unpaid labor contributed to the business of the other spouse.

Uzbekistan: A. 1-3 of the Family law envisage relationships built on mutuality and equality between husband and wife. Based on the Soviet Family Code, there is a mutual obligation of spousal maintenance.

Gambia: Under S. 4 of the colonial Maintenance of Deserted Wives Act 1916 a magistrate, if satisfied that the husband, being able wholly or in part to maintain his wife or his wife and family, has wilfully refused or neglected so to do may make an order that he pays the deserted wife a weekly sum not exceeding D20 or a monthly sum not exceeding D100. S. 18(1) of the Maintenance Causes Act 1986 entitles either party to a marriage to petition the court for an order on the ground that the other party to the marriage has wilfully neglected to provide, or to make a proper contribution towards, reasonable maintenance for the petitioner or any child of the household. S. 21 allows the court, whenever it thinks just and equitable, to award maintenance pending suit or financial provision to either party to the marriage. But in determining this, the court must consider the standard of living of the parties and their circumstances.

Tunisia: Under A. 37-42 of the CSP, a husband shall be obliged to provide maintenance for his wife after the consummation of his marriage. The husband shall not be obliged to provide maintenance if he is destitute. An exception to this shall be if the judge has granted him two months' deferment; and upon completion of that time, he is still unable to provide maintenance, then the judge shall dissolve the marriage. If the wife is aware of his hardship at the time of contracting the marriage, she shall have no right to demand divorce. If the husband is away from his wife and has no money and leaves no maintenance, and if no one else provides maintenance during his absence, the judge shall grant a delay of one month, in case he might reappear, and then shall divorce her from him. To do so the judge must have verified what has occurred and must have taken the oath of the wife with regard to this. Under A. 42 maintenance for the wife shall not lapse due to the passing of time.

Senegal: Under A. 375 of the CF, both spouses are to contribute to the maintenance of the family, but the husband bears the primary responsibility. Under A. 166, non-maintenance is grounds for divorce (only available to wives). Insufficient maintenance is equivalent to a lack of maintenance if the husband otherwise has the means to maintain the family, and the amount given does not meet the calculated needs of the family (TPI/Dakar mai 1978 RJS. Credila 1982 vol III p.158).

Bangladesh: Under S. 9 of the MFLO, if a husband fails to maintain his wife adequately, or where there is more than one wife, if he fails to maintain them equitably; the wife/wives can apply to the local Union Council or to the local Family Court for a grant of maintenance certificate that specifies the amount of maintenance which is due. The former route is often quicker and does not require a lawyer. However, the amounts awarded are usually smaller, and if a wife needs maintenance for children, she still must apply to the Family Court. Maintenance can be sought while the wife is living with the husband. Neither the MFLO nor case law refer to 'obedience.' However, if the couple is separated, the wife has to show that she left the marital home with 'reasonable cause;' generally the courts interpret this provision in a woman's favour (Sirajul Islam v Halena Begum & Others DLR 1996, 48). It is possible to obtain an order for past maintenance (for a period of time during which the wife was not adequately maintained), as well as an order for future maintenance. There are no provisions for interim maintenance.

Pakistan: The same provisions as for Bangladesh (see, above) apply, but under amendments to the FCA, which came into force in 2002, S. 17 A states that the court may pass an interim order for maintenance, and if the husband does not pay that interim maintenance within the specified period, the wife's suit for maintenance will be decreed. If the ordered maintenance still is not paid, the maintenance is recoverable as arrears of land revenue. Maintenance has been widely defined to include that which is necessary for mental well-being (1992 MLD 219). Maintenance orders by the Union Council Nazim can be revised within 30 days of the order. Maintenance decrees by a Family Court cannot be appealed if the amount is below Rs 1,000 (US$17.90) per month. Under the amended FCA, a husband now has the statutory option to reply to a wife's suit for maintenance with a claim for restitution of conjugal rights.

The link between maintenance and 'obedience' is implied but not explicit

Algeria: Under A.37 of the CF, the husband is required to provide maintenance for the wife within the limits of his ability, except from such time as it is established that she has abandoned the matrimonial home. Under A. 39, the wife is required to obey the husband and accord him the respect due to him as head of household. Under A. 74, the husband is obliged to provide maintenance for his wife from the time the marriage is consummated or at any time that she is in need of it (on the basis of evidence). Under A. 78, maintenance consists of food, clothing, medical care, accommodation or rent and, all that is considered necessary according to custom and convention. Under A. 79, the amount of maintenance depends upon the circumstances of the spouses and the conditions of their life; a wife or husband cannot have this amount reviewed for 1 year after the judgment. Under A. 80, maintenance is payable from the date of filing the claim and for a period not exceeding one year prior to the filing of the claim.

Morocco: Under A. 35 of the Moudawana ('the rights of a woman with regard to her husband'), the wife has a right to maintenance comprised of food, clothing, medical care, and accommodation. Under A. 36 ('the rights of a man with regard to his wife'), the husband has a right to "the wife's preservation of herself and her chastity and the wife's obedience to the husband in the conventional manner." A.53 only mentions procedures in the event of that a wife files for dissolution on the grounds of non-maintenance.

Philippines: A wife's right to maintenance is specified in A 67(1) CMPL. It is the wife's duty to a) dutifully manage the affairs of the house and b) purchase things necessary for the maintenance of the family, and the husband is bound to reimburse those costs incurred in the fulfillment of these duties. Maintenance under the Family Code (applicable to other communities) is gender neutral.

Sri Lanka: The husband is given the obligation of supporting his wife. The law does not define maintenance, which has been developed through case law, although S. 47(1)(g) of the MMDA specifically includes lying-in-expenses in maintenance. Under S. 34 a wife cannot claim maintenance for any period when she was living with the husband (there is no such bar in the General Law of Sri Lanka). Maintenance can be denied on the ground of 'disobedience,' but this is only understood to mean refusal to live with the husband on grounds that cannot be justified. Ill-treatment by the husband or his relatives, his failure to provide a residence separate from in-laws, non-payment of prompt mahr, and a husband's violence are all justifiable grounds for wife to refuse to live with husband and still be entitled to maintenance (3 MMDR 82 & 2 MMDR 102). Maintenance is dealt with by the Quazi courts under S.47(1), and it is possible to apply for an increase or a reduction by showing good and sufficient cause (S. 47(1)(e)). However, S.36 bars claims for past maintenance. Under S. 64(1) and 66, if the husband fails to heed a maintenance order, the wife can apply to the Quazi for an enforcement order, and the Quazi then applies to the magistrate in the area where the husband lives to recover the amount as a fine. The effect of S. 64(1) and S. 66 is that the wife has to apply for maintenance to the Quazi of the husband's place of residence and recovered maintenance is remitted to the Quazi who then pays the wife; these processes are cumbersome. If the husband is unemployed, the amount of maintenance is determined by his potential earning capacity (Kamer v Sithy Zain 4 MMDR 92).

☹ Maintenance is conditional upon 'obedience'

Malaysia: Under S. 59-70 of the IFLA, a wife (or a former wife during idda) is entitled to reasonable maintenance from the husband. The Court can order a man to pay maintenance to his wife. A wife shall not be entitled to maintenance when she is nushuz, or unreasonably refuses to obey the lawful wishes or commands of her husband. She can be thus categorized by: withholding her association with her husband; leaving her husband's home against his will; or refusing to move with him to another home or place, without any valid reason according to Hukum Syariah. As soon as the wife repents and obeys the lawful wishes and commands of her husband, she ceases to be nushuz. In determining the amount of maintenance to be paid, the court shall base its assessment primarily on the means and needs of the parties, regardless of the income of husband. The court can order interim maintenance, security for maintenance, compounding of maintenance, recovery of arrears, and variation because of a material change in the circumstances of either party.

Fiji: A wife who is cohabitating with her husband cannot get a maintenance order unless she files for divorce. A wife who separates from her husband and subsequently files for maintenance must prove that her husband is at fault. A wife cannot claim back/past maintenance if proven adulterous (even if adultery takes place after separating from the husband due to the husband's fault). However in case law, the wife being a 'drunkard' has not been a bar to her securing maintenance, and the court has not deemed a wife's desire to live separately from her in-laws 'unreasonable' (Raj Mati v Amika Prasad 7 FLR 28, 1961).

Nigeria (marriages under the MCA): While during the subsistence of a marriage, either party may petition for a maintenance order on behalf of the children of the marriage (MCA Part IV Section 70 of 1970); the wife can seek maintenance for herself only after judicial separation.

Egypt: A husband is obliged to provide his wife with maintenance if she submits herself to him. Maintenance shall include food, clothing, accommodation, medical treatment, and any other necessity prescribed by Sharia. A wife's illness shall not prevent her from entitlement to maintenance. Maintenance is not due to her if she apostasies, if she fails to submit herself without justification, if the husband is not at fault, and she leaves the matrimonial home without his permission (except if the circumstance is permitted by Sharia). A husband cannot withhold maintenance if the wife goes out for lawful work, provided that it does not appear that this right is being abused or that her working is contrary to the interest of the family, and also provided that her husband has not asked her to refrain from exercising this right. A claim of maintenance shall not be heard for a past period exceeding one year ending on the date the claim was filed. A husband's debt of past maintenance to his wife has priority and takes precedence over other debts of maintenance. If a husband does not pay maintenance, and there is a ruling against him, his assets may be attached to this debt. If he has only non-visible assets, or if he is wealthy but refuses to pay, or if he claims an inability to pay (and substantiates that inability), the judge shall grant the wife an immediate divorce. However, if he cannot substantiate such a claim, the judge can grant him a period of one month to pay. If he still fails to comply, the judge shall divorce her. If the husband is absent, his visible assets can be attached to his debt. If not, he may be granted a grace period. If he still does not pay, the judge shall grant her a divorce upon expiration of the time period. These provisions are contained in Law No. 25 of 1929, as amended by Law No.100 of 1985, concerning provisions on maintenance and certain matters of personal status.

Iran: Under A. 1114, 1005 of the CC, a wife must reside in her husband's home (tamkin, which implies that she is sexually available to him) to qualify for maintenance.

Sudan: Under S. 92 of the MPLA, the husband is obliged to maintain his wife unless his wife is 'disobedient' (nashiz). Under S. 75, 'disobedience' includes leaving the matrimonial home without a legal justification, working outside the home without her husband's permission and approval, and/or refusing to travel with her husband, without a legally justified reason. The nashiz wife is considered neither divorced nor married. She is to be deprived from the right to maintenance, matrimonial residence, and custody of her children.

Yemen: Under A. 149-156 of the LPS, the husband has a duty to provide maintenance for his wife, and this maintenance shall include food, clothing, accommodation, furnishing, medical care, and [domestic] services. The husband's circumstances (in terms of affluence or hardship) shall be taken into account when deciding the amount of maintenance. Maintenance of a wife shall take priority over other kinds of maintenance. A wife shall not be entitled to maintenance (a) if she refuses to move to the matrimonial home without an acceptable justification; (b) if she leaves the matrimonial home without acceptable justification (c) if the she refuses to consummate the marriage or to live in the matrimonial home, without acceptable justification; (d) if she works outside the home without the consent of her husband, provided that they had not agreed that she would be allowed to work; and/or (e) if she refuses to travel with her husband without acceptable justification. The judge cannot award more than 1 year's past maintenance, unless the spouses have agreed otherwise. If the husband fails to heed a maintenance order or is absent, and it is evident that he is not providing his wife with maintenance, a judge shall award maintenance for her out of his property. The word of the wife shall be accepted if she asserts that maintenance has not been paid for past periods.

Nigeria (marriages under Muslim laws): A wife is entitled to maintenance from her husband. This shall include food, shelter, and clothing; provided in accordance with the financial ability of the husband, the status of the wife prior to the marriage, and community custom. Because in sickness a wife may be unable to discharge her conjugal duties, under such circumstances she does not have a legal right to claim maintenance. However, because some jurists have agreed that compassion and accountability (in the case that her sickness may have been caused in part by poor maintenance) demand that a husband continue to provide a sick wife with maintenance, the court may require him to do so.

Women of the Maghreb Formulate a Progressive Family Code

In 1991, a group of women's associations and women researchers from the three Maghreb countries (Algeria, Morocco, Tunisia) met in Rabat at the invitation of the Moroccan Women's Democratic Association (ADFM) and decided to set up the "Collectif 95 Maghreb Egalite". They noted that although women's conditions and status in the region had undergone major changes, social and political resistance remained very strong, while new threats to Maghrebi women's gains and rights had become apparent.

In anticipation of the 1995 Beijing Fourth World Conference on Women, "Collectif 95 Maghreb Egalite" decided to highlight the struggle of women in the region at the NGO Forum by presenting three documents, including 'Cent Mesures et Dispositions: Pour une codification maghrebine egalitaire du Statut personnel at du Droit de la famille' (One Hundred Measures and Proposals for an egalitarian Maghrebi codification of personal status and family law).

Their proposals were based on the belief that women's struggle for true equality and a meaningful citizenship must be founded on respect for women's rights, in both public and private life. The legal inferiority of women within the family is the basis for discrimination against women in the public sphere. While the Maghreb is generally perceived to be entirely homogeneous, "arabised" and "islamised", it is in fact at the same time Berber, Arabo-Muslim, Mediterranean and African. Moreover, while other legal fields have seen transformation, mainly due to colonial influences, family law continued to be governed by an interpretation of Muslim laws which condemned women of Muslim communities across the Maghreb to an inferior status, symbolized by: the practice of wali; the requirement that the wife must obey the husband; women's lack of guardianship rights; and unequal inheritance.

"Collectif 95 Maghreb Egalite" believed that the challenges of modernity require proof of "the ability of Islam to question itself and to rediscover its evolutionary dynamic". A beginning has been made to varying degrees in the three countries, where recently legislation concerning women has begun to be developed and put in place that is based on equality, freedom and non-discrimination, and that keeps in mind the need to harmonize local legal norms with international norms. However, in today's Maghreb, the question of equality between women and men in all fields is linked to the fundamental problem of secularization of the family law.

The proposals envisaged by "Collectif 95 Maghreb Egalite" call for the equality of men and women in rights, duties and before the law; equality between the spouses through the abolition of he notion of head of the family and right of obedience, and the possibility for the woman to also be responsible for the maintenance of the family; the replacement of the notion of paternal authority with parental responsibility; equality in inheritance; equality of rights between women and men in the attribution of nationality to children; rejection of any form of racial discrimination or religious discrimination in the field of family relations (i.e.,, the abolition of separate codes for different communities); and the legal protection of children before and after birth by recognition of natural filiation.

Based upon this reconceptualization of the family, "Collectif 95 Maghreb Egalite" proposed that in the area of maintenance:

Art 69. Maintenance includes all that is necessary for life, notably food, clothing, medical care, education and housing.

Art 70. The spouses have a mutual obligation of maintenance. Ascendants and descendants also all have the right to maintenance.

Art 71. The amount of maintenance is to be calculated according to the income of the person who owes it and according to the need of the person who receives it, taking into account their circumstances of living.

Art 72. An ascendant must maintain descendants who are minor and who are incapable of supporting themselves.

Maintenance shall continue to be owed to a descendant until the completion of their studies, provided they have not passed the age of twenty-five years.

Maintenance shall continue to be owed to disabled descendants who are incapable of supporting themselves, whatever their age.

Art 73. When they are several, children shall contribute to the maintenance of ascendants according to their financial capacity and not depending upon their number.

Art 74. The obligation of maintenance cannot lapse between spouses.

Art 75. In case of either parent's lack of capacity to support the children, the parent who has the financial capacity to do so shall support the children.

Art 76. In the event of voluntary failure to provide maintenance or alimony following divorce, for more than one month beginning from the day it is due, the defaulter is liable to imprisonment of three months to one year.

Payment of the maintenance due terminates the suit for recovery or the execution of the sentence. A state fund will automatically pay the maintenance or alimony to its legal recipient. The fund has the right to recover the amount paid from the defaulter.

Extracted from Cent Mesures et Dispositions: Pour une codification maghrebine egalitaire du Statut personnel at du Droit de la famille, "Collectif 95 Maghreb Egalite" (ed. Women Living Under Muslim Laws), WLUML, Grabels.

8 STATUS OF CHILDREN

introduction

This chapter deals with the establishment and acknowledgement of paternity, adoption, and maintenance of children. Accordingly, we look at the status of children in four different circumstances: where the child is born from a valid marriage; where the mother is the only known parent; where the child is not born from a valid marriage but paternity is acknowledged; and where the child has been adopted. The term 'legitimacy' has been deliberately avoided wherever possible to indicate our rejection of social attitudes that condemn children born of unions not sanctioned as valid marriages. However, in the Laws section at the end of the chapter, the term has been used where the law itself uses it.

This chapter provides only a brief introduction to these issues. Issues concerning children are of particular concern to women for a number of reasons. These include the biological reality of their reproductive role, their social role as the primary care providers for children, and the common problems they share with their children in the event that the husband/father abandons the family.

Giving a child a certain status may or may not give that child the full rights associated with being a legally recognized biological child. For example, a child who has been acknowledged as a member of a family unit is entitled to maintenance in some systems (Malaysia). However, this acceptance into the family does not mean that this child can inherit if she/he is not considered legitimate under the legitimacy rules or affiliation proceedings in Muslim family law (Malaysia, Singapore). In such a case, it would be necessary for the child's interest in the estate to be specifically provided for in a will, as she/he is not a 'true' beneficiary. Also, an adopted child may receive a portion of the estate of her/his adoptive parent by way of gift (Malaysia, Singapore, Philippines).

The rights of children (specifically to maintenance and inheritance) and the rights of parents to custody and guardianship are clearly established when the children result from a valid marriage. Validity will depend upon the system's requirements regarding requisites for marriage (see p.59) and registration (see p.133).

An unmarried woman has full and sole guardianship and custody rights over her child, and the child inherits from the mother's estate.

Many questions about the paternity status of children involve a complex range of possible situations: a) both parents are known and there is no dispute over paternity, but the legal validity of their relationship is in doubt; b) a child is born during a valid marriage, but the father disputes paternity; c) the mother is not married to the father, but she or a third person seeks to establish paternity; d) the mother is not married to the father, but the father acknowledges paternity; the father acknowledges paternity, but a third party (or the court) refutes the acknowledgement. Some systems attempt to address all of these situations and the relevant conditions involved (Malaysia, Philippines).

gender discrimination and the status of children

There are clearly gender related dimensions to issues concerning the status of children.

Firstly, despite the expectation that mothers will invest more energy in a child's upbringing than will fathers, children are often seen as the property of their fathers. This perception of the father's ownership is reflected in systems where only the child's father is recognized as having certain administrative rights and responsibilities (Iran), or where administrative forms use the father's name and not the mother's as a means of identification.

Secondly, social attitudes towards children born outside a valid marriage are closely linked to laws and attitudes towards sexuality. In Iran, some Malaysian and Nigerian States, Pakistan, and Sudan, all consenting sex outside a valid marriage carries heavy legal penalties. Children born from such relationships are effectively punished for their circumstances of birth. But in many more communities and systems, it is only women's sexual activity outside of a valid marriage, rather than all such activity, that is strongly condemned. This bias against women is reflected in court attitudes where paternity suits against influential fathers rarely succeed (Indonesia), or where a woman seeking to establish paternity may find herself criticised by the court (Egypt).

Thirdly, in some systems (whether through the law or through judicial interpretation), greater weight may be given to the man's word than to the woman's when paternity is disputed.

Despite a general social conservatism that is reflected in laws and attitudes towards women's status within the family, most laws are generous about their presumption of children's status. This is particularly true for laws based on Muslim laws. For example, the concept of 'sleeping embryo' derived from an interpretation of Maliki laws can enable paternity to be established sometimes years after a woman's marriage has been dissolved. In Nigeria, among the Hausa the concept is known as kwatance and can be as long as seven years although the courts in the North have generally limited this period to one year. Generosity is also the norm in laws that define the status of children born from a marriage of doubtful validity.

However, this generosity is often conditional upon the father's acknowledgement of paternity. Although in practical terms it is only the mother who can really know who is the father, sometimes the law allows the man's word to determine a case of disputed paternity. If the father refuses to recognize paternity, in the absence of scientific methods (such as DNA testing) to establish paternity, there may be little the mother can do. Recognition of the injustice of disputed paternity (and thereby denial of children's maintenance and inheritance rights) has been one of the main factors behind legal reforms introducing compulsory marriage registration (see p.133).

Some systems curb a man's power to deny paternity. For example, case law in Pakistan has consistently insisted that Muslim laws have a strong presumption of legitimacy and do not accept mere denial of paternity by the man as sufficient grounds to deny a child the status of legitimacy. Instead, if the husband wishes to deny paternity, he must prove that he had no access to his wife during the period of time when conception could have taken place.

In some systems the man's power to reject paternity is time-bound, and the child can be rejected only within 2 months of her/his birth (Iran).

Some systems, particularly those based on Muslim laws, are not so generous in the case of children born from adulterous relationships. While the mother's husband may deny paternity, another man may not acknowledge paternity of a child born to a married woman (Malaysia). The Tunisian Supreme Court has attempted to curb the recognition of children from illicit relationships, but, in practice, if the father acknowledges the child at the time of her/his birth registration, the child is effectively legitimized in the eyes of the state.

In Turkey, reformers have consciously attempted to end both the stigma attached to children not born in a valid marriages and the injustice of giving different weight to the claims of men and women. The new Civil Code has discarded the term 'illegitimate' and instead talks of establishing descent. Paternity can be established through marriage with the mother, recognition by the father, or a court ruling. The child then has the same inheritance and maintenance rights, as well as rights to the father's name, as a child born from a valid marriage does. Similarly, the superior courts in Pakistan have noted that Muslim laws do not permit the use of the word 'illegitimate' as it stigmatizes the child. Instead, if a child is born to a woman who was convicted of zina, the word 'sabatunnasab' (whose descent is proved) is to be used.

the rights of children from a marriage of doubtful validity

Some systems attempt to protect the rights of children born from marriages that are of doubtful validity. Marriages of doubtful validity include marriages that are registered but subsequently an irregularity or obstruction to validity has been discovered that renders the marriage liable to being declared invalid (Senegal provided at least one party was acting in good faith, Tunisia, Yemen). Many laws in Arabic-speaking countries declare all marriages that fail to meet validity requirements, including those that would be identified as 'irregular' under Muslim laws, to be invalid. Nevertheless, these systems usually protect the rights of any children, even when the marriage is liable to be annulled by a court ruling, by establishing paternity, maintenance, and inheritance rights (India, marriages under the Special Marriages Act).

The rights of children from marriages that are unregistered but subsequently proven through a court process are equally protected (Bangladesh, Malaysia, Pakistan, Senegal) (see p.135). In Nigerian Muslim communities, following the general principles of Muslim laws, a child born of an irregular marriage has the same rights as a child born of a valid marriage.

Where a system does not recognize 'religious' marriages (e.g., a marriage only solemnized in a mosque), the children may be socially guaranteed their rights while accessing their rights through the courts remains extremely difficult. But in Fiji and Turkey, for example, if the parents subsequently go through the required civil marriage ceremony, the status of children born prior to the civil ceremony is secured.

the presumption of paternity

Many systems that have codified provisions concerning paternity and acknowledgement presume filiation in the event that a child is born within marriage or within a certain number of months or years following dissolution of marriage by death or divorce (see below).

Thus, in systems where paternity is governed by a civil law applicable to all communities, that a child is born during the continuance of a valid marriage between her/his mother and any man, or within 280 days after the dissolution of their marriage (provided the mother remains unmarried), is conclusive proof that the child is the legitimate child of that man (India, Sri Lanka, Singapore).

Systems based on Muslim laws also presume paternity is established for a child born within marriage, but they differ on the minimum and maximum time limits, for example:

- after 6 lunar months of marriage and within 4 lunar years after dissolution (Malaysia);
- after 6 months of marriage and within two years after dissolution (Philippines);
- after 6 months of marriage and within 10 months after sexual relations between the wife and husband (Iran, but this is extendable).

Laws that presume paternity soon after the marriage or long after divorce are option-giving for the mothers of such children. However, in systems based on Muslim laws, the father usually has a codified right to deny paternity. Whether or not in practice this codified right gives men greater power in disputes over children's status depends upon the court's interpretation. The W&L research did not address this issue in depth. However, at least in Pakistan, it is clear that the courts are highly reluctant to deny a child status, even if the husband files a case of zina against his wife.

Where weight is given to the husband's word, and procedures for revocation of divorce are unclear, women and the rights of their children become extremely vulnerable. Perhaps partly to address this vulnerability, Malaysia's Islamic Family Law (Federal Territories) Act, 1984 (Act 303) provides criminal punishment for divorced spouses who resume cohabitation without going through the required ruju (revocation) procedures.

the rejection of paternity

Although most systems (whether through the text of the law or case law) require firm proof before a man can reject paternity, systems which recognize li'an proceedings as a means of rejecting paternity cannot be seen as option-giving (Malaysia, Nigeria,

Pakistan, Philippines). Li'an is a form of divorce under Muslim laws whereby the husband swears on the Qur'an that his wife has committed zina, and she, in response, swears on the Qur'an that she has not. This process is repeated a further two times and if neither retracts their oath, the court automatically pronounces the marriage dissolved. The essence of li'an is that the husband has no proof of his accusation. By recognizing li'an a law may permit the paternity of the child who is the subject of li'an proceedings to be rejected without evidence. Again, much depends upon how the courts have interpreted these provisions. The understanding in some systems is that while li'an proceedings mean the child cannot be ascribed to the husband, the child is not technically dismissed as illegitimate but simply of unknown paternity.

A similar lack of options occurs in situations where there is no claim of marriage, but the mother seeks to have paternity established. While systems not based on Muslim laws generally permit any parent to establish paternity through court proceedings, systems based on Muslim laws generally only establish paternity if it is acknowledged by the father (Tunisia).

the acknowledgement of paternity

Systems that unconditionally allow fathers to acknowledge paternity of any child, and do not require their wife's consent can be a double-edged sword (Cameroon). On the one hand, the acknowledged children benefit from the rights and status they gain, but on the other hand, the provision of these benefits may affect the financial security of any children from the father's existing marriage (maintenance and inheritance will have to be shared). In addition, the possibility of acknowledging children may undermine state efforts to regulate polygyny (Cameroon). Indeed, in an effort to strengthen provisions outlawing polygyny (Article 9), Lebanon's unsuccessfully proposed 1998 civil marriage law stated that children born from an illegal second marriage are illegitimate (Article 61). In Cameroon, magistrates may not bother to properly determine what is the woman's share of the marital property on the husband's death, and thus, a woman may find her share being divided among children she never knew existed, but who had been acknowledged at some point by her husband.

Other systems make acknowledgement of paternity conditional, for example, upon a reasonable age gap between the father and the child (Malaysia, Philippines), or upon the possibility that the parents could have been lawfully married at the time of conception (Malaysia). This latter condition would appear to rule out the possibility of a man acknowledging a child born while her/his mother was married to another man. Children born to adulterous mothers are, therefore, at a greater disadvantage than children born to unmarried mothers.

Some systems have attempted to restrict the circumstances under which acknowledgement of paternity can be refuted by the court or a third person. For example, under the Philippines Code of Muslim Personal Laws, the only grounds on which paternity can be disclaimed is if it proved that there could have been no physical access between the parents at or about the time of the child's conception.

adoption

This chapter discusses the rights of adopted children relative to those of biological children. For a discussion of adoptive relationships and how they create bars to marriage on the grounds of consanguinity and affinity, see p.96.

Generally, systems based on Muslim laws only permit fosterage, and the inheritance rights of such children is limited by legal and social provisions pertaining to gifts and wills. Tunisia is the sole exception where full adoption is a legal possibility. (Lebanon's unsuccessful 1998 uniform civil code also sought to legalize adoption).

However, in some other systems, a civil law on adoption may apply to Muslim communities because all citizens are governed by a single set of laws that are not based on Muslim laws (Cameroon, Central Asian Republics). In yet other systems, laws regarding adoption may apply to all citizens even if the adopting parents are married under Muslim laws (Singapore). Case law in Sri Lanka has confused the situation because, although all citizens can adopt under the Adoption

Ordinance, 1941, the Supreme Court has ruled that children adopted by Muslims have no right to intestate succession (i.e., automatically inheriting as biological children would, in the absence of a will). However, they continue to be able to inherit under a will. While adoption is generally not recognized in Muslim laws, other traditions (notably Hindu customs) have influenced some Muslim communities, and they now practice adoption whereby the adopted child has the same social status as biological children, and generous provisions may be made for inheritance (Indonesia, Sri Lanka, certain parts of Pakistan).

In systems such as Singapore, a potential conflict of laws arises, and there may be confusion about affinity and consanguinity rules and an adopted child's inheritance rights.

For female children, unless full adoption is recognized, there may be confusion (in systems that recognize ijbar and make the wali's consent a marriage requisite, see p.66) about who holds the power of ijbar and who is to act as the wali for the girl/woman's marriage. In some systems the court acts as the wali (Malaysia, Singapore).

Algeria's provisions list detailed rights and responsibilities of foster parents and children, which apart from the issue of inheritance, result in a foster child's status coming very close to that of a biological child. However, social acceptance of these provisions lags behind.

In many Muslim communities, it is common for close relatives of a couple who cannot have biological children of their own to allow one of their children to live with the couple as a foster child (Pakistan, Philippines). These children receive maintenance and support for education from their foster parents, but whether or not they receive lifetime gifts (hiba) and/or one-third of the foster parent's property (permitted under principles of inheritance) depends upon local social practice and the family involved. For example, because of property concerns, a paternal (rather than maternal) nephew/niece is preferred as a foster child in Pakistan's Punjab and Sindh provinces. But in Pakistan's NWFP and among Hazarajats, a brother's children are not adopted because of strong traditions which regard brothers as rivals in inheritance. In Iran, bequests tend to be limited to one-quarter of the adoptive parent's estate.

Laws and attitudes towards fosterage in systems based on Muslim laws have changed both for the better and for the worse, sometimes because of Islamization. Customary laws in Indonesia (adat law) traditionally permitted adopted children to receive the same share of inheritance as biological children. However, other laws have regulated adoption since 1991. Under the new law, adopted children receive an obligatory bequest of one-third of their adoptive parent's estate, but they can no longer receive more than this through lifetime gifts. These changes can be variously interpreted as either the Islamization of inheritance laws or a response to locally-generated concerns regarding unfairness resulting from adat law (see bibliography).

Until the codification of Muslim laws began in India (which then included Bangladesh and Pakistan) in the 1930s, various customary laws governed inheritance. Under some customary laws in parts of Pakistan that have been strongly influenced by Hindu customs, adopted children were given a share of inheritance. However, once Muslim inheritance laws were codified, and particularly since the social atmosphere has changed following Islamization in more recent decades, this aspect of customary law is now dismissed as 'unIslamic,' and adopted children are no longer guaranteed a part of the inheritance. However, elsewhere in the country, notably in major urban centres, despite the widespread knowledge of the position of Muslim laws regarding adoption, there is a growing acceptance of adopting unrelated children. Edhi Centres (charity shelters) have baskets outside where babies can be placed anonymously without formalities and questions, and the children are subsequently put up for adoption. Wills may be made, and a family will generally uphold lifetime gifts to the adopted child if they are publicly made.

maintenance of children

Whether or not children's maintenance rights are enforced depends primarily upon the validity of their parents' marriage and/or whether or not their paternity has been acknowledged. Women may face extreme difficulty in securing and enforcing maintenance decrees for their children in systems where only registered marriages are valid (Central Asian Republics, Fiji, Senegal). However, as long as the marriage was considered valid, a child's right to maintenance continues after divorce.

Some systems provide that maintenance is an obligation shared by both parents as part of an overall right of joint guardianship and custody (see p.338). Other systems deem that children have a right to maintenance principally, or only, from their father (as guardian) and their father's male relatives.

A stereotyping of gender roles is visible in many maintenance laws, where the duration of maintenance is different for daughters and sons. The length of time for which children are entitled to maintenance varies as follows:

- daughters, until they are married, and sons, until puberty or until the sons finish their studies, unless the sons are physically incapacitated (Sri Lanka)
- daughters, until they are married and again if they are divorced and have no financial resources; and sons until they are capable of earning money for themselves, and in cases where the son is physically or mentally handicapped, the father's support continues (Sudan)
- until children are married (Fiji)
- until completion of their education (gender-neutral in the Philippines, only sons in Malaysia)
- daughters, until the consummation of their marriage, and sons, until age of majority; or both sons and daughters, until they have finished their education or have means to provide for themselves (Algeria).

Systems differ over whether there are provisions for the maintenance of children not born within a valid marriage (India and Bangladesh have such a provision, while it has been removed from the statute in Pakistan).

problems regarding enforcement of maintenance decrees

While most parents/fathers accept their duty to maintain their children, when they do not, enforcing a child's right to maintenance becomes very problematic. Enforcement problems often become especially difficult to solve following a divorce (see p.312). As with orders for the recovery of a married women's maintenance (and her maintenance during the waiting period or her alimony), child maintenance awards are usually low (up to 25% of the father's salary in Sudan and 20% in Sri Lanka); an exception may be Indonesia's government regulations regarding civil servants under which an ex-husband must pay one-third of his salary to his ex-wife and an additional one-third to his children.

These awards are also extremely difficult to enforce if the paying parent is self-employed or abandons the family (see Maintenance, p.219 and Financial Rights and Settlements, p.311). In Nigeria under customary and Muslim laws, the father is unequivocally responsible for child maintenance. However, even if a court makes a maintenance award, it is unclear how such an award is to be enforced where the majority of the population works in subsistence agriculture, and thus they have no bank accounts. The children of migrant workers are particularly vulnerable (Bangladesh, Pakistan, Sri Lanka). In contrast, where the economy is highly regulated, for example in Singapore, the court has access to the Central Provident Fund (CPF) records of all citizens and can check income reported to the CPF authorities. This information can facilitate recovery in the case of self-employed parents.

Some systems allow a father's salary or property to be attached in the event that maintenance is not forthcoming (Bangladesh, Malaysia, Pakistan, Singapore, Senegal). Such a provisions may be found in Muslim family laws (Malaysia) or in general civil laws on maintenance (India, Singapore). Where the courts that decide and have the power to enforce maintenance decrees are different from the courts that have jurisdiction over family law matters for Muslims, Muslim mothers often must take on the difficult task of coordinating the two courts, in order to secure maintenance for their children. In Malaysia, there are provisions in the various State Muslim laws to order that property be used as security for maintenance. However, these provisions have rarely been accessed because the State Syariah courts (who make maintenance awards) have no power over land matters. Moreover, they have very little or no other powers to enforce maintenance orders by other means.

Lobbying for Strengthening Children's Legal Rights

In Nigeria's federal structure, the matter of 'children' remains on the residual list, i.e., the list of matters on which the various States can legislate independently. Consequently, States in Nigeria may have different laws governing adoption, guardianship, etc. The current federal legislation, the Children and Young Persons Law, 1957, is extremely outdated.

A Children's Bill, containing extensive provisions regarding fosterage, custody, guardianship, adoption, maintenance, inheritance, etc was recently prepared, to be used as a model in the various States. Unfortunately, when it was submitted to the National Assembly for consideration, the representatives rejected it on the grounds that its contents did not take into account Nigerian 'traditions', 'culture' and 'values'.

Rights activists are now preparing to renew their lobbying and advocacy efforts with legislators and hope that after proper sensitization, they will reconsider the Bill. However, if passed, the federal legislation would only provide protection to children in the federal capital territory.

Activists are also planning to meet all the Speakers of the State Houses of Assembly to promote reform in the individual States.

NOTES

LAWS: Presumption and Acknowledgment of Paternity

Criteria

All the laws dealt with here presume paternity of children within a valid marriage. Generally, the wider the time period during which a child's conception would be considered during a valid marriage, the more option-giving this is for women.

☺ More option-giving are those laws which:
- Do not make filiation dependent upon valid marriage.

😐 The middle ground is occupied by those laws which:
- Favour a presumption of paternity, but also codify li'an as a means of rejecting paternity; or
- Favour a presumption of paternity, but do not provide mechanisms for women to be able to establish paternity.

☹ Less option-giving are those laws which:
- Codify the point that children born outside of a valid marriage are illegitimate; or
- Regard all unregistered marriages as void.

☺ **Paternity and legitimacy are not dependent upon a valid marriage or the father's acknowledgement**

Turkey: The new Civil Code has discarded the term 'illegitimate' and instead discusses the establishment of descent. Under A. 282 maternal descent is established by birth, and paternal descent can be established through marriage with the mother, acknowledgement, or a court ruling. Under A. 329 if the unmarried mother of a child is looking after the child, she has the right to claim maintenance for the child. Under A. 498, children whose filiation has been established have the same inheritance rights as children born from a valid marriage.

India (marriages under the SMA, 1954): Children of a marriage that has been declared void are legitimate if conceived before the court decree. There are provisions for permanent alimony and maintenance of such children.

Cameroon: The paternity of children born outside of marriage can be established directly after birth by the parents' declaration in the mayor's office (civil status registry), or later, through a court decision, based upon a declaration by the parents; the declaration must be corroborated by at least 2 witnesses. Acknowledgement of paternity does not need the wife's consent.

😐 **Paternity is presumed if the child is born within marriage, unless the parties could not have had access to each other**

India (all marriages): S. 112 of the Evidence Act, 1872 states that the fact that any person was born during the continuance of a valid marriage between his mother and any man, or within 280 days after its dissolution, the mother remaining unmarried, shall be conclusive proof that he is the legitimate son of that man, unless it can be shown that the parties to the marriage had no access to each other at any time when he could have been begotten (although the law uses 'son,' it also applied to daughters).

Paternity is presumed; husbands can deny paternity via li'an

Pakistan: Under A. 128 of the Qanun-e-Shahadat Order, 1984 (Law of Evidence), the fact that a child was born during the continuance of a valid marriage between her/his mother and any man and not earlier than the expiration of six lunar months from the date of the marriage or within two years after its dissolution, the mother remaining unmarried, shall, be conclusive proof that she/he is the legitimate child of that man, unless, the husband has refused, or refuses to own the child; or the child was born after the expiration of six lunar months from the date on which the woman had accepted that the period of idda had come to an end. Anything contained in this above clause does not apply to non-Muslims if it is inconsistent with their faith. Courts, pre-1947 (Independence) and since then, have been consistently reluctant to declare a child illegitimate and have held that mere denial of paternity by the husband would not take away the status of legitimacy from the child (Mst. Hamida Begum v Mst. Murad Begum and others PLD 1975 SC 624 - an inheritance dispute; Shahnawaz Khan and another v Nawab Khan PLD 1976 SC 767). Only li'an proceedings can remove the paternity status of a child, and then the marriage is also dissolved. In a case of zina filed by a husband against his wife who had given birth to a full-term baby six months after marrying him, the complaint was dismissed by the Sessions Court and again by the superior Federal Shariat Court, which held that the husband must prove that he had no access to the wife (Shamsul Haq v Mst. Nazima Shaheen and another 1992 PSC (Criminal) 382). Irregular marriage and co-habitation are also sufficient grounds to establish paternity. Cases regarding acknowledgement by a Muslim father date back to the 19th century (Wuheedun v Wusee Hossein, 1871, 15 W R 403; Mst. Qadul and 7 others v Allah Bachaya PLD 1973 Baghdad ul Jadid 48). Since 1979, extra-marital sex carries heavy penalties, which in effect hinders mothers from attempting to establish paternity of a child born out of wedlock.

Paternity is presumed but presumption and acknowledgement of paternity is conditional; husbands can deny paternity via li'an

Philippines: Under A. 59 (2) of the CMPL, children born after 6 months following the consummation of a marriage or within 2 years after divorce or death of the husband shall be presumed to be legitimate. The only evidence that can disprove this presumption is that of the physical impossibility of access between the parents at or about the time of conception. Under A. 59(1), claims that a child is illegitimate or that their paternity is doubtful must be proved. Under A. 63, acknowledgement (iqrar) of a child by the father shall establish paternity and confer upon each the right to inherit from the other, provided: (a) the father publicly acknowledges the child, who does not doubt it; and (b) the relationship does not appear impossible by reason of disparity of age. A. 94 affirms the possibility of inheritance between the acknowledged child and the father and their relatives, following the principles of Muslim laws of inheritance. However, a child who was the subject of the li'an proceedings that led to his mother being divorced inherits only from his mother and her relatives (i.e., paternity is denied).

Malaysia: Under most State Muslim laws, for a child who is born 6 or more qamariah (lunar) months after her/his mother's marriage to a man or within 4 qamariah years after divorce or his death, paternity (nasab) is established in that man, provided the mother remained unmarried during that period. Most states have the following requirements for any claim of paternity or acknowledgement of paternity within the period of legitimacy (as above) or after four qamariah years: a) the paternity of the child is not established in any one else; b) there is a sufficient age gap between the man and the child that they could actually be parent and child; c) where the child has reached the age of discretion (mumaiyiz), the child accepts to be acknowledged; d) the man and the mother of the child could have been lawfully married at the time of conception; and e) the man is competent to make a contract; f) the acknowledgement is specifically that the child is the legitimate child of his body and is with the intention of conferring legitimacy. The presumption or acknowledgement can be rebutted only by: a disclaimer on the part of the child; proof that the man and child are so close in age that paternity is physically impossible; proof that the child is in fact some other person's child; or proof that the child's mother could not possibly have been the lawful wife of the acknowledging father at the time when the child could have been conceived. However, a man may by way of li'an or imprecation, disavow or disclaim the child before the court.

Paternity is presumed; fathers can only deny paternity within time limits; children regarded as property of fathers

Iran: A. 1158-1167 of the CC deals with parentage. Under S. 1158 a child born during marriage belongs to the husband, provided that the interval between the date of conception and the birth of the child is not less than 6 months and not more than 10 months. Under administrative measures, only the father can have the child's birth certificate issued, register the child in school, consent to the child's marriage, or send the child to work. Under A. 1162-1163, a man may only reject paternity within 2 months of the child's birth or within 2 months of coming to know of her/his true date of birth. Extra-marital sex carries heavy penalties, which effectively prevent any claim or acknowledgement of paternity of a child born out of wedlock; and, under A. 1167, a child born as a result of fornication does not belong to the fornicator (i.e., the man).

Paternity is presumed; acknowledgement or denial of paternity depends upon the father's statement

Egypt: A man can recognize paternity through a court declaration. The law is silent about any conditions for claims acknowledging or denying paternity.

Nigeria (marriages under Muslim laws): Provided the man does not dispute paternity, a child is presumed legitimate up to 4 years after divorce. However, a child born as a result of extra-marital relationship between the parents who subsequently married is regarded as illegitimate because such a marriage is regarded as not valid, due to an interpretation of Maliki prohibitions to valid marriage. Children born from irregular marriages (which are rare) would be considered to have full rights. In the now famous Amina Lawal case, Amina's child's father initially acknowledged paternity but withdrew the acknowledgement when it became clear that this would leave him liable to strict punishment for zina. In the North, the prospect of illegitimacy is a major issue. Some communities in the south west of Nigeria customarily prefer to ensure that the bride is pregnant before marriage to ensure that she is fertile. This practice is sometimes accompanied by the abuse of children for whom the mother cannot identify the father. Under post-1999 Sharia criminal legislation in some states in the North, extra-marital sex carries heavy penalties, and these effectively prevent any claim to or acknowledgement of the paternity of a child born out of wedlock. The Constitution of the Federal Republic states that no child (or person) shall be discriminated against on the basis (among others) of the circumstances of its birth.

Tunisia: Under A. 68-74 of the CSP, filiation of a child can be established by the father, who has to prove cohabitation, or by at least 2 witnesses. Under A.69, filiation is not established if a married woman's child is disowned by her husband after proving that there was no cohabitation, or if a child is born any later than one year after the death of the husband or the divorce of parents. Men can acknowledge a child at any time, and the child then has the right to inherit from his/her father. A Supreme Court judgment of 1973 formally declared relationships outside of marriage illicit and described such relationships as 'fornication.' By defining conception under these circumstances as fornication, this ruling eliminates any possible legitimate relationship between such a child and his/her father. However, in practice, the child has the benefits of legitimacy if the father declares himself to be the child's father (at the time of birth) in the civil status registry.

☹ Children born outside valid marriage are presumed illegitimate, but paternity can be claimed

Fiji: Children are legitimate if born when the parents are validly married or if the parents subsequently marry. Children born of parents who have only gone through a nikah ceremony and who have not had a registry marriage are illegitimate in the eyes of the law. However, a suit to claim paternity can be filed, and the father can acknowledge the child.

Indonesia: Under A. 43(1), a child born out of wedlock shall have civil law relationships only with the mother and her family. Fathers of illegitimate children have no financial responsibility. In cases of contested paternity, the court has discretion to demand medical tests to prove paternity. However, the court usually will not do so if the putative father is influential.

LAWS: Adoption

Criteria

☺ More option-giving are those laws which:
- Legally recognize adoption.

☹ Less option-giving are those laws which:
- Do not legally recognize adoption.

☺ **Adoption is legally recognized**

Cameroon: Adopted children have the same inheritance rights as biological children.

Nigeria (laws not based on Muslim laws or customary laws): Children adopted under the statute law can be included in the adoptive parent's will without any limitation. Some States (mostly in the south east and also Lagos) have passed Adoption Acts.

Sri Lanka: Muslims can legally adopt (no exceptions under the Adoption Ordinance 1941), but the Supreme Court in Ghouse v Ghouse (1988) (1 Sri L.R. 25) added confusion: Muslims cannot confer on adopted children the right to intestate succession in a manner that conflicts with Muslim laws, although Muslims have the right to make a will, and adopted children can inherit under a will.

Tunisia: Under A. 8 of Loi No. 1958-0027 du 4 mars 1958, a married man or woman who is an adult and is mentally and physically capable to provide materially for an adopted child, may adopt. The other spouse's authorization is necessary. The court may also permit adoption by a widower or divorced man, but not a woman of similar status. Adoption gives the adopting parent and the adopted child the relationship of a legitimate filiation. A Tunisian can adopt a foreign child, but a foreigner cannot adopt a Tunisian child. The adopting parent must be at least 15 years older than the adopted child, except where the child is that of the adopter's spouse. The adopted child must be a minor, and the consent of the child's biological parents must be obtained, if they are alive. An abandoned child can be adopted after the adopting parents obtain the authorization of the administrative officer of the area. The child takes the name of the adopting parent. Adoption cannot be revoked.

Turkey: Under A. 305-307 of the CC, the minimum age for adopting a child has been reduced from 35 to 30, and single persons and people who already have children can also adopt. Spouses can only jointly adopt and must be married for at least 5 years before doing so.

☹ **Adoption is not recognized in laws**

Indonesia: A. 209 of the KHI prescribes an 'obligatory bequest' in favour of adopted children when the adopted child has not been named in a will by the adoptive parents (concept adopted from 1946 Egyptian law providing for obligatory bequest for children of predeceased parents). The bequest is limited to one-third of the parent's estate. Adoptive parents can also give up to one-third of their estate as a gift to the adopted child. Previously, following adat law (customary law), Indonesian Muslims could give away their entire property as a gift during their lifetime.

Iran: An adopted person may inherit whatever is in their name and additionally the adoptive parent may leave a will giving them up to one-third of their estate. Blood relatives often succeed in contesting bequests over this amount in court.

Nigeria (marriages under Muslim laws): Foster children do not inherit from the foster parents, but foster parents may make lifetime gifts (with no qualification regarding quantity) and/or leave a bequest for the foster child, not exceeding one-third of the net estate of the deceased.

Pakistan: There are no codified provisions, but following Muslim laws, adopted children cannot be regarded as full children of adoptive parents. If a foster parent makes a written provision, courts will uphold lifetime gifts and bequests for up to one-third of the property.

Philippines: Under A. 64 of the CMPL, adoption does not confer the status and rights of a legitimate child under Muslim law, except that the child may receive a gift (hiba). This provision contrasts with the possibility of adoption available to members of other communities.

Algeria: Muslims who have the financial and moral capacity may become foster parents through a legal deed via a court or notary public. They are then responsible for the upkeep, education, and protection of a minor child, just as they would be for a biological son or daughter. If the child has known living parents, the biological father's consent is necessary. The child keeps her/his biological parentage if the parents are known. But the Executive Decree of 13/1/92 completing that of 3/6/71 concerning the change of name, provides that it is possible to change the name of a fostered infant born of an unknown father; the mother's authorization is necessary, and this authorization must be given in an authentic deed. The foster parents then become the legal guardians of the child, and they benefit from rights, such as family allowances for the child, just as they would from parenting biological children. The foster father administers the child's property. He can will or make donations of up to one third of his property to the child. If he exceeds this proportion, the will or donation becomes null and void, unless his heirs consent to it. If the biological parents request the reintegration of their child into their family and the child is of age, the child has to decide for herself/himself if they want to do this or not. In the case of the death of a foster parent, legal rights and responsibilities are transferred to the heirs.

LAWS: Maintenance of Children

Algeria: The father has a duty to provide maintenance for his children unless they have other resources at their disposal. For male children, maintenance continues until they attain the age of maturity, and for girls, until they consummate their marriages. The father remains subject to his obligation as long as the child remains physically or mentally handicapped or is still receiving education. The obligation of maintenance only ceases when the child is able to provide for herself/himself. Maintenance is to include food, clothing, medical care, accommodation, and all that is considered necessary according to custom and convention. In assessing maintenance, the judge takes into account the circumstances of the spouses and the conditions of their life. A review of assessment is not possible within one year of the judgement. Maintenance is payable from the date of application. Under A. 75 of the CF, the judge may, however, rule (on the basis of evidence presented) for the father to pay back maintenance for a period not to exceed one year prior to the filing of the claim.

Bangladesh: Under S. 488 of the CrPC, a Magistrate may order the maintenance of legitimate or illegitimate children. Women are able to come forward to claim maintenance

Fiji: The father is obliged to maintain children if the parents are married until the children are 16, and if divorced, until they are 18. Court practice is to order not more than one-third of the father's income as maintenance. It is possible to obtain a variation or revision of an order on proving change of circumstance. The wife may be able to have an absconding husband, who is trying to leave the country and avoid maintenance, arrested (Chiman Lal v Pan Bhai 1978 24 FLR 121).

India (all marriages): Magistrates have the power to order maintenance in the case of both legitimate and illegitimate children under S. 125 of the CrPC, under which dependent wives, children, and aged parents, who are unable to maintain themselves, can apply.

Malaysia: Under A. 72-80 of the IFLA, it is the duty of a man to maintain his children by providing them with accommodation, clothing, food, medical attention, and education according to his means and station in life. An order for maintenance will expire when the daughter has been married, in the case of a son, when he reaches 18 years. However, the court can extend the father's liability beyond this for a further reasonable period to enable the son to pursue further or higher education or training. The court has the power to order security for maintenance and can attach property. Maintenance orders can be lowered or raised where the court is satisfied that the order was based on a misrepresentation or mistake, or where there has been a change in circumstances.

Morocco: Under A. 126(1), a father is bound to maintain his minor children who cannot earn. Girls' right to maintenance continues until it becomes binding on their husbands and that of sons until they become major and capable of earning. Where a child is a diligent student, his right to maintenance shall continue until the completion of his education or until he attains 21 years of age.

Pakistan: S. 488 of the CrPC has been repealed, in effect leaving no provision of maintenance for children born outside a valid marriage. The father's obligation to maintain children is constructed from Muslim laws and is dealt with by the Family Courts who have jurisdiction over issues of maintenance under the Schedule to the Family Courts Act.

Philippines: Under A.62 (b), (c) CMPL, a legitimate child shall have the right to receive support from his/her father, or, in his default, from his heirs. Additionally, he/she shall have the right to inherit and to other rights of succession, which the Code recognizes in his/her favour. Under A. 65, support is defined to include everything that is indispensable for sustenance, dwelling, clothing, and medical attention, according to the social standing of the person obliged to give support, as well as the education of the person entitled to the support until he/she completes his/her education and/or training for vocation, even beyond the age of majority.

Sri Lanka: The father has a duty to maintain daughters until they are married and sons until the age of puberty, unless they are incapable of earning because of physical infirmity, disease, or engagement in studies. Maintenance awards are made from the date of application. There is also a provision for mothers to apply for an increase in their child's maintenance by showing 'good and sufficient cause.'

Sudan: Under S. 81 and 84 of the MPLA, providing child maintenance is the responsibility of the father. A girl is to be supported by the father until she is married. If the daughter's husband dies, or she is divorced and has no financial resources, then she is entitled to support from her father. The boy is to remain under his father's support up to the age when he can work and earn money for himself. If a boy is sick or disabled, the father's support is to be continued. The mother is under a duty to provide support only when the father is dead or unable to do so.

9a DISSOLUTION OF MARRIAGE: AN OVERVIEW

The great diversity of laws and practices across Muslim countries and communities is clearly visible in the area of dissolution of marriage.

Although customary practices regarding divorce tend to be more restrictive for women than are codified laws, this is not always the case. In one community it may be unthinkable for a woman to leave her marriage, but in another the option of walking out of an unhappy marriage with the support of her natal family may be perfectly possible and socially acceptable.

Chapters 9 and 10 of the Handbook look at the various forms of dissolution of marriage, including all those recognized under Muslim laws as well as the 'equal grounds' form of divorce that is recognized under systems not based on Muslim laws. The related issues of financial settlements on dissolution, custody and guardianship of children, and waiting periods also affect women's individual strategies in the event of dissolution. Indeed, these issues affect a woman's options just as much as do the laws and practices governing the divorce itself. Accordingly, these have been included in this volume of the Handbook.

the diversity of laws concerning dissolution and its related matters

The various laws governing divorce lie along a continuum. At one extreme, men may have completely unrestricted authority to terminate their marriages at will (without providing any reason before any authority), while women in the same community can dissolve their marriages only through lengthy court procedures and then only on a few narrowly defined grounds. At the opposite end of the spectrum, both men and women may access divorce (only through the courts) and they can do so on equal grounds.

But divorce involves much more than just the question of who can divorce whom and on what grounds. As mentioned above, such closely related issues as financial settlements, custody of children, and waiting periods must be factored in. To understand the reality of divorce and related matters for women one must remember that while one system may have more option-giving provisions or practices in one area related to divorce, the same system may have less option-giving provisions or practices in another related area. For example, in some systems the law may give women few rights to divorce and deny them any hope of retaining custody of their children while giving them the possibility of winning a considerable financial settlements on talaq. In another system, the law may allow a woman the possibility of terminating her marriage without having to establish fault and give her an equal chance of retaining custody while denying her any access to marital property.

social attitudes and changes through legal reform

In systems governed by Muslim laws, as well as those governed by other sources of law, dissolution of marriage has been the focus of considerable legal reform over the past 100 years or so.

In some contexts women have been able to access divorce even without reforms. For example, among the Hausa in northern Nigeria, when a woman leaves the marital home and refuses to return, the husband is shamed and teased into pronouncing talaq ("are you so much under her influence that you cannot let her go?"). Accordingly, a Hausa woman would need to resort to initiating divorce proceedings only if her husband still refused to pronounce talaq.

But in many other contexts, divorce was very difficult to access before legal reformers recognised that restricting access to divorce does not fix unhappy marriages. The impossibility of divorce, whether due to strict laws or social attitudes, simply leads to desertion, polygyny (where this is possible), domestic violence forcing women to abandon their marital homes, or even conversion to another religion (in an attempt to evade restrictive provisions). In early 20th century colonial India, Muslim women were unable to access divorce and large numbers began converting to other religions in the belief that their marriages would automatically stand dissolved. It was the Indian Ulema, in their efforts to counter this trend, who pressed the colonial authorities to introduce a new law codifying the grounds for divorce that would be accessible to women. Elsewhere in Muslim communities, reform has focused both on widening women's access to divorce and on controlling the arbitrary exercise of talaq by men. Even in countries governed by laws based on Christian concepts of marriage, which unlike laws based on Muslim laws have only recognised the possibility of dissolution of marriage in the past 150 years, changes have made divorce far more accessible.

Despite these changes, both laws and practices still tend to make divorce easier to access for men than it is for women, and to make life tougher for women than for men in the post-divorce period. That this is true both for systems based on Muslim laws and for those based on other sources reflects a commonality of patriarchal control asserted through laws, practices and social attitudes.

In systems based on Muslim laws, these attitudes are often illustrated by the widespread misconception that talaq is the only 'Muslim' form of divorce. Indeed, many laws still require the husband to pronounce a talaq, even when a couple mutually agrees to divorce; this may involve the court 'requesting' the husband to pronounce talaq. These misconceptions persist despite agreement by the various Schools that Muslim laws do recognise forms of dissolution available to women. In many communities, it is only when women want to dissolve their marriages that hadith citing divorce as the most hateful thing to the deity are remembered and repeated. But attitudes can change; in Malaysia, for example, following reform in the 1980s, faskh is now accepted as a form of dissolution available to women married under Muslim laws.

Even in Muslim majority countries, not all divorce provisions are based on Muslim laws. But at the same time, the complexity of Muslim laws and misconceptions about these tend to influence, and at times confuse, the application of divorce provisions in Muslim countries and communities. Therefore, we have included a brief outline of the relevant provisions in Muslim laws concerning the various forms of divorce available to men and women. This outline does not reflect any work towards progressive reinterpretation of Muslim laws, but simply the standard, commonly agreed upon principles.

dissolution procedures and expanding women's rights

Regardless of the individual circumstances under which a divorce occurs (does the woman want to dissolve the marriage or to prevent her husband from doing so), the nature of the actual procedure is extremely important for women's rights in dissolution. In general (excluding situations where customary practices may operate equitably), it is more option-giving for divorce to be regulated through the courts, rather than through any other forum or rather than remaining unregulated. This is true despite the inevitable restrictions that result from judicial attitudes. Dissolution through the courts, when all extra-judicial steps are not recognized as valid, ensures a proper record of the proceedings and gives greater clarity to the date of effectiveness and any rights due to either spouse. However, not all systems require court-based dissolution. Others only require women to go through the courts, and this requirement effectively favours men.

On the other hand, it is more difficult to categorically state whether or not counselling and reconciliation procedures are beneficial to women. This depends on the procedures, who is to be involved as arbitrators and what powers they have regarding the final decision. For women wanting to end a violent (or otherwise unbearable) marriage, obligatory reconciliation procedures may needlessly prolong a painful situation. On the other hand, for women being discarded through talaq, reconciliation procedures may be their only chance to be heard.

One of the most contentious issues in dissolutions based on Muslim laws is the question of revocation: which forms of dissolution are revocable, who has the power of revocation and for how long a period of time can this be exercised. Some laws have attempted to clarify these issues while others reflect the apparent lack of consensus among jurists (or perhaps fail to address the prevailing confusion). Certainly, laws that permit men to discard their wives through unfettered talaq and equally allow men to revoke talaq without taking the woman's will into account, give men an extraordinary tool of control over women.

This imbalance severely violates the equality inherent in the concept of Muslim marriage as a contract. Indeed, emphasising the contractual nature of Muslim marriage has been a major strategy for women's rights activists and legal reformers in Muslim countries and communities. Highly significant changes have been made to the standard marriage contract in recent decades in Bangladesh, Iran, Malaysia, and Pakistan. In both India and South Africa, women's rights activists are currently attempting to promote progressive standard marriage contracts. Many laws also have articles expressly permitting women to negotiate written conditions to their marriage contracts. Marriage contracts are important to a woman's rights in divorce because the contract may include conditions that give a wife a delegated right to divorce (talaq tafwid), or ta'liq, or provisions restricting or conditioning the husband's right to divorce (as seen in Negotiated Rights and Responsibilities, p.167). Scholars have shown that women across Muslim communities and throughout Muslim history have successfully used the marriage contract to negotiate the terms and conditions of the dissolution of marriage. We define those systems that allow or facilitate the negotiation of such rights as option-giving for women. Where women can add such negotiated conditions, they are strengthened both in their position at the time of dissolution and, perhaps more importantly, in their position within the intact marriage. This strengthened position may even prevent situations that lead to dissolution. In Saudi Arabia negotiated clauses in the marriage contract are quite commonly used to ensure women have rights that tradition would normally deny them, including easier access to divorce.

Laws in the sections on Dissolution on Equal Grounds for Women and Men, and Other Forms of Dissolution for Women are listed alphabetically and not listed according to whether they are more or less option-giving for women because each law has such a range of provisions within it that they are not strictly comparable. For example, whereas one country's law may not require a woman to wait for more than 6 months before she can apply for dissolution on the grounds of desertion, that same country's law may have a very narrow construction of cruelty. The impossible question would then arise as to how to 'grade' that country's law.

dissolution on equal grounds for women and men

This section discusses systems in which the grounds for dissolution do not make significant distinctions between men and women; the sole exception being the grounds of non-maintenance, which, because maintenance is usually the responsibility of the husband, is available only to women. Provisions concerning adultery may also have subtle differences for women and men.

These systems fall into two distinct categories. The first includes those systems where the laws are based on sources other than Muslim laws, although there may be a sizeable Muslim community (Central Asian Republics, Fiji, Turkey). Laws that are applicable to Muslims who have the option to marry under non-Muslim laws (Bangladesh, Cameroon, Gambia, India, Nigeria) also fall into this category. The second category includes those systems where laws are based on Muslim laws, but the grounds for dissolution of marriage are available equally to men and women – at least in theory (Indonesia, Tunisia).

Senegal's Code de la Famille has been inspired by Muslim laws, by the Napoleonic Code, and by Wolof and other customary laws. Since it offers almost equal grounds to men and women, its provisions are discussed in this section. Similarly, the grounds of 'constant disputes and quarrels' (niza' wa shiqaq) are available to men and women in laws derived from the Ottoman Code (applicable to the Palestinian community in Israel and some other Arabic-speaking countries) so this is discussed in this section.

All laws discussed in this section (with the exception of laws in Fiji) recognize the concept of 'irretrievable marital breakdown', 'constant disputes and quarrels', 'discord and strife' (niza' wa shiqaq), or the possibility of dissolution without having to prove specific grounds. In general, whether based on Muslim laws or other laws, these systems in effect accept that where one spouse is determined to dissolve the marriage, there is little that the courts can do except enforce arbitration and reconciliation procedures and assess the damages due to the other spouse. No such acceptance informs the concepts of faskh, ta'liq, and suspended talaq, which are available to women in Muslim laws. In each of these, the wife must provide substantial evidence of one or more very specific grounds.

mubarat and mutually agreed divorce

Muslim laws have for centuries recognized the possibility of spouses mutually agreeing to divorce without having to establish fault on the part of either party. However, it is only recently that mutually agreed divorce has been accepted in systems based on other sources of law (notably where Christian concepts define marriage as a sacrament).

In most books on family laws in Muslim countries and communities, the first form of divorce discussed is talaq. In many ways this helps reinforce the misconception that talaq is the only 'acceptable' form of dissolution. We deliberately begin the sections in this chapter of the Handbook with mubarat. This is to emphasize our view that, while all breakdown in marriage is unfortunate, it is preferable to allow a couple to mutually agree to part from one another without the having to endure the pain of publicly establishing fault.

talaq and talaq tafwid/('esma)

In a number countries (Indonesia, Tunisia, the former South Yemen), family laws governing Muslims are largely based on Muslim laws, but talaq is not recognized and dissolution of marriage can take place only through the courts and largely the same grounds are available to men and women.

Although we have discussed these provisions in detail in the section on Dissolution on Equal Grounds for Women and Men, we have also mentioned them in the section on Talaq in order to illustrate how far some Muslim countries have moved towards ending the injustices of talaq even while retaining Muslim laws as the source of their inspiration.

The section on Talaq Tafwid (also known as 'esma, literally 'the permission' in many Arabic-speaking countries) immediately follows the section on Talaq in order to highlight its importance as a form of dissolution that is both available to women and based on Muslim laws. Talaq tafwid is the delegation, by a husband of his power of talaq to his wife, unconditionally or conditionally. Usually the husband delegates this power through a negotiated clause in the marriage contract, but he can delegate it to the wife at any time during the marriage. There is a strong misperception among communities that by granting this power to his wife, the husband somehow loses his own power of talaq, which is not correct. Although talaq tafwid is dependent upon the husband agreeing to delegate his right, once delegated it cannot be taken back. If the delegation is unconditional, the wife is given effectively the same rights to divorce as her husband has (in systems where talaq is recognized). Accordingly, the option of talaq tafwid can serve to partly redress the power imbalance in a marriage.

The section on Talaq Tafwid includes both unconditionally and conditionally delegated talaq, but not the ta'liq and 'suspended' talaq available through the Malaysian and Iranian marriage contracts (see paragraph below).

other forms of dissolution available to women

Muslim laws recognize the concept of khul', the wife's right to seek release from the marriage tie by compensating her husband, but not all systems based on Muslim laws and not all practices in Muslim communities make this a possibility. Although legal systems and communities may confuse khul' with mubarat, the essential distinction is that under Muslim laws khul' requires adjudication by a third party (the qazi or judge). On the other hand, mubarat is theoretically conceptualised as a form of dissolution that does not require the intervention of any third party to establish the circumstances of the dissolution – although actual laws may require the couple to go through some official forum.

In addition to mubarat, talaq tafwid and khul', there are other forms of dissolution that may be available to women in systems based on Muslim laws. A variety of terms are used, including faskh, tafriq, ta'liq (see Muslim Laws on Dissolution, p.249), and judicial divorce. Despite their differences, these forms of divorce share that they can be accessed by a woman only through an adjudicating forum (a court, qazi or jamaat). Additionally, a woman must provide concrete evidence of some fault or defect on the part of the husband or his failure to meet the terms of the marriage contract. With this established, the wife, as the injured party to the contract, generally retains all financial rights due from the contract, including mahr and whatever other financial settlements are recognized by the particular system.

Under the standard marriage contract in Iran and Malaysia, following reforms in the past two decades, the husband effectively pronounces a suspended talaq or conditionally delegates his right of talaq. This right becomes operable in the event that, for example, he fails to maintain his wife for a certain period of time. These contractual provisions are discussed in Other Forms of Dissolution for Women (p.281) because, in effect, they are closer to the fault and defect-based faskh and tafriq.

financial rights & settlements on dissolution, custody & guardianship, the waiting period (idda), and intervening marriage

It would be impossible to discuss dissolution of marriage without considering related matters such as financial settlements and child custody since, for women, problems related to these issues often limit women's ability to access any right to divorce they may have. Financial settlements, and custody and guardianship are two areas where there is a great deal of variation in laws, some being noticeably more favourable to women than others. Their favourability does not depend upon whether the laws are based on Muslim laws, customary laws or other sources.

The chapter on matters related to dissolution of marriage begins with discussing the waiting period, during which a divorced or widowed woman cannot remarry. We begin this chapter with the waiting period because, at least in Muslim laws, certain financial rights are specifically related to the waiting period. Known as idda in Muslim laws, the waiting period is also found in laws based on the Napoleonic Code, although in that case the waiting time is extended to 300 days, rather than the three months required under Muslim laws.

Finally, we discuss remarriage here only in the context of the much-disputed notion of intervening marriage, hilala, i.e., the question of whether or not a woman can validly remarry the same husband without first having to marry and be divorced from another man. Given our lack of information on laws and practices concerning remarriage, we have only briefly mentioned other matters relating to remarriage under the sections on Capacity (of divorced or widowed women to contract their own marriage, p.68) and Capacity to Marry – Other Prohibitions (remarriage during the waiting period, p.97).

9b DISSOLUTION OF MARRIAGE: MUSLIM LAWS ON DISSOLUTION - AN OVERVIEW

procedure for talaq

Talaq procedures are derived from Qur'anic verses and the Sunnah, which in essence require:

- a statement of divorce; and
- attempts at reconciliation, mediated by representatives; and
- a waiting period of 3 menstrual cycles.

The various Schools are agreed that pronouncement of divorce must be made before witnesses. However, there is no agreement among jurists and the various Schools as to whether the statement of divorce should be oral or written (or both). It is also not agreed upon as to how many times the statement should be made; when the waiting period begins; whether or not, and under what conditions, a husband can revoke his talaq; and when an intervening marriage is required before a divorced husband and wife can remarry.

Thus, various forms of talaq have developed including ahsan, hasan and bid'a.

- **Ahsan** is a single statement of talaq that is made at a point between two menstruations (tuhur), followed by an idda period. In talaq, the waiting period has a dual function. It is firstly designed to provide a 'cooling off' period during which the husband can rethink his action and perhaps revoke the talaq. If he does not change his mind, the idda period helps to ensure that there is no confusion over paternity in the event that the divorced wife remarries. Once the idda expires, the talaq becomes baynuna sughra (also known as the 'lesser finality'). Should the couple choose to remarry each other after a talaq ahsan, they would be required only to make a fresh contract. However, if a talaq takes place in this manner for the third time (i.e., the couple have divorced, remarried, divorced, remarried and are now divorcing for the third time), the talaq becomes baynuna kubra (also known as the 'greater finality'). After a talaq baynuna kubra, the couple cannot remarry unless (and until) the woman has married another man, consummated that marriage and which is later dissolved. This intervening marriage is known as hilala.

- **Hasan** is a single statement of talaq that is made at a point between two menstruations (tuhur), followed by a further single statement of talaq during the subsequent tuhur, followed by a final statement of talaq during the third successive tuhur. Provided there has been no revocation or sexual intercourse during the entire period up to the third pronouncement, the divorce becomes irrevocable upon the third pronouncement and then the period of idda begins. In effect, a talaq hasan is only revocable within a maximum of two menstrual cycles whereas a talaq ahsan is revocable within during three cycles. Should the couple choose to remarry each other after going through talaq hasan, the woman would first have to undergo hilala.

- **Bid'a** is a series of three pronouncements of talaq given at one time and followed by idda. Here too, should the couple choose to remarry each other; the woman would have to undergo hilala. Bid'a means 'disapproved' or 'innovation,' which implies that it is further removed from the Qur'anic source than other forms of talaq. Jurists have not agreed as to whether or not a talaq bid'a is an acceptable form of talaq.

Most jurists agree that talaq remains revocable after the first and second pronouncements, but becomes irrevocable on the third pronouncement. There is a lack of clarity as to whether or not a husband is obliged to pay maintenance during the idda that follows an irrevocable divorce.

some forms of dissolution available to women

The principle of khul' is also derived from Qur'anic sources (Surah al-Baqarah: 229, and Surah al-Baqarah: 187) and the Sunnah, according to which, a wife may seek a release from the marriage tie by giving her husband some compensation. The same conditions requiring reconciliation efforts and observance of idda are applied as in other forms of divorce under Muslim laws.

However, jurists disagree as to whether or not khul' requires a husband's permission. Additionally, opinions vary as to the precise conditions for khul' to be accepted by a qazi and as to whether or not a khul' dissolution is revocable by the wife, as well as what form the compensation should take. Among jurists, there are subtly distinct understandings of khul' which explain some of the differences apparent in laws and practices.

"Khul' literally means 'laying off', as in taking off a garment (this is the connection to Surah al-Baqarah: 187 which speaks of the husband and wife being raiment or garments to each other). The issue disputed among jurists is the question of agency: who is laying off what? Is it the husband laying down his marital authority over the wife, or is it the couple untying the marital knot on the wife's asking? Does the qazi have authority to untie the marital knot on the wife's asking?

If a couple agrees to a khul' and the relevant compensation to be paid by the wife to the husband without the intervention of a third party, then most interpretations accept this as a valid dissolution. The real questions arise when the couple cannot agree and require some form of intervention or hakam. Where interpretations regard khul' as the husband laying down his marital authority over the wife, laws may require that the husband must consent to the khul' (whether this is done extra-judicially or through a qazi). This more patriarchal interpretation of the Qur'anic provisions appears to be currently dominant in most laws. Indeed, the husband's authority is emphasized by the fact that in some instances the khul' is effected by the declaration of talaq by the husband before the qazi. In contrast, where interpretations focus on the wife's agency in khul' (inspired by the mutuality implicit in Surah al-Baqarah: 187), then laws tend to regard the husband's consent as irrelevant and empower the qazi/hakam to pronounce the marital tie as dissolved.

Thus there remains the question of compensation (also known as zar-i-khula and khului): what is an acceptable form of compensation, whether or not this is the return or waiver of mahr, and whether or not the qazi can determine the compensation according to the circumstances of the case. The Qur'anic provisions do not specify the return or waiver of mahr, and indeed there is no indication that the consideration or compensation for khul' must be the return of something which the wife has received from the husband; she might have to compensate her husband even when she has not received anything or may not have to return anything when she has actually received something.

Some other forms of dissolution that are available to women are derived from the Qur'anic concept of marriage as a contract, as well as from Qur'anic references to the responsibilities of husbands. These forms of dissolution include: talaq tafwid (delegated right of divorce, or 'esma), faskh (judicial dissolution, generally related to an irregularity in the contract or the violation of a contractual clause), tafriq (judicial divorce generally related to problems between the spouses, specifically a spouse's failure to fulfil certain marital responsibilities) and ta'liq (a suspended or conditional talaq, e.g., "you are divorced if I fail to maintain you for 4 months"). Schools differ as to the extent of grounds available to a wife, with the Hanafi school offering the narrowest grounds. Since husbands may already have a unilateral right of talaq, then faskh, tafriq and ta'liq are generally seen as divorce options for women. However, husbands also may access some of these forms. For example, an incurable disease on the part of one's spouse is a grounds for tafriq that is available to both husband and wife.

9c DISSOLUTION OF MARRIAGE: MUBARAT AND DIVORCE BY MUTUAL AGREEMENT

introduction

Many systems, both those based on Muslim laws and those based on other sources, recognize the possibility of divorce by mutual consent (known as mubarat in Muslim laws). This type of dissolution conforms to the idea that marriage is a contract; consequently, it allows spouses to negotiate the conditions and effects of their divorce. Although either party may initiate this type of dissolution, in systems that require court endorsement or some other formal proceedings, both spouses must apply jointly.

While some systems based on Muslim laws may not actually use the term 'mubarat,' they still may allow the spouses to mutually dissolve their marriage and then go to court for a confirmation of such a dissolution. In this situation, the court may require the husband to pronounce a talaq (Sri Lanka, Singapore for Muslim marriages, Malaysia, Nigeria for marriages under Muslim laws). When the divorce operates as a talaq, the claims flowing from a talaq divorce ensue. In the Philippines some cases that are initiated as talaq become a divorce by mutual consent after an intervention by the court. They are then recorded as a divorce by mutual consent in the court order.

In other systems, such a divorce is either termed irretrievable breakdown or divorce by mutual consent (Senegal, Tunisia, Turkey). In Turkey, this type of divorce is only available to spouses who have been married for more than 1 year.

There are obvious advantages to mubarat if it actually facilitates dissolution by mutual consent. Mutual consent presumes an agreement of the termination of the marriage and assumes a less contentious process. When this is the case, parties are able to negotiate the settlements, claims, and property rights between them. However, where parties are not in an equal bargaining position, how mutual the agreement is may be in question, and a woman's rights may be bargained away or compromised. Such inequalities may have inspired a provision in the 1998 proposed uniform civil code for Lebanon (never passed), which sought to do away with mubarat. Mubarat or divorce by mutual agreement is not commonly accessed in any system dealt with here. This unfortunate fact illustrates how little social room there is for a divorce to be uncontested. However, it may be that in communities where divorce routinely takes place without court intervention and without strong social condemnation (certain communities in Nigeria and Pakistan), mutual divorce is more common.

procedure

Some countries require a court intervention (Senegal, Tunisia, Turkey) or a registration procedure (Bangladesh, Pakistan) for mubarat. In Bangladesh and Pakistan, the parties do not have to appear before the local council, and they can notify the authorities through the mail or through an authorized agent. Furthermore, the spouses can nominate representatives to appear at reconciliation proceedings. In other systems, there is no formal regulation of mubarat, in which case the parties may declare their intention to mutually dissolve their marriage in an oral or written agreement (marriages under Muslim laws in India and Nigeria).

In Senegal and Tunisia, if the spouses apply for divorce by mutual consent, the court can merely confirm their extra-judicial agreement and register the divorce.

In many areas of Nigeria, it is customary for the wife's family to negotiate a mubarat, as well as a mutual settlement of the financial arrangements that will follow the dissolution. In such cases, the husband is required to pronounce talaq, but his pronouncement does not necessarily have to be through a court. In Iran a divorce by mutual consent of the parties is often treated as a khul'.

Such treatment nullifies the intent and effect of dissolution by mutual consent, which emphasizes the agency of both spouses and avoids fixing blame on either one. Also, transforming mubarat into a talaq or khul' can result in confusion about such effects of the dissolution as financial rights and the revocability of the divorce.

In Pakistan, mubarat is rarely accessed and procedural forums (local councils) appear confused over who can revoke a mubarat. Problems stemming from the complicated wording of the Muslim Family Laws Ordinance's provisions concerning procedure for mubarat are compounded by the staffs of the local councils (including the elected heads, or Nazims) being both ignorant of statutory laws and conservative in their social attitudes.

NOTES

LAWS: Mubarat and Divorce by Mutual Agreement

Criteria

☺ More option-giving are those laws which:
- Explicitly permit mubarat, or divorce by mutual agreement.

😐 The middle ground is occupied by those laws which:
- Permit divorce by mutual agreement, but place conditions to such an agreement.

☹ Less option-giving are those laws which:
- Are silent about the possibility of mubarat.

☺ The law recognizes mubarat/divorce by mutual agreement

Algeria: A. 48 of the CF recognizes the possibility of divorce by mutual consent. All forms of divorce require a court process and a period of up to 3 months for reconciliation. Mubarat appears to be revocable by the husband.

Bangladesh & Pakistan: Mubarat is recognized under S. 8 of the MFLO and by the DMMA. The procedure is extra-judicial, requiring only notification to the Union Council/Prasad. Because S. 8 does not clearly spell out who has the authority to revoke a mubarat and whether or not reconciliation proceedings are required, the procedural authorities and public remain confused, although a logical reading of S.8 would imply that reconciliation proceedings are required, and a mubarat can only be revoked by both spouses acting jointly.

India & Nigeria (marriages under Muslim laws): Mubarat is possible with or without the involvement of a court or extra-judicial forum. The parties may agree to the terms mutually, but generally there is no refund of mahr already received.

Malaysia: Under S. 47(3) of the IFLA, if the other party consents to the divorce and the court is satisfied that the marriage has irretrievably broken down, the court shall advise the husband to pronounce one talaq before the court. This is revocable divorce and the parties may resume cohabitation if they mutually consent to a ruju' which must also be reported and registered.

Senegal: The CF recognizes divorce by mutual consent. The role of the judge is merely to ensure that the couple are acting of their own free will and that public morality and norms are respected in the agreement they have reached and then to endorse the agreement. The agreement must also cover custody of children and decide the fate of marital property.

Tunisia: Under A. 31 of the CSP, divorce by mutual consent is recognized. Divorce is only possible through the court and after reconciliation efforts by the judge. The judge may confirm an agreement between the spouses relating to ancillary matters such as custody, maintenance, etc.

😐 Permit divorce by mutual agreement, but place conditions to such an agreement

Turkey: Following a 1988 amendment adding this grounds, under A. 166 of the CC, spouses may apply for divorce on the grounds of irretrievable breakdown, provided they have been married for more than 1 year.

☹ The law is silent about the possibility of mubarat

Gambia (marriages under Muslim laws), Morocco, Sri Lanka: The law does not mention the possibility of mubarat, but each law has an overriding principle that where the law is silent, the principles of Muslim laws apply.

IMPLEMENTATION & PRACTICES

Pakistan: Middle-class professionals or the feudal elite may negotiate a mubarat in order to avoid the public embarrassment of a contested divorce or the shame of a one-sided divorce. This usually only occurs when the spouses and their families are social equals.

Philippines: In many instances a divorce by talaq becomes a divorce by mubarat after the intervention of the court.

Sri Lanka: The parties agree to a divorce, and then the husband pronounces a talaq.

Singapore: Mubarat is not specifically provided for in the law. However, the court does recognize the possibility that either party may apply for a divorce while both agree to terminate the marriage. If the husband initiated the application, the husband is required to pronounce a talaq.

9d DISSOLUTION OF MARRIAGE: TALAQ

introduction

Talaq, or repudiation, is the unilateral termination of a marriage contract by the husband. This section deals only with laws and customs that are both based on Muslim laws and recognize the right of a husband to exercise talaq. See p.267 for unconditional and conditional delegation of the right of talaq to the wife or any third party (talaq tafwid or 'esma). For statute laws based on other sources or for systems that are also inspired by Muslim laws, but instead give women and men equal grounds for dissolution, see p.293.

Talaq is one of the major factors that result in women's unequal status in marriage. Although Muslim marriage is seen as a contractual relationship that must be entered into by two consenting parties; talaq gives the power to unilaterally terminate this contract to only one of the parties, the husband. It is particularly unjust that this power is unaffected by whether the marriage has lasted for one day or for 50 years. Some have tried to argue that the exercise of talaq tafwid (the husband delegating the right of talaq to his wife) is equally 'unjust.' However, such an argument is not sustainable because ultimately it is the husband who can choose whether or not to delegate his power of talaq to his wife. Most likely, he would only choose to do so if he trusted his wife not to use such a power arbitrarily. The wife never has such a choice.

Additionally, where husbands are given the right to pronounce talaq unilaterally, the power to revoke the talaq (and take back the wife) is likewise seen as his alone. The wife then has no say in whether or not she wants to remain married to a man who has gone as far as to begin the process of discarding her. When in such a position, a woman's powerlessness and vulnerability are exacerbated by laws that fail to recognize marital rape.

Even if the so-called 'right of talaq' is never exercised, a husband can use such a power as a tool of control throughout the marriage. Wherever laws or practices accept that unilateral repudiation cannot be prevented (i.e., it is a husband's inherent 'right'), a wife is vulnerable to having her marriage terminated without her having been consulted or given any power to prevent it. When we remember that few laws and customs fully protect women's economic rights on divorce (see p.311), we see clearly the potentially devastating impact of talaq. Such potentially devastating consequences must be suffered in tandem with the equally devastating emotional consequences of being discarded without being given any power to respond.

regulation of talaq

In all systems where statute laws on family matters are based on Muslim laws, there has been some attempt to regulate the procedure for talaq. Such procedural regulation reflects a state's recognition that talaq is a source of litigation and that allowing men the unfettered right to talaq is not desirable.

Some systems, in which family laws are based on Muslim laws, do not recognize talaq (Indonesia, Tunisia, and South Yemen prior to reunification in 1990). These require all dissolution to go through the courts, and they also make the same grounds available to both men and women. However, by acknowledging the possibility of dissolution without fault, thcy provide the means to seek dissolution arbitrarily. By offering such a possibility where social attitudes continue to support the concept of talaq, states fail to truly terminate the use of talaq, even if they do not recognize talaq bid'a by law.

Muslims in Israel, for example, are governed by laws that penalize talaq in theory while permitting it to continue in practice. Israeli law does not permit a wife to be divorced against her will. Accordingly, if a Palestinian Muslim man talaqs his wife, she can file a complaint with the Police, and he will be liable to a 3-month prison sentence. However, the talaq remains valid. To avoid criminal penalties, husbands file for dissolution on the grounds of 'discord and strife' (niza' wa shiqaq) and take advantage of patriarchal stereotypes of women's role in the family to achieve a favorable decision (see Dissolution on Equal Grounds for Women and Men, p.293).

However, in other systems, even where all dissolutions have to go through the courts, talaq continues to be conceptualized as an inherent 'right' of the husband; and accordingly, it is still recognized by the law. Thus, the court reserves the right to reject a woman's plea for dissolution of marriage if she fails to prove the grounds on which she is exercising faskh or tafriq while reserving no such right (and indeed failing to require any proof of wrong doing) when a man exercises talaq. In such systems, regulation can do little more than delay or put a check on the exercise of talaq, or increase the financial settlements (Iran, Malaysia, Singapore).

On the other hand, negotiated conditions may be inserted into the marriage contract that result in the husband being prevented (in practice) from exercising talaq. For example, a husband may be effectively prevented from pronouncing talaq by conditions that prohibit him from doing so within a specified time frame or by conditions that would require an unaffordable payment of compensation in the event of talaq.

Some systems recognize talaq but do not recognize a talaq pronounced in anger or in a state of intoxication (Morocco and systems where Ottoman law applies).

Regulatory procedures vary greatly in both their requirements and their impact on women. For example, all systems theoretically agree that there have to be efforts towards reconciliation and that these efforts must involve others (in addition to the husband and wife). However, in many systems the provisions pertaining to talaq result in this requirement becoming meaningless.

In systems where there is no codified procedure, talaq remains unregulated unless a wife brings a challenge in court (India and Nigeria for marriages under Muslim laws). In Nigeria, a challenge by the wife may be heard by the Muslim courts; while in India, the local community (jamaat) may require that some procedure be followed or that the wife approach the general courts for relief.

This section focuses on systems that both recognize talaq and regulate it through various provisions.

regulatory procedures and obligations of husbands

The major difference between various provisions regarding talaq involves the question of when, and under what conditions, the talaq will take effect.

Some systems require talaq to be carried out through the courts (Algeria; Iran; Malaysia; South Yemen, prior to reunification in 1990). Any earlier pronouncement or declaration regarding talaq made by the husband is considered immaterial and does not affect the status of the marriage. (At the most, such statements are viewed as a declaration of the intention to pronounce talaq, as in Tanzania). Such systems are preferable because any subsequent dispute about the form of the talaq (revocable or irrevocable) and the date that the talaq took effect can be prevented because the proceedings took place before an official forum and were recorded.

Those systems that only recognize court-based talaq can be further divided into two categories. The first requires all financial matters associated with the divorce to be settled before the divorce certificate can be issued (Iran, an amendment introduced following protests by women's groups regarding the injustice of arbitrary talaq). Such provisions act as a bar to arbitrary talaq in effect because a husband would first have to settle any mahr, division of marital property, and mata'a before getting a certificate of divorce. In the second group, the divorce is not conditional upon the resolution of associated matters, and recovery of mahr and other financial issues requires a separate suit.

Systems that recognize extra-judicial pronouncement of talaq may still have certain regulatory procedures (e.g., notification to the wife and registration with the authorities) that come into operation once the pronouncement has been made (Bangladesh, Egypt, Pakistan, Philippines, and Sri Lanka). But such systems often differ over whether or not a talaq remains valid if the husband fails to follow this subsequent procedure. Even where the talaq would not remain valid, such systems usually leave procedural loopholes that may be easily exploited by unscrupulous husbands.

procedures open to abuse by husbands

Whereas in Sri Lanka failure to follow the provided registration procedure before the Quazi does not affect the validity of the talaq, the situation in Pakistan is not so clear. Under the MFLO, a husband is responsible for notifying the Union Council (of the area where his wife is resident) that he has pronounced talaq. Ironically, this leaves the law open to abuse by husbands because it can leave a divorced women's status unclear. Until Islamization in the late 1970s, the courts tended to insist that failure to follow the registration procedure invalidated the talaq. However, since the Zina (Enforcement of Hadd) Ordinance, 1979, women have been vulnerable to severe penalties for adultery when they remarried following an oral, unregistered talaq. In many cases, husbands who have discarded their wives through talaq have sought to continue to control them by deliberately failing to follow the registration procedure. To save women from such penalties, the courts have in some cases accepted a talaq that has not followed the required procedure (see box below).

Even in other situations, Pakistani courts have accepted a talaq that failed to follow the required procedure. In one case (Muhammad Salahuddin Khan v Muhammad Nazir Siddiq 1984 SCMR 584), the wife received a written divorce deed from her husband and then took sleeping pills, went into a coma, and died seven months later. Her husband claimed a share of her property using the plea that he had never routed his talaq through the Union Council when such a routing is a mandatory requirement of law. His plea was rejected, but the Supreme Court reiterated its position from earlier cases where it had held that the application of S.7 is mandatory. The court simply refused to grant leave to appeal against the High Court's decision. The High Court had ruled that the talaq had indeed taken place, and therefore, the husband was not a legal heir of the deceased.

In contrast to the situation in Pakistan, social attitudes are different in Sri Lanka where almost all husbands exercising talaq automatically approach the Quazi courts for registration of talaq.

Whether or not a system recognizes unregistered talaq as valid, it clearly offers greater protection of women's rights (in the event of talaq) if husbands who fail to follow the required procedures are liable to significant penalties (fines and/or imprisonment).

Whereas following procedures for talaq is not mandatory in many systems, following procedures for forms of dissolution initiated by women is almost always mandatory in those same systems. Accordingly, any woman-initiated divorce that was decreed without correctly following procedures would be invalid.

The Interaction of Talaq Registration and Provisions for Zina: Pakistan

A woman who remarries following a talaq in which the procedure was faulty can be liable for bigamy under S. 494 of the Pakistan Penal Code. Since the introduction of the Zina Ordinance in 1979, she also can be prosecuted for adultery. In such a case, adultery is usually registered under S. 10(2) of the Zina Ordinance, which means she is charged with zina liable to tazir (convictions under tazir require less stringent evidence and the punishments are not as severe as under hadd). If the wife and her new husband confess to having lived as husband and wife, they both may be liable to hadd, which in the case of a married woman committing zina could be stoning to death.

It is exactly such a series of events that led to the famous Shahida Parveen case (Mohammad Sarwar v the State PLD 1988 FSC 42). On the basis of the couple's confession to having lived as husband and wife, each was sentenced to death. In appeal before the Federal Shariat Court, the case was remanded to the trial court for retrial. Shahida had a written divorce from her first husband on a stamp paper, but the talaq had not been routed through the Union Council. The FSC relied on another case (Mirza Qamar Raza v Tahira Begum PLD 1988 Karachi 169) where it was held by a High Court that the application of S. 7 of the MFLO was not required. (That the precedent set by this case would be followed to help Shahida is somewhat ironic because women's groups have criticised it for undermining the protective spirit of the MFLO's talaq registration requirements. Indeed, the Supreme Court later overturned this ruling in Federation of Pakistan v Tahira Begum 1994 SCMR 1740.)

In the Shahida Parveen case, the FSC also allowed the couple to retract their confession. This retraction was allowed because the rules require that a person being accused of zina be aware of the consequences of his/her confession.

In another case a former husband registered separate cases of bigamy and zina and both went through different lines of trial and appeal, the former up to the Supreme Court and the latter up to the Federal Shariat Court. In the zina case, the woman was acquitted because of the lack of evidence indicating that she had lived, as a wife, with the subsequent husband. However, the conviction under bigamy was upheld through the various appeal stages up to the Supreme Court level because the subsequent marriage had been proven, and the wife did not deny it.

She was convicted while her subsequent husband was acquitted on the basis that it was not in his knowledge that his wife's first marriage was not dissolved (Malik Javaid Ali and another v Abdul Kadir and another 1987 SCMR 518).

forms of talaq, revocation, and idda

Since the Qur'an contains no specific procedure for talaq, multiple forms for talaq have been developed by the jurists (see Muslim Laws on Dissolution, p.249). The question of whether or not a triple, irrevocable, and immediately effective talaq (talaq bid'a) is permissible is still unresolved. Most codified laws have attempted to do away with this highly unjust form of repudiation, but customarily it continues to be practiced (especially in Bangladesh, India, Pakistan and Nigeria). It is even formally recognized in some systems (Sudan, Yemen).

The form of talaq determines whether or not the talaq can be revoked. If the law recognizes any form of pronouncement, the wife may be left uncertain as to whether or not and until when her husband can change his mind and take her back. Few laws specify the precise procedure for revocation (Malaysia is an exception), and this can cause additional uncertainty and violation of a wife's human rights. Revocation through the court appears to be the most option-giving because the husband's intention would have to be clear and documented, and the wife would have to be present and thus aware of the situation. Malaysia does not recognize unilateral revocation and explicitly states that the court cannot force a wife to return to a husband. Such a provision is certainly more option-giving.

If the law is also unclear as to when idda starts and is completed, this can affect a woman's claim to idda maintenance. Additionally, as long as a woman's status is unclear, she will not have the capacity to validly remarry. All this uncertainty results in the husband retaining control over the wife who he has discarded through talaq.

Some laws (Bangladesh, Philippines, Pakistan) have attempted to avoid this minefield by insisting that no matter what the form of pronouncement, a registered talaq is counted as a talaq that can be revoked by the husband up until the expiration of idda. Sri Lanka's laws are unclear on this point, while Malaysia and Singapore allow husbands to choose which form of talaq they are pronouncing, revocable or irrevocable. In contrast, Indonesia does not recognize revocable divorce. (For further details on idda see p.301).

reconciliation procedures

Even though there is a consensus among the various schools of Muslim jurisprudence that efforts must be made to facilitate reconciliation before dissolution can become effective, only some systems make such efforts obligatory (Indonesia, the Philippines, and Malaysia when one party contests the divorce). Other systems do not require that attempts at reconciliation be made prior to finalizing the divorce (Egypt, Morocco). Still others allow for reconciliation efforts, but do not make them mandatory (Sri Lanka).

Generally, reconciliation is facilitated by one arbiter from each party, with a third person appointed by the state having the final word. However, in many systems the parties are encouraged to pursue reconciliation, but no mechanism for doing so is provided. As with other aspects of dissolution, it is generally more option-giving if reconciliation efforts include a formal, statutory procedure so that there can be no subsequent dispute over any agreement that was reached.

Some systems require a husband to state his grounds for seeking dissolution (Tunisia, Malaysia). Other systems explicitly prohibit judges or qazis from recording such reasons (Sri Lanka). Even where a husband must state his grounds, this requirement is designed only to facilitate the reconciliation process and his statement cannot be used to reject his plea.

Generally, where arbiters have no powers to prevent a talaq and no powers to influence any financial settlements, their usefulness is limited to preventing an impulsive talaq. Most women will have already tried to use their social networks to dissuade the husband, but some may welcome one final opportunity to reconcile the marriage or to voice their anger at the situation.

trends and practices

In many communities talaq continues to be the only form of dissolution that is socially recognized. In fact, many divorces registered as talaqs are either mutually agreed upon or are requested by the wife. Often negotiations within the family ensure that court proceedings are not required, but it is presumed that talaq is the only 'proper' way to end the marriage.

Despite widespread efforts to regulate, and in some instances, do away with talaq, procedural loopholes and social attitudes still leave women vulnerable to talaq. The wave of Islamization and rising identity politics has, in places, undermined reform efforts. Procedures for talaq have even been declared 'unIslamic,' as in Pakistan (Allah Rakha and another v Federation of Pakistan and others PLD 2000 FSC 1). This case is currently in appeal and the FSC's decision is suspended.

Still, there have been successes. Women married under Muslim laws in India have approached the civil courts to have their unregulated talaqs declared invalid on the basis of constitutional guarantees of fundamental rights (see p.264, India). Women in Iran have sought to redress some of the imbalance in dissolution through the 1993 'wages for housework' provisions (see p.165).

The Prevalence of Dissolution: The Philippines

Research by the Pilipina Legal Resources Centre found that in one Shari'a court in the Muslim city of Marawi, Philippines, there were 80 cases of registered divorce between 1995 and 2000. 78 of these were registered as divorce by talaq; two were registered as faskh (by the wife). Of the 78 registered as talaq, 59 were considered by the court to be mutually agreed upon, and comments to that effect appear in the order of divorce.

Out of cases that went to trial, 50 were cases of divorce that had been filed by women and only one that had been filed by a man. These cases can be broken down as follows:

28 were divorce by faskh;

13 were divorce with demand for recovery of mahr;

8 were petitions for divorce by judicial decree (mubarat); and

1 was a petition for tafwid.

Most cases in the 5th Shari'a circuit court of Shariff Aguak, Maguindanao are based upon registration of talaq. For instance, from July 1998 to July 1999, (SHCC Civil Cases no. 98-492 to 99-527) 50% of the cases filed were based upon registration of a man's unilateral talaq. No case of tafwid was filed. The PLRC determined that even educated women are often unaware that it is possible for them to orally divorce their husbands. The remaining cases dealt with mutual agreements to dissolve marriage, petitions to resume marital relationships, and petitions to contract subsequent marriages (polygyny). Clearly, the interpretation and administration of justice in the CMPL has had a profound impact on women.

NOTES

LAWS: Talaq

Criteria

☺ More option-giving are those laws which:
- Do not recognize talaq.

😐 The top middle ground is occupied by those laws which:
- Require a court procedure for talaq and for reconciliation and do not recognize any extra-judicial procedures; and
- Clearly state what constitutes a valid form of pronouncement.

The lower middle ground is occupied by those laws which:
- Require notification and registration of a talaq with the authorities; but
- Leave the form and effects unclear.

☹ Less option-giving are those laws which:
- Have only minimal regulation of talaq; or
- Do not regulate talaq.

☺ Family laws are based on Muslim laws, but talaq is not recognized

Indonesia: Under the ML, all divorces must go through the court. A husband married under Muslim laws must provide the religious court with a written notification of his intention to divorce, which must include his reasons for wishing to do so. If the reasons accord with one of the six grounds available to husbands and wives, both parties are called separately for reconciliation meetings with counselors. If reconciliation fails, the court will call the parties to witness the divorce. Revocable divorce is not recognized. A minimum three-month period must lapse between the admission of a suit and public notification.

Tunisia: Under A. 30 of the CSP, divorce shall only take place in court. A. 31 establishes equal grounds for husband and wife, including 'at the will of the husband or at the request of the wife.' Under A. 32, all adjunct matters are to be decided along with the case for dissolution. In the application to court, the husband is to provide relevant information that will assist the court's reconciliation efforts. The law does not envisage revocation.

Tanzania: Under S. 107, for Muslim marriages a pronouncement of talaq is treated as an announcement of the intention to divorce, but the divorce is not final until a Marriage Conciliatory Board has met the spouses, and the court has issued a decree of irreparable breakdown.

Yemen (South Yemen, prior to reunification): Unilateral divorce was prohibited, and all divorces were required to go through the courts. Violation of these laws was punishable by a fine or imprisonment, or both. Husbands and wives were given access to the same grounds for divorce. Violation of these provisions was punishable with a fine of up to 100 dinars or imprisonment of up to 1 year, or both.

😐 Talaq takes place through court proceedings

Algeria: Under A. 48 of the CF, one of the grounds for divorce is 'the will of the husband.' Under A. 49, divorce can be established only through a court judgment, which must be preceded by a judge's attempt to reconcile the couple. (The time period in which reconciliation is attempted shall not exceed the period of three months.) The court's rulings are not subject to appeal. Revocation is permitted only during the reconciliation period.

Iran: Under Article 1133 of the CC (law amended in 1993 following women's activism), the husband can divorce his wife without ascribing any reasons, provided he first settles all her financial rights. All divorce cases have to go through the court. The Registrar can only register a divorce after permission has been issued from a court and after any mahr, maintenance, and/or wages for housework have been paid to the wife. But A. 1133 is interpreted to mean that no court can force a man not to divorce his wife. Under A. 1145, if a man initiates divorce, it is revocable, unless before consummation, or after the wife has reached menopause, or it is the third divorce between the same husband and wife.

Notification and registration of talaq are required; some standardization of forms and effects has been attempted

Bangladesh & Pakistan: Under S. 7 of the MFLO, the husband must provide a written notification of having pronounced talaq 'in any form whatsoever' to the Union Council/Prasad, and a copy of this notification must be provided to the wife. No matter what the form of the pronouncement, the talaq is not final until the expiry of 90 days from the receipt of the notification by the Union Council/Prasad Chairman (now called a Nazim in Pakistan), or in the case that the wife is pregnant, until she delivers, whichever is later. During this waiting period, talaq can be revoked, expressly or otherwise. In Pakistan, case law has undermined the requirement of registration, notably Allah Rakha and another v Federation of Pakistan and others PLD 2000 FSC 1, which struck down S.7 as 'unIslamic,' although this case is in appeal and the effect of the judgment remains suspended.

Egypt: Under A. 5 of Law No. 25 of 1929 as amended by law No. 1200 of 1985, a divorcing husband must have the written certification of his talaq notarized by a qualified notary within 30 days of his pronouncement of talaq. The wife is deemed to be aware of talaq if she attends the notarization, is given personal notification of talaq, or if a representative of the wife is given a copy of the certificate of talaq. All talaq shall be revocable except the third. A talaq to which a number is added verbally or by gesture shall be effective as a single talaq. The consequences of the talaq come into force from the date that the wife is made aware of it. The following talaqs are not effective: talaq by a man who is intoxicated or under coercion; talaq which is not immediately effective (e.g. based on a condition that a certain action takes place or does not take place).

Philippines: Under A. 46 of the CMPL, repudiation of the wife can be filed as a written notification to the clerk of the Sharia Court. An arbitration council is constituted. This council makes a report, and then the court issues an order. A. 46 prescribes the ahsan form of talaq and clarifies that 'any number of repudiations made during one tuhr shall constitute only one repudiation and shall become irrevocable only after the expiration of the prescribed iddah.' A.54 outlines the effects of an irrevocable talaq, or dissolution of marriage.

Malaysia: Divorce outside the court and without court permission is an offence punishable by fine of up to RM 1,000 (approximately US$ 265) or imprisonment (up to 6 months), or both. These same penalties apply both to husbands who have failed to register a divorce and to any other person who registers an extra-judicial divorce. Under S. 47, the husband must apply in writing for a divorce, and he must state his reasons for divorce. If the wife does not consent before the court, the court shall appoint a conciliatory committee consisting of a Religious Officer and two others (one for each spouse, preferably close relatives). This committee is given six months to attempt reconciliation (this time period may be extended by the court). No advocate or solicitor can appear for either party without the committee's permission. If the committee is unable to agree, or the court is not satisfied with their conduct, the court may appoint another committee to replace it. If the court is satisfied that the marriage has broken down irretrievably, it will advise the husband to pronounce one talaq, which shall then be registered. This is a revocable divorce and the parties may resume cohabitation if they mutually consent to a ruju,' which must also be reported and registered. S. 51 provides detailed procedures for revocation and discourages unregulated revocation by providing that those who fail to follow revocation procedures shall be liable to fines and/or imprisonment, which shall be doubled if the wife was never aware of the divorce. Court decisions on matters related to the divorce are to be appended to the certificate.

☹ Regulation of talaq is weak

Morocco: A. 44 of the Moudawana recognizes talaq, but A. 46 provides a confusing definition. In addition, A. 48 requires two male witnesses of good character to witness the registration of a talaq.

The Moudawana requires the repudiation to take place in the presence of the wife and with a judge's authorization. If a wife is summoned to court and does not attend, and her husband insists on the repudiation, her presence is immaterial. Talaq is invalid if pronounced during the wife's menstruation (A. 47) or if pronounced in anger, under coercion, or while in an intoxicated state (A. 49). Ila is not effective as talaq (A. 50). Additionally, suspended talaq that is dependent upon the performance or non-performance of some action is not effective. Each registered talaq is treated as a single talaq.

Sri Lanka: Talaq is recognized under S. 27 of the MMDA, and the procedures for enacting talaq are laid out in the 2nd Schedule to the MMDA. After notice has been given to the Quazi of the wife's residence, the Quazi is to attempt reconciliation. If there is no reconciliation within 30 days of the date of notice, the talaq is recorded before two witnesses. The wife need not be present, but she is to be notified of the pronouncement. The divorce is registered 60 days after this pronouncement. The Act also provides for further attempts at reconciliation by the Quazi after talaq is pronounced. The Quazi is not to record the reasons for talaq. These procedures are directory and not mandatory because although S. 29 requires all divorces to be registered, S. 16 recognizes unregistered divorces as valid. In case law, a talaq in the absence of the wife was recognized as valid even if it had not been communicated to her. Under S. 30 the husband's claim to have pronounced talaq earlier is to be believed, but the date that the divorce became effective is not clear, although the husband is required to then follow the 2nd Schedule. There is a history of conflicting case law over the validity of an oral talaq that does not follow the procedure in 2nd schedule of MMDA.

Sudan: Talaq is regulated by the MPLA. A talaq can be revoked by the husband within the specified waiting period, provided it is not the third talaq (talaq bain baynona kubra, see Muslim Laws on Dissolution, p.249), which is irrevocable. Talaq is presumed to take place where all reconciliation efforts have failed. The husband is not obliged to justify the talaq. As soon as the husband pronounces talaq (whether revocable or irrevocable), the wife is considered divorced and immediately the idda period begins. The husband may or may not register the talaq during the idda period. However, after the idda period he must provide the wife with a written talaq document, and he is required to register it and notify an official.

Gambia (marriages under Muslim laws): Under the MMDO, no grounds or conditions for divorce are stipulated except "those permissible under Sharia." All attempts to reconcile the marriage must have failed in order for a divorce to be permitted. The divorce is complete and takes effect three months from the day on which it was pronounced.

Nigeria (marriages under Muslim laws): There are no registration or court procedures required for talaq.

India (marriages under Muslim laws): The Shariat Act of 1937 states that "in all questions regarding ...dissolution of marriage, including talaq... the rule of decisions in cases where the parties are Muslims shall be the Muslim Personal law." But recent case law has disputed the validity of talaq bid'a. In 1994 Justice Tilhari of the Allahabad High Court held that talaq through triple pronouncement was contrary to Article 14 (equality before the law), Article 15 (prohibition of discrimination on grounds of religion, race, caste, sex or birth) and Article 21 (protection of life and personal liberty) of the Constitution of India. Moreover, a May 2002 judgment by a full bench of the Bombay High Court (now binding for the state of Maharashtra) in the case of Dagdhu Pathan, requires husbands to prove in a court of law that all requirements for divorce under Muslim laws have been fulfilled before pronouncement of talaq. This implies proving efforts towards reconciliation and the payment of mahr; without such proof, any registration and certificates issued under the Waqf Act will have no value in the eyes of the law and a wife can continue to demand maintenance. In general practice, however, talaq does not require the involvement of any state authority and, depending upon the particular community's practices, the husband may either pronounce an oral talaq without any additional procedures, or he may go before the jamaat or some other forum (where attempts at reconciliation may take place, or payment of dower may be made). The wife's presence is usually seen as irrelevant. Case law has established the validity of talaq pronounced under intoxication, compulsion, or in anger.

IMPLEMENTATION

Case law is contradictory on the validity of unregistered talaq

Sri Lanka: A considerable body of case law regarding similar provisions in the Muslim Marriage and Divorce Ordinance of 1929 had held that statutory procedures can be dispensed with (Nansoora v Sithy Jaria (1945, 3, MMDR 40); Kappalneiyina v Avvakudy 1937 2 MMDR 50; Seyadu Ahmed v Ruwaida Umma 1949 3 MMDR 99). The only procedural requirement that had to be followed was that talaq had to be pronounced before reliable and credible witnesses (Wapkany v Pathuma Nachchia, 1938, 2 MMDR 62; Rahimaniyaumma v Pitche, 1938, 2 MMDR 86; Jiffri v Ummu Ayesha, 1958, 4 MMDR 154).

However, under the current MMDA, case law has been less settled. The Board of Quazis has held that talaq that has been granted by a Quazi, even without following procedures, cannot be challenged (Fathima Rizniya v Mohamed Naushad (837/98/T)). Other cases have stressed the importance of following the procedure, particularly the provisions relating to reconciliation (M.B.M. Meera Saibo v Ummu Azmiya Ahmed Mohiden, 1997, case No. 3364 Board of Quazis November 1997, unreported).

Pakistan: Before the 1979 Zina Ordinance, the courts tended to follow Syed Ali Nawaz Gardezi v Lt.Col. Muhammad Yusuf PLD 1963 SC 51, which held that failure to follow the S.7 MFLO procedure (that requires registration of talaq) would render a divorce invalid. However, faced with cases where vindictive husbands attempted to exploit the non-registration of talaq in order to register cases of zina against former wives who had remarried, the courts have been more lenient regarding the application of S. 7 of the MFLO (Muhammad Sarwar v The State PLD 1988 FSC 42; Noor Khan v Haq Nawaz PLD 1982 FSC 265; Alladad v Mukhtar 1992 SCMR 1273; Mohammad Rafique v Ahmad Yar PLD 1982 Lahore 825; Amanullah Shah v Eidat Shah NLR 1981 Criminal 164; Mukhtar Ahmad v Ghafoor Ahmad PLD 1990 Lahore 484).

Talaq not routed through the Union Council has also been accepted as valid in other instances, for example where a husband sought to claim that the talaq was invalid so that he could claim a share in the wife's estate after she died (Muhammad Salahuddin Khan v Muhammad Nazir Siddiq 1984 SCMR 584). At the same time, when the Union Council had been provided written notification of talaq, but the husband died before the expiry of 90 days, the courts have held that the marriage subsisted and declared the wife to be a widow who is entitled to inheritance.

S. 7 also requires that Arbitration Council proceedings attempt reconciliation. However, it has been held that these proceedings are directory in nature and not mandatory (Mst. Farida Parwin v Qadeeruddin Ahmad Siddiqi PLD 1971 Karachi 118). If arbitration does not take place, it does not render the talaq ineffective. Although S.7 of the MFLO requires written notification, there has been litigation concerning whether or not notification to the Union Council is accepted as a valid talaq for Shias, who traditionally require oral talaq, through the recitation of a particular formula in Arabic (Mirza Qamar Raza v Tahira Begum PLD 1988 Karachi 169, and Federation of Pakistan v Tahira Begum 1994 SCMR 1740); Maryam Bano v Hussain Ali 1984 CLC 1961).

Courts try to support women

Sri Lanka: Some Quazis ignore the fact that they explicitly are not to examine the grounds of the talaq. They take their own initiative to conduct an inquiry, and use Qur'anic references to equality between men and women as a justification.

PRACTICES

Negative talaq practices

India: The cultural diversity of the Muslim community in India means that talaq practices differ from community to community, although 'triple talaq' (talaq bid'a) is uniformly recognized. Talaq by post has recently become popular. In this practice, a wife is first sent to her natal home where she will receive a postal talaqnama, which may mention the reasons for divorce. Since the woman is not in the matrimonial home when she receives this letter, she has little chance of retrieving her property and belongings that she left behind. In Ernakulam (Kerala), a talaqnama is sometimes drawn up, and this requires the husband to return the dowry and the wife to return the mahr (this latter is completely contrary to Muslim laws).

Nigeria: Talaq without registration or regulation is widely practiced among Muslims in Nigeria, with much lower rates in Kwara, Oyo, and Osun states. It is the most common form of divorce in Muslim communities (although it includes divorce as a reaction to the wife's refusal to return to the marital home). Jurists hold that a divorce bidi (not following the proper form, or bid'a) is legally valid, though it is a moral wrong. Although women technically can sue over a divorce bidi, it is unclear how this would benefit them.

Pakistan: Communities tend to regard oral talaq that has not been registered as valid. Women then remarry believing themselves to be validly divorced. However, men appear to be more aware (possibly through legal advice) that oral talaq may prove useful later as a means of manipulating zina provisions against the former wife. Because talaq is the most socially recognized form of dissolution, a divorce may be formally registered as a talaq, even when the couple have either mutually agreed to divorce or the wife has requested a divorce (and a settlement has been mediated by the community or family).

Senegal: Field research by GREFELS found that talaq is widely recognized by communities and imams. The talaq is pronounced by the husband three times, saying each time,"I set you free" in the Wolof language. Pronouncement of divorce is seen as the right of men only. The husband does not have to specify reasons. 58% of respondents in focus group discussions did not mention the requirement of witnesses in divorce, while 22.8% thought that one man or five women were required, and 41% felt there should be witnesses, but did not mention their number or sex.

Sri Lanka: 'Triple talaq' is common in Akurana and the Eastern province. Most likely this prevalence is influenced by the widely held misperception that a triple talaq absolves the husband of his obligation to provide maintenance during the idda period. The woman is generally not given a choice regarding reconciliation. Instead, her family makes the decisions. Often talaq is pronounced orally, and this leads to disputes over the date of the divorce and the validity of any revocation.

Tanzania: Most Muslims think talaq is still legally recognized.

Positive talaq practices

India: In some areas of India, before a divorce is finalized, there may be efforts to reconcile the parties through the intervention of family members, local leaders, a religious body, or even politicians. Some communities also insist that the talaq be documented. To some extent, such documentation helps clarify a woman's status and the related matters of idda and maintenance.

Pakistan: Communities generally uphold marriage contracts that contain negotiated clauses regarding payment in the event of talaq or restrictions on the husband's exercise of talaq.

Dialoguing with Quazis

Since the 1930s, Quazi Courts have been adjudicating on matters of marriage and divorce between Muslims in Sri Lanka, and play a major role in implementing the fundamental principles of Muslim laws in Sri Lanka. Quazis are male Muslims of good character and don't necessarily have to be a lawyers. There are approximately 50 Quazis administering Muslim laws around the country. Appeal lies from the decisions of Quazis to the Board of Quazis and thereafter to the Court of Appeal and the Supreme Court.

The Muslim Women's Research and Action Forum in Sri Lanka has been engaging in a dialogue with Quazis since 1994 as they implement the law, many of whose provisions are discriminatory towards women. As a group they can violate even the rights available to women under the law due to their ignorance or confusion about its provisions. The methodology for dialogue was designed to both share perceptions regarding personal laws and Muslim women's rights and to provide Quazis information in areas where the Women & Law research had revealed confusion, as well as information about progressive legislation and interpretations in other Muslim countries and communities. Extracts from the initial dialogues have been published as booklets in English and Tamil by MWRAF, and provide insights into the Quazis' perceptions and the strategies they sometimes use as individual judges when confronted with injustice to women in the family.

Through the process of dialoguing with Quazis, MWRAF has developed important professional and personal relationships with some of them and is able to rely on their assistance in resolving problems facing individual women who approach MWRAF for counseling on family law issues. MWRAF is also confident that these Quazis will be an important ally in MWRAF's advocacy for Muslim personal law reforms in Sri Lanka in the future.

9e DISSOLUTION OF MARRIAGE: TALAQ TAFWID ('ESMA AND THE DELEGATED RIGHT OF DIVORCE)

introduction

In systems based on Muslim laws, a husband may delegate his unilateral right to talaq to his wife, permitting her to pronounce talaq upon herself. This contractual agreement can be made through the marriage contract, or it can be negotiated subsequently. Talaq tafwid is also commonly referred to in Arabic-speaking communities as 'esma, which simply means 'the permission.'

Several systems based on Muslim laws make specific provisions for talaq tafwid, which may be:

- Unconditional and absolute, i.e., the wife can use it whenever she wishes; or
- Conditional, i.e., exercised only when a particular event happens (e.g., the husband takes a second wife), or on the breach of a promise (e.g., non-payment of mahr after a specified period of time).

This section does not discuss systems that are based on sources of law other than Muslim laws because these do not recognize talaq, and, therefore, do not recognize talaq tafwid. This section also does not discuss 'suspended talaq', ta'liq, or the dissolution options that are provided to women through Iranian and Malaysian marriage contracts. These divorce options are closer in effect to a grounds-based dissolution (see Other Forms of Dissolution for Women, p.281).

Often those who oppose husbands delegating their powers in this manner believe (or try to convince others) that a husband who has delegated his right of talaq to his wife loses his own power of talaq. This is not true.

In the absence of legislation and social practices that grant women equity and security in their marriages, talaq tafwid can correct that part of the imbalance in marriage that is caused by a husband's power to unilaterally terminate the marriage.

unconditional talaq tafwid

Unconditional talaq tafwid has the effect of giving women the same authority and power that men have to terminate their marriages. Thus, talaq tafwid frees women from the need to establish grounds for divorce. Still, a woman's right to financial entitlements (such as mahr, idda maintenance, and mata'a) is preserved because the husband remains under the same obligations that he would be under if he had pronounced the talaq himself.

The possibility of delegating talaq to the wife is explicitly recognized in the statute laws of countries such as: Bangladesh, Iraq, Jordan, Morocco, Pakistan, Philippines, and Syria. Other systems may recognize talaq tafwid also if spouses are permitted to negotiate rights through their marriage contract (see Negotiated Rights and Responsibilities, p.168).

conditional talaq tafwid

Talaq tafwid can be granted also as a means of enforcing specific stipulations in a marriage contract. In such a case, the wife is given the power to exercise talaq tafwid if the husband breaks a condition in the marriage contract. However, she will have to go to court (or through some other formal procedure) to demonstrate that a condition or a promise from her marriage contract has been broken.

This form of talaq tafwid is clearly not as useful as an unconditional grant of talaq tafwid. However, it can expand a woman's right to divorce by including grounds that are traditionally not available to women under Muslim laws (such as the grounds that the husband has refused to allow the wife to work or study).

talaq tafwid delegated to a third party

A husband can delegate his power of talaq to the wife or to another person. That other person would then have the power to unilaterally terminate the marriage. When such a power is delegated to a third person, it is almost always a conditional talaq tafwid. This practice appears to have been practiced more in the past when other forms of dissolution had not been codified and made available to women.

This form of talaq tafwid is sometimes less option-giving than a conditional talaq tafwid delegated to the wife because it requires the wife to convince someone else (usually a family member) to take steps to dissolve the marriage. Nevertheless, delegation to a third party may offer the wife some socially acceptable access to dissolution in situations where women have otherwise very limited divorce options.

procedure for talaq tafwid

To exercise her right, a woman who has been granted talaq tafwid generally has to go through the same procedure that is required for the husband to exercise talaq. However, where the law is silent on the required procedures, social attitudes may obstruct a woman from accessing talaq tafwid.

Where talaq is regulated through the courts or some other official forum, women must produce documentary evidence that the right of talaq has been delegated to them. In the case of a conditional talaq tafwid, the wife must make a declaration that the condition has been met. Unless the law is clear that she is not required to actually prove that the conditions have been met, the courts may start demanding the level of evidence required for a faskh or tafriq dissolution (see Other Forms of Dissolution for Women, p.281).

Even though talaq tafwid is a principle recognized in Muslim laws and many statute laws, social attitudes often cause judges and other procedural forums to resist a wife's attempt to exercise talaq tafwid. Most often these same authorities offer no resistance to a husband's exercise of talaq.

Frequently, women face problems in accessing their delegated right of talaq because it has not been clearly stipulated in their marriage contract. This lack of clarity gives implementing forums room to make objections.

revocability

Although talaq by a man is usually revocable, the various schools of Muslim jurisprudence are not clear about the revocability of talaq tafwid – that is, whether or not it is revocable, and if so, by whom. Moroccan law specifically states that a delegated divorce is not revocable. In Pakistan and Bangladesh under the Muslim Family Laws Ordinance, the wife may revoke a talaq tafwid within the 90-day period after she has notified the local authorities. But local implementing forums continue to differ in their treatment of such cases because of their ignorance of this form of divorce and because of their disapproval of women having agency in a divorce. In other systems, the law is silent; this also creates confusion.

prevalence

The practice of talaq tafwid varies from being widely recognized (Bangladesh) to being absolutely unknown (Malaysia, Nigeria).

In South Asia there is a long tradition of talaq tafwid, and accordingly, there is a wealth of case law, particularly from India. The practice of granting women talaq tafwid at the time that the marriage is contracted has seen a resurgence in Bangladesh in recent years due to the advocacy efforts of women's human rights groups. This resurgence reflects a positive change in attitudes towards women's access to divorce among entire communities since negotiations over contractual conditions to a marriage are not dependent merely upon the wishes of the bride but also of the families of both parties to the marriage. The strategies that Bangladeshi activists used to increase the prevalence of talaq tafwid could be adapted by women in other Muslim countries and communities.

In Pakistan, there is a growing prevalence of talaq tafwid in both rural and urban areas and across classes, although it still is not as common as it is in Bangladesh. Sometimes even if the families have agreed to talaq tafwid, the imam performing the nikah ceremony will try to prevent it from being written into the marriage contract. In order to eliminate an imam's ability to do this, activists in Pakistan are calling for a change in the standard marriage contract form that will result in the husband's delegation of talaq tafwid being automatically presumed unless he has specifically crossed out the relevant marriage contract clause.

Talaq tafwid may also be possible in systems where it is not specifically provided for in statutory laws. Where Muslim laws are not codified, where the law is codified but there is a clause to the effect that 'where ever the statute is silent general principles of Muslim laws apply' (Sri Lanka, Morocco), or where the law generally recognizes conditions that are permissible under Muslim laws (Malaysia, Sudan), women could argue for access to talaq tafwid. Unfortunately talaq tafwid is unknown and not practiced in many Muslim countries and communities.

In Sudan (where talaq tafwid is known as 'esma), it is socially unacceptable for women to utilize the 'esma. In Nigeria the principle is unknown, and there is strong resistance to efforts to draw attention to the possibility of talaq tafwid.

Talaq Tafwid and Changing Trends

Since at least the 16th century, contracts containing talaq tafwid have been recognized in the Indian subcontinent. The topic is thoroughly discussed in local Hanafi texts, and a whole chapter is devoted to this subject in the Fatawa-e-Alamgiri, which was prepared during Mughal Emperor Aurganzeb's rule (1658-1707) and promulgated by Imperial Authority at that time.

But the colonial courts in India, staffed by judges obviously influenced by Anglo-Christian ideas of marriage, were uncomfortable with such a concept. They insisted that the delegation was valid only if the specified conditions under which the wife was authorized to pronounce talaq were 'reasonable' and not contrary to 'public policy.' They also required that the option not be absolute or unconditional.

However, in recent years the Indian courts have gradually started to acknowledge that spouses have the power to settle the terms governing their future marital relations. Recent Indian cases have upheld that even an unconditional grant of talaq tafwid is valid. In a 1992 case, a Magistrate rejected a woman's application under S. 3(1) of the Muslim Women's (Protection of Rights on Divorce) Act 1986 for return of her dowry, payment of outstanding mahr, and maintenance for herself and the child of the marriage on the grounds that he did not recognize her divorce by talaq tafwid (Mangila Bibi v Noor Hossain All India Reporter, 1992 Calcutta 92).

On appeal, the High Court found that the marriage contract delegated an unrestricted power to the wife to pronounce talaq. The High Court held that a blanket delegation was valid since it "was not prohibited by the personal law of the parties." It was important that there had been a written marriage contract, and this had been registered under the procedures for voluntary registration of Muslim marriages and divorces available in Bengal.

NOTES

LAWS: Talaq Tafwid/ 'Esma and the Delegated Right of Divorce

Criteria

☺ More option-giving are those laws which:

- Explicitly recognize talaq tafwid; and
- Include it in the standard marriage contract.

😐 The middle ground is occupied by those laws which:

- Explicitly recognize talaq tafwid without including it in the standard marriage contract or providing clear mechanisms for its use.

☹ Less option-giving are those laws which:

- Are silent about talaq tafwid.

The following systems do not recognize talaq; thus, they do not recognize talaq tafwid: **Cameroon**, **Central Asian Republics**, **Fiji**, the **Gambia** (marriages under MMDO), **Indonesia**, **Nigeria** (marriages under the MCA and customary laws), **Senegal**, **Tunisia**, and **Turkey**.

☺ **Recognized in law and provided for in the standard marriage contract**

Bangladesh & Pakistan: In Bangladesh talaq tafwid procedures are governed by S.6 of the MMDRA and in Pakistan by S. 8 of the MFLO. An optional clause in the standard marriage contract form in both countries asks 'whether or not the husband has delegated the power of talaq to the wife, and, if so, under what conditions.' Delegation to a Kitabia wife is recognized as well as is delegation through a written agreement after the marriage. S.6 of the MMDRA was also intended to clarify the mechanism for accessing a power of talaq delegated before 1961 (when the MFLO recognized talaq tafwid).

😐 **Recognized in law**

India (marriages under Muslim laws): Under the 1937 Shariat Act "in all questions regarding ...dissolution of marriage, including talaq... the rule of decisions in cases where the parties are Muslims shall be the Muslim Personal law." Talaq tafwid is recognized and upheld by the courts.

Philippines: Under A. 51 of the CPML, if the husband has delegated (tafwid) to the wife the right to effect a talaq (at the time of the celebration of the marriage or thereafter), she may repudiate the marriage and the repudiation would have the same effect as if it were pronounced by the husband himself.

Iraq: Divorce terminates the bond of marriage when pronounced by the husband or by the wife who has been assigned or delegated an authority in that regard or by the Qadi. No divorce shall be effective except when pronounced through the legally prescribed formula (The Code of Personal Status of 1959 (amended in 1980), S. 34).

Morocco: The Moudawana mentions talaq tafwid but does not clarify if the procedure for talaq outlined in A. 46 – 52 also applies to talaq tafwid. Under A. 44 divorce is defined as the dissolution of marriage by repudiation by the husband or by his agent or by a person having an authority delegated by the husband or by the wife having an option to do so. Under A. 67, a delegated divorce is not revocable. Under A. 82, all cases, which cannot be resolved by the present code, will be determined by reference to dominant opinion within the Maliki School.

☹ **Law is silent; possibility of talaq tafwid remains**

Algeria: The CF does not mention talaq tafwid in A. 47-57 on dissolution of marriage. Under A. 222, in the absence of a provision in the law, reference shall be made 'to the provisions of the Sharia.'

Sri Lanka: There is no specific reference to talaq tafwid in the MMDA, but it can be recognized under S. 28(2), which recognizes a woman's right to obtain a divorce under Muslim laws.

Malaysia: The IFLA is silent about talaq tafwid. However, since marriages solemnized under Hukum Syara' are recognized as valid, a talaq tafwid can be entered into the marriage contract.

Nigeria (marriages under Muslim laws): Standard texts used by courts that hear cases related to Muslim marriages state that both parties can make stipulation(s) in the marriage contract, provided this does not invalidate the marriage and stand contrary to the purpose of marriage.

Sudan: The MPLA does not mention talaq tafwid, but under S. 24 the woman has the right to declare conditions to her marriage.

9f DISSOLUTION OF MARRIAGE: KHUL'

introduction

In many systems based on Muslim laws, a woman may seek a divorce from her husband (without having to prove fault on his part) by offering him some form of compensation. This form of divorce is referred to as khul'. In most systems, a woman must access khul' through the courts. Khul' is not available in Indonesia and Tunisia, where the laws provide equal grounds-based dissolution to men and women (see p.293).

The prevalence of khul' in any given context depends on a variety of factors. These include how accessible other forms of dissolution are for women both socially and legally and whether or not the courts and the community regard the husband's permission as necessary for khul'.

Whereas in Pakistan khul' is the most common form of dissolution accessed by women through the courts, in Bangladesh (because of the increasing trend of granting the wife talaq tafwid) khul' divorces have been largely replaced by divorces effected through talaq tafwid. At the same time, a new form of khul' is emerging outside of the court system in Bangladesh because of a trend in which community religious figures have been advising husbands who are seeking to exercise talaq to get their wives to seek khul' instead. These kazis have been telling husbands that they will not be obliged to pay mahr if they can convince or trick their wives into signing for a khul' divorce. Some husbands have even taken their wives' signatures on pieces of paper and then forged requests for khul'. In such cases, when the wife goes to recover her mahr after being divorced, she is informed that she is not entitled to it because the divorce was achieved through khul'.

In Sri Lanka, khul' is hardly used. Instead, women tend to access grounds-based dissolutions. In contrast, khul' is the most common form of dissolution accessed by women in Nigeria. This may be the case partly because the financial benefits of tafriq and faskh are little known and partly because khul' is a faster and easier process.

advantages and disadvantages for women

For women seeking divorce, the main benefit of accessing khul' is that it does not require the wife to prove a particular, narrowly defined fault on the part of the husband (unlike faskh, tafriq, and ta'liq, see Other Forms of Dissolution for Women, p.281). Accordingly, khul' allows a woman to access dissolution on the basis of a more general breakdown in the marital relationship. In systems not based on Muslim laws, a woman may demand dissolution on similar grounds, such as 'incompatibility' or 'marital breakdown' (see Dissolution on Equal Grounds for Women and Men, p.293).

Even in situations where a woman has a legitimate reason to seek a grounds-based dissolution, she may not be able to produce the necessary proof. For example, dissolution on the grounds of domestic violence (cruelty) might require a medical certificate. Women are rarely in a position to obtain such a certificate unless it is an extreme case and/or they have access to state-recognized doctors. In such a case, khul' may offer a way out because lesser evidence (such as testimony from witnesses) is acceptable in most systems. Indeed, in some systems no evidence is required to access khul', and the assertion "I don't like his face" (based on a reported hadith) can be acceptable to the court. Moreover, in most systems, khul' (largely because of the lesser evidence requirements) offers a quicker means of dissolution for women.

However, khul' most definitely has its disadvantages for women. Firstly, khul' usually involves some financial loss for the wife. Systems differ greatly over the precise form this loss may take and as to whether or not such loss is inevitable (see Compensation Due, below). The usefulness of this form of divorce therefore depends upon both the wife's financial position and the system's provisions regarding compensation.

Secondly, in most systems khul' is not a 'right' on the same footing as a husband's unilateral power of talaq. Depending upon the local interpretation, often a woman must convince a third party (a court or another forum) that she cannot continue her marriage and/or secure her husband's agreement to release her from the marriage tie. (This is in contrast to provisions regarding talaq, where the courts or wives have no such powers over husbands.) The approach of Muslim courts in Nigeria is an exception; there khul' is available simply on the wife's demand and is conditional only upon the wife's payment of compensation (the amount of which is decided by the court).

Although access to khul' can give women (especially those who are financially more secure) more options than does access to fault-based dissolution, it is not as advantageous for them as is access to unconditional talaq tafwid.

the confusion with mubarat

In systems where Muslim laws are uncodified, khul' is often recognized by communities and accessed through community forums (India, Senegal) or through Muslim courts (Nigeria). Even in systems with codified laws that are based on Muslim laws, khul' is sometimes practiced extra-judicially (Bangladesh).

All codified systems based on Muslim laws do require some form of registration of divorce. However, sometimes an extra-judicial khul', if ever registered, is ultimately registered as a talaq or mubarat.

In many contexts, there is a tendency to confuse khul' with mubarat. This confusion stems from the subtle differences in laws across Muslim countries and communities. In some systems, mubarat is not even mentioned and the possibility of dissolution in which both parties abandon their financial rights against each other is discussed under provisions on khul' (Jordan, Syria). Legal practitioners and even courts in Bangladesh and Pakistan sometimes confusingly refer to 'khula-mubarat,' and Nigerian jurists comment that khul' is possible both through the court and through extra-judicial forums, even if in practice khul' is adjudicated through the courts. The situation is further muddled by the fact that many systems do not oblige the wife to compensate the husband if he has not demanded such compensation.

the question of the husband's permission

The lack of clarity over the precise nature of khul' is also reflected in variations of the procedures that govern khul' and the various roles that courts play in a khul'.

Most systems agree that at some point the court can be given the power to intervene and settle questions of compensation. But there are differences over whether it is the court or the husband who agrees or disagrees with the woman's plea that the marriage should be dissolved, and whether or not the courts are needed at all.

In many systems, khul' requires agreement between the spouses, in other words the husband's agreement is required (Algeria, Morocco, Sri Lanka, Yemen). However, in some of these systems, such an agreement has to be processed through the courts (Algeria, Sri Lanka), while in others khul' does not require court procedures (Morocco, Yemen) apart from subsequent registration.

The husband's opinion or agreement is irrelevant in some systems (Bangladesh, Malaysia, Pakistan, Philippines). In 2000, courts in Egypt recognized a woman's right to obtain a khul' divorce even if she has not obtained her husband's consent. In these systems the court plays a central role because it both determines whether or not the petition for khul' will be granted and (in the case that khul' is granted) it determines what compensation the wife will have to pay. In Nigeria khul' does not require a husband's permission and the courts cannot refuse a woman's plea. Their only role is to adjudicate the matter of compensation.

Laws in Sri Lanka are possibly the least option-giving because they require not only the husband's agreement but also the Quazi's. The Quazi must be satisfied that sufficient evidence has been presented before granting a khul', and, in practice, khul' appears just as difficult to access as a grounds-based divorce.

proof required for khul'

Where a court is required to assess a woman's plea for khul', she usually has to prove that hatred is felt between she and her husband and/or that she 'cannot live within the limits prescribed by God.' Often proving such feelings and/or inabilities entails lengthy procedures that involve assessors and arbitrators (Malaysia, Sri Lanka).

Thus, it is clear that in most systems khul' requires a more subjective assessment by the court or qazi than does a fault-based divorce. Accordingly, a woman who is seeking khul' is dependent upon the court or qazi's understanding of her position. Even within the same system, courts can vary widely in the criteria they use to decide whether or not they are willing to grant khul'.

In Pakistan more than forty years ago the courts held that khul' can be granted by a court irrespective of the husband's opinion. However, there continues to be disagreement (even in the superior courts) as to whether or not a plea for khul' is itself sufficient evidence of hatred to warrant granting a divorce.

compensation due (zar-i-khula)

Although many systems and communities regard the return of mahr (or surrender of unpaid mahr) as the appropriate compensation for khul', the Qur'anic source (2:229) does not specify a precise form of compensation (see Muslim Laws on Dissolution, p.250).

In systems where mahr is the presumed form of compensation, the usefulness of this form of divorce largely depends upon the woman's economic position and the amount of mahr that was specified in her marriage contract. If a woman's mahr is small, or if the woman has sufficient financial resources to pay back her mahr, khul' may be the simplest and quickest means for her to end her marriage. However, if the mahr is substantial, having to return it or having to forego any unpaid portion of it may be impossible or at least very difficult. Thus, a woman's economic insecurity can severely limit her access to khul'.

Some laws specify the form of or limit the amount of compensation (proper dower, Algeria), while others specify that 'anything which is the valid subject of a contract' is legitimate payment (Morocco). Still others allow the court to determine the form and amount of compensation due (Malaysia, Nigeria). In Nigeria the trend is away from fixing the compensation at more than the mahr amount. Some judges (and village heads) calculate the compensation due by subtracting the value of the marriage gifts that were provided by the bride's family from the value of a mahr (and/or kayan sadauki provided by the groom and family). They may even fix a token amount for the compensation or order that the wife pay nothing at all. Others may look at the length of the marriage when assessing compensation due, setting smaller and smaller compensation the longer that the couple has been married. In contrast, the courts use mahr as the guideline for determining compensation in most systems. Occasionally, a woman may be required to surrender her claim to idda maintenance and other financial rights as well (Iran, Sri Lanka).

When deciding the issue of compensation, the courts in Malaysia, Nigeria, and Pakistan appear to consider which of the spouses was at 'fault.' This approach can both benefit and damage women's interests.

On the one hand, this approach accepts that while wives may not be able to establish a specific fault, actions by husbands can be a source of conflict and therefore little compensation is due from wives accessing khul'. One innovative judge in Pakistan took into account the benefits that had been received by the husband (such as her having borne and reared their children, housekeeping, etc.) and subtracted a value for these from the compensation that was due to the husband (M. Saqlain Zaheer v Zaibun Nisa 1988 MLD 427). In some instances, the Pakistani courts have held that no compensation was due.

On the other hand, such an approach by the judiciary fails to challenge the narrow interpretation of fault-based dissolution and results in women continuing to risk the surrender of their financial rights in order to part from abusive husbands. In Pakistan, lawyers tend to encourage women to file for khul' rather than for a grounds-based dissolution, even if, for example, the husband has failed to maintain the family. In Nigeria, women usually have no lawyer and the alkali (judge, who is in principle bound to ensure justice and not to seem neutral as in British style courts) often fails to mention the alternative possibilities provided by fault-based divorce. This failure may be due to the alkali's patriarchal sympathies, his receipt of a bribe from the husband, and/or his desire to avoid lengthy litigation.

Other important compensation issues include what evidence is needed to prove the amount of mahr and who's evidence is be accepted in both determining the amount of mahr and proving what amount, if any, remains unpaid. Additionally, one must consider if non-payment of the compensation affects the validity of the khul'.

khul' and revocation

In most systems the khul' form of divorce is regarded as irrevocable, or bain sughra (meaning that once granted by the court, the divorce cannot be revoked during the idda period by either the husband or the wife). Thus, if the spouses want to get together again after khul' has been granted, they will have to remarry. However, the wife is not required to undergo an intervening marriage before remarrying unless this is the third such dissolution between the same husband and wife. This irrevocability contrasts unfairly with the husband's power to pronounce a talaq and then revoke it. Thus, if a woman chooses to pursue khul', she cannot change her mind during the idda period that follows the court's granting of divorce.

However, in some systems all divorces are revocable during the idda. In these systems the wife retains the right to revoke a khul' divorce during the idda because it was she who initiated the divorce (Bangladesh, Pakistan). Confusingly, some judgments in these systems use the term 'irrevocable' to describe khul' because the husband does not have the right to revoke it as he does in other situations (Princess Aiysha Yasmin Abbasi v Maqbool Hussain Qureshi PLD 1979 Lahore 241).

Cross-Country Precedent Does Not Always Work

After the 1967 landmark Khurshid Bibi case in Pakistan, which confirmed that the husband's agreement is of no concern in khul', women in Sri Lanka have attempted to access the principles that it established - without success (Ansar v Mirza, 1971, 75 NLR 295).

After examining the Qur'anic verses on the subject, the related ahadith of Jamilah and Habibah, the writings of the Shafi jurists, and the legal provisions applicable in Sri Lanka, the Sri Lankan Supreme Court refused to follow the Pakistani precedent. One of the two judges concluded that under Shafi law, consent of the husband is absolutely essential for khul', and since Sri Lankans are governed strictly by the law of their sect, a Shafi woman could not obtain a khul' if her husband does not agree to it. He went on to say that the Pakistani decision was given against a different statutory backdrop and that accordingly, he was not bound to follow it.

But the other Supreme Court judge hearing the case acknowledged that there was some support in Muslim laws for the concept of granting the wife the right "to obtain a khul' divorce unilaterally." He said that interpreting the law in this manner would require that this right be widely accepted by the Muslim community, which did not appear to be possible at that time in Sri Lanka. But he pointed out that given "the rapid pace at which traditional notions are shed these days, the possibility of an extension of the law might not be too distant."

It has been more than 30 years since the judgment was delivered, and an extension of the law as envisaged by Justice Samarawickrama has yet to materialize.

NOTES

LAWS: Dissolution of Marriage - Khul'

Criteria

☺ More option-giving are those laws which:
- Do not require the husband's agreement for khul';
- Allow khul' at the wife's request and without establishing fault;
- Allow the courts to fix compensation according to the circumstances.

😐 The middle ground is occupied by those laws which:
- Require the husband's agreement, but offer alternative mechanisms if he refuses to give it;
- Set the amount of the mahr as the maximum compensation.

☹ Less option-giving are those laws which:
- Require the husband's agreement;
- Require the wife to pay the compensation before the decree can be issued.

☺ **Husband's agreement is not required; court fixes compensation; khul' available on request**

Nigeria: Case law establishes that the question of release from the marriage tie should be considered separately from the issue of compensation. Therefore, it is for the judge to fix the amount of compensation, which could be more or less than the mahr (Mohammed Dan Kubura v Bello Idirs T/ Wada suit No.CA/K/1/197 Court of Appeal, Kaduna). (In older cases, compensation was sometimes more than the mahr.) Some recent Sharia court cases have found that the khul' payment should not be more than the original value of the mahr that was received or promised at the time of the marriage ceremony. In Babajo v Hassana the court found that the maximum that Hassana should pay her husband was the amount of the mahr that she had received, which in this case was N100 (less than US$ 1), and that to demand more was unjust and amounted to promoting immorality (Kaduna State, Sharia Court of Appeal, case No. 57 in 1982). Judges may also make the payment a mere token amount. (In one case, the court fixed the compensation at N10, which is less than US 1cent, a worthless amount even for Nigeria's poor.)

Husband's agreement is not relevant; court fixes compensation; but courts demand varying degrees of evidence

Bangladesh & Pakistan: The Family Court has the power to grant a khul' divorce, and the husband's consent is not relevant. It is for the court to decide what compensation, if any, the wife has to pay if this is demanded by the husband (Bilquis Fatima v Najmul Ikram Qureshi PLD 1959 West Pakistan; Khurshid Bibi v babu Mohammed Amin PLD 1967 SC 97). In the Bilquis Fatima case (para. 42), the court clarified, "the right is not granted to a wife to come to court at any time and obtain khula [...]. There is an important limitation on her right of khula. It is only if the judge apprehends that the limits of God will not be observed, that is, in their relation towards one another [...] a harmonious state, as envisaged by Islam, will not be possible, that he will grant a dissolution. The wife cannot have a divorce for every passing impulse. The judge will consider whether the rift between the parties is a serious one, though he may not consider the reasons for the rift." However, there is contradictory case law regarding the extent of evidence that the wife is required to provide in order to prove a breakdown; the lower courts are more inclined to demand extensive proof. Restrictive interpretations include Aali v. ADJ-1 Quetta 1986 CLC 27 (Pakistan) and Mohammad Kutubuddin Jaigirdar v. Nurjahan Begum 1973 25 DLR 21 (Bangladesh). More generous interpretations include Safia Begum v Khadim Hussain 1985 CLC 1869; Syed Muhammed Rizvan v Mst. Samina Khatoon 1989 SCMR 25; Ghulam Zohra v. Faiz Rasool 1988 MLD 1353; Rashidan Bibi v. Bashir Ahmed PLD 1983 Lahore 549; Mohammad Mumtaz v. Parveen Akhtar 1985 CLC 415; Naziran Bibi v. Mohammad Roshan 1984 CLC 3330.

Bangladesh: It is standard case law that the wife has to forfeit something in order to be granted a khul' divorce. This may be the whole mahr (Hasina Ahmed v SA Fazal 1980 32 DLR 294) or her claim to unpaid dower (Sheerin Alam v Captain Shamsul Alam 1996 48 DLR 79).

Pakistan: Until an amendment to the Family Courts Act, which came into effect in October 2002, khul' did not explicitly appear in any statutory text, and rights activists had long demanded precise and certain provisions regarding the right of khul'. Previous case law had held that it was not necessary for a wife to return mahr to obtain a khul' divorce, and the wife's failure to pay compensation did not invalidate the divorce (1985 MLD 2486; Razia Katoon v Muhammad Yousuf 1987 MLD 2486; Samia Akbar v Muhammad Zubair PLD 1990 Lahore 71). However, the amended FCA directly refers to khul' and has inserted S. 10(4) in the FCA, which states that the court 'shall also restore to the husband the Haq Mehr received by the wife in consideration of marriage at the time of marriage.' It is anticipated that due to this amendment there will be serious litigation over the precise amount of mahr to be returned. The first part of the new provision might refer only to the mahr received before the wife files for dissolution, but the latter phrase ('at the time of marriage') brings in confusion. The standard marriage contract records total mahr, as well as the amount paid at the time of marriage, plus the division (if any) of mahr into prompt and deferred portions. It is not clear which of these parts of mahr the phrase 'at the time of marriage' refers to.

Malaysia: Under S. 49 of the IFLA, the court shall order a khul' if the parties agree. A khul' is irrevocable (bain sughra). If the parties cannot agree to the amount of compensation, the court will assess the amount, keeping in mind the status and means of the parties. If the husband does not agree to khul', a conciliatory committee is appointed under S. 47(5) which allows 6 months or more for reconciliation. If the husband still refuses to pronounce talaq, two arbitrators (Hakam) are appointed with the aim of resolving the dispute. Ultimately courts do not obstruct a khul' and may order the wife to pay only a symbolic compensation.

Philippines: Under Art 50 of the CMPL the wife may, after having offered to return or renounce her mahr or to pay any other lawful consideration for her release from the marriage, petition the court for divorce. The court shall issue the decree in meritorious cases after fixing the compensation.

Egypt: Following an amendment to personal status law in January 2000, a woman can obtain a divorce on the grounds of 'incompatibility.' After her application the judge allows 6 months for a court-appointed arbiter to attempt reconciliation. If this reconciliation effort fails, the woman then publicly declares her hatred for her husband and states that she fears she cannot fulfil her conjugal duties as laid down by God. The wife is to return her mahr and waive her rights to post-divorce maintenance.

The husband's agreement is required

Algeria: Under A. 54 of the CF, khul' is a judicial decree following agreement between the spouses. If the couple do not agree on the compensation, the judge will fix a sum, which will not exceed the mahr ul mithl that is calculated at the time of the judgment.

Morocco: Under A. 61-65 of the Moudawana, the spouses may agree to divorce by khul' and anything that is a valid subject of a contract may be offered as legitimate compensation. If the wife is poor, the payment cannot be made using something to which the children of the marriage have a right.

Iran: Where the wife initiates a divorce and fails to establish grounds, she loses her right to wages for housework, idda maintenance, etc.

Sri Lanka: Statute law makes no specific reference to a wife's right to obtain a khul' divorce. However, under S. 28 (2) of the MMDA, a wife has the right to obtain a divorce of any description that is permitted to a wife under Muslim law. The Supreme Court has established that the husband must consent to khul' and that there has to be evidence that the parties are unable to observe the limits of God (Ansar v Mirza 1971 75 NLR 295). There are no reported cases of successful applications for khul' divorce, and, therefore, it is unclear what compensation a wife would be expected to give. However a required procedure has been laid out in the Third Schedule to the MMDA for making an application to the Quazi Court (exactly the same procedure as for faskh in Sri Lanka). The Quazi appoints three Muslim assessors to assist him in hearing the application.

A Successful Struggle to Expand Women's Rights to Divorce: Egypt

In January 2000, the Egyptian parliament enacted a law that allows women to obtain divorce from their husbands on the grounds of incompatibility; the divorce is granted upon the wife's return of her mahr. The amendment to the Personal Status Law took place amidst widespread controversy and debate, both within and outside parliament.

Prior to the new law, women had to wait years for judges to decide their applications for divorce under the 75-year-old Personal Status Law. A successful application required conclusive proof and independent corroboration of a husband's ill treatment or physical abuse of his wife (see p.286). In contrast, under the same law a husband could simply obtain a divorce by filing a paper with the marriage registrar; he did not even need to inform his wife. The husband can still obtain a divorce in this manner.

Due to this inequity, women's grassroots movements had been applying considerable and continued pressure to the government to recognize a wife's right to khul' from the early 1990s until the reform in 2000.

The government supported the women's campaign despite vocal opposition from sociologists, writers, and religious and political figures who were associated with conservative politico-religious groups. The opposition alleged that granting women the right to khul' would lead to social instability, emasculate men, and lead to the breakdown of families.

Progressive women's groups and their supporters argued that recognizing a women's right to khul' would bring justice, stability, and harmony to Egyptian households, without in any way diminishing men's God-given rights.

Their most powerful strategy for winning public opinion was to emphasis the basis of khul' in Muslim laws. The Sheikh of Al-Ahzar agreed to reiterate that the right to khul' is enshrined in Islam and he claimed to follow the Prophet's own example by endorsing this right (reference was made to the hadith where Thabet Ibn Qay's wife requested divorce for no reason other than that she had grown to dislike/hate him and could not continue to live with him).

Although the new law is a big step forward for Egyptian women, it still requires that they forfeit both their mahr and their right to post-divorce maintenance in order to obtain a khul' divorce (see Financial Rights and Responsibilities, p.311). Because the right to access khul' is attached to this financial disadvantage, some activists have argued that the new law will only benefit wealthy women who can afford to forego financial support.

9g DISSOLUTION OF MARRIAGE: OTHER FORMS OF DISSOLUTION FOR WOMEN

introduction

In addition to mubarat, talaq tafwid, and khul', women governed by systems based on Muslim laws may also access certain forms of dissolution that are loosely grouped as fault-based dissolution. Although men may also access certain fault-based grounds, this section focuses on the circumstances under which women have access to such grounds.

Faskh and tafriq are two forms of fault-based dissolution that are found in systems based on Muslim laws. While generally faskh is based upon an irregularity in a marriage contract (including some physical condition which impairs sexual relations in the marriage) or upon the violation of a contractual clause, generally tafriq is based upon relationship problems between spouses, specifically one spouse's failure to fulfil certain marital responsibilities. However, these two terms may be used interchangeably both in popular usage and in some laws. Other terms used to describe the fault-based divorces that are discussed in this section include 'judicial divorce.' For the sake of clarity, we shall use the term 'fault-based dissolution.'

Many systems provide that only women can apply to a court for faskh, the reason being that men can divorce by talaq. However, in Malaysia laws allow either spouse to apply for faskh, based upon the other spouse's incapacity to perform sexual obligations. The grounds for fault-based dissolution are generally similar to those provided for divorce under laws that offer equal grounds to men and women (such as those in Indonesia, Senegal, and Tunisia, see Dissolution on Equal Grounds for Women and Men, p.293). However, third parties may also access faskh in some systems.

This section will deal with the different grounds available in various systems. Some of these grounds may already be established in a marriage contract or in a 'conditional divorce' or ta'liq (Malaysia, Singapore, Indonesia, Philippines) or in the Iranian style conditional tafwid. In the Gambia, when the marriage is contracted, husbands may make a witnessed verbal promise to uphold the wife's right to his provision of maintenance and to his fulfillment of his marital responsibilities. Although his breaking of such a promise may be accepted as grounds for dissolution in theory, such grounds are hardly (if ever) accessed by women because women are almost always unaware of their rights to access fault-based dissolution.

the advantages and disadvantages for women

The main advantage of a fault-based dissolution is that if the divorce is granted, the woman does not lose her rights to mahr, idda maintenance, and mata'a (see Financial Rights and Responsibilities, p.311). She retains these rights because the husband is seen as 'responsible' for the divorce.

In some systems, fault-based dissolution is becoming the most frequently used form of divorce by women because the courts are interpreting 'fault' increasingly widely.

However, such dissolution always requires the intervention of a court or a qazi, thus 'fault' has to be proven by evidence. It can be very difficult for women to provide the kind of hard evidence required to prove a specific fault. Inevitably, a fault-based dissolution involves lengthy hearings, and women may abandon efforts to secure a fault-based dissolution. These women may either opt for khul' (if that is socially and legally available) or a life-long separation that offers no hope of securing financial rights. Even if courts accept oral evidence rather than insisting on documentary proof to establish a claim (Nigeria)(in cruelty cases for example), oral testimony from witnesses may be hard to find.

The process is made even longer when arbitration or hakam is involved. Unless the court can order interim financial maintenance, women can be left in a financially insecure position by prolonged divorce proceedings. These difficulties that women face in the process of divorcing through a grounds-based dissolution seem especially unjust when the same system recognizes a husband's right to exercise unfettered extra-judicial talaq. Where alternative forms of dissolution are socially and legally available to women (such as talaq tafwid or khul), fault-based dissolution or ta'liq is less frequently accessed.

Where women lack family support for their case, providing the required evidence may become very difficult. In addition, women may fear possible family reprisals for bringing 'family matters' into the public arena. However, in some communities, a fault-based dissolution relieves the wife from the stigma of being divorced by talaq because it places the blame squarely on the husband. Accordingly, women prefer fault-based divorce in such contexts.

Many women are prevented from initiating dissolution, even if the 'fault' lies with the husband because of their belief that they will lose custody of their children. However, custody and guardianship operate on different sets of principles (see p.337), and a woman does not automatically lose custody if she initiates a divorce.

grounds for dissolution

In various systems women have obtained divorces that were based upon the following grounds:

- Conjugal: where husbands fail to fulfill conjugal obligations for a specified period of time (4 months, Algeria; 6 months, the Philippines; 1 year, Malaysia; 3 years, Bangladesh, India, Pakistan). 'Reasonable cause' excuses the husband from such grounds. Although conjugal obligations are largely interpreted to include only cohabitation and sexual access. The law in the Philippines has defined failure to perform marital duties widely so that this category includes the husband's failure to live with and respect the wife; to be faithful; to help and support the wife; to refrain from bringing danger, dishonour or material harm to the wife; to satisfy mahr; and/or to offer and maintain a conjugal dwelling befitting the wife's social status.
- Imprisonment: where husbands are imprisoned (Sudan); (at least 1 year: Philippines, Algeria); (at least 3 years: Malaysia); (over 7 years: Bangladesh, India, Pakistan).
- Desertion: (Sri Lanka); (for more than 1 year: Algeria, Malaysia); (6 months: Iran); (for more than 4 years: Bangladesh, India, Pakistan). In some systems where a country is at war or there are hostilities, a disappearance, if explained, does not qualify as desertion for the purposes of faskh (Jordan).

Desertion is one of the most common forms of divorce by husbands in customary practices. In many systems the incidence of desertion is increasing, due to economic pressures and the possibility of migration. Communities often set a longer waiting period than do laws during which a woman cannot seek dissolution or rebuild her life. However, a husband who returns after a prolonged unexplained absence might be subject to community sanctions (Pakistan). In Adamawa State (Nigeria), a woman who is deserted may seek divorce after as little as three to four months.

- Husband's failure to provide maintenance: (Egypt, Sudan, Algeria, Sri Lanka); (for 3 months: Malaysia); (for 6 consecutive months: Philippines): (for more than 2 continuous years: Bangladesh, India, Pakistan).
- Polygyny: marrying other wives (without justification: Algeria); (without permission: Bangladesh, India, Iran, Pakistan); (inequitable treatment in polygynous marriage: Bangladesh, India, Iran, Pakistan, Malaysia).
- Interference in the wife's autonomy: the husband's interference in the wife's exclusive property (Bangladesh, India, Nigeria, Pakistan, Philippines); refusal to allow her to pursue her education or profession (only available in systems that do not recognize the husband as 'head of household' or in those that allow such

a condition to be added to a marriage contract); or obstructs the wife in her religious obligations.

- Unusual cruelty (Philippines), cruelty (Malaysia, Nigeria, Pakistan, Sri Lanka, Sudan), cruelty or ill treatment (Iran). Cruelty may be defined in the text of the law (Bangladesh, India, Malaysia, Pakistan) and in most systems this definition has been further elaborated in case law to include verbal and mental cruelty.
- The husband's behaviour: adultery; drunkenness; narcotics addiction (Iran); association with women of ill repute (Bangladesh, India, Malaysia, Pakistan).
- Defects in the husband: impotency (Malaysia, Philippines, Sudan, Sri Lanka); insanity (Egypt, Philippines, Sri Lanka); incurable disease (Sudan); leprosy and virulent venereal disease (Bangladesh, India, Pakistan). In some (Bangladesh, India, Malaysia, Pakistan) the grounds of insanity is only available if the problem has lasted for 2 years or more.

In some systems the grounds for fault-based or judicial dissolution are inclusive of "any other grounds acceptable" under Muslim laws. Depending upon other provisions in the laws, this may be understood to include khul', the option of puberty, talaq tafwid and/or the grounds of ila', zihar, and li'an. Li'an is in effect no longer an accessible grounds for women in Iran and Pakistan because li'an provisions conflict with laws criminalizing extra-marital sexual relationships.

In Iran and Malaysia, the standard marriage contracts introduce a ta'liq or conditional talaq tafwid, which can be accessed by a wife in the event that her husband fails to meet the obligations in the contract. The grounds included in the standard marriage contract (Iran) or ta'liq (signed as a separate document at the time that the marriage is contracted, Malaysia) are similar to the grounds that are found under fault-based dissolution. The woman's rights also remain similar in terms of financial settlements. However, there may be slight procedural differences, so each woman must decide what is most beneficial for her according to her own circumstances.

There are usually three grounds stipulated in the ta'liq certificate: desertion, non-maintenance, and failure to provide consortium rights (sexual in nature). The ta'liq certificate is recorded in the official register, and copies are given to both parties or just to the husband. The husband is required to sign the ta'liq directly after the marriage ceremony. Some ta'liq certificates may contain a formula where if any of one or more grounds of the ta'liq is proved upon a complaint to the court, the wife may pay the husband a nominal sum of RM 1-3, and this converts the divorce into an irrevocable divorce (or a khul' as the courts term it in Malaysia). An oral ta'liq is accepted if it can be proved by witnesses. Ta'liq is a practice that precedes the codification of Muslim laws in Malaysia; the practice remains popular despite the provisions of the current law on faskh and khul'.

In some systems, provisions for judicial divorce include grounds that relate to requisites of marriage, e.g., the option of puberty, or forced consent (see p.128 & p.90).

procedures

In some systems, the procedures that must be followed in order to establish certain grounds may effectively extend the time period required for the grounds to become accessible. For example, under the Dissolution of Muslim Marriages Act 1939, a decree for dissolution on the grounds of desertion is not effective until 6 months after it is issued; if the husband appears during this period, the woman's case is lost (Bangladesh, India, Pakistan). Similarly, a decree on the grounds of impotence gives the husband a further year in which to prove he is no longer impotent before the order becomes final. In Malaysia, faskh on the grounds of imprisonment is only available after the husband has served 1 year of the sentence. In the Sudan a woman may have to wait 3-5 years after she first raises her case before it can become final.

All systems offering fault-based dissolution (whether codified or uncodified) require that there be an opportunity offered for reconciliation. The reluctance of judicial bodies, formal and informal, to give credence to women's requests to end unhappy marriages often leads to protracted reconciliation/arbitration procedures. These procedures are often held-up further by the husband's reluctance to attend sessions or his unwillingness to co-operate with the process in other ways.

The subtle differences in reconciliation and arbitration procedures can have an immediate effect on the success of a woman's plea for dissolution. In Sri Lanka, the Quazi appoints two Muslim 'assessors' (usually local notables), whose role is to assist the judge in assessing the veracity of the woman's claims (not just to attempt reconciliation). The involvement of such local 'notables' can work to the detriment of women's claims.

If the reconciliation process takes place outside the court, it may either cause confusion (because the details are not properly recorded) or lead the wife to be subjected to local social pressures and increase the trauma involved in a divorce. On the other hand, extra-judicial processes may be less intimidating and quicker than court-based procedures. We believe that it can be assumed that if a woman is seeking dissolution on the grounds of fault, the marriage is beyond rescue. We, therefore, feel that reconciliation procedures merely prolong the legal process and increase the social problems faced by divorcing woman.

Many systems consider a dissolution that is based on the grounds of fault to be irrevocable. However, systems are sometimes unclear as to whether this means that only the husband is prevented from revoking the divorce or that the wife too is prevented from revoking the divorce (even though she initiated the proceedings). In Morocco a dissolution initiated by a wife on the grounds on non-maintenance or ila' can be revoked by the husband. The common limitations placed on a woman's right to revoke a dissolution contrast unfairly with provisions that protect a man's right to revoke a talaq. However, in Bangladesh and Pakistan the wife may revoke a divorce within the 90-day period that follows the court decree being received by the local authorities and that precedes the divorce becoming final.

The Kelantan Ta'liq

The printed ta'liq form in the Malaysian state of Kelantan (each state has slightly differing versions):

"I (full name of husband) hereby make the declaration of ta'liq that whenever I leave my wife (full name of wife) for four months or more, willfully or under duress, or I or my representative do not give her compulsory maintenance for such period whereas she is faithful to me, or I cause hurt to her body, or I neglect her for four months or more, and she later makes a complaint to the Kadi Hakim Syarak (Syariah judge), which is found to be true, and she gave to the Kadi on my behalf an amount of Ringgit Malaysia 1, then immediately she is divorced by a talaq khuli (khul')."

Sometimes the formula for khul' may be cancelled at the time of the promise of ta'liq (at the time the marriage is contracted). However, the bride is not necessarily consulted about this.

NOTES

LAWS: Other Forms of Dissolution for Women

Criteria

The laws is this section have not been listed according to the criteria of more or less option-giving for women because each law has such a range of provisions within it that they are not strictly comparable. For example, whereas one country's law may not require a woman to wait for more than 6 months before she can apply for dissolution on the grounds of desertion, that same country's law may have a very narrow construction of cruelty. The impossible question would then arise as to how to 'grade' that country's law. Instead, countries and their provisions have been listed alphabetically.

Algeria: Under A. 53 of the CF, a wife can petition for divorce based on the following grounds:

- Non-payment of maintenance for which judgment has been made, unless the wife was aware of her husband's hardship at the time of contracting the marriage;
- Infirmity which prevents the achievement of the aims of marriage;
- The refusal of the husband to come to his wife's bed for a period of more than four months;
- The sentencing of the husband to prison for a period of more than one year (in which he leaves her without maintenance);
- The absence of the husband for more than one year, without valid justification or without maintenance;
- Any harm, which is legally recognized as such – e.g. not providing maintenance or marrying other wives without justification;
- Any moral impropriety, which is grave and reprehensible and which is proven.

Bangladesh, India, and Pakistan: Under the DMMA, the grounds are:

- Desertion by the husband for more than four years;
- Husband's failure to pay maintenance for more than two continuous years;
- Husband's taking of an additional wife without permission of an Arbitration Council (only Bangladesh & Pakistan);
- Husband's having been sentenced to imprisonment for seven years or more;
- Husband's failure to perform marital obligations for a period of three years, without reasonable cause;
- Husband's impotence at time of marriage (and his continuing to be so);
- Husband's insanity for a period of two years or his suffering from leprosy or a virulent venereal disease;
- Husband's cruel treatment of wife, meaning habitual assault or cruel conduct (even if does not amount to physical ill treatment), his association with women of ill repute, or his forcing his wife to lead an immoral life; his disposal of her property or prevention of her exercising her legal rights over it; his obstruction of her in the observance of her religious profession or practice; and/or if he has more than one wife, his failure to treat a wife equitably, in accordance with the injunctions of the Qur'an;
- Any other grounds recognized as valid under Muslim Law.

Egypt: Grounds for divorce are:

- Deep-seated defect in the husband (which may not be cured or which may be cured only after a long period and which may cause the wife harm, e.g. insanity, leprosy (whether it occurred before she was unaware of it or after marriage and does not accept it, but no divorce will be granted if she explicitly or implicitly accepted it)).
- Lack of maintenance;

- Harm caused by discord between spouses;
- The absence of a husband for a year or more without reasonable justification may lead to irrevocable divorce if the woman suffers harm due to his absence, even if she has money with which to support herself;
- If a husband is sentenced to jail for a period of at least 3 years, the judge may irrevocably divorce him from his wife after he has served one year of his sentence, even if she has money with which to support herself.

Gambia (marriages under Muslim laws): There are no specific grounds outlined under the MMDO, which simply states that 'Sharia' is to be followed. At the time that the marriage is contracted, a husband may make a verbal promise to maintain his wife and fulfil his marital responsibilities. A husband's failure to fulfil these promises is rarely, if ever, applied as grounds for dissolution by the forums hearing a woman's plea for dissolution.

Iran: A wife can initiate divorce on two basic grounds:

- Under A. 1130 of the CC (as mended on 12 November, 1991), on the grounds of harm where the continuation of the marriage would cause difficulty and hardship for the wife. If the harm is established, the court can compel the husband to divorce his wife. Where this is impractical (e.g., desertion), the court may pronounce her divorced. Drug addiction is only accepted as harm if it is proved that the addiction has financially ruined the husband and made him incapable of supporting the family.
- Breach of marriage contract: Since 1987, the standard marriage contract opens the right to divorce (effectively a conditional talaq tafwid) on 9 grounds, including ill-treatment; desertion (6 months); failure of maintenance (6 months without reason); disease affecting marital life; insanity; the wife and the court finding that the husband's job is objectionable and his subsequent refusal to leave it; childlessness due to the husband's fault after 5 years of marriage; inequality of treatment in polygynous marriage; polygyny without wife's permission. If the wife can prove these conditions have been violated, and they were not struck out on the marriage contract form at the time of marriage, the court issues a permit enabling her to divorce herself on behalf of the husband. The woman retains her right to mahr, maintenance, and mata'a. A breach of the marriage contract can be a wider grounds than harm because it may include the violation of additional negotiated clauses.
- Li'an is recognized under A. 1052 of the CC and creates a permanent prohibition of marriage between the parties. The law is interpreted to mean that the wife does not have a similar right to accuse the husband without proof. If she makes such a claim and fails to prove it, she will be liable to be punished for qazf.

Malaysia: Under S. 52 of the IFLA, faskh is available where:

- The whereabouts of the husband have not been known for a period of more than one year;
- The husband has neglected to or failed to provide for the wife's maintenance for a period of three months;
- The husband has been sentenced to imprisonment for a period of three years or more (not available until the sentence has become final and the husband has already served one year of the sentence);
- The husband has failed to perform, without reasonable cause, his marital obligations (*nufkah batin*) for a period of one year;
- The husband was impotent at the time of marriage and remains so, and the wife was not aware at the time that she married him that he was impotent (the husband has a further 6 months to prove that he is no longer impotent);
- The husband has been insane for a period of two years, or is suffering from leprosy or vitilago, or is suffering from a venereal disease in a communicable form;
- The husband treats her with cruelty, including habitual assault; makes her life miserable by cruelty of conduct; associates with women of evil repute or leads what, according to Hukum Syara', is an infamous life; attempts to force her to lead an immoral life; disposes of her property or prevents her from exercising her legal rights over it; obstruct her in the observance of her

religious obligations or practice; if he has more wives than one and does not treat her equitably in accordance with the requirements of Hukum Syara; that even after the lapse of four months, the marriage has still not been consummated owing to the willful refusal of the husband to consummate it;

- The wife did not consent to the marriage or her consent was not valid, whether in consequence of duress, mistake, soundness of mind, or any other circumstance recognized by Hukum Syara';
- At the time that the marriage was contracted, the wife, though capable of giving a valid consent, was, whether continuously or intermittently, a mentally disordered person within the meaning of the Mental Disorders Ordinance, 1952; and her mental disorder was of such a kind or to such extent as to render her unfit for marriage;
- There is any other grounds that is recognized as valid for dissolution of marriages or fasakh under Hukum Syara'.

Under S. 126, the husband's willful refusal to co-habit after a court order, makes him liable to a fine of RM 500 and/or imprisonment of up to 6 months.

Morocco: Under S. 53-58 of the Moudawana, the wife can access judicial divorce (tatliq) on the grounds of:

- Non-payment of maintenance (if the husband proves his inability to pay, he is granted up to 3 more months to provide maintenance) (a faskh on this grounds is revocable by the husband);
- Defect (mental or physical and that is incurable or only curable after more than 1 year), no matter whether the defect occurred at the time of marriage or later, provided that the wife did not explicitly or implicitly accept the defect (divorce may be deferred for 1 year in the hope of a cure) (a faskh on this grounds is irrevocable);
- Harm making it impossible to continue married life (arbitration may be ordered);
- A husband's absence, without valid reason for more than 1 year (where the husband can be contacted a further period may be allowed by the judge);
- Ila', allowing the wife to apply for dissolution. A time period of 4 months is set. If the husband does not comply, the judge grants a revocable divorce.

Nigeria (marriages under Muslim laws): The wife can institute dissolution on the following grounds:

- The husband fails to maintain the wife (e.g., provide shelter, food, medical expenses, and clothing). In Yahaya v Adamu Salisu, the wife called witnesses to prove lack of provision of food or adequate medical care. The Sharia Court of Appeal, Kano, affirmed the divorce.
- There is a manifest defect in the husband (either mental or physical disability). If the wife knew of the defect before the marriage but remained silent, she cannot access this ground. If the complaint is impotence or insanity, the case may be adjourned for 1 year.
- Failure to provide sexual satisfaction. In Modu Fugurambe v Amina Alirambe, the wife complained to Lamisula Area Court II Maiduguri that her husband was 'not her match sexually.' She swore on the Holy Qur'an that her complaint was true and the marriage was dissolved.
- The husband injures the wife by molestation;
- The husband is absent for a long period of time (desertion). For example, Aisha Umar complained to Area Court 1 Sokoto that her husband had left her for 2 years and 3 months. She produced witnesses and was granted a divorce.
- The husband obstructs the wife's fulfillment of her religious obligations (i.e., refuses to permit her to go on pilgrimage);
- Li'an, zihar, and ila' are recognized but seldom used.
- Injury or discord between the wife and husband. For instance, Luba Mamman complained to the Area Court, Sokoto that her husband often verbally abused her father and accused her of committing adultery. The husband, Tukur Ibrahim, protested against the divorce. The Sharia Court of Appeal ruled that the wife could have the divorce. In Hadiza v Lawal Aminu, the wife sued for divorce on the grounds of cruelty and destruction of property, and the Area Court Zaria granted the divorce.

Philippines: Under A. 52 of the CMPL, the court may, upon petition of the wife, decree a divorce by faskh on any of the following grounds:

- Neglect or failure of the husband to provide support for the family for at least six consecutive months;
- Conviction of the husband by final judgment, sentencing him to imprisonment for at least one year;
- Failure of the husband to perform for six months (without reasonable cause) his marital obligation in accordance with this Code;
- Impotency of the husband;
- Insanity or affliction of the husband with an incurable disease, which would make the continuance of the marriage relationship injurious to the family;
- Unusual cruelty of the husband as defined under the text of the succeeding article; or
- Any cause recognized under Muslim law for the dissolution of marriage by faskh, either at the instance of the wife or of the proper wali (includes la'an without witnesses).

A. 53 allows for faskh on the ground of unusual cruelty, if the husband:

- Habitually assaults her or makes her life miserable by cruel conduct, even if this does not result in physical injury; associates with persons of ill-repute or leads an infamous life, or attempts to force the wife to live an immoral life; compels her to dispose of her exclusive property or prevents her from exercising her legal rights over it; obstructs her in the observance of her religious practices; and/or does not treat her justly and equitably as enjoined by Islamic law.

Sri Lanka: Under S. 28(1) of the MMDA, the wife is permitted to apply for divorce on the basis of any act or omission that amounts to fault or ill treatment on the part of the husband as recognized under Muslim laws. Because the law of the spouses' sect applies (without any further clarification), there can be confusion about the precise grounds available to women. The grounds have not been codified and are established through case law. These are:

- Non-maintenance;
- Desertion;
- Physical or mental cruelty, including allegations of adultery;
- Leprosy, insanity, impotence;
- Li'an (Mohamed v Elsie Fathumal 1939 2 MMDR 98).

Procedures are specified in the Third Schedule to the MMDA and do not make any distinction between faskh, khul', tafwid, etc. Dissolution initiated by a wife requires an inquiry by the Quazi, who is assisted by two male Muslim assessors that he appoints. Unless the husband admits the allegations, the wife must have two independent witnesses (not necessarily Muslims) to the facts. If a husband is missing, the Quazi may have notice served on the husband's nearest relative or dispense with the necessity of serving notice.

Sudan: According to the MPLA there are specific grounds for judicial divorce:

- Incurable disease and/or defects (S. 151-161);
- Impotence: Section 153-161;
- Cruelty, mistreatment, and disunity (S. 162-169);
- Lack of financial maintenance and economic hardship (S. 174-184);
- Absenteeism or imprisonment, (S. 185-191)

A dissolution decreed by a court is a talaq bain baynuna sughra (irrevocable, but the couple can remarry each other through a fresh contract.).

IMPLEMENTATION

Negative trends in implementation

Iran: In practice, only if a husband seriously and repeatedly batters his wife, and there is medical evidence to this effect, is a petition for divorce accepted on the grounds of ill treatment. The process may take several years, and judicial discretion is wide.

Pakistan: Evidence requirements are stringent, and a case may take many years. Divorce under the DMMA, 1939 is, therefore, the form of divorce that women access the least. Lawyers also tend to discourage women from filing under the DMMA. If they choose to follow this advise, they lose their rights to financial settlements.

Sri Lanka: Although fault-based dissolution is widely accessed by women, even where a woman is able to very clearly establish fault on the part of the husband, Quazis may be reluctant to grant a faskh divorce if the husband is against it, and they may unnecessarily delay the proceedings, causing inconvenience and mental hardship for the wife.

Positive trends in implementation

Sri Lanka: The landmark Supreme Court decision of King v. Miskin Umma 1925 26 NLR 330 led to restricting the traditional right of women to obtain divorce through the intervention of the mosque imam. This decision reflected the conservatism regarding divorce that was found in colonial law at that time. The Muslim community resisted efforts to give the jurisdiction of divorce over to ordinary (colonial) courts. This reluctance led to the 1929 Muslim Marriage and Divorce Ordinance, which established special Quazi Courts with jurisdiction to grant 'fasah' and the 1951 MMDA refined this. A wife may reject the assessors who are chosen by a Quazi for a fasah case. If a woman applies for faskh, and the husband twice fails to appear, the Quazi proceeds with ex-parte hearings and grants the divorce, not waiting the required 3 months for the husband to appear.

PRACTICES

Gambia: Communities rarely, if ever, apply the various grounds for dissolution available to women under Muslim laws. This is despite the practice in which the husband makes a verbal promise, at the time of the marriage ceremony, to meet his responsibilities.

Malaysia: Since the introduction of fault-based grounds through the 1980s reforms, and with changing social attitudes, it is becoming increasingly acceptable for women to initiate divorce.

Pakistan: Fasah (the ground that the husband has been unfaithful) is hardly ever accessed because wives are not expected to speak about such conduct by their husband in public. Women of the elite classes who are married to cousins may share their problems with elders who may take some action short of divorce. Among the Hazarajat, action may be taken if the husband is caught red-handed by someone other than the wife. Li'an is hardly accessed because of customary practices endorsing violent responses to (even presumed) adultery by women (see Volume II: Violence Against Women). However, in some areas (Mianwali, Attock, Makran, and also Thar) if the wife is not caught red-handed, li'an may lead to divorce/separation. In Charsadda a woman's oath on the Qur'an is given value; in Swabi, on unproven suspicion of adultery, the husband may take a second wife. Ila' is usually resolved by family mediation. Men sometimes use zihar in anger, and communities vary over whether this is regarded as a valid or invalid divorce. Generally, zihar is socially condemned and not accepted as a form of divorce. Men may occasionally utter zihar as part of a revenge vow ("you are my sister until I have avenged my father's death").

A Desperate but Enterprising Move

Although women in many communities in Pakistan are unaware of their legal rights to dissolution (and equally unaware of the associated procedures that are required), communities may have some basic knowledge of the grounds for divorce available under Muslim laws.

One young woman from a conservative rural community in Pakistan's North-West Frontier Province was happily married until one day her husband announced that he was going to marry another wife. The new wife came to live with the couple, and the young woman decided to take action - in the only way she knew how.

At the time, she was breastfeeding her child. When asked to prepare morning tea for the newly married couple, she made the tea but mixed her own milk in with the tea and served it to both her husband and his new wife.

Once they had drunk the tea, she announced that they were now haram to each other, having shared the same woman's milk, and that her husband was haram to her, as she was now his 'mother.'

The community upheld this action as a valid divorce.

9h DISSOLUTION OF MARRIAGE: DISSOLUTION ON EQUAL GROUNDS FOR WOMEN AND MEN

introduction

Systems in which all divorce provisions make the same grounds available to both men and women are generally found only in systems that are not based on Muslim laws. Laws in Indonesia and Tunisia are exceptions to this rule; in both countries attempts have been made to address the discriminatory aspects of unilateral talaq.

While Senegal's Code de la Famille is inspired by Muslim laws, the Napoleonic Code, and Wolof and other customary laws, it offers almost equal grounds to men and women so its provisions are also discussed in this section. Similarly, the grounds of 'constant disputes and quarrels' (niza' wa shiqaq) are available to men and women in laws derived from the Ottoman Code (applicable to the Palestinian community in Israel and some Arabic-speaking countries, as well as Malaysia), and these are briefly discussed in this section as well.

equal grounds does not mean equal rights in divorce

The promise of equal grounds can be deceptive. In some systems the conditions for proving adultery are discriminatory, and, as such, they make it almost impossible for a wife to access divorce based on such a claim against her husband while making it comparatively easy for a husband to do so (Cameroon, Fiji). Also, in practice, the availability of equal grounds does not resolve the problem of social attitudes, which continue both to obstruct women's access to divorce and to facilitate men's access.

Divorce by mutual consent in systems that do not distinguish between women and men in their provision of grounds are discussed in Mubarat and Divorce by Mutual Agreement, p.<>. However, not all systems that do not distinguish between men and women in their provision of grounds recognize the possibility of mutual agreement to divorce. Instead, some systems presume divorce is always contested. This presumption forces spouses to humiliate one another in court in order to establish 'fault.' In Fijian case law, the courts have rejected uncontested divorce applications, even when they are based on such sensitive grounds as one spouse's refusal to consummate the marriage.

Thus, in many of these systems, divorce involves lengthy and complex procedures. Some systems first require a judicial separation and then require a long period of waiting before a decree can become final (up to 3 years in Turkey). Lengthy procedures cannot work to women's advantage. No matter who initiated the divorce, social attitudes make it easier for men to begin rebuilding their lives (particularly by finding a new partner) while the proceedings continue. Also, women usually have fewer financial resources to enable them to survive until a final financial settlement is reached.

grounds for divorce

The grounds for divorce in systems that do not distinguish between the grounds available to men and those available to women are generally similar across countries and communities. These tend to resemble the grounds available under Muslim laws and are generally based on a failure to fulfill marital responsibilities. Usually, these grounds include a set of provisions concerning cohabitation and sexual access (desertion, or the spouse being jailed, willful refusal to cohabit, impotence, insanity, etc.); a set concerning mutual treatment (the spouse's cruelty, immoral lifestyle); and a set concerning mutual financial support (non-maintenance, willful failure to contribute to the household expenditure).

Most laws in these systems also provide further for a more general grounds, such as marital breakdown or constant quarrels (Fiji does not). Although Malaysia and some Middle Eastern systems do not have equal grounds for divorce, both spouses can access the grounds of shiqaq. Although the availability of such grounds can prove useful for women who cannot prove fault, it can also advantage men who usually face smaller financial settlements under this type of divorce than they do under talaq.

Despite the similarities, not all these systems recognize all of the grounds mentioned above; they may include them under other grounds or not recognize them at all. Also, some systems provide for additional grounds. For example, in Indonesia very specific grounds are provided for drug addiction, gambling, and drunkenness; but the law does not specify non-maintenance as grounds for divorce. Indonesian laws also list consent obtained through illegal threat or misinformation as grounds for divorce because they do not provide for annulment (although a 6 month time limit applies).

There are also subtle differences in the way each of these grounds may be restricted, sometimes to women's advantage and sometimes not. In the Central Asian Republics, a man cannot divorce his wife during pregnancy or when they have a child under 1 year old. In Cameroon and Fiji, a wife has to catch her husband in the act of committing adultery in the family home or prove that the adultery took place with one woman over a period of time in order to be able to use adultery as a grounds for divorce. In contrast, in these same systems a single proven incident of adultery that was committed by the wife in any location is sufficient grounds for the husband to access divorce.

Based on outdated English law, laws in some systems do not permit divorce applications within the first 2 years of marriage (the Gambia – marriages under the Civil Marriage Act, Nigeria – marriages under the Matrimonial Causes Act). Others do not allow cruelty as grounds within the first 3 years of marriage (Fiji, which only accepts habitual cruelty as grounds). Under 'exceptional circumstances' the grounds of cruelty can be accessed earlier, but to do so requires separate permission from the court. There are no such time limits provided in other systems (Cameroon, Indonesia, Senegal, Tunisia).

procedure

The availability of divorce on equal grounds does not solve the problem that for various reasons many women find it harder than men do to prove their grounds. In systems based on English common law, the evidence requirements are such that the court must be 'reasonably satisfied' that the grounds are proven. But proof can be difficult to establish in private matters, and the courts (especially lower courts) often are not clear as to what constitutes an acceptable standard of proof (Fiji). For example, the law may not require objective proof of injury, and it may accept mental torture as cruelty, but the courts still may tend to narrowly interpret cruelty to include only physical injury; they may further require medical certificates, etc. In Tunisia, when the generous grounds allowed under the Maliki School were enacted, the very demanding Maliki evidence requirements were also applied.

Procedural issues are extremely important in all personal status matters because they can make the difference between a women being able to access her rights or not being able to do so. In Senegal the woman chooses which court is to hear her application (that of her area of current residence or that of the marital home). In contrast, in Tunisia only the court of husband's residence has jurisdiction. In Turkey laws offer the widest choice as either spouse may apply to the court in either of the spouses' domicile or to the court in the location where they last lived together for at least 6 months. In Cameroon spouses must agree to be judged either by (a) the more easily accessible Court of First Instance, which bases its judgments largely on customary and Muslim laws, or (b) by the High Court, which follows the Civil Status Ordinance.

Systems differ over whether all matters related to the divorce (custody, property settlements, etc.) are to be decided along with the application for divorce or are to be decided separately. In some systems rejection of the divorce application means rejection of all associated suits, including those pertaining to child custody and maintenance. These suits are rejected even if the couple is no longer living together. On the other hand, these same systems may prevent the final divorce decree from being issued until all related issues are settled; this can considerably delay the process (Fiji).

Reconciliation efforts are usually mandatory (Indonesia; Cameroon - High Court process only; Tunisia; Turkey) and often cause the same problems as do reconciliation procedures in other forms of divorce (see p.283-284). Some systems allow the judge to issue interim orders concerning such issues as child custody and maintenance during the reconciliation period. Such orders can ease the burden of lengthy reconciliation processes. Laws in Indonesia and Tunisia make all divorces irrevocable; and by doing so, they close a potential avenue of spousal abuse (see p259).

When Equal Grounds are Not so Equal

A number of systems in the Middle East that derive their family laws from the Ottoman Code (Iraq, Jordan, the Palestinian community in Israel, Syria) make the grounds of niza' wa shiqaq (constant discord and strife) available to both spouses. In addition, talaq is available to the husband, and khul' and other grounds for dissolution are available to the wife.

The procedures in these systems are generally similar. The judge first establishes that there is discord and then appoints arbiters to attempt reconciliation. Among the Palestinian community in Israel, the arbiters are also expected to assess the extent of blame on both sides. The financial compensation due to either spouse will be based on this assessment. If the wife is assessed as being 30% responsible for the discord, she will only get 70% of any financial settlement due to her on divorce. The arbitration decision is final and appeal is only possible on procedural grounds.

For women the grounds of 'discord and strife' has the advantage that very specific proof is not required (as in fault-based dissolution, see p.281). A wife may be able to convince the arbiters that the husband is at least partly responsible (thereby not having to return/surrender all of her mahr).

But assessment by the arbiters can be an extremely lengthy - and arbitrary - process, depending upon the attitude of the arbiters. Given patriarchal stereotypes about women's roles and responsibilities within the family, there is a tendency for the arbiters to see the discord from the husband's perspective and award compensation accordingly.

In the Palestinian community in Israel, men frequently use the 'discord and strife' provision to avoid the possibility of incurring criminal penalties for pronouncing talaq (under Israeli law, a divorce against the will of the wife is liable to a 3-month prison sentence) and to reduce the size of the financial settlement they will have to make.

NOTES

. . . .

. . . .

. . . .

. . . .

. . . .

LAWS: Dissolution on Equal Grounds for Women and Men

Criteria

Laws have not been ranked according to whether they are more or less option-giving for women because their multiple provisions are not strictly comparable. However, those laws which do not place any time restrictions on the grounds and which offer general grounds such as 'marital breakdown' are certainly more option-giving.

Bangladesh (marriages under the SMA): Under S. 10 of the Divorce Act, 1869 (commonly called the Christian Divorce Act), the husband may petition for divorce on the grounds of his wife's adultery. S. 11 requires him to name the alleged adulterer who becomes a co-respondent in the divorce suit. Under S. 10, a wife cannot sue for divorce on the grounds of adultery alone; she must also prove any of the following: bigamy and adultery with another woman; cruelty; desertion without reasonable cause for more than 2 years; that he is guilty of rape, sodomy, or bestiality; incestuous adultery by the husband; or that the husband has changed his religion from Christianity and married another woman. Case law since the 19th century has constructed cruelty very narrowly and excludes mental and verbal abuse, violence while drunk, and single incidents of violence. Under S. 12, the court must be satisfied that the spouses are not colluding to achieve a divorce. Under S. 19, nullity may also be sought on the grounds of continuing impotence since the time of marriage.

Cameroon: The grounds for divorce are the same for wives and for husbands, except in cases of adultery. The grounds include: unreasonable refusal to cohabit; imprisonment of one of the spouses; physical cruelty or assaults; insult which constitutes a serious violation of the rights and obligations resulting from the marriage and renders the marriage tie unbearable (this can include physical or moral violence, written or verbal insult, and insult can be construed from a spouse's actions); and adultery. In the case of adultery, it suffices for the husband to prove that the wife had sexual intercourse with another man one or more times. The wife has to prove that her husband had sexual intercourse in the matrimonial home or with the same woman over a period of time. An application for divorce can be filed either before the High Court or the Court of First Degree (the spouses have to agree on which court has jurisdiction). The Court of First Degree usually hears cases under customary or Muslim laws. In divorce through the High Court, the Court is obliged to try and reconcile the parties. If reconciliation is not possible, the judge passes a non-reconciliation order authorizing the divorce application to proceed and making provisional orders based on the demands of the parties. These orders usually relate to separate residence, custody of children, maintenance of children, and spousal maintenance (usually the woman). Following divorce, the wife can use her maiden name if she so desires, but she cannot be forced to do so unless she is using the husband's name fraudulently.

Central Asian Republics: Divorce is available on demand for both women and men, except the husband cannot divorce the wife if she is pregnant or there is a child under 1 year old.

Fiji: Divorce is fault-based and inherited from English common law. The grounds include adultery; willful refusal to consummate the marriage; cruelty (a single incident is not sufficient unless the wife had the husband convicted for that one incident, and she must apply for divorce within 1 year of the conviction, plus cruelty cannot be a grounds until after 3 years of marriage, except on application to the High Court for 'exceptional grounds'); and constructive desertion (where the wife is forced to leave due to the husband's cruelty, for example after one violent incident).

The summons brings the parties to court 10 days after they are issued. After court hearings, a decree nisi is granted, and this is followed by a minimum 3-month waiting period before the divorce becomes final and absolute. The decree absolute is not issued until all attendant matters are settled (custody, maintenance, property, etc.).

Gambia (marriages under the CiMA and MCA: The grounds for divorce are clearly spelt out under the MCA, 1986. Under S. 3 either party to a marriage can present a petition for divorce on the sole grounds that the marriage has broken down beyond reconciliation. The petitioner must prove one or more of the following under S. (1(a-f)): adultery; behavior that means the petitioner cannot reasonably be expected to live with the respondent; desertion for a continuous period of 2 years; or that the couple has not lived together as man and wife or reconciled their differences. Under S. 11(1) of the Act, no petition for divorce shall be presented to the court within 2 years from the beginning of the marriage, except on application to the court on the grounds of substantial hardship by the petitioner or deprivation on the part of the respondent.

Nigeria: Similar provisions apply under the MCA, 1970.

India (marriages under the SMA): The SMA provides the grounds and procedure for divorce and judicial separation. Grounds for divorce, which are available to both spouses under S. 27, are voluntary sexual intercourse with any person other than his or her own spouse; desertion for a period of 2 years; the spouse undergoing a prison sentence of 7 years or more; cruel treatment; incurably unsound mind, mental disorder, venereal diseases, or leprosy, not having been contracted from the petitioner; or not having been heard to be alive for a period of 7 years. Other grounds available to both spouses are: no resumption of cohabitation for a period of 1 year or more after passing of a decree of judicial separation; or no restitution of conjugal rights after a period of 1 year or more from the date of a decree for restitution of conjugal rights. Some grounds available to a wife alone include: the husband being guilty of rape, sodomy, or bestiality; or a maintenance order or decree against him, not withstanding that the parties were living apart. In a divorce petition, alternate relief in the form of judicial separation can also be granted. The Divorce Act, 1869, has been amended by the Indian Divorce (Amendment) Act, 2001. The grounds are similar to the Divorce Act applicable in Bangladesh (see above). However, the grounds are now available equally to the husband or wife, and each grounds is sufficient for a decree to be granted (e.g., the wife no longer has to prove adultery compounded with cruelty; either is sufficient grounds on its own).

Indonesia: (Article 38) All divorce is to go through the courts, and grounds do not distinguish between husband and wife; these include if the marriage ceremony was performed under illegal threat or following misinformation regarding one of the spouses (the suit must be filed within 6 months of discovering the misinformation); adultery, drunkenness, narcotics addiction, gambling, and other vices; desertion for more than 2 consecutive years; one of the spouses being sentenced to jail for 5 years or more; violence or ill-treatment that endangers the safety of the other spouse; incurable disease or disability preventing marital duties; or constant and heated arguments. The law also recognizes the power of a spouse's senior relatives to request dissolution of a marriage but is silent on whether or not their son/daughter's approval is required for such an application. The spouse wishing to divorce sends a letter to the Court of their own district, notifying their intention to divorce and the reasons. The court is to hold a hearing within 30 days. Both parties are called separately for reconciliation meetings with counselors (wife's counselors are women). The law does away with the concept of revocable divorce.

Malaysia: Under S. 48 of the IFLA, if the court is satisfied that there are constant quarrels between the spouses, it may appoint two Hakam to act for them (usually close relatives) with the aims of arbitration and of convincing the husband to pronounce a revocable divorce.

Senegal: Under A. 166 of the CF, there are 9 grounds for divorce equally available to men and women, and a 10th ground available to women only (non-maintenance by the husband): proven adultery; a spouse sentenced for a socially humiliating crime (e.g., rape, theft, murder); a spouse's refusal to meet financial agreements relating to the conclusion of the marriage (e.g., refusal to pay mahr); violation of the duty to cohabit and provide support and assistance; ill-treatment, vices, and harm rendering marital life impossible; absence for 2 years following a judicial decree of desertion, or 4 years from the date of last contact; incurable and proven sterility; grave and incurable illness discovered during the marriage; or general incompatibility rendering marital life impossible. Opposition by one of the spouses cannot obstruct the process, and it is for the judge to assess responsibility and pronounce the divorce by finding either or both of the spouses at fault. No matter who files for divorce, the wife has the right to choose whether the case is to be heard in the court of her area or the area of the marital home. An application can be written or verbal, and the judge is obliged to attempt reconciliation (without lawyers present). If reconciliation fails, the judge may pass interim orders regarding custody, maintenance, etc. The judge may reject the claimed grounds (and these cannot be used again in a fresh application); or may adjourn a decision for a maximum of 12 months to allow reconciliation. The final decree must fix the date of the waiting period.

Tunisia: Under A. 31 of the CSP (as amended by Loi No. 81-7 of 18 fevrier 1981), divorce can be pronounced by the court under three alternative circumstances: by mutual consent; on the grounds of harm (understood to relate to the failure to fulfill rights and responsibilities of the spouses laid out in the law); or at the will of the husband or the wife. For the grounds of harm, the court may reject the petition. For divorce at will, the judge has a duty to accept the divorce and must only decide on the damages due to the other spouse. Whoever applies for the divorce, the competent court is the one in the husband's area of residence. The summons to appear must be served by a process server. Under A. 32, a divorce decree cannot be made until reconciliation efforts have been made; lawyers are not to be present. Even if not requested by the couple, the court is to decide all related matters along with the divorce (housing, maintenance, custody of children, visitation rights) except where the parties have agreed among themselves.

Turkey: Under A. 161-166 of the CC, there is no distinction between the grounds available to men and women: adultery; ill-treatment or behavior detrimental to the spouse's honour; leading a dishonourable life (including sentencing for a socially humiliating crime) making cohabitating impossible; insanity; or irretrievable breakdown. Irretrievable breakdown was not available until a 1988 amendment, and accessing this grounds requires the marriage to have lasted more than 1 year and the spouses to have agreed regarding the division of marital property. Divorce on the grounds of desertion requires an official request for the spouse to return to the marital home. Once the official request has been made, the procedural period (required by law before suing for divorce on this ground) begins. Once a fault-based ground has been established, the judge may order a divorce or legal separation for a period of one to three years to allow for reconciliation (but if the petitioner only requested legal separation, the judge cannot order a divorce). If during this period the couple are still not reconciled, the judge may grant a divorce on the grounds of irretrievable breakdown, if one of them requests that he do so.

IMPLEMENTATION

Court attitudes tend to restrict access to divorce

Cameroon: Women usually prefer to have their divorce applications heard by the Court of First Instance because it is cheaper (lawyers are not required), faster (as it is less formal), and simpler (the application and evidence can be verbal).

Fiji: The courts routinely turn down applications for divorce on the basis of fault if the court believes the couple has mutually agreed to use a fault as a means of achieving a quick divorce. Therefore, for divorce on the grounds of adultery, the courts usually insist that a co-respondent (the adulterous spouse's lover) is named and will not proceed if the co-respondent is not named. Similarly, in a case between an Indo-Fijian couple regarding one spouse's willful refusal to consummate the marriage, the court refused to grant a divorce, even though the refusing spouse did not contest the grounds.

The courts tend to interpret cruelty very narrowly, defining it to include physical cruelty only. Moreover, they demand objective proof of injury. While it is possible to access the grounds of cruelty during the first three years of marriage, the husband must have been convicted of physical harm in order to do so. This provision is not very useful given the low rate of reporting and conviction for such crimes. In addition, the courts are uncertain as to how to apply common law evidence requirements (the court must be 'reasonably satisfied'), and this uncertainty tends to work to a woman's disadvantage because often it is difficult to produce sufficient proof in private matters.

Indonesia: In order to access the grounds of incompatibility, the law requires the reasons for discord to be 'sufficiently clear to the court.' This formulation allows for patriarchal interpretations of marital roles and makes women dependent on the testimonies of those who witness the discord (generally, either no one witnesses it, or only a wife's in-laws do). Women counsellors often pressure the wife to withdraw her claim during the reconciliation process. These counsellors encourage the wife to return to her husband, and they reiterate her duty to obey. Moreover, they often claim that divorce is not acceptable in Islam.

Senegal: The vague formulation of the grounds of grave and incurable disease leaves interpretation up to judicial discretion, which may or may not work to a woman's advantage. In one case a judge pronounced a divorce, holding the wife to be exclusively to blame because she had refused to cook for her husband, who had been maintaining her normally. The judge ruled that she was guilty of excess and that her neglect had caused her husband grave harm and rendered marital life intolerable (TPI Dakar No. 2097 du 13 juillet 1982. Epoux Camara).

Turkey: The general rule is that an application for divorce is filed by the party who is less responsible for the breakdown of the marriage against the party who is more responsible for its failure. In the reverse case, when the party more responsible files for divorce, and the party less responsible does not agree to the divorce, the case may be dismissed. However, if the couple is not reconciled within three years of the rejection, the court automatically rules in favor of a divorce, if one of the parties requests it.

Tunisia: The standards set by judges to prove damages and fault tend to be higher for women than for men.

PRACTICES

Central Asian Republics: Women are expected to avoid 'creating the circumstances' for divorce and are expected to tolerate polygyny and violence rather than demand divorce. The rate of divorce is half that in Russia, and divorced women (regardless of the grounds on which their divorce was based) have low social status. Customarily, infertility is an acceptable grounds for the husband to seek divorce. Infidelity by the wife leads to divorce (notably in Uzbekistan and Turkmenistan), whereas the wife is expected to tolerate infidelity by the husband. The customary lack of divorce options for women and high rates of domestic violence can lead to suicide. Self-immolation is a traditional form of 'protest' suicide among rural Uzbek and Turkmen women. It is used to highlight the fact that the woman would rather burn in the fires of hell than continue living with her husband. The ancient cultural influence of Zoroastrianism in the region assigns a purifying role to fire, and thus suicide by fire is also a symbolic means of ridding the woman of the hateful marital union. Uzbek film directors have made a film Plamen ('The Flame') about this widespread practice.

Fiji: A common cause of divorce among the Indo-Fijian community is the practice of forced marriage. Forced marriage leads one or both of the spouses to subsequently seek divorce on the grounds of cruelty. Sometimes one of the spouses refuses to go through with the religious ceremony after the legal marriage has taken place (implying willful refusal to consummate since customarily, consummation does not take place until after the religious ceremony).

Sometimes divorce will result from a husband refusing to take his wife home after the marriage ceremony.

Senegal: Divorces that are obtained through the courts and registered under the law are limited to the major cities of Dakar, Kaolack, and St. Louis, where the most common grounds are non-maintenance, desertion, incompatibility, and harm. Men most frequently access incompatibility (which is understood to be closest to the socially recognized practice of talaq). The majority of divorces are extra-judicial. Whereas Senegalese law allows for the late registration of oral and customary marriage, there is no such provision for divorce, and only divorces that go through the court and are registered are valid. This leaves women vulnerable to charges and penalties for bigamy if they remarry following a divorce under customary or Muslim laws. This vulnerability may explain why women outnumber men as applicants for divorce through the courts (70% of applications filed with departmental tribunals in Kaolack and St. louis between 1997-1999). At the same time, men file 95% of the (rare) cases filed for bigamy.

In field research by GREFELS for the Women & Law Project, focus groups listed the following as common grounds for divorce under customary laws: the husband's lengthy absence; non-maintenance; ill-treatment, domestic violence; misunderstandings between the spouses; adultery; 'indiscipline' on the part of the wife; conflict with in-laws; jealousy; polygyny; and bad behaviour by either spouse. Under the local understanding of Muslim laws, a woman does not have the capacity to pronounce divorce, although khul' is recognized.

Judicial Attitudes Will Take Time to Change

Patriarchal court attitudes also obstruct women's access to divorce, even where women are given access to the same grounds. A case that appeared before a Turkish court exemplifies such obstruction. The case concerned a pregnant woman who had filed for divorce from her husband. The judge rejected her plea, and in the court minutes he was quoted using an expression that can be roughly translated as, "You should never leave a woman free from a slap on her back and a child in her belly."

It later emerged that that was not the first time that the woman had applied for a divorce from her husband. After each previous application, she had changed her mind, returned to her husband, and had a child. Apparently, the judge had lost his temper with the woman when he saw that she was once again pregnant, and he used the expression mentioned above.

Perhaps, it is difficult for a male judge to understand how a woman can have sex with her husband at the same time that she wants a divorce. The judge demonstrated an attitude towards women (typical of the male-dominated society in which he lives) that reflects a crude understanding of the most effective means of exercising control over women.

Arin, C. (1996), The Legal Status of Women in Turkey, Women for Women's Human Rights Reports Vol. 1, Istanbul

10a MATTERS RELATED TO DISSOLUTION OF MARRIAGE: IDDA AND THE WAITING PERIOD

introduction

Some systems, both those based on Muslim laws and those based on other sources, require a compulsory waiting period following the dissolution of a woman's marriage (as a result of divorce or the death of her husband), during which she cannot remarry. Men are not subject to such a waiting period following a final divorce decree.

Communities may also enforce a compulsory waiting period during which certain rituals and practises must be observed.

Generally, where Muslim laws are applied, the waiting period (or idda) lasts 3 menstrual cycles or 3 months in the case of dissolution of a marriage, and 4 months 10 days in the event of the husband's death. In both instances, if the woman is pregnant, she must observe idda until the child is born. The husband continues to be liable for the maintenance of the wife during the period of idda (unless this has been waived by the court after khul'), and she must be supported from his estate if he dies. After the idda has been completed, a woman is free to remarry.

In some systems that are not based on Muslim laws (Central Asian Republics, Gambia - marriages under the Civil Marriage Act, Fiji), there is no waiting period after the dissolution of a marriage, whether by divorce or by the death of the husband. However, communities have a range of practices that recognise waiting periods and mourning rituals that may or may not be based on an understanding of Muslim laws.

Nevertheless, other systems influenced by the Napoleonic Code (Cameroon, Senegal, Turkey) require a waiting period of 300 days after the dissolution of marriage. This waiting period is justified as a necessary precaution to avoid confusion over paternity. In Turkey, however, a woman wishing to remarry before the expiry of the 300 days can do so after providing a medical certificate that verifies that she is not pregnant.

In these systems, post-divorce alimony is not limited to the waiting period. But in systems based on Muslim laws, maintenance (rather than mata'a and any other financial settlements) is limited to the length of the idda. In some systems based on Muslim laws, a woman may be disqualified from receiving maintenance, even during the idda period, if she has been judged 'disobedient' (see Financial Rights and Settlements, p.312 for details regarding idda maintenance and the right to remain in the matrimonial home).

a period of rest or enforced seclusion?

Some view the observation of a waiting period as a positive practice that allows a woman a period in which she is freed from some social obligations while she continues to be entitled to support by her husband or his heirs. In addition they claim that idda prevents confusion over the paternity of any child, and, in the case of talaq, reconciliation may take place. But because community practices often mandate that a woman remain secluded or follow other restrictive rituals during the waiting period, others argue that a required waiting period allows a husband or his family to maintain control over a woman's sexuality and public mobility even after divorce or death.

In many Muslim communities, it is believed that idda facilitates reconciliation. However, this belief is based on the presumption that the wife will always want to reconcile and that by ensuring that she remains available, idda offers her the chance that her husband will decide to revoke his talaq. However, where idda is spent in the marital home (perhaps with the idea of facilitating reconciliation (Nigeria)), it may expose women to the risk of continued domestic violence (see Financial Rights & Settlements, p.313). In the systems covered in this Handbook that are based on Muslim laws, none of the laws defines the purpose of idda; although some specify that during this period the woman may not remarry (Philippines).

Often idda is marked by a socially enforced seclusion, which may impede women from working, going about their daily business, and/or participating in their normal social interactions. Some women have had to ignore such laws and/or customs (as well as risk public scorn) in order to leave the home to work so as to ensure the survival of their families when their husbands (or their husband's families) refuse to support them. Sometimes widowed women are expected to wait to settle the affairs of the husband's estate (such as taking out a grant of administration) until the idda following their husband's death is completed. Such expectations have no clear basis in Muslim laws and appear to be based on customary practices.

Invariably, where a community requires a waiting period, decisions about whether or not it has to be observed, at what point it begins, and the precise rituals involved are not made by the divorced or widowed woman. In instances where a family is aware that there are requirements, but they are uncertain as to the precise application in their situation, they may consult a local religious or other community authority.

the waiting period on becoming a widow

Although the same justifications are used to explain the waiting period that follows both divorce and widowhood (and indeed, in the case of Cameroon, Senegal and Turkey; the length of time is the same), the waiting period rituals practiced on divorce and death are often quite different.

Many widows face an uncomfortable dilemma: if they remain in their husband's household, they may be financially supported but probably pressured into surrendering any inheritance claims they may have. Far from being a period of rest, the waiting period following the death of one's husband can be a time of extreme social pressure. Both law and custom are often unclear about the waiting period required for widows that are not menstruating. Moreover, the actual duration of the waiting period observed may depend upon a combination of class, community and individual social status, and the economic activities of the woman involved.

procedural problems

In the case of divorce, a precise date for when the waiting period begins is essential. If the law is unclear, the woman's right to maintenance during this period is threatened; usually when there is a dispute over the date that talaq was pronounced. Any system that recognizes triple talaq/talaq bid'a strengthens the practice of denying women idda maintenance altogether. Because such a divorce is irrevocable, many communities presume a husband's responsibilities automatically end with the pronouncement of such a talaq.

There is generally less dispute about the waiting period when a divorce has been initiated by a woman (since this almost always requires a court process) or in systems that require all divorces to go through the courts. This is because the court process fixes a clear date for the beginning of the waiting period.

In contexts where women do not keep records of their menstrual cycles, a law that specifies that idda should last three menstrual cycles can create considerable confusion. Again such confusion raises doubts about maintenance rights. Although setting idda at 90 days can only represent an average, doing so may be simpler and clearer for all concerned, and therefore easier to enforce.

Communities vary in how seriously they take the prohibition on remarriage during the waiting period. The effects of a marriage that is contracted during the idda period may also vary considerably. In Turkey, it is now possible to produce a medical certificate of non-pregnancy after three months have passed since the dissolution of a marriage and thereby shorten the waiting period. In Senegal, however, marriages contracted during the 300-day waiting period are invalid and cannot be registered; yet women routinely remarry after three months and risk being prosecuted for bigamy because they are not yet properly divorced. In Pakistan and Iran, such marriages carry even higher risks because bigamy is covered under laws on zina, which carry very heavy penalties. These risks could be reduced by requiring compulsory marriage registration procedures that clarify the bride's status (see p.148).

Systems vary slightly on the length of the waiting period in the event of pregnancy. In some, delivery itself is taken to signify the end of the period (even if it occurs two days after the divorce from or death of the husband). With a newborn to take care of, a longer waiting period and the possibility of continued financial support is probably more to women's advantage. Other systems provide this longer period by defining 'delivery' in such a away as to include the lying-in period after a child is born. In some, idda is calculated to last until 90 days after dissolution or until delivery, whichever is later. This latter formulation is more in keeping with the concept of idda being a 'breathing space' for a divorced or widowed woman.

Idda is also closely associated with the revocation of divorce in Muslim laws, as it is only during the idda that revocation can take place. A clear starting date for idda clarifies the time limits for revocation. Laws that do not allow couples to have their final divorce certificate until the idda has been completed attempt to make things absolutely clear. However, couples often do not return to claim their final certificate and in ignorance presume that once the court or official forum has accepted their divorce application, the divorce is complete.

The problems presented by a lack of clarity in provisions concerning idda are a focus of demands for reform in the Philippines Code of Muslim Personal Laws. The PLRC has proposed that A. 57(b) of the Code should be amended to include the specific time when to start the counting of idda. In the case of divorce by talaq, the PLRC recommends that the period of idda should be counted from the time the written notice is filed by the husband with the Shari'a Circuit Court. However, in the case of divorce by faskh and those other forms of divorce which require the wife to petition the court, the PLRC recommends that duration of idda should be up to the time a final decree of divorce is granted by the Shari'ah Court provided, that it shall not be less than three months from the time the petition was filed in the court.

maintenance and inheritance rights of widows

Clearly it is more option-giving if widows have a legally protected right to remain in the marital home during the waiting period; such a right prevents them from facing immediate economic hardship and homelessness following the death of their husbands. However, if remaining in the marital home is an obligation rather than a choice, it cannot be option-giving. Customs may also dictate that the widow has a 'choice' between either being provided with lifelong maintenance by remaining with the in-laws and foregoing her inheritance rights or foregoing maintenance and claiming her inheritance.

In contrast to custom and tradition, Senegal's Code de la Famille has detailed provisions ensuring the maintenance of a widow (including accommodation and food) for the entire 300-day waiting period and these provisions are to be deducted from the deceased husband's estate.

Both law and custom are often unclear as to whether or not a widow is entitled to maintenance during idda upon death or only entitled to her share of the estate (Iran). Older cases in Malaysia are muddled, but there has been a concerted effort to streamline judicial opinion and make judgements on the basis that the widow is due inheritance, and not maintenance, during the idda that follows a husband's death. Another area of confusion is whether or not the idda maintenance is to be deducted from the wife's share of the estate or is a separate debt on his property. According to some texts used by Muslim courts (e.g., Abu-Hassan, Iziyya), a widow is expected to maintain herself from her own share of the deceased's property. However, this is not strictly followed. In most cases, wives and children are maintained by the deceased's property before it is shared.

In principle, idda on divorce implies that the marriage still subsists and therefore if the husband dies during this period, the wife is still entitled to inherit, even though socially she is considered divorced.

In the Gambia, custom requires that the family of the deceased cater to the needs of the widow during the mourning period. In practice, the sadaqa (money given to charity for the benefit of one's soul) given during the burial ceremony is utilised to take care of the widow and any children she may have. After the waiting period, the remaining money is shared between the widow (widows if it is a polygynous relationship) and other family members. The expenses for the forty-day ceremony are also drawn from these funds. So often there is nothing or very little left for the widow/s to fall back on. However, with the increasing poverty in the region, the families of the deceased often fail to fulfill these obligations. Thus, women are now moving out to fend for themselves as soon as the forty-day ceremony is over. Widows feed their families and take care of other familial obligations that the late husband had been responsible for. This trend can be observed among literate and illiterate women.

NOTES

LAWS: Idda and the Waiting Period

Criteria

Given the differences of opinion regarding the benefits to women of a waiting period, we have not ranked provisions according to whether they are more or les option-giving. However, where such provisions do exist, they are more option-giving where the laws:

- Have a clear starting date for the waiting period following divorce; and
- Express the waiting period as 90 days (rather than 3 cycles); and state that the waiting period is 90 days or delivery, whichever is later; or
- Permit the woman to shorten a 300-day waiting period through proof of non-pregnancy.

And less option-giving where the laws:

- Have no clear starting date for the waiting period; or
- Do not provide a mechanism for women to shorten a 300-day waiting period in the event of non-pregnancy.

Length of the waiting period on divorce is 3 months/90 days; starting date is clear

Bangladesh & Pakistan: Under S. 7(3) of the MFLO, idda lasts until 90 days have passed (or if a wife is pregnant, until delivery, whichever is later) from the date of notification of talaq to the Union Council. Under S. 8 it is apparent that the same idda applies following other forms of dissolution, and case law establishes that idda is to be counted from the date the local Council receives the court decree of dissolution.

Indonesia: The waiting period shall last for 3 menstrual cycles, the duration of which shall be at least 90 days. The 90-day minimum also applies when the wife has stopped menstruating. Since all divorce is handled through the courts, the starting date is clear.

Three menstrual cycles; starting date can be disputed

Algeria, Morocco: The waiting period for a woman who is not pregnant lasts for 3 menstrual cycles. For a woman who is not menstruating, the waiting period is 3 months from the date of the pronouncement of talaq. In the case of Morocco, where talaq may be pronounced extra-judicially, the starting date of idda is not clear.

Gambia (marriages under Muslim laws): The waiting period following divorce lasts 3 months or 90 days.

Iran: Under A. 1151 of the CC, the idda following the death of or divorce from a husband lasts for 3 consecutive tuhur after menstruation, except where the woman has reached the age of menopause and does not menstruate, in which case the idda will be 3 months. Under A. 1155, there is no idda after divorce for postmenopausal women.

Sri Lanka: The waiting period for a divorced woman is 3 months. Under S. 22 of the MMDA, registration of a marriage of a woman during her waiting period is prohibited; the penalty for contravention is a fine not exceeding 100 rupees (approx US$ 1) (S.87). Case law establishes that idda begins from the date of the first talaq and not from the date of registration (Jabbar v Jainambu 4 MMDR 145, 1958). The text of the law is contradictory regarding the period of maintenance because under S. 47(1)(d), the Quazi has the power to make an order for maintenance of a divorced wife until the registration of the divorce, or for the duration of her idda period.

Nigeria (marriages under Muslim laws), Philippines, Sudan: The waiting period shall be 3 monthly cycles. Since Nigeria and Sudan recognize various forms of talaq, the starting date may be disputed if there are no witnesses to the pronouncement of talaq. In **Sudan**, if the talaq is the third pronouncement, there is no possibility of revocation, and the full idda must be served. For the first and second pronouncements, idda may be ended by revocation. In the **Philippines**, A. 56 of the CMPL, defines idda as the period of waiting prescribed for a woman whose marriage has been dissolved by death or by divorce, the completion of which shall enable her to contract a new marriage. Under A. 57 every wife shall be obliged to observe idda in the case that her marriage is terminated by divorce, for 3 monthly courses; or in case that she is pregnant, for a period extending until her delivery. Under A. 57(2), should the husband die while the wife is observing idda for divorce, another idda for death shall be observed.

The waiting period is longer than 90 days and only to ensure paternity is determined

Turkey: Under A. 132 of the CC, the waiting period shall be 300 days to ensure that a woman is not pregnant. Women who do not want to wait must produce medical proof that they are not pregnant before they can remarry.

Cameroon, Senegal: The waiting period shall last for 300 days or until delivery (whichever is earlier). During this time a woman cannot validly remarry. In Senegal, under A. 112(1) of the CF, the waiting period begins with the court order of non-reconciliation. Under A. 176(2), the woman can reduce the waiting period to 3 months, which will begin on the day that the judgment is final.

Algeria, Nigeria (marriages under Muslim laws): Under laws based on Maliki laws, a woman, who has been deserted by her husband and who has secured a dissolution on such grounds must serve an idda of 4 months and 10 days before the marriage becomes dissolved.

Morocco: Under A. 73 of the Moudawana, a woman whose menstruation is delayed or who is unable to distinguish one cycle from another shall wait 9 months and shall then complete a waiting period of 3 months.

Length of the waiting period in the event of pregnancy

Bangladesh & Pakistan: Under S. 7(3) of the MFLO, idda shall last 90 days (or until delivery, whichever is later) from the date of notification of talaq to the Union Council or the Union Council's receipt of the court decree of dissolution. Case law establishes that 'delivery' includes the lying-in period.

Algeria, Indonesia, Iran, Morocco, Philippines, Sri Lanka, Sudan: In the event that a woman is pregnant, her idda period shall last until delivery, even if this occurs before 90 days have passed.

Nigeria (marriages under Muslim laws): In the event of pregnancy, a woman's waiting period shall end immediately after delivery.

The waiting period after the death of the husband

Algeria, Bangladesh, Gambia (marriages under Muslim laws) Iran, Morocco, Nigeria (marriages under Muslim laws), Pakistan, Philippines, Sri Lanka, Sudan: The waiting period shall last for four months and 10 days after the death of the husband or until the delivery of the child, if the woman is pregnant.

Additional provisions regarding the waiting period and widowhood

Algeria: Under A. 61 of the CF, a widow is not obliged to leave the matrimonial home during her waiting period except in the case of proven moral impropriety.

Indonesia: The waiting period for widows shall last for 130 days and there shall be no distinction between menstruating and non-menstruating women.

Morocco: Under A. 77 of the Moudawana, any woman who has been divorced by a revocable form of divorce and whose husband dies during the waiting period shall then deduct the time already observed in idda from the idda that follows a husband's death.

Philippines: Under A. 57 of the CMPL, if the husband dies while the wife is observing idda for divorce, another idda for death shall be observed.

Senegal: Under A. 262(4) of the CF, a widow is entitled to maintenance (including accommodation and food) for the entire 300-day waiting period and the cost of this shall be deducted from the deceased husband's estate. The widow loses this right if she remarries during the waiting period. Working women benefit from two regulations regarding the waiting period on widowhood: Decree No. 72 215 du 7 mars 1972 permits a widow to request a widow's leave no matter what her religion and Circular Letter No. 974/PR du 18 octobre 1967 allows Muslim women an absence of 3 days.

Sudan: The length of the waiting period is not stipulated in the MPLA and generally Muslim communities follow Muslim laws and begin the waiting period on the day that the husband dies. The widow has the right to spend the waiting period in the matrimonial home. If she is employed, she is required to take leave from work and her social interaction with men is prohibited.

PRACTICES

Gambia: Some elderly widows are exempted from mourning and from observing the idda that follows a husband's death, if he requested such an exception prior to his death. However, very few women benefit from such a practice because tradition and religion are believed to require women to observe idda.

India: During field research by the Women's Research & Action Group for the W&L, a Baroda based woman complained, "The custom should not be imposed so rigidly on women. (For) a woman who is the sole supporter of her family...(idda) can drive her and her family to the brink of starvation..."

Nigeria: A widow is entitled to her share of the inheritance, and up to one year's maintenance out of her deceased husband's property if she remains in the marital home (usually understood to mean the family house as opposed to a rented home in the city or accommodation provided through the husband's work). Maintenance beyond idda is available if the husband's estate has not yet been shared and/or if the widow retains a close link with her in-laws. However, widows are sometimes neglected, especially if there are no friends and relatives to help them. A widow is expected to live an extremely modest life and refrain from going out.

Pakistan: There is a lack of knowledge about the idda procedure, leading to frequent remarriage during idda, which can lead to subsequent zina cases (i.e., for bigamy). There is often confusion over the required length of idda for widows, especially in the case that the widow has undergone a hysterectomy (a common medical procedure for women over 40). The degree of seclusion that a woman must observe during her idda depends upon the community and class she is from. It can range from complete seclusion for the entire period to being able to work very soon. Seclusion requirements are more likely to be overlooked when a widow has minor children to support. Widows receive life-long maintenance if they remain with their in-laws, and such an arrangement presumes that she will not claim her share of the deceased husband's property.

In Swat, NWFP, men may also observe idda and not remarry for 1 year after being widowed.

Philippines: The widow stays in the matrimonial home and is maintained by the husband's family if she is not working.

Senegal: Women are not aware of the legal obligation to observe a 300 day long waiting period and only observe the idda required under custom and Muslim laws (3 months after divorce, or 4 months and 10 days after widowhood). If they are pregnant and remarry after this shorter period, they may encounter problems because the law then assumes that the previous husband did not father the child.

Sri Lanka: There is confusion among Quazis concerning what idda requires: does it require only that a woman not remarry or does it also require that she remain in seclusion and observe customary practices (e.g., wearing white clothes)? If a woman does not follow community rules concerning idda, she may not be able to recover idda maintenance. Most women do not observe seclusion on divorce, particularly educated middle class women, who may refuse to stop working. In some areas, lower class women may also refuse to observe idda. For widows, there is no strict observation amongst the urban poor of the 4 months 10 days period; idda is more strictly observed by older women.

Sudan: Traditionally, women who are observing idda are expected to remain confined to their homes; often they are expected to stay in the room where they start their idda. Customarily, idda is part of the traditional mourning practices, according to which women are supposed to sleep on only a white unrefined cotton cloth, refrain from any traditional beautification practices (in some cases this includes not using soaps when showering), and not listen to the radio or watch television. Although, not reflected in the Muslim Personal Law Act, there is a religious fatwa used by sheiks that gives a woman permission to work during idda if she is the family breadwinner. The conditions of this fatwa are that there should be no other way to support the family and that the woman should be at home before sunset. Despite this fatwa, very few women are willing to work or continue working during the idda period. Often other female relatives will take over a widow's domestic responsibilities during the idda period.

10b MATTERS RELATED TO DISSOLUTION OF MARRIAGE: FINANCIAL RIGHTS AND SETTLEMENTS

introduction

Divorce involves a tangle of personal and legal ties that need to be rearranged, if not severed, so that spouses may continue their lives independently of each other. This includes a redistribution of the control and ownership of the matrimonial home and other assets, as well agreements concerning the maintenance of children. Muslim laws introduce two further elements to divorce. The first is that of mahr, which is an essential element of Muslim marriage. Issues relating to mahr on dissolution of marriage include the payment of unpaid mahr by the husband, or the possible return of mahr to the husband, or the foregoing of unpaid mahr by the wife. What happens to the mahr will depend on the circumstances of the divorce and the specific laws under which the dissolution takes place (see Khul', p.273). The second issue is that of mata'a, which is variously interpreted as either a consolatory gift or an opening of a door to the long-term maintenance of a divorced woman. In Iran, women may in addition claim 'wages for housework' (see p.165).

It should be noted that none of these issues (namely mahr, mata'a, maintenance during idda, alimony, and property rights on divorce), exist in a vacuum. The precise nature of what a divorced wife can receive and recover on dissolution depends not only on the form of dissolution but also on the form of her marriage (oral or written, and under which laws) and the local provisions based on Muslim, customary, and other laws. In some systems, customary and Muslim laws regarding financial rights on dissolution are incorporated into or accessed through civil laws applicable to all citizens.

Monies paid to a woman during her waiting period are considered part of the maintenance due to her as a wife (or nafaqa, under Muslim laws). This is not a form of alimony, nor is it technically correct to call this 'post-divorce maintenance.' However, since it is a financial issue that is raised following the dissolution of a marriage, maintenance during the waiting period is discussed here.

Alimony refers to the financial maintenance of a divorced wife, and alimony provisions are derived from European laws. The concept of alimony is based upon the premise that women cannot hold property autonomously and depend on men to provide them with maintenance. Thus, a divorced husband is released from his responsibility to maintain his former wife only after she has remarried. In the interim she receives alimony.

Muslim laws (based upon the Qur'anic verse 2:241) require that a divorced woman receive mata'a from her husband following talaq, talaq tafwid or ta'liq, or following faskh and tafriq, under certain circumstances. Mata'a is a form of compensation that in Tunisia may be paid in monthly installments, or as a single payment, or in the form of property. Mata'a may be interpreted to include any of these payments or a combination of them, and its payment effectively allows a divorced woman to receive maintenance beyond the waiting period. However, laws may restrict or eliminate mata'a payments by awarding only lump sums (Sri Lanka) or by refusing to recognize mata'a at all (Nigeria, Pakistan).

Even where laws envisage generous financial settlements on the dissolution of a marriage, such settlements are useless if the law does not facilitate actual recovery. Women can benefit from systems that require that all settlements and related issues be resolved during divorce proceedings (Fiji, Iran, Malaysia, Sri Lanka, Tunisia). Laws in Iran, which make the actual payment of financial settlements a condition to the final decree of divorce, are particularly beneficial to women following talaq or faskh.

However, such requirements can burden women who are initiating khul' or being divorced according to a judgment that labels them as being 'at fault.' Husbands can also use the settlement process as an opportunity to delay proceedings.

For women, provisions regarding interim maintenance and other interim arrangements can be just as important as those that govern the long-term outcome of proceedings. Laws in Egypt, Indonesia, Malaysia, Pakistan, and Senegal provide for such interim arrangements while laws in Bangladesh do not.

Finally, where women from Muslim communities are subject to laws different to those governing women of other communities (India, Sri Lanka), it is important to note whether or not this different legal position places them at a comparative disadvantage. For example, under the General Law in Sri Lanka, the court has wide discretion to award a divorced woman an annual sum, a monthly sum, a lump sum, and/or a settlement of property (S.615 of the Civil Procedure Code No.2 of 1899 as amended by Law No. 20 of 1977). On the other hand, the Muslim Marriages and Divorce Act, 1951 only provides for awards of maintenance during idda or until the divorce is registered.

maintenance during the waiting period

In all systems where the law requires a waiting period following the dissolution of a marriage (whether based on Muslim laws or other sources), the man is responsible for maintaining the woman during this period. However, if the woman has initiated the divorce, or she is found to be 'at fault,' or she engages in a subsequent sexual relationship; her right to maintenance during this period may be lost. However, where a husband alleges his divorced wife's immorality in a mala fide attempt to escape his maintenance obligations, the courts may not relieve him of his obligation (Pakistan).

Systems that do not require a waiting period (Fiji, marriages under the Special Marriages Act in India, the Civil Marriage Act in Gambia, and the Matrimonial Causes Act in Nigeria) instead recognize the possibility of alimony once the decree is final.

The main problem that women face regarding maintenance during the waiting period is uncertainty over the precise length of time that they will be entitled to receive maintenance. This uncertainty stems from a lack of clarity concerning the precise point in the divorce process at which the waiting period begins (see Idda and The Waiting Period, p.302). Generally, such problems are eliminated in systems where the entire divorce procedure must take place through the courts (Senegal, Indonesia, Tunisia, Turkey) because the date of the decree establishes the date of the waiting period. In systems that recognize irrevocable, talaq bid'a (triple talaq), idda is still required. However, it is a popular misperception in such systems that since this form of talaq is irrevocable/immediately effective, the husband's responsibilities towards his wife (including maintenance) are over at the moment that the talaq is pronounced (India, Nigeria although she may remain in the marital home). Avoidance of having to pay idda maintenance is one of the main reasons men continue to support of the unjust practice of talaq bid'a.

Systems differ over the effect of pregnancy on maintenance rights during the waiting period. In some (Bangladesh, Pakistan) maintenance continues for 90 days or until delivery, 'whichever is later.' In the Philippines and the Sudan, maintenance can be extended for up to two years if the divorced wife breastfeeds a child from the marriage. However, in most systems the waiting period (and thereby maintenance) automatically ceases on delivery. Such provisions reflect a narrow view of wives as childbearing vessels. 'Delivery' may be more widely interpreted to include the lying-in period after the birth or more narrowly interpreted to mean only the actual birth. The interpretation of such terms clearly affects the length of time during which a wife is entitled to maintenance.

Regardless of how generous or lean a maintenance award may be, women often encounter problems with recovery and enforcement (see Maintenance, p.219). These problems are compounded by social attitudes that condone a husband's non-payment of maintenance to divorced wives.

the right to remain in the marital home

Given that the marital home is usually owned or leased in the husband's name, it is clearly option-giving if women have a legally protected right to remain there during the waiting period. Such a right prevents divorced women from facing immediate economic hardship and homelessness. While in Bangladesh, Fiji, and Pakistan, the law is silent concerning a divorced woman's right to accommodation; laws in Egypt, Morocco, Malaysia, and Algeria provide specifically for such a wife's accommodation. In Nigeria, divorced wives have clear rights to remain in the marital home, but they almost never do so. However, accommodation arrangements are not part of final divorce settlements, and they may be revoked if a woman re-marries or her behavior is deemed morally improper (Algeria, Malaysia). In some systems the right to accommodation does not give a woman any rights to the matrimonial home (Algeria), or such rights end at the conclusion of the idda period (Malaysia).

However, where remaining in the marital home is an obligation rather than a choice and where maintenance is only available while a woman remains in the marital home, such provisions are not option-giving.

In Morocco, for example, the wife must either live with relatives who have been nominated by the husband or in a 'safe house' ordered by the judge until the divorce is finalized. If she refuses to do so, she loses her right to accommodation. Moreover, such accommodation is the only form of maintenance envisaged by the law.

In many communities, women cannot remain in the matrimonial home during the waiting period. Practical considerations have led to three exceptions where a woman may retain some access to the matrimonial home. These include: where the couple agree to the divorced wife remaining in the matrimonial home (Philippines), where a woman has sons who give her access to the marital land (Gambia), or where circumstances force the divorced spouses to continue to reside together in the marital apartment (Central Asian Republics). Since these arrangements are usually informal, they depend on the good will of individuals and societal sanction. Because both of these may fluctuate, women remain vulnerable when they depend on informal accommodation arrangements.

A Steady Slide Backwards for Yemeni Women

In Socialist South Yemen, a civil law bill was passed in 1978 that awarded the marital home to the woman on divorce if there were children from the marriage, even if she initiated the divorce. The subsequent steep rise in divorce led to a revision of the article giving the courts more scope for deciding such matters based on the facts of the case— in other words, reintroducing customary notions of 'fault.'

The reformed Article 30(a) of the civil code stated that where the husband was at fault, the court could order 'proper compensation' for a period not to exceed 1 year. If the wife caused the demise of the marriage, the compensation was not to exceed the amount of the mahr. The centralized state also provided small amounts of maintenance for destitute divorcees.

Under the 1992 Personal Status Law that was introduced after reunification, a divorced wife can receive compensation worth up to one year's maintenance only if she has been divorced arbitrarily and suffers distress as a result. Additionally, the husband's circumstances are taken into account when making any such award. Moreover, maintenance during idda is only due if the woman remains 'obedient' and if the talaq was revocable.

alimony

In systems not based on Muslim laws, courts may or may not order maintenance or alimony beyond the waiting period. Indeed, they may not order any maintenance at all. Where maintenance is awarded, such awards are generally conditional upon a woman's proper behavior and her lack of responsibility for the divorce; an assessment of either of these conditions can be highly subjective.

Although the Fiji courts are empowered to provide and enforce maintenance orders without consideration of a woman's sexual activity, they rarely do so because of social attitudes.

In most cases, maintenance awards are inadequate (Turkey, Central Asian Republics), and enforcement is difficult. The new Turkish Civil Code has attempted to make access easier for women by requiring alimony cases to be heard by the court of the area where the party claiming alimony is domiciled, not by the court of the area of the marital home.

mahr

In systems based on Muslim laws, a wife can recover unpaid mahr (whether prompt or deferred) following talaq, talaq tafwid, or ta'liq. Usually, she can also recover her mahr following a divorce under most grounds of tafriq or faskh. Obviously, wherever communities practice the full payment of mahr at the time of marriage, this avoids the wife having to worry about recovery on dissolution (see Mahr, p.179). However, in some systems there is a misperception that the woman is obliged to return the mahr, even if the husband initiates the divorce (Gambia).

In some communities, there may be a considerable lapse of time between the date when the marriage is contracted and the actual wedding ceremony, and the wife does not begin living with the husband (implying consummation) until after this ceremony (Pakistan, Sudan). If divorce takes place before the social ceremony in such systems, half the mahr is recoverable. This provision concerning mahr is codified in certain systems—notably, Algeria, Morocco, and Tunisia.

Although clear laws facilitate a woman's recovery of mahr after divorce, even silent or unclear laws generally recognize a divorced woman's right to recover her mahr. Accordingly, in most systems based on Muslim laws, mahr is recoverable through the courts as mahr ul mithl (proper dower), even if the amount has not been specified in the marriage contract.

Mahr may not be recoverable at all where laws are based on sources other than Muslim laws and consequently do not recognize mahr (Turkey).

Mahr also may be unrecoverable following a divorce that was granted on the grounds of 'discord and strife'/incompatibility (Indonesia, Malaysia, Palestinian communities in Israel, Senegal), especially if the court judges the wife to be 'at fault.' In a divorce by khul', unpaid mahr is not recoverable; and depending upon the circumstances of the case and the court's appreciation of the issues, a woman may even be required to return or surrender that portion of her mahr that has already been paid to her.

Additionally, proving the amount of mahr that has already been received by the wife (and therefore the amount that remains unpaid and due to the wife) can be problematic. The sum of mahr reflected on the marriage registration form may differ from the amount actually agreed upon by the parties or paid to the woman (Malaysia, Pakistan, Sri Lanka, Sudan). In Sudan a lower amount may be written to avoid registration fees that are calculated on the basis of the mahr, while in Pakistan a higher amount may be written in the nikahnama for the purposes of public prestige.

Thus, on divorce women may not be able to prove the whole sum that remains unpaid. Some systems place the burden of proving mahr balances on the woman. Often these systems also accept the husband's word if the wife is unable to provide proof (Egypt, Morocco). Whereas Egyptian laws will not accept the husband's claims if he claims a mahr amount that clearly conflicts with his wife's status, Morocco's laws place no such conditions on accepting a husband's word. In contrast, case law in Pakistan places the burden of proving the amount and payment of mahr on the husband.

In Sri Lanka, only a Quazi may initiate recovery of unpaid mahr on behalf of a divorced woman. In practice, women are not advised that they can claim unpaid mahr, and Quazis often do not initiate the recovery of this mahr for them.

In some systems, laws place a time limit on the recovery of mahr after a divorce or after the death of a husband (3 years in Bangladesh, India, Pakistan, and Sri Lanka). In the case of Sri Lanka, it is interesting to note that there is no such time limit in relation to recovery of the customary kaikuli.

In terms of practices, if women have a substantial mahr, they sometimes arrange not to claim it in exchange for retaining custody of their children (Pakistan, Iran). But a substantial mahr can have its drawbacks and actually may obstruct divorce. For example, among some Pukhtuns in Pakistan, immovable property is transferred into the bride's name as deferred mahr in the marriage contract. Since social status among the Pukhtun is determined by control of women and land, and since divorce results in the loss of both; divorce is made nearly impossible by social constraints. At best, a wife may hope to separate from her husband. In other communities, husbands may resort to minor but constant cruelty in an effort to force their wives to leave the marital home. If a wife leaves under such circumstances and then cannot prove the grounds for dissolution, she cannot claim her mahr.

Following protests by women, particularly protests against the injustice of wives being discarded by talaq after many years of marriage, the courts in Iran have begun to determine the amount of mahr that is due on divorce by calculating the effect of inflation on the original amount written in the contract. However, enforcement is problematic because men continue to evade registering their divorces. A husband who effects an unregistered divorce is only liable to a fine while the talaq itself remains valid.

mata'a

Muslim laws require that a husband pay a wife mata'a following a divorce that he initiated or following a divorce in which the wife is not 'at fault.' Mata'a is distinct from both the maintenance provided during the waiting period and mahr, and it is unrelated to the division of the matrimonial assets.

Not all systems codify mata'a. As a result there is confusion regarding whether or not paying it is obligatory, the amount and circumstances in which it should be paid, and what forms are permissible (lump sum or property settlement, or monthly payments). Despite a Qur'anic basis for the payment of mata'a, systems based on Muslim laws do not always provide a woman with the right to claim mata'a (Malaysia, Nigeria, Pakistan). In Nigeria, mata'a is dismissed as a Christian practice because of its similarities to alimony. In other contexts, courts and/or qazis may have the power to order the payment of mata'a, but they choose to exercise this power infrequently (Sri Lanka).

Where legislation provides for mata'a, it often states that the amount of mata'a shall be determined by the husband's financial means and the wife's circumstances (Morocco). Unfortunately, women often cannot provide proof of their husbands' financial resources, so husbands escape this obligation. Placing such a burden of proof on a woman who most likely has no access to the matrimonial home and no immediate or direct access to documents that would assist her claim clearly impedes her from successfully claiming mata'a.

Each woman's individual circumstances will determine which form of mata'a is best for her (lump sum, property settlement, or monthly payments), but laws which allow flexibility in this regard are more option-giving. It is equally beneficial if laws clarify that mata'a is a debt against a deceased husband's estate.

Some argue that mata'a opens a door to the long-term maintenance of a divorced wife. Indeed, such laws as those in Tunisia that allow mata'a to be paid in monthly installments for an indefinite amount of time appear to support such an argument. However, such long-term maintenance should not be confused with idda maintenance that has been extended beyond the usual three months or extended beyond the delivery of a child (Egypt, Philippines, Sudan). Where mata'a installments are conditional upon the divorced wife not remarrying or not having subsequent sexual relationships, mata'a becomes far closer to the European concept of alimony, with its assumption of women's economic dependence on men. Thus, laws that permit monthly installments of mata'a may facilitate a husband's continued control over his divorced wife. In such a case, mata'a no longer remains purely a consolatory payment by the husband to the wife for the divorce.

division of matrimonial assets on divorce

Many systems recognize the right of women to claim a share of matrimonial assets.

Division of property on divorce may be determined by courts acting on their own discretion (Central Asian Republics, Fiji, Gambia, Malaysia, Singapore, Tanzania, Yemen) with or without guidelines being provided in the statute. Unusually, Malaysian law allows for the division of all assets, including those acquired by either spouse individually.

In other systems, assets are divided according to the spouses' chosen matrimonial property regimes (communal/joint, or separate – see Glossary) (Cameroon, Iran, Philippines, Senegal). Whether or not this is option-giving for a woman will depend upon the space for her to negotiate a regime to her benefit and the individual circumstances of the couple.

Generally, marital assets are divided inequitably, with women receiving the smaller share. Such inequitable distribution results, in part, from the under-valuing of women's contributions in at least two distinct ways. Firstly, some systems link division of marital property with 'fault' rather than the comparative contribution of each spouse (Iran), and if the wife is judged to be responsible for the divorce, she may not be given her share. Already the other financial settlements possible on divorce (recovery or surrender of mahr, waiting period maintenance, alimony and mata'a) are conditional to a woman's 'proper behaviour.' By additionally treating the division of marital property conditionally, systems fail to recognize a woman's right to her share of matrimonial assets as absolute and presume that only a man's right to such property is absolute.

Secondly, when dividing marital assets, courts and others tend to focus on women's direct financial contributions through wages and to undervalue or fail to recognize altogether their contributions through unpaid domestic labour. In Fiji, for example, unemployed wives are not recognized as having contributed to the marriage, and Senegal's Code de la Famille only envisages a woman's ownership of assets that she acquired through the exercise of a paid profession. In such systems, husbands benefit from a wife's contribution of her labor and time to the family and any family business, yet these benefits are given no value when a marriage ends. In Malaysia, even assets acquired individually by one party may be divided, as long as the party who actually purchased the asset receives a greater share. Though this may seem just and equitable in theory, it leaves room for an insensitive judge to undervalue a woman's contribution and accordingly award her with very little.

However, a woman's household and familial efforts are sometimes taken into account (Iran, Malaysia, Singapore). Since 1993, courts in Iran have been able to require a divorcing husband to pay wages to his wife for the housework she has contributed to the marital union, provided she is not found to be at fault in the divorce. In 1995 it was made compulsory for divorcing husbands to pay the determined wages for housework along with the wife's other rights, such as mahr and nafaqa, before the divorce could be registered. In Tanzania in a case involving a Muslim couple, domestic chores were regarded as a contribution towards the acquisition of property (Bi Hawa Mohamed v Ally Sefu Civil Appeal No. 9 of 1983, Dar es Salaarn Registry, unreported).

Opting for a joint property regime (where all marital assets are considered to belong to the spouses equally) does not necessarily solve a woman's problems, especially where polygyny is practiced. Most often, social attitudes dictate that neither party applies for the division of the joint estate However, since most often it is the husband who remains in the marital home and controls the assets, this lack of division usually results in the wife leaving the marital home with nothing. Also, courts do not always divide joint property equally on divorce, and a woman may have problems proving her contribution towards a property's acquisition (Cameroon, Senegal).

Since women generally return to their natal homes after separation or divorce, they usually lose their share of the matrimonial property as it falls to the husband or his family's control (Central Asian Republics). This tendency for property to remain with the husband and his family can make the enforcement of a court settlement that favors the wife difficult.

Generally, the concept of dividing marital property is not socially recognized in South Asia. Before a recent amendment in Pakistan's Family Court's Act, such division had not been incorporated in the procedural laws, which were largely the same in Bangladesh and in Pakistan. In Bangladesh women's organizations have proposed legal reforms that would require the assets that had been acquired during a marriage to be divided equally between the two spouses on the dissolution of the marriage. Conservative politico-religious groups have strongly resisted these proposals and even demanded a public apology from those proposing the reforms. In Nigeria there is also no concept of dividing marital property on the dissolution of marriages under Muslim laws. This may be partly because assets acquired during the marriage are usually demarcated as belonging to either the wife or the husband. Any attempt to suggest that the wife may deserve a share in the husband's property or in assets that have not been clearly demarcated as hers is dismissed as a 'Christian' and/or 'Western' imposition, which, in any case, would be unfair to co-wives in the context of polygyny.

recovery of assets brought into the marriage

Laws that recognize a wife's absolute ownership of those customary goods and assets that she brought into her marriage (e.g., customary dowry, kaikuli, pemberian) can facilitate her recovery of these assets on divorce. (This is of course in addition to other moveable and immoveable assets she may have already owned). However, because the giving of such customary goods and assets is financially and socially burdensome, some systems have sought to either ban them or limit the value of them (Bangladesh, Central Asian Republics, Pakistan). These laws have failed to control such practices, and instead they often obstruct a wife's recovery of the full amount on divorce. Courts in Pakistan have recognized that husbands attempt to misuse this legislation, and the courts have insisted that they (husbands) return the full dowry (jehez), even if the value was above the legal limit.

Generally, the recovery of the assets brought into a marriage is negotiated outside the courts. In many communities it is socially accepted that what the wife brings into the marriage (whether it be pots and pans or a car) is hers to keep on divorce. However, in other communities the actual recovery of such goods may be determined by the relative strength of the respective families and the willingness of the woman's family to support her claim.

linking financial settlements to registration of divorce

Claims for the recovery of mahr and mata'a (if recognized), for the division of matrimonial property, and for settlements regarding custody and maintenance may be handled as part of the divorce proceedings (Fiji, Iran, Malaysia, Tunisia), or they may have to be made separately through other legal actions. Both approaches have advantages and disadvantages for women.

Instituting separate actions for divorce and financial settlements is expensive and complex and adds to the emotional cost of dissolution. These suits may be further complicated where matrimonial property and custody are not covered by family laws and thus require a separate suit. Since women do not always have familial or societal support for legal action, they may end up simply suing for divorce and abandoning other claims. Some Quazis in Sri Lanka have informally attempted to address this. The Muslim Marriage and Divorce Act 1951, requires Quazis to recover only mahr before the registration of talaq. But since mahr in Sri Lanka is often minimal, this offers women little protection. To address this, some Quazis also delay the registration process until mata'a has been paid and kaikuli returned; such delays offer women greater financial security.

Provisions which require all matters related to divorce to be settled together apparently aim at removing the burden of separate suits and ensuring that each party's rights have been addressed, with no 'loose ends' remaining. Indeed in Iran, it was women's pressure that brought about the 1995 amendment that requires husbands to settle all financial claims before a divorce can be registered.

But where a woman's claim for matrimonial property is ancillary to divorce proceedings, she stands to lose all claims to the matrimonial property if her suit fails. A woman's losses can be made even greater in systems like Fiji's where the divorcing woman does not even have the right to her personal belongings if she has moved out of the matrimonial home. Thus, if her suit for divorce fails, she loses everything.

Alternatively, the divorce may be withheld or the proceedings delayed simply because the husband is not willing to meet the obligations that are ancillary to the granting of a divorce. By giving the husband the power to drag out the divorce process, such systems give him considerable leverage to press his wife into surrendering her financial claims, simply to end the painful proceedings.

With these various considerations in mind, we would say that the more option-giving systems are those that allow the courts flexibility to approach each case on its own merits and that encourage gender sensitivity in judges.

Getting a Fair Share: Muslim Women in Singapore

In addition to idda maintenance, mata'a and the recovery of mahr, women married under Muslim laws in Singapore (as women of other communities in the country) are frequently able to recover a substantial share of matrimonial assets, even when they have not contributed to the family's income through paid employment.

Following amendments to the Administration of Muslim Law Act 1966 (no. 27/66) in 1999, the definition of matrimonial assets was clarified and the factors that the courts could take into account while deciding the division of these assets was also elaborated.

With the 1999 Amendments, the factors that are to be taken into account are (Section 52(8)(a) ADMLA):

(a) the extent of contribution made by each party in money, property or work towards acquiring, improving or maintaining the property.

(b) Any debt owing or obligation incurred or undertaken by either party for their joint benefit or for the benefit of any child of the marriage.

(c) The needs of the children, if any.

(d) The extent of contributions made by each party to the welfare of the family, including looking after the home or caring for the family or any aged or infirm relative or dependent of either party.

(e) Any agreement between the parties with respect to the ownership and division of the property made in contemplation of divorce.

(f) Any period of rent free occupation or other benefit enjoyed by one party in the matrimonial home to the exclusion of the other party.

(g) The giving of assistance or support by one party to the other party (whether or not of a material kind) including the giving of assistance or support which aids the other party in the carrying on of his or her occupation or business.

(h) The income, earning capacity, property and other financial resources which each of the parties has or is likely to have in the foreseeable future.

(i) The financial needs, obligations and responsibilities which each of the parties has or is likely to have in the foreseeable future.

(j) The standard of living enjoyed by the family before the breakdown of the marriage.

(k) The age of each party and the duration of the marriage.

(l) Any physical or mental disability of either of the parties the value to either of the parties of any benefit (such as a pension) which, by reason of the dissolution of the marriage, that party will lose the chance of acquiring.

The 1999 Amendment defines matrimonial assets as (Section 52(14) DMLA):

(a) any asset acquired before the marriage by one party or both parties to the marriage which had been substantially improved during the marriage by the other party or by both parties to the marriage.

(b) Any asset of any nature acquired during the marriage by one party or both parties to the marriage.

However, this does not include any asset (not being the matrimonial home) that has been acquired by one party at any time by gift or inheritance and that has not been substantially improved during the marriage by the other party or by both parties to the marriage.

NOTES

LAWS: Matters Related to Dissolution - Mahr and Mata'a

Criteria

☺ More option-giving are those laws which:

- Provide for the recovery of mahr and mata'a; and
- Do not specify a maximum time-limit or particular form of mata'a; or
- Recognize the possibility of damages to be paid by the party at 'fault' (systems not based on Muslim laws).

😐 The middle ground is occupied by those laws which:

- Provide for the recovery of mahr and mata'a; but
- Place limitations on the form and/or amount of mata'a, or make it only available following talaq.

☹ Less option-giving are those laws which:

- Provide for the recovery of mahr; but
- Do not recognize the concept of mata'a.

☺ **Recovery of mahr and compensatory settlements are recognized in law**

Tunisia: Under A. 31 of the CSP, the court determines the financial compensation the parties shall owe each other in the event of divorce. Courts interpret this to mean that if a woman is 'wrongfully' divorced, she may be awarded mata'a in the form of a lump sum, a property transfer or monthly installments. Payment of monthly installments may be increased or decreased and end on death of the husband, the wife's remarriage, or at any time that the wife ceases to require maintenance. The amount may be determined by the standard of living that the wife was accustomed to. Under A. 32, even if not requested, the judge is to rule on the divorce and all related matters including custody, maintenance, and housing and visitation rights.

Malaysia: Under S. 56 and 57 of the IFLA, a woman divorced 'without just cause' may apply for mata'a, and she retains her right to mas kahwin (mahr). The amount of mata'a is to be fair and just. Under S. 47(1)(f), the spouses are to inform the court of any agreement or demands regarding maintenance and accommodation for the wife and children, custody and division of marital assets. Under S. 47(11), the conciliatory committee appends its recommendations regarding matters related to the divorce to the non-reconciliation certificate.

Iran: Unpaid mahr is recoverable on divorce, provided that the woman is not held to be at fault. If the mahr was not stipulated, under A. 1091 of the CC, mahr ul mithl will be recoverable. In 1993 'wages for housework' (ujjat ul mithl) was confirmed in the law for women who were not at fault for the divorce. The court fixes the amount based on the period of time the couple co-habited, the wife's activities, and the husband's financial situation. Where the husband has no money, the woman will not be paid any 'wages for housework.' Following an amendment in 1995, all financial matters related to divorce must be settled before the divorce can be registered.

Gambia (marriages under Muslim laws): Mahr is not to be returned by the woman on divorce, and the Qur'anic precept that a husband must give his divorced wife a suitable gift on divorce is applied.

Laws not based on Muslim laws

Turkey: Under A. 174 of the CC, the party least at fault and who has suffered injury to their actual or potential interests due to the divorce can claim reasonable compensation, which can be paid monthly or in a single payment. Under A. 176, lump sum damages can also be claimed for infringement of personality rights.

Senegal: Both spouses are liable to pay damages to the injured party in divorce, as assessed by the court.

Recovery of mahr and compensatory settlements are recognized in law; mata'a is restricted in form and/or amount

Egypt: If the couples divorce on the grounds of harm, the arbiters appointed by the court fix any compensation due to each other as part of the proceedings. Under A. 18(2) of the 1920 law on Personal Status as amended by Law No. 100 of 1985, a woman divorced by talaq or without fault is entitled to mata'a. However, mata'a is envisaged as extended maintenance rather than a lump sum. It as at least two years' maintenance, with the amount and duration being determined by taking into consideration the husband's wealth, the circumstances of the divorce, and the length of the marriage.

Sudan: Provided the divorce was not based on some physical defect in the wife, on the grounds of the husband's poverty, on the grounds of non-maintenance, or through khul', mata'a is to be decided by the judge on the basis of the husband's means for a maximum of six months' maintenance.

Recovery of mahr is recognized; mata'a only available on talaq

Algeria: A. 14 of the CF governs the wife's right to mahr. Under A 52, the woman shall be awarded damages for harm if the judge considers the husband to have abused his right of talaq.

Morocco: A. 20 and 22 of the Moudawana governs the woman's right to mahr. Under A. 60, compensation from the husband in accordance with his means and the wife's circumstances is obligatory in the event of talaq. Compensation in the event of fault-based dissolution is not clear and recovery of mahr and mata'a are separate to any divorce proceedings.

Yemen: A. 33-39 of the LPS recognizes the wife's right to mahr and mahr ul mithl where mahr was not specified. Under A. 71, the judge may award mata'a only in the event of a talaq that causes a wife distress and hardship. The amount is determined in accordance with the husband's means, with a maximum value equivalent to up to 1 year's maintenance for a woman of her status.

Recovery of mahr is recognized; mata'a is not recognized in law

Sri Lanka: Under Rule 4, Schedule 2 of the MMDA, when a husband divorces his wife, the Quazi has the duty to initiate the recovery of unpaid mahr, even if the wife does not demand such recovery. Under S. 47(1), the Quazi determines whether or not and how much mahr should be paid. Under S. 39, the woman can only claim mahr within three years after the dissolution of the marriage. Mata'a is not mentioned in the MMDA.

Bangladesh & Pakistan: Mahr may be recovered after a divorce by talaq or talaq tafwid, or after divorce under the DMMA (either through a separate suit or as part of the dissolution suit through the Family Courts). If no mahr or only part of it was given in compensation for a khul', the wife may still recover the remaining amount. If the amount of mahr was not specified in the marriage contract, the court will determine the mahr ul mithl. Mahr is considered to be covered by the colonial Limitations Act 1908, whereby an application for recovery must be made within 3 years of divorce or death, or the woman forfeits her right. The husband bears the burden of proving the amount of mahr already paid. Mata'a is not recognized.

Nigeria (marriages under Muslim laws): Mahr is invariably paid in full at the time of marriage and remains with the woman on divorce by talaq or where the husband breaches the terms of the marriage. Mata'a is not recognized as a concept.

LAWS: Maintenance During the Waiting Period & Alimony

Criteria

While it may be option-giving for some women for the period of post-divorce maintenance to be extended beyond the waiting period or idda, as discussed in the introduction to this section and the chapter on Maintenance, p.217, the conceptualization of maintenance may reinforce negative gender stereotypes and strengthen a former husband's control over his ex-wife. Moreover, it is difficult to compare the concepts of alimony and idda maintenance. We have therefore decided not to rank these provisions according to more and less option-giving criteria.

NOTE: For the length of the waiting period in which maintenance is due, see The Waiting Period, p.306

Maintenance may extend beyond 3 months/delivery; access to the matrimonial home is recognized

Sudan: Under S. 73 of the MPLA, a divorced woman is entitled to maintenance during idda. The amount is fixed according to the husband's capacity, and the overall payment period should not exceed one year, except when the woman gives birth to a child, in which case she is entitled to a maximum of two years and three months of maintenance starting from the date of the child's birth. The code grants women the right to spend the idda period in the matrimonial home. During this period the woman is to be physically restricted to her residence. Working women undergoing idda are required to be on leave for the specified period.

Laws not based on Muslim laws: alimony available under certain circumstances

Turkey: Under A. 175 of the CC, either party may be liable to pay maintenance to the party who is not at fault and who is left destitute as a result of the divorce. (A previous clause, which made a woman only liable to pay her ex-husband maintenance if she was wealthy, was deleted on the grounds of 'discrimination against men.') The amount is determined by the financial means of the payee and may be paid monthly or in a single payment. A party may be deprived of any mutually agreed upon or court awarded maintenance or material recompense where they: cease to be poor; adopt an immoral lifestyle; live with another person without first being married to them; remarry; or die. Under A. 178, applications for maintenance must be filed within 1 year of the final divorce decree.

Cameroon: The woman may be granted post-divorce maintenance if her husband is the party at fault in the divorce. The court determines the amount of maintenance by taking into account the ex-husband's financial resources and the woman's needs. Payment of maintenance continues as long as the woman remains needy and does not remarry.

Fiji: The 'clean break' principle is used in divorce. Therefore, courts often prefer payment of a lump sum of maintenance to periodical payments. Payment of maintenance ends on admission or proof of a wife's adultery, the former wife's remarriage, death of the husband, or the husband's incapacity to pay.

Nigeria (marriages under the MCA): Either spouse may be liable to pay the other alimony depending upon their relative economic strength.

Senegal: Under A. 178 of the CF, the court may award maintenance for a maximum 300 days (equivalent to the waiting period) if the divorce was initiated by the husband due to incompatibility or due to the wife's grave and incurable illness. The amount may be raised or lowered according to the parties' circumstances. If reconciliation efforts fail during divorce, the judge may make interim orders for custody, maintenance and division of marital property.

Laws based on Muslim laws: maintenance may continue beyond idda, closer to concept of alimony

Tunisia: In addition to idda maintenance, if the woman is not at fault for the divorce, compensation may be in the form of monthly payments conceptually close to extended maintenance (see p.217).

Indonesia: Under A. 41(c) of the MA, either party may be obliged by a court to pay maintenance to the other party.

Philippines: Under A. 67 of the CMPL, idda maintenance may extend to two years after the birth of a child, provided the woman continues to breastfeed and depending upon judicial discretion. Maintenance may be paid daily, weekly, or monthly. Under A. 69, if the payee dies, his or her heirs cannot claim back any maintenance that has already been paid. Under A. 70 payment of maintenance ceases on the death of the recipient; where the payee is the woman and she can no longer afford to support her divorced husband without neglecting her own and her family's needs (but needy husbands are still obliged to maintain their wives); where the recipient commits any act which, under Muslim law, disqualifies them from inheritance or support.

Egypt: A divorced woman is entitled to nafaqa for up to 1 year; the amount of these payments shall be based on the ex-husband's capacity but shall not be less than is needed to meet the woman's needs. Interim maintenance orders are to be passed within 2 weeks of the wife's claim, the amount of which will be deducted from the final amount of maintenance due. A woman who is not found to be at fault is entitled to compensation for at least 2 years. This compensation shall be in addition to idda maintenance and in the form of monthly payments; accordingly, such payment is conceptually similar to extended maintenance (see p.217).

Maintenance is limited to idda

Bangladesh & Pakistan: A divorced woman is only entitled to maintenance during the idda period. This period begins either on the date on which the Union Council is notified of the talaq or on the date when it receives a court decree for dissolution and extends until either 90 days have passed, or, in the case that the wife is pregnant, until the delivery of the baby, which ever is later. The law does not condition a divorced woman's right to maintenance on her behaviour. However, a woman may lose her right to idda maintenance if this was part of the court's order for a khul' decree.

Pakistan: Through an amendment to the Family Courts Act, which came into effect in 2002, the courts may order interim maintenance at any stage in a maintenance case or as part of a suit for dissolution.

Sri Lanka: Under S. 47(1)(d) of the MMDA, maintenance may be claimed only through the Quazi courts until the registration of a divorce, or during idda. Under S. 47(1)(g), such maintenance may include lying-in expenses. Women married under the MMDA may not access the General Law, which provides for alimony. The law does not condition a divorced woman's right to maintenance on her behaviour.

Iran: A divorced woman's right to maintenance is limited to the idda period and the amount of this maintenance must be settled before the divorce can be registered. A woman who is at fault or nushuz is usually denied idda maintenance.

Algeria: Under A. 61 of the CF, a divorced woman has the right to remain in the marital home, provided that moral impropriety on her part is not proved. She also has the right to maintenance during the waiting period. The amount of maintenance to be paid is based on the circumstances of the spouses and their conditions of life. If the marital home is the sole residence, it is excluded from the above provisions.

Malaysia: Under S. 65(1) of the IFLA, maintenance is paid to a woman until the expiry of her idda; however a court declaration that she is nushuz terminates maintenance rights. S. 70 provides for interim maintenance which may be deducted from any final maintenance award as long as the amount received by the woman after deductions is sufficient for her basic needs. Under S. 65(2), a woman's right to her pemberian ceases on her remarriage, on her living with someone in an adulterous relationship, or until such date as agreed.

Morocco: Under A. 59 of the Moudawana, where divorce proceedings have been initiated, and the spouses cannot continue to cohabit, the husband must nominate some of his relatives with whom the wife can reside until the divorce is finalized. If the wife chooses not to live with any of the relatives nominated by the husband, a judge may order her to stay at a 'safe-house.' In either case, the husband must maintain his wife until the divorce is finalized. If the wife retains custody of any children, the former husband must make provision for their accommodation during the period of custody.

Nigeria (marriages under Muslim laws): If a woman is divorced through a revocable talaq, she spends the idda in her husband's house and is entitled to maintenance. If she is irrevocably divorced, she spends the idda in her husband's house but is not entitled to maintenance, unless she is pregnant. In which case, the husband is required to maintain her until she gives birth to the child.

Yemen: Under A. 86 and 87 of the LPS, idda maintenance and accommodation are only due following a revocable talaq, and even then only if the woman remains obedient.

LAWS: Property Settlements on Divorce

Criteria

☺ More option-giving are those laws which:

- Provide for the division of matrimonial assets on dissolution, taking into account women's unpaid, domestic labour.

😐 The middle ground is occupied by those laws which:

- Provide for the division of matrimonial assets on dissolution, but do not take into account women's unpaid, domestic labour; or
- Require or allow couples to choose a matrimonial property regime at the time of marriage.

☹ Less option-giving are those laws which:

- Do not provide for the division of matrimonial property on dissolution; or
- Are silent regarding the division of marital property.

☺ Courts can order division of marital property, taking into account women's domestic labour

Central Asian Republics: All marital property acquired by the spouses during the marriage belongs to both parties in equal share and is to be divided upon divorce. Judges have the prerogative to divide property unequally in certain circumstances. For example, if the woman has custody of the children, she will be awarded the family apartment.

Malaysia: Under S. 58 of the IFLA, following divorce the court has power to order the division of assets or the division of the proceeds of the sale of any assets acquired by joint effort of the parties during a marriage. Under S. 58(2), the court must incline toward an equitable division, taking into account: the extent of the contributions made by each party in money, labour, or property toward acquisition of the assets; debts incurred by either party for their joint benefit; and the needs of any minor children of the marriage. Under S. 58(3) and (4), assets acquired by the sole effort of one party to the marriage may also be divided, taking into account: the extent of the contribution to the welfare of the family made by the party who did not acquire the assets and the needs of any minor children of the family. However, the division must be reasonable, and the party by whose efforts assets were acquired must receive a greater proportion. Under S. 58(5) assets to be divided can include assets owned before the marriage by one party but which have been substantially improved during the marriage by either the other party or by the parties' joint effort.

Singapore: Amendments to the ADMLA in 1999 incorporated provisions in the Women's Charter concerning the division of matrimonial assets and which empower the Syariah Courts to take into account a wide variety of factors in the division of matrimonial assets including domestic labour (Section 52(8) and 52(14) of the ADMLA) (see p.318). The amendments have also facilitated recovery of assets by granting the lower courts powers to enforce decrees. Even under previous provisions, case law routinely granted women who made no direct monetary contribution to the family up to 50% of the proceeds of the sale of matrimonial assets (in addition to mata'a and idda maintenance), taking into account the length of the marriage, their domestic contribution and other factors (such as the circumstances of the divorce and the likelihood that mata'a and idda maintenance will be recoverable). Where a wife made an approximately 40% financial contribution to the family income, she was awarded 70% of the net proceeds of the sale of matrimonial assets (Zulkifli B. Abu Bakar v Siti Rohani Bt. Jaafar, Appeal case No. 57 of 1996; Zaiton Bt. Hashim v Salleh Bin Jaafar, Appeal case No. 24 of 1998); where a wife has made little or not direct financial contribution, she has been granted between 33% - 50% of the net proceeds (Asmah Bee Bt Moh'd Din v Selamat Bin Sarkawi, Appeal case No. 11 of 1995; Noor Afisah Bt Omar v Rohaizat Bin Wardi, Appeal Case No. 16A of 1996).

☹ Courts can order division of marital property; women's domestic labour is not taken into account

Fiji: Under S. 86(1) MCA (Cap. 51), the court may order a settlement of property that it considers just and equitable in the circumstances. A claim for marital property is ancillary to divorce proceedings, and if the wife's divorce suit fails then her claim to marital property also fails. However, a woman can place a caveat on the marital home to warn potential buyers of her interest in the property. The caveat applies for a limited period and must be continually renewed. The wife has no right of immediate access to her personal belongings after leaving the matrimonial home. Application of the principle of constructive trust may provide grounds for a wife to obtain a share in the joint property. She must prove that any property that she claims was held in trust by the other spouse and that she contributed to the acquisition of it. Courts tend to grant woman a share in the matrimonial property if she has made a direct financial contribution. Her share may be half of the property where she can prove her contribution or only one third where her contribution cannot be proved. Women who are homemakers have not received any share of matrimonial property.

Gambia (marriages under the CMA): Courts have discretion to make a just and equitable order for the division of assets under the MCA and the Laws of Gambia 1990. Under S. 22 of the MCA, 1986 (Cap 43), the order may include movable and immovable property, and the spouse not maintaining ownership of non-divisible assets may be compensated for their share of such assets through a single payment or multiple installments. Under S. 28, the court may issue a restraining order to prevent one party from disposing of or permitting the disposition of property with the intention of defeating a financial or property settlement. Under S. 2 of the Married Women's Property Act 1885 (Cap 41: 05), the wife can acquire, hold, and dispose of moveable and immovable property at will, whether it be real or personal

Indonesia: Under A. 37, joint property is to be dealt with according to the different laws of Indonesia's various communities. Under Article 42(2), regulation No 9 of 1975, Concerning Implementation of Law of Marriage, applications for interim custody, alimony and for safeguard of spouses' property are heard as part of the same suit.

Pakistan: Under the amended Family Courts Act, which came into effect in 2002, a suit for dissolution may address the recovery of the wife's property and 'any other property of the party to the suit,' which could include any property obtained by the couple during marriage to which the wife contributed. Previously, if there was any such dispute, the wife's only option was to file a separate suit in the civil courts; now the Family Courts can handle such disputes. These provisions have yet to be tested in court, so the question of whether unpaid domestic labour is taken into account is not known. Also, now Family Courts may pass an interim order to preserve and protect any disputed property that may be affected by an eventual decree. Under Pakistan's Dowry and Bridal Gifts (Restriction) Act, 1976, the woman is the sole owner of any dowry. Although the law places limits on the value of dowry, case law permits women to recover, through the Family Courts, dowry in excess of the legal limit. Dowry can be claimed up to three years after the divorce.

Spouses can decide property regime at time of marriage

Iran: The standard marriage contract includes an optional clause stating that wealth accumulated during the marriage will be divided in half on divorce.

Philippines: A. 38 of the CMPL provides that in the absence of any other written agreement between the spouses (either made in the marriage contract or subsequently), the couple shall be governed by a complete separation of property regime. Under A. 41, each spouse retains whatever property they brought in to the marriage, all income from employment or trade, any money inherited during the marriage, any income from their personal property, and nuptial gifts; the wife retains her mahr. Under A. 43, each spouse also retains that household property which is customarily used by that spouse. Couples may choose a regime of absolute community of property, which would mean that on divorce all property brought into the marriage and acquired during the marriage is to be divided equally upon dissolution.

Cameroon: The spouses are to choose the marital property regime as part of the marriage documents: joint, or separate property. Where there is no prenuptial deed the courts assume a joint property regime. Once divorce proceedings have commenced, one of the spouses must apply for the division of the joint estate. In a joint property regime, each spouse is to receive half of the property. In a separate property regime, the parties leave the marriage with whatever assets are in their separate names and their respective share of assets held in both names.

Senegal: The spouses are to choose the marital property regime as part of the marriage documents: joint or separate property or regime dotal (the husband controls all assets given to the wife at the time of marriage which are to be restored to her on dissolution). Where there is no prenuptial deed, the courts assume a separate property regime. However, no matter what the chosen option, under A. 381(3) of the CF, all assets in the husband's main residence are presumed to belong to the husband (whereas each wife is presumed to own the furniture in the house chosen by her husband if this is outside his main residence). Under A. 382, in the absence of proof, a disputed asset 'belongs indivisibly' to both spouses and shall be shared between them on divorce. Under A. 393(2), all personal property (e.g., jewelry) and fixed assets brought into the marriage are excluded from community property. If one of the spouses has a business, a judgment regarding its division following divorce does not come into effect for 3 months from the date it has been legally notified. In the event of divorce through mutual agreement, the judge must also confirm the spouses' consent to the division of assets.

☹ No division of marital property provided in law

Bangladesh: Family laws do not provide for post-divorce property settlements. However, a case may be filed under civil law to recover a woman's share of marital property. S. 3, 4, and 5 of the Dowry Prohibition Act of 1980 make the promising, giving, receiving, and demanding of money or other property to the groom, in consideration of a marriage, a non-bailable offence that is liable to imprisonment and fine.

Sri Lanka: Family laws do not provide for post-divorce property settlements. The MMDA specifically recognizes that kaikuli (in the form of money or movable property) is to be he held in trust by the husband for his wife. The Board of Quazis has ruled that Quazis can inquire into and adjudicate upon a claim for kaikuli only if it is mentioned in the marriage contract. Kaikuli recovered on divorce is to be deposited with the district courts and may only be withdrawn on the Quazi's permission. If Kaikuli is not mentioned in the marriage register, the woman may apply to the District Courts for relief.

Sudan, Yemen: The law is silent on the division of marital property on divorce.

IMPLEMENTATION

The courts expand women's financial rights on divorce

Cameroon: Even if the spouses have not chosen a community property regime, the courts usually order that the property be divided between them and refer the parties to a notary to determine and give effect to the actual division of the property.

Iran: Following pressure from women's groups, the court (either at the request of the wife or at its own discretion) calculates the recoverable mahr according to what it was worth at the time the couple married; this only applies if the mahr has been written out in monetary value and not in gold and real estate. For instance, if at the time that the couple married the sum of mahr could buy 300g of gold, the equivalent sum should be paid at the time of dissolution, rather than the original written amount unadjusted for inflation.

Malaysia: No pronouncement of talaq, order of divorce, or annulment will be registered unless the Chief Registrar is satisfied that final order(s) for custody and maintenance of dependent children, for maintenance and accommodation of the divorced wife, and for her mata'a have been made.

Pakistan: Where life long maintenance for a divorced wife is incorporated as a condition in a marriage contract, the courts recognize the wife's right to such payment. This recognition is based on pre-Independence case law that held that: "the marital rights ended with the divorce, but the contract subsists till the plaintiff dies or breaks it, and so long as the right to maintenance lasts, it cannot be treated as devoid of consideration or opposed to public policy" (Muhammad Muinuddin v Jamal Fatima (1921) 43 All. 650).

Philippines: Although complete separation of property is the norm in marriages under the CMPL, which would then not entitle a wife to a share in her husband's assets on divorce, in one case decided by a Shari'a court, the wife was given a one-third share of the value of the properties used in her husband's business. The court stated that she had helped manage and run the business.

Sri Lanka: The MMDA, 1956 does not allow the registration of divorce to be withheld on account of non-payment of mahr. In practice, Quazis refuse to register a talaq until some mata'a payment is made available to the woman or the kaikuli is repaid. While the MMDA, 1956 does not specifically provide for mata'a, Quazis incorporate mata'a into divorce proceedings by referring to a Shafi treatise, Minhaj el Talibin. This payment is usually a lump sum, which is calculated according to the duration of the marriage. Quazis fix an amount of kaikuli and enforce its return even if the original amount of kaikuli has not been properly recorded in the marriage contract.

Court practices and interpretation restrict women's access to financial rights on divorce

Cameroon: In a joint property regime, the woman does not receive half of the property. Judges may require her to show how she participated in the acquisition of the joint property, irrespective of the couple's choice of marital proprietary regime.

Central Asian Republics: The courts have not resolved the issue of ownership of the family apartment: does it belong to the spouses equally, as individuals, or to both of them as a family unit? This lack of clarity affects women's rights to the family home on divorce.

Fiji: The Lower Courts and High Court can hear cases relating to property settlements. The lower courts are cheaper and more accessible to women, but the magistrates are less knowledgeable and less sensitive. In certain circumstances, the courts have the power to award maintenance irrespective of the wife's adultery. This power is rarely utilized because of social attitudes. Periodical payments are usually small sums that are less than the basic minimum needed for survival. Payments are made irregularly and are not enforced, and courts tend to protect the ex-husband's income from any claims by a divorced wife.

Gambia: The duty to pay mata'a is derived from the Qur'an. It is not applied uniformly because the amount to be paid is usually left to the man to determine.

Pakistan: Civil cases for the recovery of marital property are extremely lengthy, discouraging women from applying. The expense and length of Family Court cases for recovery of unpaid mahr on divorce discourages women from pursuing their claims unless the mahr is very substantial.

Senegal: The law limits mahr, wedding expenses, and engagement gifts for the wife to a maximum of 3,000 fCFA (approx US$ 4.50), 15,000 fCFA (approx US$ 22), and 5,000 fCFA (approx US$ 7.30) respectively. In one case (TPI Dakar 20-12-1977 RJS. Credila 1982 vol III p.188 Diop v Fall), the court ordered the woman to return the entire mahr, wedding expenses, and engagement gifts; although the amount returned could not exceed the legal limit.

Sri Lanka: The form on which marriages are registered provides space for the mahr to be specified; addition space is provided to record whether the mahr is to be paid immediately or not. This record can be used as evidence during proceedings for the recovery of mahr. Case law is not clear about the admissibility of oral evidence in the case that amount of mahr differed from that recorded on the marriage registration form. Some Qazis do not advise women that they may claim unpaid mahr when they initiate divorce proceedings on the basis of the husband's fault. A divorced wife's entitlement to idda maintenance is outlined in S. 47(1)(d) of the MMDA, 1956 (see p.323). However, it is unclear how long this maintenance period lasts. The legislative intent may have been to ensure that in the event that a divorce takes longer than three months to be finalized, the woman continues to receive maintenance and equally that if the divorce is registered before three months have passed, she nevertheless continues to receive maintenance for the full three month period. However, this has not been fully debated in case law and the section's wording merely creates confusion.

PRACTICES

Customary practices are overwhelmingly negative

Cameroon: In practice, it is difficult to maintain the distinction between each spouse's property within the joint property regime. Husbands do not account for their administration of the joint property, and women are often not asked for their opinions on or permission for the sale of joint property. Generally, neither party applies for division of the joint estate and women consequently leave the marriage without taking anything with them.

Central Asian Republics: In practice, a deserted wife returns to her parents' home and does not exercise her right to half the matrimonial property. This property falls under the control of the husband and his family. Couples may divorce but be forced to reside in the same apartment for lack of alternatives.

Fiji: Even after divorce, maintenance payments are customarily dependent on the ex-wife not beginning any new relationship.

Gambia: Custom dictates that on divorce, even if the husband was at fault, and especially where the woman remarries, the mahr must be returned. This is probably because of the customary confusing of bride-price with mahr. During marriage, a woman is generally provided with land from her husband's family. She is not the owner of the land, but she can use it and enjoys rights and duties similar to those enjoyed by an owner. All usufruct rights to the husband's or his family's land are lost on divorce. However, the divorced woman may retain access to the marital home and land through her sons. Should the divorced husband die, his brother or the family head will hold the land, and the woman will lose all access to it.

India: In Chennai/Madras (Tamil Nadu), the divorce deed does not mention payment of mahr or return of dowry. On divorce, dowry given to the husband and his family is not returned and mahr is not paid. In most parts of India, women are not given maintenance in any form after divorce, although field research by WRAG found that women in many parts of the country, especially Gujarat and Orissa, feel maintenance should be given. Where some money is given, it continues to be maintenance restricted to the idda period, and the payment of any deferred dower. Divorced men tend to think that their obligations end on divorce. But in some parts of the country, even the mahr is not paid. In Lucknow for example, most poor women are not paid their mahr, while richer ones are. In Bhopal, there are occasional cases of settlements made after talaq if the woman applies to the local mufti.

Iran: The optional clause in the standard marriage contract allowing for equal division of assets accumulated during the marriage on divorce is usually struck out at the time of marriage.

Kyrgyz Republic: Family property is usually registered in the husband's name, which causes problems for division and recovery of marital assets following divorce.

Nigeria: Women are generally not maintained after divorce because they return to their natal homes. As far as property brought in to the marriage is concerned, women in practice tend to remove their property directly (piece-by-piece secretly in advance, where they initiate the divorce) and in the company of friends/relatives of their choosing (who can act as witnesses/protectors in case of attack where the divorce was acrimonious) when divorce is a talaq. Such removal tends to be done when the former husband is away from the marital home.

Philippines: Women usually cannot remain in the marital home on divorce unless the separating couple comes to an informal agreement. Couples rarely bother to identify which assets belong to whom, which causes problems on the division of property.

Pakistan: Husbands generally do not maintain their wives during idda, largely because women tend to return to their natal home following the breakdown of a marriage; women are either unaware of or unable to access their right to maintenance. Recovery of dowry depends on the relative strength of the couple's respective families and enforcement of judgments granting return of dowry is difficult because of social attitudes. Among the Pukhtuns dower in the form of property is transferred into the bride's name, though she does not control the property in practice. This practice actually obstructs divorce since men refuse to lose control of their land. Civil cases for the recovery of marital property are extremely rare (although becoming more frequent through the support of women lawyers) and are generally only filed by women who work outside the home. Women often surrender their claims to unpaid mahr in return for undisputed custody of any children of the marriage.

Senegal: Under custom the divorced woman has to leave the marital home on dissolution. However, imams who were surveyed by GREFELS stated that the woman must be given accommodation and food if she is pregnant, and must also be given mahr ul mithl if she has not already received her mahr.

Women face enormous problems in recovery of maintenance where husbands work in the private sector. Even if the woman presents all the due documents, the managers refuse to execute the order for maintenance. During a survey by GREFELS, women reported instances where former husbands preferred to leave their jobs rather than pay alimony. Women do not keep receipts of household assets bought with their money and are therefore unable to reclaim them on divorce.

Few women understand the regime dotal option and activists are seeking its removal from the Code de la Famille.

Sri Lanka: In practice, the mahr reflected in the marriage registration form is nominal. Larger sums than stated may be promised, creating problems for recovery.

Turkey: Maintenance payments are generally insufficient. This is due to the difficulties women have in proving their husband's financial means in a largely unregulated economy.

Customary practices to women's advantage

Pakistan: In a practice that pre-dates independence in 1947, maintenance continuing beyond idda is negotiated and enforced by the community in certain communities in the Punjab (Mianwali and Kalabagh areas). These agreements may be recorded as part of the divorce settlement or recorded separately.

Philippines: Accepting the complete separation of property as the norm, Filipina Muslims often use this as a justification to demand the right to have a job or engage in business so that they can have their own independent income.

Senegal: In certain regions (Fatick and Kaolack), the woman may take all the household goods with her on divorce. Although under the CF husbands may equally demand damages in the event of divorce, they rarely do.

The Shah Bano Case: Muslim Women's Financial Rights Become the Focus of Identity politics

A 1973 proposed amendment to S. 125 of the Indian Criminal Procedure Code sought to introduce a uniform law of maintenance for all citizens of India, irrespective of their personal laws. Whereas previously Muslim women had been able to claim maintenance only during idda, the new law allowed indefinite maintenance (with a maximum of Rs. 500 per month – approximately US$5) to dependent wives. Some Muslim members of Parliament strongly objected to a definition of 'wife' that includes a woman who has been divorced but has not remarried, and argued that Muslims must be exempted from the law.

Although the Law Minister highlighted the social problems facing divorced women (Lok Sabha debate, Vol 36, August 30, 1973), opposition from conservative Muslims and politico-religious forces inside and outside the parliament led to the inclusion of S. 127(3)(b), under which S. 125 will not apply if the divorced woman receives 'the whole of the sum which, under any customary or personal law applicable to the parties, was payable on such divorce.' In the case of Muslims, because mata'a is not customarily recognized in the region, this was taken to mean if the woman has received her mahr, she is not entitled to receive anything beyond idda maintenance.

But interpreting S. 125 and 127(3), the Supreme Court held in two cases that unless the mahr is equivalent to reasonable maintenance, the husband still had to pay maintenance (Bai Tahira v Ali Husain Fissalli Clothia, 1979 Cr LJ 151; Fuzlunbi v Khader Vali AIR 1980 SC 1730). Subsequently, this position was reiterated by the Indian SC in the famous Shah Bano case, which involved a woman who had been abandoned and left destitute after many years of marriage. The Indore Magistrate's Court had awarded her with Rs. 25 (approximately $0.50) per month after she had been married for 46 years. Her husband was estimated to be earning Rs. 5,000 per month (approximately US$100). On appeal to the High Court, this was 'raised' to Rs. 179.20 per month, which her husband appealed as 'excessive' to the Supreme Court.

The strongly negative reaction to the Shah Bano judgment among certain sections of the Muslim community in India appears to have been because the court referred to the need for a uniform civil code, which was taken as an attack on the minority's identity in an already tense context of rising Hindu fundamentalism. The fact that a non-Muslim judge was apparently interpreting the Qur'an was used as a point to further inflame sentiments. The judge however defended his decision warning that such criticism would lead to sectarian courts in the country.

Following violent demonstrations and under pressure from several religious leaders, Shah Bano herself publicly stated that divorced Muslim women should be excluded from the purview of S.125 and that the government should guarantee that it would not interfere with Muslim laws in any way. Fearing rejection by the Muslim community in the forthcoming elections, the government passed the Muslim Women (Protection of Rights on Divorce) Act 1986. Under S 3(1) of the Act a divorced Muslim woman can claim from her husband on divorce:

- a reasonable and fair provision and maintenance to be made and paid to her within the iddat period by her former husband
- an amount equivalent to the sum of mahr or dower agreed to be paid to her at the time of her marriage or any time thereafter according to Muslim law, and
- all the properties given to her before or at the time of marriage or after her marriage by her relatives or the husband or his friends (i.e. dowry or jehez and other gifts)

Beyond the idda period, if a woman had no means of support and had not remarried, the Act held her relatives (rather than her ex-husband) responsible for maintaining her, and if they were destitute too, then the Waqf Board or Muslim Welfare Trust was responsible. The Act was interpreted by activists as in effect forcing Muslim women to walk from door to door for survival by denying them their right to appeal for alimony under India's criminal code, a right enjoyed by divorcees of all other communities.

In the first decision to be given under the new Act, the Lucknow Magistrate Court (Fahima Hussain v Shafat Ahmed) appeared to completely subvert the purpose of the Act. The petitioner was awarded idda maintenance at the rate of Rs. 1000 per month for three months, Rs, 30,000 in a lump sum as fair and reasonable provision and her mahr of Rs.52,000.

The Bombay High Court (in the Jaitunbi Mubarak Shaikh case) appears to have gone beyond even this, and held "As far as the making of a reasonable and fair provision... the liability is not restricted to the iddat period [because] the dictionary meaning of the word 'provision' would make it clear that the Muslim husband is required to visualize the future needs of his wife."

The Shah Bano case raised women's awareness both in India and the region. In Kerala for example, a number of cases have been filed subsequently, and in Calicut, Kerala there has been a mata'a settlement for hundreds of thousands of rupees.

In Bangladesh where the Shah Bano case had been watched closely, the restriction of maintenance to the period of idda was challenged in a 1995 High Court case (Hefzur Rahman v Shamsunnahar Begum (DLR 1995, 54, Vol. 47) where the court held that:

"a person after divorcing his wife is bound to maintain her on a reasonable scale beyond the period of iddat for an indefinite period, that is to say, until she loses the status of a divorcee by remarrying another person."

Women's rights activists and human rights activists hailed this decision, which went against more than 100 years of judicial precedent, as a landmark decision. But a full Bench of the Supreme Court of Bangladesh overturned the decision in December 1999, and this decision again limited maintenance for divorced women to the idda period. It appears that by emphasizing maintenance rather than mata'a, the case had been lost.

10c MATTERS RELATED TO DISSOLUTION OF MARRIAGE: HILALA (INTERVENING MARRIAGE)

introduction

Intervening marriage, or hilala refers to a prohibition that prevents an irrevocably divorced couple (irrevocably divorced through talaq baynona kubra/a third talaq or dissolution) from remarrying unless the former wife has subsequently married another man, consummated that marriage, and then been either divorced or widowed from him. Originally, this prohibition was intended to curb a husband's unfettered right of talaq (particularly the disapproved talaq bid'a/ triple talaq) by putting his divorced wife out of his reach. Thus, hilala requirements grew out of the need to penalize erring husbands who disposed of their wives in an irresponsible manner. In spite of its original purpose, hilala has become oppressive to women in many communities.

Hilala creates problems where there is confusion in Muslim laws about the various forms of talaq and their revocability. This prohibition on remarriage between spouses already thrice divorced applies only in systems based on Muslim laws. In systems that do not recognize talaq as a form of dissolution, the question of revocation does not arise. By effectively abolishing revocable divorces, both Indonesia and Tunisia have done away with the practice of hilala.

In South Asia and South East Asia (Malaysia and Singapore) for instance, among Muslim communities a triple oral talaq is recognized as a valid divorce, even where the law does not recognize it as valid. In Hanafi-majority South Asia, even if a triple talaq is pronounced in rage or intoxication, it is still regarded by communities as an irrevocable talaq. Accordingly, it is effective from the moment it is pronounced. Because of this community perception (which is promoted by mosque imams and even some 'religious scholars'), there is a common presumption that if a couple wishes to reconcile after such an argument, the wife will have to undergo hilala.

In some instances, women are willing to go through the humiliation of a ritualized intervening marriage because they wish to remain with their first husband and because they accept the belief that reconciling with him without a hilala would be against religious precepts (haram). The choice of whether or not this intervening marriage is really consummated may not be for the woman to make. However, in other instances, women choose to stay with the intervening 'husband' and do not go back to their ex-husband.

In Pakistan and Bangladesh, the Muslim Family Law Ordinance 1961 attempts to abolish hilala in all but extreme situations. Each talaq under the MFLO, no matter how pronounced (triple or otherwise), operates as a single, revocable divorce and only becomes effective after the idda is completed. The law is clear that, should the couple thus divorced wish to remarry, they can do so without an intervening marriage, unless they have been divorced three times under the MFLO procedure. Nevertheless, intervening marriage continues to be widely accepted as obligatory because of the widespread practice of talaq bid'a (triple oral talaq) and the presumption that such a talaq is an irrevocable talaq.

customary practices regarding hilala

In Pakistan, couples that have had a serious argument, during which the husband in a fit of rage pronounced a triple talaq, may consult a maulvi (mosque imam or local religious figure) and ask him to pronounce a fatwa on the situation. The maulvi may then pronounce that an intervening marriage is required (ignoring the legal provisions) and volunteer to act as the intervening husband. If hilala does occur, it is not uncommon for the intervening 'husband' to deceive the woman as to his intentions; this deception can result in the forced consummation of such convenience marriages. Often once such a consummation has occurred, the first husband sometimes refuses to take his former wife back. Alternatively in some communities, couples seek to have the initial divorce revoked by securing a fatwa from a local imam that invalidates the talaq on the grounds that it was pronounced when the husband had a high fever and was therefore not of sound mind. Even if the community knows that the couple has lived apart for months, the fatwa may be accepted.

In Bangladesh, newspapers almost daily report cases where intervening marriages lasted just 24 hours and cases where the former wife is forcibly married to a child in order to meet the requirements of hilala. Where the spouses do not submit to the dictates of the village mullas, they can be ostracized and sometimes punished (in the name of the Shar'ia) with lashing, stoning, or having to go round the village with strings of shoes around their necks.

In Malaysia, Singapore, and Sri Lanka, a husband is only required to pronounce one talaq; and therefore, if the couple wants to remarry, they can do so. In Singapore the registrar cannot register a triple divorce. Such a matter will have to be brought to court. In practice three pronouncements in one sitting is considered as one talaq and is registered as such. But in Malaysia despite the legal provisions, the practice of hilala is so widely recognized that a pejorative name exists for intervening husbands: 'blind Chinamen' (kahwin China buta).

In Sudan, intervening marriages that are explicitly contracted for the purposes of tahlil (absolving the first husband from pronouncing a rash irrevocable talaq) are socially regarded as against religious precepts—that is, haram. The intervening 'husband' in such a situation is also socially condemned, and the intervening marriage is dismissed as a 'tatyees marriage,' implying that such a husband is a mere puppet.

A Judge Hits Out at the Fatwa Givers

Many popular newspapers and magazines in Pakistan run columns for people seeking advice as to 'what the Sharia has to say' about their various problems.

Unfortunately, many women unquestioningly accept the fatwas given by these so-called religious scholars, even when they contradict the statute law or present a very narrow (and often anti-women) interpretation of Muslim laws.

One judge in Karachi (while hearing two constitutional cases on the validity of judicial decrees for khul') harshly criticized these newspaper columns and their writers for their level of understanding about Islam. He warned that only court verdicts are legally binding on people.

In particular, he quoted a response in one leading daily, in which a woman who had secured a khul' decree had been told that she would go to hell if she believed the court decree was valid. She had been further instructed to return to her husband because she was not validly divorced. The judge noted other incidents where women who have followed the law of the land have been threatened with accusations their actions might be considered zina and their children illegitimate.

The judge also addressed the issue of hilala and clarified that if a woman wished to remarry following a khul' decree, there was nothing to prevent her from doing so, whether she wished to marry another man or remarry the same man

Dr. Maqbool Ahmed Abid and another v Mrs. Rehana Kausar and others KLR 1996 Civil Cases 50.

NOTES

LAWS: Hilala and Intervening Marriage

Criteria

Most laws regarding hilala are unclear. Partly, this is because many laws do not clarify whether a triple talaq/talaq bid'a counts as a single divorce or three divorces, and therefore whether the hilala rule applies or not. Similarly, laws are not always clear regarding the requirement of hilala if a woman has initiated the divorce. This lack of clarity means that deciding whether a law is more or less option-giving for women will largely depend upopn implementation. Certainly, laws which clarify when hilala applies are more option-giving. As we do not have sufficient information regarding implementation, we have only listed the countries alphabetically.

Algeria: Article 51 of the CF states that any man who has divorced his wife by talaq three times in succession may not take her back unless she has subsequently been married to another man by whom she has then been divorced or who has then died after the consummation of the marriage.

Bangladesh & Pakistan: Under S. 7 of the MFLO, nothing shall debar a wife whose marriage has been terminated by talaq, effective under this [Ordinance], from remarrying the same husband, without an intervening marriage with a third person, unless such termination is effective for the third time. Under S. 7(1), after 'pronouncement of talaq in any form whatsoever' the parties must follow the procedure for notification to the local authorities, reconciliation and idda before the dissolution becomes effective and the certificate can be issued (whether for a talaq or judicial decree). Each time a dissolution is registered under the MFLO following this procedure, it counts as a single talaq/dissolution.

Iran: Under Article 1057 of the CC, a woman who has been the wife of a man three consecutive times and has been divorced will be forbidden to be the wife of that man again unless she first marries, by a permanent marriage, another man and after consummating that marriage, she is separated from him by divorce, rescission of marriage, or death.

Malaysia: Under S. 47(14), where reconciliation fails in talaq, the court advises the husband to pronounce one talaq, which is considered a revocable divorce. Under S. 14(c), a woman divorced by three talaqs may not remarry her previous husband unless she has first lawfully married another person and then that marriage has been dissolved (after being consummated), and she has observed the idda following such dissolution.

Morocco: Article 71 of the Moudawana states that the third talaq shall terminate the marriage immediately and shall prevent the making of a new contract unless the woman has completed the waiting period that follows the termination of a marriage (to another husband, with whom the marriage must have been legally consummated) by divorce.

Philippines: Under A. 30 of the CMPL, where a husband has thrice repudiated (talaq bain kubra) a wife on three different occasions, he cannot remarry her unless she has first married another person who has since divorced her (after consummating the intervening marriage), and she must have then observed the idda that follows such a divorce. The CMPL addresses hilala under A. 30 and 32 (irregular marriages after a triple divorce between the same parties) and A. 33 (removing impediment to an irregular marriage).

Sri Lanka: Under S. 28 of the MMDA, 1956 and its Second Schedule, the form of pronouncement for talaq is talaq ahsan, a single talaq; and therefore, hilala is not required if the couple wishes to remarry.

Sudan: In the event of talaq bain (revocable single talaq by the husband) or talaq baynona sugra (decree by the court), the spouses do not require hilala if they want to remarry each other. Hilala is only required if the talaq is a talaq baynona kubra. The MPLA appears to condemn any intervening marriage that is merely a formality to enable the first husband to remarry his thrice divorced wife.

If Hilala Does Not Stop Him, Maybe a Financial Penalty Will

Although this Malaysian case came to the courts as a case for recovery of a contractual payment, it touched upon the issue of hilala and reveals a woman's attempts to control her husband's repeated use of talaq (Hamzah bin Musa v Fatimah Zaharah [1982] 1 MLJ 361).

Fatimah Zaharah had been divorced three times (bain kubra) by her husband. The husband had altogether had nine wives (sometimes four at a time). After the third talaq, the husband claimed that he wanted to remarry his former wife because she was carrying his child. The ex-wife went through 'a shady marriage ceremony, which is called China Buta.' This was done by the parties making an arrangement with another man who was willing to marry her on the condition that after the marriage had been solemnized, the man would then divorce the woman and the former husband would then be able to remarry her.

The court in its judgment noted that this practice is frowned upon by most Muslims as an attempt to circumvent religious laws. The practice is at present on the decline in Malaysia... but it is nonetheless practiced by short-tempered couples and by husbands who make hasty decisions and later regret these decisions.

After the intervening marriage and after remarrying her former husband, the woman drew up an agreement, which the husband signed. Among the terms of this agreement, the husband agreed to pay her RM 5,000 should he yet again divorce her by talaq.

When her husband did divorce her by talaq, she approached the court to claim this amount under the agreement. The Court of Appeal held that it was a valid agreement under the Contracts Act; it was not opposed to public policy, being neither immoral nor in contravention of Muslim laws. Judge Mohamed Zahir said, "...there is no law in the Muslim religion which prohibits a wife or would-be-wife from entering into contract with her husband...It is a contract in which the plaintiff agreed to marry the defendant on the stipulation that were he to divorce her, (he is) to pay her RM 5,000. She had fulfilled her term of the obligation by marrying him and upon divorcing her, the defendant is obliged to fulfil his term of the contract." Perhaps, after paying the RM 5,000 Hamzah bin Musa learned how to control himself.

10d MATTERS RELATED TO DISSOLUTION OF MARRIAGE: CUSTODY & GUARDIANSHIP OF CHILDREN

introduction

Custody refers to the day-to-day responsibility and physical care of a child. In contrast, guardianship refers to a set of supervisory rights over the person and property of a child.

Custody (and to a far lesser extent guardianship) is an area where in recent years there have been significant changes in favour of mothers. This has been particularly so where court interpretations are at least partially based on the 'best interests' or 'welfare of the child.' In addition, courts have tended to limit those situations under which a woman is disqualified from being awarded custody (and guardianship, where this is possible). In most systems covered in this Handbook, the trend (seen in some developed countries) towards recognizing that in certain circumstances fathers may be suitable primary caregivers has yet to appear.

The principle divide regarding custody is not between systems based on Muslim laws and those based on other sources, but between systems where the principle that guides custody decisions is the welfare of the child (Bangladesh, Cameroon, India, some states of Malaysia, Pakistan, Senegal, Sri Lanka, Tunisia, Turkey) and those where other considerations are prioritized (Egypt, Iran, Philippines, Sudan). However, in the area of guardianship, there is a noticeable difference between systems based on Muslim laws and those based on other sources.

In all the systems covered in this Handbook, a mother has both custody and guardianship rights to any child born of a marriage which is void for failure to fulfill the marriage requisites (see p.59), or for failure to fulfill registration requirements (where registration is necessary for validity, see p.133).

the gender stereotyping of parental roles

This section discusses the issues of custody and guardianship in the context of divorce. However, in order to understand issues of custody, it is first necessary to understand the rights and responsibilities of mothers and fathers within the family unit.

Some systems (both those based on Muslim laws and those based on other sources) distinguish between custody and guardianship. Such a distinction is generally made where the father is regarded as having greater decision-making power and financial responsibility within the family than is the mother. Such systems see the father as the 'natural guardian' or the 'head of household,' and, therefore, the mother has lesser rights over the children.

In Senegal, for example, the mother and father do not have the same legal rights in regard to their children during the marriage. As the 'head of the family,' the father's authority is supreme. The mother can have final authority only if the father is declared an incompetent guardian by a court. A salaried woman cannot include her children on her state medical insurance, and the children require the father's permission to leave the country. Following women's protests, a proposed law on parental authority (guardianship) was presented to parliament, but it faced strong opposition. The new constitution, which was accepted by a national vote in 2000, stipulates that both parents have equal legal responsibility for their children; but the law on guardianship remains unchanged.

As a result of this patriarchal vision of the family, divorced mothers often find themselves having the responsibility of custody while enjoying few supervisory rights.

Custody and guardianship are issues that are dominated by stereotyped gender roles: women are defined as caregivers, and men are defined as providers. At a practical level, these stereotypes can bring advantages and disadvantages for women (discussed below). Importantly, women are rarely given a choice as to whether or not they want to be caregivers and/or providers.

In some communities a woman is expected to leave her children with their father if she divorces him (Nigeria). In other communities it is presumed that the children will remain with their mother after a divorce (Central Asian Republics). In neither context is the woman given much choice in the matter and stereotypes prevail. In the Central Asian Republics, if a woman chooses not to take custody of their children because of economic hardship, she is stigmatized and accused of rejecting her 'natural' role as a caregiver. Moreover, laws frequently overlook the reality that mothers are often also providers.

Although men also suffer from gender stereotyping in issues of custody and guardianship issues (some may want to be caregivers and are suitable), this Handbook focuses on women's perspectives. Often men are able to use custody as a means of harassing and burdening their former wives, either by abandoning any responsibility for the children or by using their socially and legally recognized rights to their children as a tool to control their ex-wives.

where both parents have equal rights to custody and guardianship

Certain systems give both parents equal rights to custody and guardianship following a divorce (Cameroon, Central Asian Republics, Senegal, Tunisia, Turkey). When deciding a case, the courts then use the principle of the best interests of the child.

In most cases the mother is given custody, and the courts order the father to continue providing maintenance for the child until she/he reaches adulthood. However, the small sums awarded for maintenance and the difficulties involved in collecting such payments often result in custody burdening mothers, even when they want to keep their children. Women in the Central Asian Republics and the Gambia frequently find that after a court has awarded them custody, the father of the children abandons them.

where the mother may retain custody

Women often mistakenly presume that they will lose custody of their children if they leave their husbands. However, in most systems, whoever has actual custody when the couple separates retains custody until the other parent files a claim for custody.

Most laws and communities presume mothers should have custody of very small children, and mothers are only denied custody of young children in extreme cases. Iran stands out as a system that rigidly applies an interpretation of Muslim laws whereby that the mother loses custody no matter what the age of the child if she remarries. The precise age at which the father can claim custody depends upon whether the system is based on Muslim laws (and which School of thought is dominant as well as the gender of the child) or is based on other sources of law. Communities in the Gambia tend to presume that on divorce, custody of girls will be given to the mother while custody of boys will be given to the father.

In systems based on sources other than Muslim laws, fathers can claim custody at any time. However, in systems based on Muslim laws, generally fathers can make such claims only once boys reach 7 years of age and once girls reach puberty, although in some systems mothers may retain custody of girls until they (the daughter/s) marry. However, Iranian laws, which are based on Shia sources, allow fathers to claim custody of girls once they reach 7 years of age and boys once they reach 2 years of age. In Indonesia children unusually stay with their mother until they reach 12 years or mumaiyiz (the age of discernment), at which time the child's preference is considered.

However, these minimums only define the age at which the father can claim custody. Whether or not he will actually be awarded custody depends on whether age limits are applied rigidly (Egypt,

Iran, Philippines, Sudan) and whether or not the best interests of the child can override other considerations.

There has been considerable recent development in the understanding of the best interests principle (Bangladesh, Malaysia, Pakistan, Singapore). Thus, custody arrangements laid out in personal laws are no longer applied rigidly. Instead, other factors are taken into account including: the child's own preference (where she/he is above the age of around 9 years); the need to keep siblings together; the need to ensure stability for the child (i.e., to avoid a change of schools or residence); the child' emotional well-being (i.e., beyond their financial well-being); and the mother's ability to contribute to their schooling and general upbringing.

The attitude and actions of the father will also be taken into account, so that deciding custody becomes a complex interaction of qualifications and disqualifications. For example, in systems where Muslim laws are recognized and custody is decided according the best interests principle (Bangladesh, India, some states of Malaysia, Pakistan, Singapore), even if a boy is over the age of 7, if the father has shown little interest until the custody claim or has failed to provide maintenance, usually the mother will be awarded custody.

Increasingly, courts appear to take into account the motives behind a father's claim for custody. If it can be established that the father's claim is being made merely as a means of harassing the mother or to counter a maintenance suit, the courts may dismiss his claim. Clearly, the application of the best interests principle allows for the accommodation of changing social attitudes and economic realities (such as the greater numbers of women in paid employment). For example, case law in Pakistan has shown that physical disabilities are not bars to the mother's custody if the child's best interests are nevertheless to be found with the mother.

Even if a system does not codify the best interests principle, trends both in customary practices and court decisions may be moving towards considering mothers to be the 'more entitled' parent and the 'better qualified' one in custody disputes, particularly where the mother is educated and/or economically self-sufficient (Nigeria).

where the mother may lose custody

Systems that rigidly codify custody arrangements according to the age of the child (Egypt, Iran, Philippines, Sudan) tend to give fathers a strong chance of gaining custody of children. These systems base such laws on extremely patriarchal presumptions: that children above a certain age (often a very tender age) receive greater benefit from their father's financial support than they do from their mother's emotional support; and that fathers have a 'natural' right to guide their heir and to shape his/her future through his (the father's) day-to-day influence.

Although such laws may provide for judicial discretion (Egypt, Iran, Sudan), they nevertheless codify age-based arrangements and do not specify that the best interests of the child should be the guiding principle. Consequently, these laws and their interpretation by conservative courts tend not to favour mothers.

Even in systems that are guided by the bests interests of the child; if Muslim laws are recognized, there may be circumstances under which a mother is presumed to lose her right to custody (of children both below and above any age limits). Often these conditions are listed in the text of the law while no disqualifications for fathers are listed, even if the disqualifications can be said to be gender-neutral, such as having behaved cruelly, having been immoral, or having renounced Islam.

Where laws list disqualifications for a mother to have custody, these commonly include:

- Having renounced Islam;
- Having married a man not related to the child within the prohibited degrees;
- Being guilty of immorality or adultery (Malaysia: 'gross and open immorality');
- Having changed her residence/ or having moved far away from the father of the children;

- Having neglected, been cruel to, and/or having failed to take proper care of the child.

While laws may say that a mother loses her right to custody under these circumstances, in practice, such changes of custody happen only when the father makes a claim of custody, and often only when allegations are proven.

Practices regarding disqualifications also have changed considerably. The most significant has been a relaxation of the second condition listed above (Bangladesh, Pakistan, Sri Lanka)—that is, if the child's best interests are served by remaining with the mother. Again, other factors may be taken into account if the welfare principle is applied. The mother may retain custody after her remarriage, particularly if the father also remarries, or if the mother is unlikely to have children with the new husband, or if the father's general conditions of living are not appropriate. Of equal importance, the understanding of 'immoral' behaviour is changing and becoming less restrictive. Even if the mother engages in socially disapproved activities (such as smoking) or professions (such as air hostessing), case law has shown that these are not regarded as 'immoral' (Pakistan and Sri Lanka, respectively).

non-muslim mothers

However, courts still tend to apply rigidly the presumption in Muslim laws that the child follows the father's religion, and therefore, a non-Muslim mother is less likely to be granted custody. Foreign mothers are also unlikely to find courts sympathetic. In some systems, the law may also distinguish between Muslim and non-Muslim mothers. In Sudan, a non-Muslim mother is only entitled to custody of her child until she/he (the child) is 5 years old (in contrast to Muslim mothers, who are entitled to custody until boys are 7 years old and girls are 9 years old).

Nevertheless, there have been developments even in this area. In Pakistan, for example, an Uzbek mother who wished to return to Uzbekistan with her child retained custody of her small child as the court argued that modern transport would allow the father to go to see his child and the 'secular atmosphere' of Uzbekistan was not a disqualification (Miss Hina Jillani, Director of AGHS Legal Aid Cell v Sohail Butt PLD 1995 Lahore 151). Later a Japanese convert to Islam was also granted custody, but to date no non-Muslim mother has been granted custody through custody proceedings.

In Nigeria, divorced non-Muslim wives increasingly have retained both custody and guardianship in practice. This holds true especially where fathers have not made court applications (most do not). However, non-Muslim mothers also have retained custody through the courts when they have been educated and/or economically self-sufficient.

mother's female relatives as alternative custodians

In some systems based on Muslim laws, if a mother is disqualified from custody, her female relatives (mother, sisters, aunts) have a prior right to custody over the father. In a case in Malaysia, the Muslim court awarded custody to the maternal-grandmother after the father had remarried and both the mother and grandmother had applied for custody (Siti Aishah v Wan Abdul Aziz, 1975). The court ruled that it was in the best interests of the child not to live with a stepmother. In Iran, on the other hand, if the father is not judged suitable, his male family members are given priority over the mother and her relatives.

Even if in principle a mother's female relatives have preference over the father for custody, such preference may not be applied in practice. In Nigeria divorced women who are poor and/or not formally educated are often compelled to leave their children in the custody their father because fathers seldom maintain children not in their custody and there are no practical mechanisms for enforcement of their maintenance responsibilities. Also, many mothers believe that if they remarry (the most common outcome for divorcees) they will automatically loose custody. Thus, children are often left in their stepmother's care, or they may go live with another relative of the father's choosing. Often women do not initiate divorce until they feel their children are old enough to handle this traumatic change in care arrangements.

guardianship

Unlike with the issue of custody, where the best interests of the child may override other provisions of Muslim laws, the issue of guardianship (in most systems based on Muslim laws) is almost always settled according to the presumption that the father has a prior right to guardianship over the mother (except where they were never married). Tunisia is an exception.

Guardianship rights may or may not be specified in the law but are generally taken to include the right to:

- Determine the child's religion;
- Determine the child's education;
- Legal control over the child's property;
- Ijbar or compulsion in marriage (confined to father and the paternal grandfather in most Schools where ijbar rights apply).

Guardianship rights tend to overshadow custody rights in that whatever rights are not included in the day-to-day responsibility of looking after the physical care of the child fall into guardianship rights. Right of access (visiting rights to the child), for example, may be interpreted as a right that flows naturally from the right of guardians.

Where fathers are presumed to have rights to guardianship, they are also presumed responsible for the maintenance of children until they can provide for themselves (until marriage for females in Nigeria; for the duration of tertiary education in some Malaysian states). However, in practice for mothers who have custody, it may be almost impossible to enforce maintenance decrees while the whole socio-legal system continues to regard the father as the guardian.

In Malaysia, for example, the division of custody and guardianship rights between mothers and fathers has added to mothers' burdens as custodians when the father cannot (or refuses) to be located. In such cases, the mother has difficulty enrolling her children in school and difficulty obtaining identity cards and travel documents for her children because the father cannot be found to give his permission.

Nevertheless, in some systems (Bangladesh, Malaysia, Pakistan, Singapore) even though the mother is not regarded as the 'natural' guardian, she may apply to be appointed as the guardian in certain situations (e.g., upon the death of the father). In some systems her application will be granted only if the father's male relatives do not challenge it (Malaysia, Singapore). In Nigeria, widows (non-Muslims as well as Muslims) increasingly retain custody and guardianship of their children, especially where they are formally educated and/or economically self-sufficient.

Turkish Court Orders Father to Return Boy

The mother of a British boy who was abducted by his father and taken to Turkey was given custody of the child after a two-year battle.

However, Belinda Chapman-Serce from Syston in Leicestershire is still waiting to be reunited with her son, who is believed to be living somewhere in Turkey. At a hearing in Istanbul, the judge decided the boy should return to England with his mother. Neither the boy nor his father were in court. Cihan Chapman-Serce, who is six, was taken by his father Salih Serce to Turkey when he was supposed to be on a weekend visit. Leicestershire police and Mrs Chapman-Serce worked with the Turkish authorities to trace the father and issue him with a court order. Denise Carter from the support group Reunite said, "The judge has ordered that the child should be returned to England so we hope he (the judge) has the power to get the police looking for Cihan. "

http://news.bbc.co.uk/1/hi/england/2471515.stm
14 November, 2002

The Child's Rights are Paramount

In Malaysia, in the Kelantan State case of Mohammed v Azizah (1979) 1 Jurnal Hukum (1) 79, both parents had remarried at the time the father applied for custody of the girl-child. The mother had custody after the divorce and had not yet remarried when custody was originally awarded to her. She had held custody for 7 years when the father applied for custody.

The Kadi asked the child for her preference and she said that she wanted to remain with her mother. The court found that her progress in school was good. He refused the father's application and ruled, "The basis and purpose of custody is for the welfare and good of the child who is to be looked after, as a fundamental right of the child, and this right must be given preference to the right of those who claim the right of custody, as is clear from what is stated in the Tuhfah and as stated by Ibn Salah and accepted as correct by Syed Sabiq in his Fiqh Al-Sunnah, vol 8: The person who has the right of custody, and the children over whom custody is claimed, both have rights; but the right of the children is stronger than that of the person claiming custody."

As translated by Ahmad Ibrahim in his book, Family Laws in Malaysia. MLJ 1997.

NOTES

LAWS: Custody and Guardianship of Children

Criteria

☺ More option-giving are those laws which:
- Recognize women and men as having equal rights to custody & guardianship; and
- Base decisions on the best interests of the child.

😐 The middle ground is occupied by those laws which:
- Base custody decisions on the best interests of the child, although aspects of personal laws may be considered;
- Presume fathers are the 'natural' guardians.

☹ Less option-giving are those laws which:
- Prioritize other considerations in custody decisions;
- Presume fathers are the 'natural' guardians.

☺ Women and men have equal rights to custody & guardianship; decisions are based on the best interests of the child

Cameroon & Central Asian Republics: Custody and guardianship can be given to either parent. The best interest of the child is the paramount consideration.

Indonesia: Under the Marriage Law, in the event of dispute, custody of children is to be decided by the court. In general, courts grant custody of children under 12 to the mother and give priority to the child's preference above that age.

Gambia: Under the Family Code if there is a disagreement, the best interest of the child is the guiding principle. Custody and guardianship of children can be awarded to the father, the mother, or a third party. S. 29:1 (Rights of Children) of the 1997 Constitution provides for taking account of the best interests of the child with regards to custody and guardianship.

Senegal: Although under the CF the father has greater rights over the children during marriage (unless he has abandoned them, A. 277), on divorce under A. 278, the judge awards custody and guardianship to either parent or a third person according to the best interests of the child. If a widow remarries, other relatives may request the court to fix certain conditions regarding the custody, maintenance, and education of the child.

Tunisia: Laws in Tunisia recognize the equal rights of parents in custody and guardianship. During the marriage, both parents have equal rights and responsibilities regarding the child. In the event of divorce, the judge shall award custody based on the best interests of the child. If the mother is awarded custody, she exercises the authority of guardianship in relation to the ward's travel, education, and financial affairs; she may be granted full powers of guardianship if the guardian is unable or unfit to exercise them.

Turkey: In the event of separation or divorce, the rules regarding custody and guardianship do not discriminate between the father and the mother. Under A. 182 of the CC, the judge awards custody to whichever parent will best look after the child. Men are not regarded as being superior to women in this respect.

😐 Custody is decided in the best interests of the child; fathers are presumed to be 'natural' guardians

Bangladesh, India and Pakistan: A. 42 of the colonial Guardians and Wards Act, 1890 (applicable to all communities), defines a guardian as a person having the care of the minor and/or the minor's property. Thus, in deciding both custody and guardianship cases under A. 17, the court is to be guided by the welfare of the minor, consistent with the law to which the minor is subject. In determining welfare, the court is to consider: the minor's age, sex and religion; the character and capacity of the proposed guardian and that guardian's relation to the minor; the wishes of any deceased parent; any relationship of the proposed guardian with the minor or his property; and the minor's wishes, if he/she is old enough to form an intelligent preference. In case law in recent decades, the courts in Bangladesh & Pakistan have consistently overruled classical Hanafi rules regarding custody (especially disqualifications affecting the mother) and granted mothers custody in the best interests of the child. Noticeable cases include Md. Abu Baker Siddique v. S.M.A. Bakar & others 38 DLR (AD) 1986; Mst. Zohra Begum v Sh. Latif Ahmed Munawar PLD 1965 Lah. 695; Bashir Ahmad v Abida Sultana 1989 ALD 432. In guardianship matters, however, the presumption that the father is the 'natural' guardian remains.

Malaysia: Most Muslim family laws specify the disqualifications of a mother as custodian and the hierarchy of female relatives as custodians and the hierarchy of male relatives as guardians. The Guardianship of Infants Act, 1960 applies to Muslims, as long as the provisions do not conflict with Muslim laws. Both Muslim and civil laws on this point make a distinction between custody and guardianship. Some Muslim family laws provide for the best interest and welfare principle in the laws itself.

Sri Lanka: Custody matters are decided in the ordinary courts, i.e. in the District Courts, not Quazi Courts, according to principles of Muslim laws, subject to the best interest of the child. Therefore, courts can grant custody to a mother if her right to custody has expired under traditional principles of Muslim law and also disregard any disqualifications placed on the mothers right to custody applicable under traditional Shafi law. The courts have consistently reiterated that custody principles under Muslim Laws can be displaced in the interests of the child. In Subair v Isthikar (1974, 77 NLR 397) the Supreme Court held that on the question of a second marriage contracted by the mother to a person who is not related to the child within the prohibited degrees, normally the woman loses custody but special considerations regarding the interest of the child may require she should retain custody. The court recognized several circumstances under which the mother would retain custody even though she has contracted a second marriage to a person not related to the minor within the prohibited degrees. The father is the guardian of the children, even when custody is awarded to the mother.

☹ The law codifies age limitations for custody; some possibility of alternatives; fathers are presumed to be 'natural' guardians

Algeria: Mothers retain custody of a boy until he reaches 16 years of age unless they (the mothers) remarry, in which case they lose the right to custody of a boy when he reaches 10 years of age. Mothers retain custody a girl until she marries unless the mother remarries, in which case she looses this right. The decision to terminate custody is subject to the ward's best interests. Guardianship is with the father, but on his death it reverts to the mother unless his will states otherwise.

Egypt: Under A. 20 of the Law on Personal Status of 1929 as amended in 1985, custody of a boy remains with the mother until he is 10 years of age. A judge has discretion to extend the period of custody until the boy reaches 15 years of age. The girl-child remains with the mother until she is 12 years of age. This may be extended by judicial discretion until the child is married.

Gambia (marriages under Muslim laws): In the event of disputed custody, Muslim laws are applied regarding age-based custody arrangements.

Iran: Under A. 1169, custody of sons over the age of 2 and daughters over the age of 7 is awarded to the father. Under A. 1170, custody of children who have not yet reached these ages reverts to the father if the mother remarries. A. 1173 permits judicial discretion in custody if the child is endangered by lack of care or moral degradation. However, courts rarely accept arguments that the father is unsuitable for custody, even in cases where there is a history of severe domestic violence or a criminal record. Even where the Court decides that the father is unsuitable, it may award custody to the paternal grandfather or uncles. However, under A. 1171, if one parent dies, the surviving parent will have custody even if the father appointed an executor for the child. Under A. 1181, the father or the paternal grandfather has the right of guardianship of children.

The guardian is the legal representative on all matters relating to financial rights of the ward. If the natural guardian is incapable of controlling the minor's wealth or is absent, the court will appoint a trustee. Non-Muslims cannot be appointed trustees for a Muslim child.

Morocco: A divorced mother has the right of custody of her daughters until they marry and the right of custody of her sons until they reach puberty.

Philippines: The care and custody of children younger than 7 years of age whose parents are divorced shall belong to the mother or in her absence, to the maternal grandmother, the paternal grandmother, the sister, or aunts. In their default it shall devolve upon the father and the nearest paternal relatives. The minor above 7 years of age but below the age of puberty may choose the parent with whom he wants to stay. The unmarried daughter who has reached the age of puberty shall stay with the father, the son, under the same circumstances shall stay with the mother (A. 78 of the CMPL). Under A.79 and 80 of the CMPL, guardianship for marriage and for property is with the father. Although parental authority is jointly exercised, the father's decision will prevail.

Sudan: Under A 109-126 of the MPLA, the mother has custody of boys until they are 7 and of girls until they are 9. The mother or alternate female relative can extend custody beyond this period if she proves to court that the continuation of her custody is in the best interests of the child and especially if she proves to the court the father is unfit as a custodian to the child. In practice, proving this is complicated and involves lengthy procedures. Remarriage of the mother or the alternate female custodian terminates the possibility of the continuation of custody unless the court decides that it is in the best interest of the child to remain with the female custodian. Under A. 118, the guardianship of children of divorced or separated parents goes to the father. The father is to oversee all matters related to the socialization, education/ schooling, and overall behaviour and conduct of the child. The father's guardianship over the boy continues until he (the boy) reaches adulthood, whereas for the girl, the guardianship does not have a time limit, whether held by the father or by any other male relative.

Rectifying a Gross Injustice: The Custody Rights of Iranian Widows

Under the pre-Revolution Family Protection Law, Iranian mothers had rights similar to paternal grandfathers in terms of custody and guardianship where the father was found to be unsuitable or had died. But the post-1979 Iranian Civil Code envisages mothers as purely temporary custodians of their children who are in effect the property of their 'natural guardians', their father and paternal grandfather.

The injustice of this situation became apparent during the Iran-Iraq War of the 1980s. Many women who had continued to support the Iranian government despite the death of their husbands in the war, then lost custody of their children to the paternal grandfather. The children of war martyrs were entitled to state financial benefits, which sometimes became the cause of custody disputes between mothers and paternal grandfathers.

The war widows mobilized formally and informally to demand justice. They asked, "Why should a mother who has already lost her husband for her beliefs in the revolution and religion also lose her child? Where is the justice in that?".

The need for more volunteers to go to the war front was a source of pressure on the religious leaders to resolve the problem. The Martyrs' Foundation (which advocated for the wives and children of the war dead) was faced with daily demands from the wives, and appealed to the legal authorities to resolve the custody issue. In 1988 the law was changed so that the custody (but not guardianship) of children whose fathers died in the war was automatically returned to the mother (amendment 1). However, the financial support and other responsibilities remain with the guardian, who is a paternal grandfather or someone appointed by him. If the children are entitled to a pension from the Martyrs' Foundation, it is paid to the mother unless the court decides the mother is incapable of providing the children with a good upbringing.

Amendment 2 confirms that the subsequent marriage of the mother does not remove her right to have custody of the children (a departure from principles of custody applied in other situations, where the mother almost automatically loses custody of her children if she remarries). Amendment 3 states that the court shall decide how much money will be paid to the mother for maintenance of the children.

Although this new law failed to address some of the fundamental problems of provisions regarding custody and guardianship, even this partial victory was cause for celebration as it addressed one of the most patriarchal aspects of the law, and may have opened the door to broader legal change in this area.

Extracted from Hoodfar, H. (1996), Personal Status Law as Defined by the Islamic Republic of Iran, in Hoodfar, H. (ed), Shifting Boundaries in Marriage and Divorce in Muslim Communities, Special Dossier, WLUML, Grabels

Annexe 1

COUNTRIES COVERED BY THE WOMEN & LAW IN THE MUSLIM WORLD PROGRAMME

- Bangladesh
- Cameroon
- Fiji
- the Gambia
- India
- Indonesia
- Iran
- Malaysia
- Morocco
- Nigeria
- Pakistan
- Philippines
- Senegal
- Sri Lanka
- Sudan
- Turkey

Additionally, partial research was also carried out in:

- Algeria, Uzbekistan, Kazakhstan and the Kyrgyz Republic

Annexe 2

LIST OF ORGANIZATIONS

The following is a list of networking organizations which took part in the W&L research as well as a selection of networking organizations who may be able to provide further information regarding issues addressed in this Handbook, or may be able to refer readers to other sources. For countries not listed below, please contact one of the WLUML Coordination offices.

wluml coordination offices:

Women Living Under Muslim Laws
International Coordination Office
PO Box 28445
London N19 5NZ

e-mail: wluml@wluml.org
www.wluml.org

Women Living Under Muslim Laws
Asia Regional Coordination Office
Shirkat Gah Women's Resource Centre
PO Box 5192
Lahore,
Pakistan

e-mail: sgah@lhr.comsats.net.pk

Women Living Under Muslim Laws
Regional Coordination Office for Africa & the Middle East
BAOBAB for Women's Human Rights
PO Box 73630
Victoria Island
Lagos
Nigeria

e-mail: baobab@baobabwomen.org

networking organizations and individuals:

algeria

e-mail: aithamou99@hotmail.com

algeria, morocco, tunisia

Collectif Maghreb Egalite' 95
2 Rue Ibn Mokala
Les Orangers
Rabat
Morocco

Tel: (+212) 37-208-645
Fax: (+212) 37-260-813
e-mail: cme95@fusion.net.ma

bangladesh

Ain O Salish Kendra (ASK)
26/3 Purana Paltan Lines
Dhaka
Bangladesh

Tel: (+880-2) 831-5158 & (+880 2) 936-0336
Fax: (+880-2) 831-8561
e-mail: ask@citechco.net

egypt

New Woman Research Center
90D Ahmed Urabi Street,
Mohandiseen,
Cairo
Egypt

Tel/Fax: (+20-2) 304-8085
Tel: (+20-2) 345-5319
e-mail: nwrc@intouch.com

list continues...

fiji

Regional Rights Resource Team
Private Mail Bag
Suva
Fiji Islands

Street Address:
2nd Floor, Pacific House
Butt Street
Suva
Fiji Islands

Tel: (+679) 3305-582 & 3305-173 & 3305-193
Fax: (+679) 3306-582 & 3305-177
e-mail: registry@rrrt.org.fj; kelera@rrrt.org.fj

Fiji Women's Rights Movement
P O Box 14194
Suva
Fiji Islands

Street Address:
115 Robertson Road
Suva
Fiji Islands

Tel: (+679) 3313-156
Fax: (+679) 3313-466
e-mail: info@fwrm.org.fj

gambia

GAMCOTRAP
(Gambian Committee on Traditional Practices Affecting the Health of Women and Children)
P.O. Box 2990
49, Garba Jahumpa Road
Bakau
Banjul
Gambia

e-mail: gamco@qanet.gm

india

Women's Research and Action Group
P.O.Box 6830
Santa Cruz (East)
Bombay/Mumbai 400 055

Tel: (+91-22) 261-55-031
Tel/Fax: (+91-22) 261-00-400
e-mail: wrag@vsnl.com

Awaaz-e-Niswan
1st floor
CVOD Jain High School
84, Samuel Street
Dongri
Mumbai 400 009
India

e-mail: niswan@vsnl.net

iran

Homa Hoodfar
Associate Prof. of Anthropology
Concordia University
1455 de Maisonneuve Blvd. W.
Montreal
Quebec H3G 1MB
Canada

Fax: (+1-514) 848-4539

malaysia

Women's Centre for Change (WCC)
(formerly Women's Crisis Centre)
24-D, Jalan Jones,
10250 Penang,
Malaysia

e-mail: wccpen@po.jaring.my
www.wccpenang.org

Sisters in Islam
(SIS Forum Malaysia Berhad)
JKR No.851, Jalan Dewan Bahasa
50460 Kuala Lumpur

Tel: (+60-3) 2142-6121 & 2148-3705
Fax: (+60-3) 2148-3601
e-mail: sistersinislam@pd.jaring.my
www.sistersinislam.org.my

morocco

LDDF
(La Ligue démocratique pour les droits de la femme
317 Rue Mustafa El Maani
1er etage N° 5
Casablanca
Morocco

e-mail: lddf@iam.net.ma

nigeria

BAOBAB for Women's Human Rights
PO Box 73630
Victoria Island
Lagos
Nigeria

e-mail: baobab@baobabwomen.org

palestine

Women's Centre for Legal Aid and Counselling
(WCLAC)
Al Dahya Intersection
Al Hirbawi Building, Third Floor
P.O. Box 54262
Jerusalem 91516
via Israel

Tel/Fax: (+972-2) 234-2172
Tel: (+972-2) 234-7438
e-mail: wclac@netvision.net.il & wclac@palnet.com
www.wclac.org

pakistan

Shirkat Gah Women's Resource Centre
PO Box 5192
Lahore,
Pakistan

e-mail: sgah@lhr.comsats.net.pk

philippines

PILIPINA Legal Resources Center, Inc. (PLRC)
3B Anda Corporate Center
F. Inigo St.,
8000 Davao City
The Philippines

Tel/Fax No: (+63 82) 224-3238
e-mail: plrcphil@info.com.ph

senegal

Grefels (Groupe de recherche sur les femmes et les lois au Sénégal)
B.P. 15275
DK-Fann
Dakar
Senegal

Tel/Fax: (+221) 825 65 33.
e-mail: grefels@sentoo.sn

sri lanka

Muslim Women's Research & Action Forum
No. 21/25 Polhengoda Gardens
Colombo 5
Sri Lanka

Tel/Fax: (+94) 74-405902
e-mail: mwraf@pan.lk

tunisia

Association tunisienne des femmes démocrates
(ATFD)
6 Rue du Liban
B.P. 107
Cité Mahragene 1082
Tunis
Tunisia

Tel: (+216-7) 179-4131
Fax: (+216-7) 179-9225
e-mail: femmes_feministes@yahoo.fr

turkey

Kadinin Insan Haklari - YENI COZUMLER
Women for Women's Human Rights (WWHR) - NEW WAYS
Inonu Cad. 37/6 Saadet Apt.
80090 Istanbul
Turkey

Tel: (+90-212) 251-0029
Fax: (+90-212) 251-0065
e-mail: wwhrist@superonline.com
www.wwhr.org

uzbekistan

Women's Resource Centre Tashkent
PO Box 7195
Abai St., 6
Tashkent
700095
Uzbekistan

e-mail: twrc@buzton.com

BIBLIOGRAPHY

This bibliography includes some of the materials consulted in the preparation of this Handbook, as well as English-language publications produced by networking organizations on the basis of their W&L research. Many of the organizations have produced additional materials on similar topics as well as materials in other languages and based on the W&L research.

Additionally, numerous unpublished papers stored at the WLUML international coordination office were consulted, some of which are listed here. Where complete citations could not be found, we have given details which may help readers trace copies.

marriage

El Alami, Dawoud Sudqi and Hinchcliffe Doreen (1996), Islamic Marriage and Divorce Laws of the Arab World, CIMEL Book Series No. 2, Kluwer Law International, London

Harvard Law School's Islamic Legal Studies Program Conference on the Islamic Marriage Contract, Cambridge, Mass., on Jan. 29-31, 1999 (unpublished papers by presenters)

Home Office (2000), A Choice by Right: The Report of the Working Group on Forced Marriage, Home Office, UK

Hoodfar, Homa (ed) (1996), Shifting Boundaries in Marriage and Divorce in Muslim Communities, Special Dossier Vol. 1 (Fall 1996), Women Living Under Muslim Laws, Grabels

Mahmood, Tahir (1987), Personal Law in Islamic Countries: History, Text and Comparative Analysis, Academy of Law and Religion, New Delhi

Moors, Annelies (1994), 'Women and Dower Property in Twentieth-Century Palestine: The case of Jabal Nablus', Islamic Law and Society (1,3) E.J. Brill, Leiden

Sisters in Islam, conference papers presented at the Regional Workshop on Islamic Family Law and Justice for Muslim Women, Kuala Lumpur, 8-10 June, 2001 (Indonesia, Malaysia, Philippines, Singapore)

Southall Black Sisters (2001), Forced Marriage: An abuse of human rights one year after 'A Choice by Right', Interim Report, Southall Black Sisters, London

Women Living Under Muslim Laws (1996), Matters Related to Marriage and Divorce in Muslim Laws: A preliminary working bibliography, WLUML, Grabels

www.unicef-icdc.org/publications/pdf/digest7e.pdf for child marriages

www.law.emory.edu/ for additional materials on specific countries and links to websites featuring texts of codes

divorce

Ahmed, K.N (1978), The Muslim Law of Divorce, Kitab Bhavan, New Delhi

Carrol, Lucy and Kapoor, Harsh (eds) (1996), Talaq-i-Tafwid, The Muslim Woman's Contractual Access to Divorce, Women Living Under Muslim Laws, Grabels

El Alami, Dawoud Sudqi and Hinchcliffe Doreen (1996), Islamic Marriage and Divorce Laws of the Arab World, CIMEL Book Series No. 2, Kluwer Law International, London

Hoodfar, Homa (ed) (1996), Shifting Boundaries in Marriage and Divorce in Muslim Communities, Special Dossier Vol. 1 (Fall 1996), Women Living Under Muslim Laws, Grabels

Mahmood, Tahir (1987), Personal Law in Islamic Countries: History, Text and Comparative Analysis, Academy of Law and Religion, New Delhi

Sisters in Islam, conference papers presented at the Regional Workshop on Islamic Family Law and Justice for Muslim Women, Kuala Lumpur, 8-10 June, 2001 (Indonesia, Malaysia, Philippines, Singapore)

Women Living Under Muslim Laws (1996), Matters Related to Marriage and Divorce in Muslim Laws: A preliminary working bibliography, WLUML, Grabels

www.law.emory.edu/ for additional materials on specific countries and links to websites featuring texts of codes

maintenance

Engineer, Asghar Ali (1999), 'Muslim Women and Maintenance', in Secular Perspectives, June 1-5, 1999

Sisters in Islam, conference papers presented at the Regional Workshop on Islamic Family Law and Justice for Muslim Women, Kuala Lumpur, 8-10 June, 2001 (Indonesia, Malaysia, Philippines, Singapore)

www.childsupportanalysis.co.uk/information_and_explanation/world/muslim.htm for summary information regarding child maintenance in various systems

custody & guardianship, children's status

Kleiner-Bossaller, A. (1993), '"Kwantacce, the 'sleeping pregnancy', a Hausa concept" in Ludwar-Ene, G. and Reh, M. (eds) Focusing on Women in Africa, Bayreuth African Studies Series 26.

Sisters in Islam, conference papers presented at the Regional Workshop on Islamic Family Law and Justice for Muslim Women, Kuala Lumpur, 8-10 June, 2001 (Indonesia, Malaysia, Philippines, Singapore)

www.childsupportanalysis.co.uk/information_and_explanation/world/muslim.htm for information regarding provisions concerning child custody and guardianship

muslim laws

Abd al-Ati, H. (1977), The Family Structure in Islam, American Trust Publications (no location)

Ameer Ali, Syed (1929), Mahomedan Law, Vol. 2, Fifth Edition, 1985 reprint, Himalayan Books, New Delhi

Mulla, D.F. (1981) Principles of Mahomedan Law, (18th edition), Mansoor Book House, Lahore

Fyzee, A.A.A. (1974), Outlines of Muhammadan Law, Fourth Edition, Oxford University Press. New Delhi, reprint 1994

Hughes, T.P. Dictionary of Islam, http://answering-islam.org/Books/Hughes (no date)

Muslim Women's Research and Action Forum (2000), The Need for Ijtihad or Intellectual Reasoning, Seminar Series No. 2, Muslim Women's Research & Action Forum, Colombo

algeria, morocco, tunisia

Association Indépendent pour le Triomphe des Droits des Femmes, Femme, connais-tu les lois qui te concernent? Guide de lois a l'usage des femmes (no date), AITDF

Collectif '95 Maghreb Egalite (1996), Cent Mesures et Dispositions: Pour une codification maghrebine egalitaire du Statut personnel et du droit de la famille, Women Living Under Muslim Laws, Grabels (English translation forthcoming, Women Living Under Muslim Laws)

http://membres.lycos.fr/lexalgeria/

www.jurisitetunisie.com contains Tunisia's Code du Statut Personnel and other relevant legislation

bangladesh

Kamal, Sultana (2001), Her Unfearing Mind, Ain-O-Salish Kendro (ASK) / Women Living Under Muslim Laws, Dhaka

Pereira, Faustina (2001), The Fractured Scales: The Search for a Uniform Personal Code, STREE, Calcutta

central asian republics

Djanaeva, Dr. Nurgul N. (2002), Kyrgyzstan Women in Transition, Bishkek

Shirkat Gah/Women Living Under Muslim Laws (1995), Assertions of Self: The nascent women's movement in Central Asia, Special Bulletin, Lahore

Tokhtakhodjaeva, Marfua (1995), Between the Slogans of Communism and the Laws of Islam: the women of Uzbekistan, Shirkat Gah/Women Living Under Muslim Laws, Lahore

Tokhtakhodjaeva, Marfua and Turgumbekova, Elmira (1996), The Daughters of Amazons: Voices from Central Asia, Shirkat Gah/Women Living Under Muslim Laws, Lahore

Tokhtakhodjaeva, Marfua (2000), 'Traditional Stereotypes and Women's Problems in Post-Soviet Uzbekistan: A Survey of the Mass Media', Dossier 22, January 2000, Women Living Under Muslim Laws, Grabels

www.lexinfosys.de/lexinfosys/ZGB.htm contains Civil Codes from the following countries, some of which are in English: Kazakhstan, Kyrgyz Republic, Tajikistan, Turkmenistan, and Uzbekistan

egypt

Chemais, Alya (1996), 'Obstacles to Divorce for Muslim Women in Egypt', in Hoodfar, Homa (ed), Shifting Boundaries in Marriage and Divorce in Muslim Communities, Special Dossier Vol. 1 (Fall 1996), Women Living Under Muslim Laws, Grabels

Communication Group for the Enhancement of the Status of Women in Egypt / Mona Zulfikar (1992), Legal Rights of Egyptian Women in Theory and Practice

Hoodfar, Homa (1996), 'Circumventing Legal Limitation: Mahr and Marriage Negotiation in Egyptian Low-Income Communities', in Hoodfar, Homa (ed) Shifting Boundaries in Marriage and Divorce in Muslim Communities, Special Dossier: Women Living Under Muslim Laws, Grabels

The Legal and Research Centre for Human Rights, Cairo, Egypt, www.geocities.com/lrrc.geo/Zaid/

fiji

Jalal, P. Imrana (1998), Law for Pacific Women: A Legal Rights Handbook, Fiji Women's Rights Movement, Suva, Fiji

www.unescap.org/pop/database/law_fiji/fiji_012_1.htm for Fiji, Matrimonial Causes Act

www.vanuatu.usp.ac.fj/paclawmat/Fiji_legislation/plmlegislation_main.html for Fiji statutory provisions

the gambia

Gambian Committee on Traditional Practices Affecting the Health of Women and Children (GAMCOTRAP) (2002), Gambian Women, Law, and Customary Practice, Bakau

United Nations Development Programme (UNDP) and Central Statistics Department (1997), The Gambia: National Human Development Report, UNDP, Banjul

india

Lateef, Shahida (1990), Muslim Women in India: Political and Private Realities 1890's – 1980's, Kali for Women, New Delhi

Mohammad, Dr. Shabbir, (1988), Muslim Personal Law and Judiciary, The Law Book Company (p) Ltd, India

Women's Research and Action Group (1996), 'Marriage and the Politics of Social Change in India's Muslim Communities', in Hoodfar, Homa (ed), Shifting Boundaries in Marriage and Divorce in Muslim Communities, Special Dossier Vol. 1 (Fall 1996), Women Living Under Muslim Laws, Grabels

Women's Research and Action Group (1997), Aspects of Culture and Society: Muslim Women in India, District Reports, Women's Research and Action Group, India

Women's Research and Action Group (1997), Women, Law and Customary Practices, Women's Research and Action Group, India

indonesia

Australian Journal of Asian Law, Vol. 4, No. 3: Islamic Law in South-East Asia

Bowen, John R. (1998), '"You may not give it away": How Social Norms Shape Islamic Law in Contemporary Indonesian Jurisprudence', in Islamic Law and Society, Vol 5 No. 3 October 1998

Katz, June S. and Katz, Ronald S (1975), 'The New Indonesian Marriage Law: A Mirror of Indonesia's Political, Cultural and Legal Systems', American Journal of Comparative Law, vol. 23 (1975): 653-681

iran

Afshar, Haleh (1985), 'The Legal, Social and Political Position of Women in Iran', International Journal of the Sociology of the Law, 1985, 13

Haeri, Shahla (1994), Law of Desire: Temporary Marriage in Shií Iran, Syracuse University

Kar, Mehranguiz and Hoodfar, Homa (1996), 'Personal Status Law as Define by the Islamic Republic of Iran: An Appraisal', in Hoodfar, Homa (ed), Shifting Boundaries in Marriage and Divorce in Muslim Communities, Special Dossier Vol. 1 (Fall 1996), Women Living Under Muslim Laws, Grabels

Kian, Azadeh, (1999), 'Women and Politics in Post-Islamic Iran: the gender conscious drive to change', Dossier 21, Women Living Under Muslim Laws, Grabels

Mir-Hosseini, Ziba (1993), Marriage on Trial: A study of Islamic family law, I.B. Tauris, London

Saidzadeh, Hojjat al-Eslam (1999), 'Foundations of the equality perspective, modern fiqh: the case of divorce', Dossier 21, Women Living Under Muslim Laws, Grabels

Taleghany, M.A.R (translator) (1995), The Civil Code of Iran

Reconstructing Fundamentalism and Feminism: the dynamics of change in Iran, Special Bulletin (1995), Shirkat Gah/Women Living Under Muslim Laws, Lahore

www.iranembassy.hu/registrationmarriage.html for requirements for Iranians when marrying foreigners

lebanon

Shehadeh, Lamia Rustum (1998), 'The Legal Status of Married Women in Lebanon,' International Journal of Middle East Studies, vol. 30, no. 4 (November): 501-519

malaysia

Devarai, Prema E. (ed.) (no date), Malaysian Women and the Law, National Council of Women's Organisations (NCWO), Penang Branch

Ibrahim, Ahmad (2001), Family Law in Malaysia, Butterworths Asia, Singapore

International Law Book Services (2002), Islamic Family Law (Federal Territories) Act 1984 (Act 303), ILBS, Petaling Jaya, Selangor

Mohamed, Maznah (2000), Muslim Women and Access to Justice: Historical, Legal and Social Experience in Malaysia, Women's Crisis Centre, Penang, Malaysia.

Siraj, Mehrun (1993), Women under Syariah law in Malaysia, School of Social Sciences, Universiti Sains Malaysia, Kanita

nigeria

Ambali, M.A. (1998), The Practice of Muslim Family Law in Nigeria, Tamaza Publishing Company, Zaria

BAOBAB for Women's Human Rights (1999), Divorce – the Dissolution of a Marriage in Muslim Personal Laws in Nigeria, Legal Literacy Series, Lagos

BAOBAB for Women's Human Rights (1999), Child Custody and Guardianship, Legal Literacy Series, Lagos

Imam, Ayesha (2000), 'Women's Rights in Muslim Laws (Sharia)' in The Place of Women Under Sharia, CRP/FNS, Lagos

Nwogugu, E.I. (1974), Family Law in Nigeria (Revised Edition), Heinemann Studies in Nigeria Law, Heinmann Educational Books, reprint 2001

pakistan

Balchin, Cassandra (ed.) (1994), A Handbook on Family Law in Pakistan, Shirkat Gah/Women Living Under Muslim Laws, Lahore

Balchin, Cassandra (ed.) (1996), Women, Law and Society: An Action Manual for NGOs, Shirkat Gah, Lahore

Government of Pakistan (1998), Report of the Commission of Inquiry for Women: August 1997, Islamabad

Jahangir, Asma and Jilani, Hina (1990), The Hudood Ordinances: A Divine Sanction?, Rhotas Books, Lahore

Shaheed, Farida et al (eds) (1998), Shaping Women's Lives: Laws, Practices and Strategies in Pakistan, Shirkat Gah, Lahore

Shirkat Gah (2000), Women's Rights in Muslim Family Law in Pakistan: 45 years of Recommendations vs. the FSC Judgment (January 2000), Special Bulletin, Shirkat Gah, Lahore

palestinian community in israel, and the west bank

Moors, Annelies (1995), Women, Property and Islam: Palestinian Experiences, 1920-1990, Cambridge University Press

Rouhana, Houda (2001), Practices in the Sharia Court of Appeal in Israel; Gendered Reading of Arbitration Decisions, (unpublished paper)

Rouhana, Houda (2002), Personal Status Laws and the Citizenship of Palestinian Women in Israel, MA thesis, the University of Greenwich, UK

Welchman, Lynn (2000), Beyond the Code: Muslim Family Law and the Shar'i Judiciary in the Palestinian West Bank, Kluwer Academic Publishers, London

philippines

Antonio, Isabelita Solamo, (no date), Women and Law in the Muslim World: The Research Abstract, PILIPINA Legal Resources Center

Antonio, Isabelita Solamo (2000), 'Image of the Legal System Among the Tri-Peoples of Mindanao', in Leonen M.V.F. (ed) 1st Alternative Law Conference: Lawyering for the Public Interest, Nov. 8-12, 1999, Alternative Law Groups, Inc. Publication, 2000, p.50-69

Antonio, Isabelita Solamo (2002), Women's Rights, Local & National Legislative Advocacy, & Networking for Effective Law Enforcement (unpublished paper presented at the Workshop On Sensitizing Police Force And Lawmakers On Women's Rights In Reproductive Health, Jogyakarta, Indonesia, 2-3 September 2002)

PILIPINA Legal Resources Center (1988), The Woman Underneath That Malong: The Implications of the Code of Muslim Personal Laws on the Muslim Women of Regions IX & XII, PLRC, Mindanao

PILIPINA Legal Resources Center (no date) 'Proposed Revised Code of Muslim Personal Laws'

saudi arabia

Wynn, I. (1996), 'Marriage Contracts and Women's Rights in Saudi Arabia', in Hoodfar, Homa (ed), Shifting Boundaries in Marriage and Divorce in Muslim Communities, Special Dossier Vol. 1 (Fall 1996), Women Living Under Muslim Laws, Grabels

senegal

Sow, F. (1996), 'Family and Law in Senegal: Continuity and Change', in Hoodfar, Homa (ed), Shifting Boundaries in Marriage and Divorce in Muslim Communities, Special Dossier Vol. 1 (Fall 1996), Women Living Under Muslim Laws, Grabels

Sow, F. with Gaye, D., Senghor, M., and Diagne, P., (forthcoming), Femmes, lois et Islam au Sénégal, Groupe de recherche sur les femmes et les lois au Sénégal (GREFELS), Dakar

sri lanka

Goonesekere, Savitri (2000), Muslim Personal Law in Sri Lanka: Some Aspects of Law on Family Relations, Muslim Women's Research & Action Forum, Sri Lanka

Kodikara, Chulani (1999), Muslim Family Law in Sri Lanka: Theory, Practice and Issues of Concern to Women, Muslim Women's Research & Action Forum/Women Living Under Muslim Laws, Sri Lanka

Muslim Women's Research & Action Forum (1999), Between Two Worlds: Muslim Women in a Multi-Ethnic Society, Muslim Women's Research & Action Forum/WLUML, Colombo

Muslim Women's Research & Action Forum (2000), Dialogue with Quazis: A report of a meeting with Quazis, Muslim Women's Research & Action Forum, Colombo

Wijayatilake, Kamalini (1996), 'Rights of Women within the Family: An Overview of the Sri Lankan Experience', in Hoodfar, Homa (ed), Shifting Boundaries in Marriage and Divorce in Muslim Communities, Special Dossier Vol. 1 (Fall 1996), Women Living Under Muslim Laws, Grabels

sudan

Fluehr-Lobban, C. (1987), Islamic Law and Society in the Sudan, Frank Cass, Ltd, London

Women and Law Sudan Country Project, Women and Law in Sudan, (Volume 1 1998, Volume 2 1999)

tanzania

Women's Research & Documentation Project, Dar es Salaam

tunisia

Kelley, Patricia (1996), 'Finding Common Ground: Islamic Values and Gender Equity in Reformed Personal Status Law in Tunisia', in Hoodfar, Homa (ed), Shifting Boundaries in Marriage and Divorce in Muslim Communities, Special Dossier Vol. 1 (Fall 1996), Women Living Under Muslim Laws, Grabels

turkey

Arin, Canan (1997), The Legal Status of Women in Turkey, Women for Women's Human Rights Reports No. 1, Women for Women's Human Rights/Women Living Under Muslim Laws

Women for Women's Human Rights, (2002), The New Legal Status of Women in Turkey, Women for Women's Human Rights – New Ways Liaison Office, Istanbul

yemen

Molyneux, Maxine (1991), 'The Law, the State and Socialist Policies With Regard to Women: The Case of the People's Democratic Republic of Yemen', in Kandiyoti, Deniz, (ed) Women Islam and the State, Temple University Press, Philadelphia

Index

See glossary pp.6-11 for terms used in this index.
"Also" is used to indicate less significant references.